W9-CGQ-257

Explorations in New Cinema History

Explorations in New Cinema History

Approaches and Case Studies

Edited by

Richard Maltby, Daniel Biltereyst and Philippe Meers

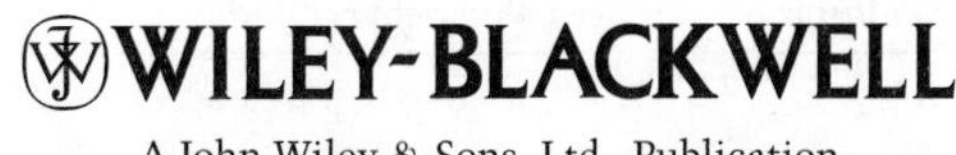

A John Wiley & Sons, Ltd., Publication

This edition first published 2011

Blackwell Publishing was acquired by John Wiley & Sons in February 2007. Blackwell's publishing program has been merged with Wiley's global Scientific, Technical, and Medical business to form Wiley-Blackwell.

Registered Office
John Wiley & Sons Ltd, The Atrium, Southern Gate, Chichester, West Sussex, PO19 8SQ, United Kingdom

Editorial Offices
350 Main Street, Malden, MA 02148-5020, USA
9600 Garsington Road, Oxford, OX4 2DQ, UK
The Atrium, Southern Gate, Chichester, West Sussex, PO19 8SQ, UK

For details of our global editorial offices, for customer services, and for information about how to apply for permission to reuse the copyright material in this book please see our website at www.wiley.com/wiley-blackwell.

Library of Congress Cataloging-in-Publication Data

Explorations in new cinema history : approaches and case studies / edited by Richard Maltby, Daniel Biltereyst and Philippe Meers.
p. cm.
Includes bibliographical references and index.
ISBN 978-1-4051-9949-0 (hardcover, alk. paper), ISBN 978-1-4051-9950-6 (paperback, alk paper)
1. Motion picture audiences. 2. Motion pictures–Distribution. 3. Motion picture theaters. 4. Motion picture industry–History–20th century. I. Maltby, Richard, 1952– II. Biltereyst, Daniel, 1962– III. Meers, Philippe.
PN1995.9.A8E97 2011
302.23′43–dc21

2010051054

A catalogue record for this book is available from the British Library.

This book is published in the following electronic formats: ePDFs 9781444396393; Wiley Online Library 9781444396416; ePub 9781444396409

Set in 11/13pt Dante by SPi Publisher Services, Pondicherry, India
Printed in Malaysia by Ho Printing (M) Sdn Bhd

1 2011

Contents

Contributors

Robert C. Allen is James Logan Godfrey Professor of American Studies, History, and Communication Studies at the University of North Carolina. He has written on the history of US radio and television (*Speaking of Soap Operas,* 1985), film history and historiography (*Film History: Theory and Practice, 1985*), and American popular theatre of the nineteenth and early twentieth centuries (*Horrible Prettiness: Burlesque and American Culture*, 1992). He is principal investigator on 'Going to the Show', a digital humanities project documenting and mapping the experience of moviegoing in North Carolina from 1896 to 1930 (http://docsouth.unc.edu/gtts/).

Daniel Biltereyst is Professor in Film, Television and Cultural Studies at the Department of Communication Studies, Ghent University, Belgium, where he is head of department and director of the Centre of Cinema and Media Studies. His work on film and screen culture, controversy and the public sphere has been published in *The European Journal of Cultural Studies*, *The Historical Journal of Film, Radio and Television*, *Media, Culture & Society, Northern Lights*, *Screen*, *Studies in French Cinema*, *Studies in Russian and Soviet Cinema*, and in edited collections, including *Understanding Rebel without a Cause* (SUNY), *Communication Theory and Research in Europe* (Sage), *Youth Culture in Global Cinema* (University of Texas Press), *Watching The Lord of the Rings* (Lang), *Going to the Movies* (Exeter UP), *The Handbook of Political Economy of Communications* (Wiley-Blackwell), *Billy Wilder, Moviemaker* (McFarland), *Je t'Aime, Moi Non Plus: Franco-British Cinematic Relations* (Berghan).

Kate Bowles is Senior Lecturer at the School of Social Sciences, Media and Communications, University of Wollongong, Australia. Her work has been published in *Jane Austen on Screen* (Cambridge University Press, 2003), *Hollywood Abroad: Audiences and Cultural Exchange* (BFI, 2004), *The Media and Communications in Australia* (Allen & Unwin, 2006), and *Studies in Australasian Cinema* (2007).

Kathryn Fuller-Seeley is Associate Professor of Moving Image Studies and Associate Chair of the Communication Department, Georgia State University. Her research interests include early US film exhibition, and historical audience reception studies. Publications include: *Hollywood in the Neighborhood: Historical Case Studies of Moviegoing in Small Town America*, ed. (University of California Press, 2007); 'Television as gendered technology: America's first audiences', in *The Columbia History of Television* (ed. Gary Edgerton; Columbia, 2007); '"What the picture did for me:" small town exhibitors and the Great Depression', in *Hollywood in the Neighborhood* (2007); 'Dish night at the movies: exhibitors and female audiences during the Great Depression', in *Looking Past the Screen: Case Studies in American Film History and Method* (eds Eric Smoodin and Jon Lewis; Duke, 2007); *At the Picture Show: Small Town Audiences and the Creation of Movie Fan Culture* (Smithsonian/Virginia 1997).

Stephen Putnam Hughes completed both his MA and PhD in Social and Cultural Anthropology at the University of Chicago, where he specialised in media history and visual anthropology with special reference to cinema in south India. He currently teaches Anthropology and Sociology at the School of Oriental and African Studies, University of London, where he is the Director of Studies for the MA programme in the Anthropology of Media. Having lived and worked in Tamil-speaking south India over the course of the last 20 years, he has conducted research on various topics related to the history of media.

Mark Jancovich is Professor of Film and Television Studies at the University of East Anglia. His publications include: *The Place of the Audience: Cultural Geographies of Film Consumption* (with Lucy Faire and Sarah Stubbings; BFI, 2003); *Defining Cult Movies: The Cultural Politics of Oppositional Taste* (MUP, 2003); *Quality Popular Television: Cult TV, the Industry and Fans* (BFI, 2003); *Horror: The Film Reader* (Routledge, 2001); *The Film Studies Reader* (Arnold, 2000); *Rational Fears: American Horror in the 1950s* (Manchester University Press, 1996); *Approaches to Popular Film* (Manchester University Press, 1995); *The Cultural Politics of the New Criticism* (Cambridge University Press, 1993); *Horror* (Batsford, 1992).

Jeffrey Klenotic is Associate Professor of Communication Arts at the University of New Hampshire in Manchester. His essays on cinema history and historiography have been published in journals such as *Film History*, *The Communication Review* and *Velvet Light Trap*, as well as in several edited anthologies and encyclopedias including *The Sounds of Early Cinema*, *The Encyclopedia of Early Cinema* and *Going to the Movies: Hollywood and the Social Experience of Moviegoing*. He is currently developing a research tool on moviegoing, social demography and cultural geography that takes the form of an interactive map, or Geographic Information System (GIS).

Arthur Knight is an Associate Professor of American Studies and English at the College of William and Mary in Virginia (USA), where he also directs the Film and

Cultural Studies Program. He has published *Disintegrating the Musical: Black Performance and American Musical Film* (Duke UP, 2002) and coedited *Soundtrack Available: Essays on Film and Popular Music* (Duke UP, 2001). He is also the director of the Williamsburg Theatre Project, a data collection project on film exhibition and moviegoing that focuses on Williamsburg, Virginia (http://moviegoing.wm.edu/wtp/), and a founding member of the Homer Project (www.homerproject.org). He is currently at work on a book, tentatively titled, *Black Star: A Cultural History of African American Fame.*

Peter Krämer teaches Film Studies at the University of East Anglia. He has published essays on American film and media history, and on the relationship between Hollywood and Europe, in *Screen, The Velvet Light Trap, Theatre History Studies, The Historical Journal of Film, Radio and Television, History Today, Film Studies, Scope, Sowi: Das Journal far Geschichte, Politik, Wirtschaft und Kultur* and numerous edited collections. He is the author of *The New Hollywood: From Bonnie and Clyde to Star Wars* (Wallflower Press, 2005), and the coeditor of *Screen Acting* (Routledge, 1999) and *The Silent Cinema Reader* (Routledge, 2004). He also cowrote a book for children entitled *American Film: An A-Z Guide* (Franklin Watts, 2003).

Annette Kuhn is Professor of Film Studies at Queen Mary, London University. She has Bachelor's and Master's degrees in Sociology from the University of Sheffield and a PhD on the history of film censorship from the University of London. Her publications include: *Ratcatcher* (BFI, 2008), *Screening World Cinema: a Screen Reader* (Routledge, 2006, with Catherine Grant), *An Everyday Magic: Cinema and Cultural Memory* (I.B. Tauris, 2002), *Screen Histories: a Reader* (Oxford University Press, 1998, with Jackie Stacey), *Women's Pictures: Feminism and Cinema* (Verso, 1994), *Alien Zone: Cultural Theory and Contemporary Science Fiction Cinema* (Verso, 1990), *Cinema, Censorship and Sexuality* (Routledge, 1988), *The Power of the Image: Essays on Representation and Sexuality* (Routledge and Kegan Paul, 1985).

Richard Maltby is Professor of Screen Studies and Executive Dean of the Faculty of Education, Humanities and Law at Flinders University, South Australia. Before moving to Australia in 1997, he was the founding Director of the Bill Douglas Centre for the History of Cinema and Popular Culture at the University of Exeter and then Research Professor of Film Studies at Sheffield Hallam University. His publications include *Hollywood Cinema: Second Edition* (Blackwell, 2003; Hua Xia Press, Beijing, 2005), *"Film Europe" and "Film America": Cinema, Commerce and Cultural Exchange, 1925–1939*, which won the Prix Jean Mitry for cinema history in 2000, and five edited books on the history of movie audiences and exhibition history, the most recent being *Going to the Movies: Hollywood and the Social Experience of Cinema* (University of Exeter Press, 2007). He is Series Editor of *Exeter Studies in Film History*, and the author of over 50 articles and essays. With Ruth Vasey he is currently completing *Reforming the Movies: Politics, Censorship, and the Governance of the American Cinema, 1908–1939*. He is currently the lead investigator on two Australian Research Council

Discovery projects examining the structure of the distribution and exhibition industry and the history of cinema audiences in Australia.

Philippe Meers is an Associate Professor in film and media studies at the University of Antwerp, Belgium, where he is deputy director of the Visual Culture Research Group. He has published on popular media culture and film audiences in *Media, Culture and Society, Illuminace, The Journal of Popular Film and Television and Screen*, and in edited collections, including *Big Brother International* (Wallflower Press, 2004); *Hollywood Abroad. Audiences and Cultural Relations* (BFI, 2004); *The Lord of the Rings: Popular Cinema in Global Culture* (Wallflower, 2007); *Watching The Lord of the Rings* (Lang, 2007), *The Contemporary Hollywood Reader* (Routledge, 2009), *The Handbook of Political Economy of Communications* (Wiley-Blackwell, 2011). With Daniel Biltereyst and Richard Maltby, he is editing *Audiences, Cinema and Modernity: New Perspectives on European Cinema History* (Routledge, 2011). His current research focuses on historical and diasporic cinema cultures.

Paul S. Moore is director of the Canadian Theatre Historical Project at Ryerson University in Toronto. He is coeditor of *Marquee: Journal of the Theatre Historical Society of America* (THSA). His essay 'Dream Palaces that Remained Dreams: Unbuilt Chicago Theatres', won the first prize in the THSA's 2006 Weiss award competition. He has published several essays on the history of film exhibition and moviegoing in Canada and has presented papers at Society for Cinema and Media Studies, Domitor, Screen and other conferences. His book, *Now Playing: Early Movie-going and the Regulation of Fun (Toronto 1906–1918)*, is forthcoming from SUNY Press.

Deron Overpeck teaches film and media studies courses in the Department of Communication and Journalism at Auburn University. His research interests include the American cinema since the end of the studio system, the relationship between the American media industry and internet journalism, and Italian cinema.

Clara Pafort-Overduin is Assistant Professor at the department of Theater, Film and Television Studies, Utrecht University, and is a founding member of ICARG (International Cinema Attendances Research Group). She is currently completing her dissertation on Dutch film and national identity in the Thirties.

John Sedgwick is Academic Leader at the Department of Economics, Finance and International Business, London Metropolitan University. He is the author of *Filmgoing in 1930s Britain: a Choice of Pleasures* (Exeter University Press, 2000) and editor of *An Economic History of Film* (Routledge, 2005, with Mike Pokorny). His work has been published in many journals, including *Economic History Review, Journal of Cultural Economics, Historical Journal of Film, Radio and Television*, and books including *Going to the Movies: Hollywood and the Social*

Experience of Movie-going (2007); *Americanisation in 20th Century Europe* (2002); and *The Unknown 1930s: An Alternative History of the British Cinema, 1929–39* (1999).

Tim Snelson is a Lecturer in Media and Culture at the University of East Anglia. His research addresses the relationship between media and social history. His publications include '"From grade B thrillers to deluxe chillers": prestige horror, female audiences and allegories of spectatorship in *The Spiral Staircase* (1946)', in *The New Review of Film and Television Studies* 7 (2), June 2009, and 'The Ghost in the Machine: World War Two, Popular Occultism and Hollywood's "Serious" Ghost Films' in *Media History* 17:1 (January 2011).

Peter Stanfield is a Reader in Film Studies at the University of Kent, the author of *Body & Soul: Jazz & Blues in American Film, 1927–63* (2005), *Horse Opera: The Strange History of the Singing Cowboy* (2002), *Hollywood, Westerns and the 1930s: The Lost Trail* (2001), and joint editor of *Mob Culture: Hidden Histories of the American Gangster Film* (2005). He is currently working on a book titled *Maximum Movies*.

Lies Van de Vijver has Master's degrees in Arts History from Ghent University and in Film Studies from the University of Antwerp. She works as a researcher on a project entitled 'Gent Kinemastad' and is preparing her doctoral thesis on the film exhibition and cinemagoing in the city of Ghent.

Deb Verhoeven is Professor and Chair in Media and Communication at Deakin University in Melbourne, Australia. Her most recent publication is *Jane Campion* (Routledge, 2009). She is President of the online journal *Senses of Cinema*, and Deputy Chair of the National Film and Sound Archive of Australia.

Mike Walsh is the Head of the Screen Studies Department at Flinders University in South Australia. He has published in numerous anthologies and journals and is currently completing a book on the international distribution network established by United Artists. He has been a coordinating editor of *The Velvet Light Trap* and currently he is a programmer and catalogue editor for the Adelaide Film Festival.

Acknowledgements

This collection launches the 'new cinema history', a body of work that focuses on the circulation and consumption of film and examines cinema as a site of social and cultural exchange. The contributors have sought to consolidate and develop lines of argument advanced in a series of books edited by Richard Maltby and Melvyn Stokes, examining the history of cinema audiences, exhibition and reception. As with many of the pieces in these earlier books, the chapters in this volume were first discussed at a groundbreaking conference, held in Ghent in December 2007, under the title 'The Glow in Their Eyes: Global Perspectives on Film Cultures, Film Exhibition and Cinema-Going'. The editors would like to thank all participants and in particular the keynote speakers, Robert C. Allen and Annette Kuhn, for contributing to the success of the conference.

We are very much indebted to all those who helped organise this event, in particular Lies Van de Vijver, Gert Willems and Carl de Keyser, the members of the Centre for Cinema and Media Studies at Ghent University, and the Visual Culture Research Group at the University of Antwerp, as well as Deb Verhoeven and Kate Bowles. We thank the Flemish Scientific Research Council (FWO-Vlaanderen), the university film-club Film-Plateau (Ghent University), and the City of Ghent for their generous support of the conference. At Wiley-Blackwell, ably aided by Margot Morse and Matthew Baskin, Jayne Fargnoli has been a model of patience and support. The editors thank Kathleen Lotze and Lies Van de Vijver for their excellent work in compiling the index.

The conference and this collection would not have been possible without the inspiration of an international group of scholars in the History of Moviegoing, Exhibition, and Reception (HOMER) project, chaired by Arthur Knight. The HOMER project, many of whose members are represented in this volume, promotes the idea that historians of the media must seek to understand what Robert Allen has called the 'social, spatial, experiential, geographic, architectural, and cultural situatedness of cinema and media'. The editors hope that this book meets this challenge and will foster more work in this direction.

Richard Maltby, Daniel Biltereyst and Philippe Meers

Part 1

Mapping Cinema Experiences

1

New Cinema Histories

RICHARD MALTBY[1]

History is not yet what it ought to be. That is no reason to make history as it can be the scapegoat for the sins which belong to bad history alone.
Marc Bloch (1953, p. 66)

Whenever I hear the word cinema, I can't help thinking hall, rather than film.
Roland Barthes (1986, p. 346)

Over the past 10 years, an emerging international trend in research into cinema history has shifted its focus away from the content of films to consider their circulation and consumption, and to examine the cinema as a site of social and cultural exchange.[2] This shared effort has engaged contributors from different points on the disciplinary compass, including history, geography, cultural studies, economics, sociology and anthropology, as well as film and media studies. Their projects have examined the commercial activities of film distribution and exhibition, the legal and political discourses that craft cinema's profile in public life, and the social and cultural histories of specific cinema audiences. Many of their projects have been collaborative, facilitated by computational analysis and the opportunities for quantitative research offered by databases and Geographical Information Systems, which allow for the compilation of new information about the history of cinema exhibition and reception in ways that would previously have been too labour intensive to undertake.[3] Having achieved critical mass and methodological maturity, this body of work has now developed a distinct identity, to which we have given the name 'the new cinema history' (Bowles *et al.*, 2011). The aim of this collection is to showcase recent work in the field, and to illustrate the questions that the new cinema history asks. As well as providing a guide to the individual contributions, this introductory essay seeks to explain what the editors believe is new about new cinema history, and what is distinctive in its approach.

Explorations in New Cinema History: Approaches and Case Studies, First Edition.
Edited by Richard Maltby, Daniel Biltereyst and Philippe Meers.

In calling this body of work new cinema history, we are deliberately distinguishing it from film history. Film history has been predominantly a history of production, producers, authorship and films. It is most often evaluative, classificatory or curatorial in its remit, and primarily concerned with understanding the complex economic, aesthetic and social systems that might cause particular films to assume the shape that they do. This activity, which has engaged historians already located within the discipline of film studies, has greatly expanded our understanding of the 'proximate forces' influencing the development and uses of the medium (Keil, 2004, p. 52). Borrowing its methods and rationale from the practices of art and literary history, historical work of this nature helps to decipher the complex aesthetic codes of the wide range of different cinematic traditions across the globe, drawing out both regularities and irregularities in the ways in which these different cinemas imitate or critique each other's stylistic habits. It can, for example, explain 'why we have dialogue hooks, montage sequences, goal-oriented protagonists, and a switch from orthochromatic to panchromatic film stock' in Hollywood movies of a particular period (Bordwell, 2005). In its close attention to the formal and ideological properties of film as a signifying system, this form of film history can reveal the ways in which the precise and subtle conventions in this system evolve over time, or change in response to external circumstances.

Placing films into a wider historical context has proven to be more problematic, however, in part because of the sceptical attention of some other historians concerned to show that films themselves do bad historical work or fail to meet adequate analytical standards to pass as works of history. As recently as 2006, the *American Historical Review* (*AHR*) removed its regular film review section, on the grounds that movies 'although undoubtedly useful as teaching devices, do not always contribute to an analytical, sophisticated understanding of history'.[4] Sceptical historians have dismissed film as a form of historical evidence on a variety of grounds: firstly, for what Ian Jarvie has described as its 'poor information load', a 'discursive weakness' that renders it a 'very clumsy medium for presenting argument' and disables it from participating in debates about historical problems. Lacking historiographical complexity, film is at best, according to Jarvie, 'a visual aid' (Jarvie, 1978, pp. 377–8). For many historians, moreover, it is too often an inaccurate visual aid, its imitation of the past fatally compromised by the inevitable distortions of fiction and anachronism. As Robert Rosenstone summarises this critique, films 'fictionalise, trivialise, and romanticise people, events, and movements. They falsify history.' (Rosenstone, 1995, p. 46). Carla and William Phillips complain that films commonly

> treat the historical record as mere raw material, to be adapted to the needs of the screenplay. Chronology is expanded, compressed, reversed, or falsified to suit the dramatic trajectory. Historical personages are revised, deified or demonized, conflated or created from whole cloth to serve the director's will. (Phillips and Phillips, 1996, p. 63)

Stephen J. Gould observes that we 'cannot hope for even a vaguely accurate portrayal of the nub of history in film so long as movies must obey the literary conventions of ordinary plotting' (Gould, 1996, p. 35). Contemplating this litany of complaint, Peter Miskell has suggested that some historians more covertly object to history films because these representations of the past are both out of their control and reach far wider audiences than historians do. To some professional academic historians, Miskell argues, 'film is a disturbing symbol of an increasingly post-literate world (in which people can read but won't)' (Miskell, 2004, p. 249). Worse still, the historical film's implied defence calls for support on the poststructuralist argument that all narrative forms, including traditional histories, deploy equivalent processes of emplotment, speculation and selection (White, 1973).

Countering the dismissal of films as impoverished and unreliable sources of information, film historians have insisted on film as a different form of evidence, requiring special training in its decoding. Haydon White has argued that the practice of 'historiophoty', the historical analysis of visual images, requires a manner of 'reading' quite different from that used in assessing written evidence, so that historians need to learn the 'lexicon, grammar and syntax' of imagistic evidence (White, 1988a, p. 1194). James Chapman, Mark Glancy and Sue Harper similarly insist that the film historian must understand 'that films are cultural artefacts with their own formal properties and aesthetics', and must therefore acquire 'skills of formal and visual analysis that are specific to the discipline' (Chapman *et al.*, 2007, p. 1). From these premises, the sympathetic treatment of film as evidence has been placed firmly on the poststructuralist side of debates over the critique of history-writing in the last quarter of the twentieth century. Film theory's practical postmodernism, offering a multiplicity of ways to arrive at 'the familiar conclusion that the "text" under analysis is full of contradictory tensions, requires active readers and produces a variety of pleasures', has naturally aligned itself with a poststructuralist questioning of the presumption that historical truth can escape the constraints of narrative convention (Willemen, 1986, p. 227; Stone, 1992, p. 194). In the face of this alliance of confident uncertainties, many historians have simply baulked at what John E. O'Connor has called the heavy 'theoretical apparatus of film studies' and the apparently unbridgeable 'chasm' it creates between the two disciplines (O'Connor, 1990, p. 8; Guynn, 2006, p. 14).

Historians' disinclination to engage with film has combined with film studies' enthusiasm for interpretation to ensure that the most common approach to film history has been one in which films are treated as involuntary testimony, bearing unconscious material witness to the *mentalité* or *zeitgeist* of the period of their production (Guynn, 2006, p. 6). Marc Bloch, co-founder of the *Annales* School, described unintentional historical evidence of this kind – artefacts from a medieval midden, the commercial correspondence of a sixteenth-century Florentine merchant – as signs that the past unwittingly drops onto the road, from which we can discover 'far more of the past than the past itself had thought good to tell us' (Bloch, 1953, pp. 62, 64). The idea that films, along with other forms of mass or popular culture, are 'eloquent social documents' reflecting the flow of contemporary history has been an implicit assumption of much writing about cinema, but explanations of how 'the film-making process taps some reservoir of cultural meaning' have remained relatively unformulated and untheorised (Barry, 1939, p. vii; Jarvie, 1978, p. 380). In the late 1940s, Siegfried Kracauer proposed that some movies, or some 'pictorial or narrative motifs' reiterated in them, might be understood as 'deep layers of collective mentality which extend more or less below the dimensions of consciousness' (Kracauer, 1947). Kracauer's proposition has remained central to what his contemporaries Martha Wolfenstein and Nathan Leites (1950, p. 11) called a 'psychoanalytic-mythological' mode of interpreting film's relationship to culture. Historian Marc Ferro, for example, has encouraged historians to treat films as historically symptomatic, suggesting that they examine the 'unconscious' of a filmic text to reveal the biases, tastes or secret fears of the cultural moment in which it was produced.[5] While such methods are readily compatible with the interpretive practices of film studies, they remain vulnerable to an empirical scrutiny of the basis on which some movies are selected as historically symptomatic while others are not. Writing in 1947, Lester Asheim questioned John Houseman's analysis of 'tough' films such as *The Big Sleep* or *The Postman Always Rings Twice* as symptoms of a postwar malaise in which 'the American people, turning from the anxiety and shock of war, were afraid to face their personal problems and the painful situations of their national life' (Houseman, 1947, p. 163). Asheim complained that Houseman was generalising from a particular example, without having demonstrated its representativeness. If historians were instead to examine *The Razor's Edge*, a big-budget production from the same year, he argued,

> they will deduce that our generation was an intensely earnest group of mystical philosophers who gladly renounced the usual pleasures of this world in order to find spiritual peace. From *State Fair* they can conjure up a nation of simple agrarians whose major problems centered around the prize hog and spiked mincemeat. And what would they make of a generation reflected in *Road to Utopia*? (Asheim, 1947, p. 416)

The concept of film as 'objectified mass dream', consensual myth or 'barometer of … social and cultural life' has nevertheless retained considerable seductive power, as has the idea of reading cultural history through textual interpretation (Nash Smith, 1950, p. 91; Landy, 2001, p. 1). Instinctively, this mode of analysis reaches for metaphor and allusion as clues to the kinds of contemporary political or moral conversations the film in question might address. As everyday film consumers, we can use films in this way by drawing on references within our cultural milieu: for example, we might consider whether *Avatar* (2009) provides an allegorical critique of either multinational capitalism or US foreign policy. Shifting this interpretive speculation into the scholarly historical register sends historians to the archives that house the textual history of public cultures, to search for correspondences between a film and the discourses that surrounded it at the time of its release. Although this is historical work, its mode of analysis often remains that of symptomatic interpretation, in the expectation that an intertextual account that juxtaposes the film's content with a different text or texts plucked from the same historical milieu 'will reveal something about the cultural conditions that produced them and attracted audiences to them'.[6] Such analyses tend to favour films that respond to their quest for allegorical or symptomatic meaning, and risk ascribing to individual films a representational significance that may be disproportionate to their capacity for historical agency. Houseman's premature invocation of what would later become *film noir* is a case in point: *film noir* has, in the main, been understood very much in Houseman's terms, while Asheim's counter-examples have remained starved of the oxygen of historical analysis.[7]

When this *zeitgeist* analysis of individual films aggregates into the study of filmic phenomena (histories of genres, authors or national cinemas, or films on particular topics and so on), the result is a series of compartmentalised thematic accounts largely detached from the circumstances of their consumption, and yet heavily dependent for their significance on the assumption that these textual encodings would have had some kind of social or cultural effect. The post hoc selection and highlighting of films that reward analysis turns the movies themselves into proxies for the missing historical audience, paying little attention to their actual modes of circulation at any time. While it may claim that films demand the historian's attention because of the cinema's mass popularity, this symptomatic approach is capable of simultaneously overlooking even the most obvious and readily available indices of that popularity. Robert Ray (1985, pp. 140–1) has noted that in the postwar period there was 'an enormous discrepancy … between the most commercially successful movies and those that have ultimately been seen as significant. Ray exaggerates only the uniqueness of this period: film history has been written almost in its entirety without regard to, and often with deliberate distaste for, the box office. Nowhere is film studies' genetic inheritance from literary analysis so much in evidence than in the deformities of attention that this produces. We need to be aware of the historical cost of this approach, and of how much has been omitted in the effort to construct film history as the story its historians want to tell: a story of crisis, innovation, anxiety, turbulence, and the elevation of the junior branch. As a means of writing the history of production, this symptomatic approach omits from serious consideration the great majority of cinema's most commercially successful products – in the case of Hollywood history, for example, the films of Janet Gaynor, Nelson Eddy, Betty Grable or Shirley Temple – perhaps because few of its historians have wanted to write the history of a cinema of complacency.

Symptomatic film history has also largely been written without acknowledging the transitory nature of any individual film's exhibition history. Both the US motion picture industry and those industries created in competition with Hollywood are built on business models that require audiences to cultivate the habit of cinemagoing as a regular and frequent social activity. From very early in their industrial history, motion pictures were understood to be consumables, viewed once, disposed of and replaced by a substitute providing a comparable experience. The routine change of programme was a critical element in the construction of the social habit of attendance, ensuring that any individual movie was likely to be part of a movie theatre audience's experience of cinema for three days or less, with little opportunity to leave a lasting impression before it disappeared indefinitely. Sustaining the habit of viewing required a constant traffic in film prints, ensuring that the evanescent images on the screen formed the most transient and expendable element of the experience of cinema. During the course of every year in the 1920s, for example, somewhere between 500 000 and 750 000 separate contracts covering approximately 11 million film bookings were written between distributors and exhibitors in the United States. For every actor, writer, electrician or painter employed in Hollywood's production industry in 1939, there were five distribution company salespeople, projectionists, ushers and box-office clerks employed in the business of despatching and exploiting motion pictures, and around 2000 people whose regular habit of ticket-buying greased the wheels of the entire operation.

Figures such as these may give some sense of scale to the larger socioeconomic system implied in Jean Mitry's 1973 proposal for a film *histoire totale*, which would be 'simultaneously a history of its industry, its technologies, its systems of expression (or, more precisely, its systems of signification), and aesthetic structures, all bound together by the forces of the economic, psychosocial and cultural order' (Mitry, 1973, p. 115). From within the *Annales* tradition of socio-cultural history, Michèle Lagny has followed Mitry in describing her version of a preferred film history located 'as part of a larger ensemble, the socio-cultural history … conceived as an articulation among three types of analysis, dealing with cultural objects, with the framework of their creation, making and circulation, and finally with their consumption' (Lagny, 1994, p. 27). The turn to reception histories has at one level begun to address the issue of the socially specific audience, and the local, national and global networks of business entrepreneurs, managers and theatre employees whom cinemagoers encountered each week at the movies (Staiger, 1992). But even histories of reception originating from within a film studies paradigm have been marked by a tendency to insist that the films themselves remain central to film history. In her 1997 *Screen* essay, 'Film History Terminable and Interminable', Barbara Klinger describes 'a cinematic *histoire totale*' that would place 'a film within multifarious intertextual and historical frames' to produce a '*Rashomon*-like effect where the researcher uncovers different historical "truths" about a film as she/he analyses how it has been deployed within past social relations' (Braudel, 1967, pp. 441–442; Klinger, 1997, p. 110). As Lagny puts it, 'the core is the film text … Working from the cinema or on the cinema means starting from the film, and going back to it' (Lagny, 1994, p. 41). Chapman, Glancy and Harper similarly insist that the primacy of 'the film text', as both source document and object of enquiry, is what differentiates film history from other forms of historical enquiry (Chapman *et al.*, 2007, p. 8).

This presumption is less likely to drive the new kinds of cinema history that are represented in this volume, in part at least because scholars in this emerging field come from more diverse disciplinary backgrounds. Cinema has become a matter of historical interest to researchers who have not been schooled in the professional orthodoxy that the proper business of film studies is the study of films. From the perspective of historical geography, social history, economics, anthropology or population studies, the observation that cinemas are sites of social and cultural significance has as much to do with the patterns of employment, urban development, transport systems and leisure practices that shape cinema's global diffusion, as it does with what happens in the evanescent encounter between an individual audience member and a film print.

The new cinema history's preoccupations with the cinema as a commercial institution and with the socio-cultural history of its audiences may seem to risk abandoning the medium-specificity of film history to what Charles Musser has warily described as 'a broader and more amorphous cultural and social history' (Musser, 2004, p. 105). The authors represented here would, however, follow Richard Abel in arguing that as mass entertainment, cinema 'has to be conceived in terms that reach beyond the production of film texts and exhibition practices' (Abel, 2006, p. 6). New cinema history offers an account that complements and is informed by many aspects of film history, particularly by investigations of global conditions of production, of technical innovation and craft and of the multiple and interconnected organisational cultures that characterise the film production industry. To these it adds knowledge of the historical operations of distribution and exhibition businesses worldwide, and of ways in which these interconnected networks of global corporate interests, local franchises and other small businesses have together managed the flow of cinema product around the world's theatres and non-theatrical venues. It uses quantitative information, articulated through the apparatus of databases, spatial analysis and geovisualisation, to advance a range of hypotheses about the relationship of cinemas to social groupings in the expectation that these hypotheses must be tested by other, qualitative means. In demonstrating the range of archival materials specific to these core areas of cinema's operational and institutional history, the new cinema history cautions strongly against the adequacy of a total history of cinema founded on the study of films.

At the same time, the new cinema history offers a counter-proposition to the assumption that what matters in the study of the audience experience should be restricted to 'reception' – that is, to what happens in the moments in which audiences are primarily focused on the screen, or are thinking afterwards about the film and its possible meanings. As Kate Bowles has suggested, film studies has most often imagined its spectators as captive and captivated creatures of its texts,

> stumbling into the theatre out of nowhere … and then vanishing back out into the crowded street and a life imagined chiefly as the place that the escapist is escaping from, not as a life furnished with other media, other pressures, or other people. (Bowles, 2009, p. 84)[8]

Oral histories with cinema audience members, on the other hand, consistently tell us that the local rhythms of motion picture circulation and the qualities of the experience of cinema attendance were place-specific and shaped by the continuities of life in the family, the workplace, the neighbourhood and community. Stories that cinemagoers recall return repeatedly to the patterns and highlights of everyday life, its relationships, pressures and resolutions. Only the occasional motion picture proves to be as memorable, and as Annette Kuhn discusses in Chapter 4, it is as likely to be memorable in its fragments as in its totality.

Kuhn's chapter seeks to address the methodological distance between the critical and theoretical analysis of individual films and the study of cinema as a social and cultural institution by examining cinema memory as a form of discourse with identifiable thematic and formal attributes, which can be analysed using 'the textual and psychoanalytic procedures familiar to most film scholars'. She develops a typology of cinema memory, distinguishing between three distinct modes in which the personal, the collective and the social intersect to different degrees and in different combinations: remembered images or brief scenes from films, situated memories of films; and memories of the activity of cinemagoing.

Remembered scenes or images from films are distinctive in being brief, fragmentary, detached from any memory of the film's plot, and still resonant and intense, evoking strong emotions or bodily sensations on the narrator's part. A common instance is a memory of having been frightened at the cinema at a very early age, but these 'private' memories are most often displaced from any recollection of the circumstances in which they took place. Victor Burgin describes such a vivid and dreamlike memory:

> I can recall nothing else of this film – no other sequence, no plot, no names of characters or actors, and no title. How can I be sure the memory is from a film? I just know that it is. Besides, the memory is in black and white. (Burgin, 2004, p. 16)

These qualities, Kuhn suggests, align this type of memory with the 'interior', preverbal psychological processes of the 'raw' dream, daydream or fantasy. Like dreams, these fragmentary memories are transformed and 'somehow diminished' when they are pressed into verbal or narrative form, 'as if the process of articulation takes the *shine* off the unspoken, unarticulated, memory image' (Burgin, 2004, p. 15).

The second type of cinema memory that Kuhn identifies is more situated, involving the recall of a film or a scene within the context of events in the subject's own life. I can, for example, recall with some precision the concern my nine-year-old self felt, on a visit to the Shirley Odeon for a friend's birthday, at the number of horses that seemed to be killed in the climactic battle in *The Commancheros* (1961).[9] I can also remember discovering my parents' expectations of cinemagoing when, in 1964 we saw a double bill of *Son of Captain Blood* (1962) and *Dr. Syn, Alias the Scarecrow* (1963). We had arrived halfway through *Dr. Syn*, and when we reached the same point in the movie three hours later, they firmly announced that 'this is where we came in', and declared that we were leaving with the narrative incomplete.[10] As Kuhn suggests, these types of cinema memories share an anecdotal rhetoric, in which the narrator is both protagonist and observer, and the story is commonly embellished with extraneous detail.

The largest category in Kuhn's typology comprises memories of the activity of cinemagoing, which are normally recounted entirely separately from memories of particular films, as recollections of a communal activity, often with repeated themes: '"We used to" is the characteristic introductory turn of phrase here … in a manner that melds the personal with the collective, or frames the personal within a collective experience.' The comparative abundance of such recollections in the discourse of cinema memory has led Kuhn and others to conclude that, in the memories of the vast majority of the cinemagoers she interviewed, 'the essentially *social* act of "going to the pictures" is of far greater consequence than the cultural activity of seeing films.' Although these accounts may sometimes underestimate the impact of particular movies on individuals or audiences at the time, they surely remind us that unlike key life events, the vast majority of films do not seek out landmark status for themselves, but are designed to fade back into the overall field of our cultural experiences. Like individual dreams that may be vivid and impressive at the time and briefly on waking, most individual movies receive little subsequent support from the processes of long-term recall and re-narration that characterise the building of our memories of significant life events. It seems that we are habituated as consumers to clear them from our memories and make way for more, and in this respect, at least, we may resemble the spectator that Roland Barthes describes leaving the movie theatre as if he were awakening from hypnosis (Barthes, 1986, p. 345).

Kuhn has elsewhere described memory as neither pure experience nor pure event, but 'always already a text … an account, always discursive' (Kuhn, 1995, p. 161). Cinema memories, like other memory texts, 'create, rework, repeat and recontextualise the stories people tell each other about the kinds of lives they lead' (Kuhn, 1995, p. 165). Each of the three types of cinema memory that Kuhn describes perform different functions across a range of private and public purposes. Putting such memories to use inevitably involves decontextualising them from their site of origin and inserting them into some other narrative or argumentative sequence. Those affective personal memories that serve to recall an emotion or its expression are least likely to circulate as public narratives, but perhaps we also remember cinema in fragments because memories of whole movies are not particularly useful in constructing our own narratives, whereas stories of cinema-going are very readily turned into narratives in which we are at the centre of events as creators of our own world (Kuhn, 1995, p. 166).

Our use of cinema memory as a component in understanding audiences and their behaviour must acknowledge the deliberately engineered ephemerality of cinema, both as a property of its commercial existence and as a phenomenon of memory. The patterns formed by individual memories of cinema, echoing those of its commercial flow, invoke less a sense of an *histoire totale* focused on an individual film text than another concept central to Fernand Braudel's historiography: the 'dialectic of duration' through which he sought to describe the simultaneous plurality of historical time (Braudel, 1980, p. 26). Social time, Braudel argued, 'does not flow at one even rate, but goes at a thousand different paces, swift or slow, which bear almost no relation to the day-to-day rhythm of a chronicle or of traditional history' (Braudel, 1980, p. 12). While the mere century of cinema's existence hardly provides a timeframe that engages the geographical time of Braudel's *longue durée*, his distinction between the cyclical, social time of 'the major forms of collective life' and the individual time of particular events provides a temporal framework within which we can examine patterns of cultural consumption (Braudel, 1980, pp. 10–11; Santamaria and Bailey, 1984).[11] Disposing of the fiction that time is homogeneous frees us from the obligation to assume that people living through periods of rapid change naturally felt disorientated; this liberation may enable us to develop a more nuanced understanding of cinema's various relations with 'modernity' in the early twentieth century (Passmore, 2003, p. 129).

All historical work, Braudel insisted, 'is concerned with breaking down time past, choosing among its chronological realities according to more or less conscious preferences and exclusions'. Traditional history, predominantly concerned with the individual, the event and the proximate explanation, has 'accustomed us to the headlong, dramatic, breathless rush of its narrative'. By contrast, the 'new economic and social history' associated with the *Annales* sought to transcend particular individuals and events in order to examine the rhythms and 'rates of respiration' of economies, institutions and social structures (Braudel, 1980, pp. 10–11, 27, 129). A segmentation of cinema history according to its economic and social phases might, for example, distinguish between the period in which cinema was available only through an act of what Robert Allen has called 'social convergence' and subsequent periods in which sociality became an optional component of the experience of cinema.

Against these larger movements of social and cultural experience, the brief life (both commercially and in memory) of individual films resembles Braudel's description of events as instants in history, 'surface disturbances ... short, sharp, nervous vibrations ... waves stirred up by the powerful movement of tides' (Braudel, 1980, p. 3). Braudel acknowledged *'l'histoire événementielle'* as the form of history that is 'by its nature the most exciting and richest in human interest', but he insisted on its capriciousness and limited explanatory power:

> I remember a night near Bahia, when I was enveloped in a firework display phosphorescent fireflies; their pale lights glowed, went out, shone again all without piercing the night with any true illumination. So it is with events; beyond their glow, darkness prevails. (Braudel, 1980, pp. 10–11)

The lacunae of memory form part of the prevailing darkness of cinema's social history, and this history is not recovered by ascribing a disproportionate historical agency to the most transitory and ephemeral component of the social experience of cinema, by making the movies themselves stand in as proxies for the missing historical audience. Finding more satisfactory ways to accommodate the culturally normative process of forgetting and moving on that so aptly mimics the rapid cycling of movies through theatres is, however, only one of the methodological issues that faces the historian of the audience experience. Writing the social history of audiences is inevitably an activity circumscribed by indeterminacy. Because audiences are evanescent, unstructured social agglomerations who assemble for each event, dissolving without apparent trace on each occasion, it is tempting to generalise the elusive empirical reality they constitute into abstract but stable social categories (Allen and Gomery, 1985, p. 156). Thus a great deal of writing on film refers to 'the audience', or sociologically derived subcohorts within this imagined totality: the female audience, the gay audience, the child audience, the Nigerian audience and so on. This abstraction has more in common with film studies' previous imagination of a hypothetical spectator crafted by the psychosexual operation of his or her ego, who nevertheless floats above the specifics of social history, and who manifests symptomatically in much the same way wherever the same movie plays.

As Robert Allen argues, film history's assumptions have inverted the accounts of popular memory, reducing the experience of cinema to an abstracted, uneventful, individual act of textual engagement. Substituting theories of spectatorship for social histories, film studies 'has invested a great deal in conceptualizing what was involved aesthetically, ideologically and sexually in playing the role of spectator', but has left largely unexplored the social preconditions that determined any instance of that role: how attendance at this or that cinema defined a class or caste identity, or how a racial or religious affiliation determined access to the apparent democracy of entertainment through social negotiations that took place outside the theatre as well as inside it. To write about historical audiences, we have to replace these imaginary spectators with ones of our own creation, located more specifically in space and time, as Richard Abel does at the beginning of *Americanizing the Movies and 'Movie-Mad' Audiences*: 'Imagine you are a young woman who has decided to join one of your store clerk or stenographer friends going to the movies after work in downtown Des Moines, Iowa, in the spring of 1913' (Abel, 2006, p. 13).

As Stephen Hughes observes in Chapter 17, exhibition histories 'tell specific stories about local people, institutions, events and communities'. This is the second challenge confronting the new cinema historian interested in the appropriate scale of an audience study: can microhistorical research from one location generate findings that are usable by others? To paraphase Abel's remark that the study of cinema exhibition and its audiences 'generally succeeds as social or cultural history more than as cinema history', this historical work at the village level may indeed succeed best as local history (Abel, 2004, pp. 108–9). Specific stories about local people stand a long way from Mitry's and Lagny's ambitious scoping of a prospective *histoire totale* for the cinema. But the fact that the larger comparative analysis that new cinema history can provide will rest on a foundation of microhistorical inquiry requires its practitioners to work out how to undertake small-scale practicable projects that, whatever their local explanatory aims, also have the capacity for comparison, aggregation and scaling. With common data standards and protocols to ensure interoperability, comparative analysis across regional, national and continental boundaries becomes possible as each 'local history' contributes to a larger picture and a more complex understanding of what Karel Dibbets, in his Dutch 'Culture in Context' project, has called 'the infrastructure of cultural life' (Dibbets, 2007).

The methodological toolkit underpinning this approach and, indeed, the ambition to enlarge the scope of what has previously been dismissed as merely local or community history is not, of course, limited to the study of cinema, but it is particularly suited to the examination of transitory cultural events, such as movie screenings. Audiences bring their individual and collective social circumstances with them to the social event that is the cinema screening, and those dispositions condition their interpretative response. The examination of context therefore needs to be both detailed and refined in order to begin to understand the interpretive frameworks likely to have been available to particular audiences. Because these occasions leave only residual contextual traces of their evanescent existence, this form of enquiry is the only way to 'capture' the cultural 'object' and weave it into a web of cultural and social relations.

While one aim of such projects is to develop broader descriptions from the aggregation of the small-scale and specific studies, the evidence seldom allows us to assume that one case study can simply stand in for others that seem like it. Far from discovering that one small town, urban neighbourhood or shopping mall is interchangeable with another, ethnographic cinema history frequently suggests that a more complex mapping of relationships is necessary. Close historical investigations of the everyday nature of local cinemagoing reveal how the resilient parochialism of individuals and communities incorporated and accommodated the passing content that occupied their screens to their local concerns and community experiences. Rather than pursuing a totalising account, the contributors to this collection would argue that the strength of cinema exhibition history lies in its aggregation of detail, in a way exactly analogous to the proposition that the more individual films we unearth and study, the more we know about films in general.

Several chapters in this collection address these methodological questions of microhistory and scale. In Chapter 13, Arthur Knight explores the limits of our knowledge of African-American moviegoing in the non-metropolitan US South, which constituted the most conspicuous instance of racially segregated cinema. His chapter charts the spectral existence of the Apollo Theatre in Williamsburg, Virginia, which made its elusive appearance in the *Film Daily Yearbook*'s lists of 'Negro' cinemas between 1936 and 1940, but is otherwise missing from the town's documentary archive or the recorded memories of its citizens. While other historians have suggested that moviegoing was more likely to have been an occasional rather than a regular activity among African Americans before the desegregation of movies theatres in the 1960s, Knight examines the 'compelling, if not quite conclusive evidence' that especially after World War II, African Americans in many places in the Southern states had 'regular and increasing access to the movies and that at least a substantial number made use of this access' despite the objectionable conditions under which their moviegoing took place. Indicating how trade data may have significantly under-represented the size of black audiences, Knight suggests that 'long before we might have suspected, there was at least a desire amongst African Americans for moviegoing to be a part of black life in the small-town South'.

In pursuing the Apollo Theatre and the possible venues that it might have been, Knight recognises the difficulties of constructing an authoritative history from hearsay. Instead, he provides an account of 'the conditions of possibility' for African-American cinemagoing in Williamsburg from the late 1930s to 1969, when the first cinema that had never been a site of segregation was built. His discussion is as much concerned with seeing and analysing the nuances of the inevitable evidentiary gaps in the audience histories that we can construct as it is with creating as full a picture as possible of black cinemagoing. The issues raised by his chapter about the representativeness of individual case studies and the extent to which generalisations can be made from them are of crucial significance to the microhistorical methodologies of the new cinema history. So is the manner of his engagement with the paucity of evidence. Even if we can establish the existence of the Apollo Theatre, we cannot know what it played, or what relationship its audiences had to what they saw, or how that relationship might have differed from those of other audiences. These gaps in our knowledge are precisely what compel us to look for new and different clues to the social experience of cinema, and to seek other ways in which we might connect this particular case to others that might seem equally marginal from the point of privilege that has been film history's normal viewing position.

In Chapter 17, Stephen Hughes explains that Indian cinema history has also largely been 'written without reference to anyone who might have watched films'. Relatively little attention has been paid to the historical composition of local film audiences in India, and until recently there have been no sustained attempts to study exhibition as a pivotal institution.[12] Under these circumstances 'the Indian audience' is particularly liable to the kind of distorting abstraction discussed earlier. For distributors and exhibitors operating in this highly diversified market, however, sensitivity to the divisions within audiences was critical to business success. Adopting a sociological rather than a formalist approach to genre, Hughes' chapter demonstrates how south Indian exhibitors in the 1920s classified film genres as part of their business practice to help them 'imagine, cultivate and socially differentiate' their cinema audiences.[13] By constructing a hierarchy of genres that blended questions of taste with social differentiation, exhibitors could operate a hierarchy of venues catering to different castes, classes and religious groups without explicitly segregating the social space that cinema provided. In conjunction with the economic hierarchy of ticket prices, exhibitors used their sociology of genre to constrain the democratic promise of a socially equalised audience by creating a space in which existing relations of caste and class could be simultaneously enacted and transgressed (Liang, 2005, p. 369). Hughes suggests that in India, just as in the United States and Europe, histories of exhibition are likely to lead scholars 'away from the main metropolitan areas into district cities, smaller market towns and rural hinterlands', to places that are not currently on any maps of film history: places in which the exercise of consumer discretion, which was a hallmark of cinema's appeal in US cities, was often reduced to choosing whether or not to go to the one available show in the community's only cinema.

Bemboka, a village of 300 people in the rural south of New South Wales, is certainly one of those places beyond the limit of existing cinematic maps. Exemplifying the way in which microhistorical studies can question dominant accounts of national cinema, Kate Bowles in Chapter 18 uses the history of the volunteer-operated weekly picture show that entertained the Bemboka community from 1956 to 1967 to reassess the long-standing belief among Australian media producers and scholars that Hollywood's dominance of their exhibition market was the outcome of coercive business practices, that Australian audiences were unwilling accomplices to America's success, and that Australian communities were culturally diminished by this. Bowles identifies the segmentation of the Australian market as lying in its challenging geography rather than in ethnic, linguistic or religious diversity. In the immediate context of her analysis, the 'tyranny of distance' in Australia meant that the effect of key transitions such as the availability of television diffused at an uneven pace, complicating any sense of what could be regarded as typical of national exhibition. The Bemboka picture show opened for business in the same year that television broadcasting began in Sydney and Melbourne, and closed in 1967 at least in part because its immediate purpose of raising funds to build a new Memorial Hall for the community had been achieved. A television signal of sorts reached Bemboka in 1961, but reception was poor and unreliable for another decade.

Given the difficulties involved in ensuring a regular supply of good quality 16-mm prints to a location as small, remote and economically marginal as Bemboka, Bowles' research is bound to ask why both the distributors and the Memorial Hall Fund Committee maintained their commercial relationship despite the obstacles of cultural incompatibility. For the distributors, she suggests, the answer lay less in the insignificant financial return than in the reputational benefits that could be gained by demonstrating their commitment and service to rural and regional Australia as a counter to the perennial complaints of Australian producers. For the schoolteacher and general store manager who ran Bemboka's picture show, the venture was a practical demonstration of community maintenance at least as much as it was an attempt to bring the modernity of *Rock Around the Clock* to its country audience. It is, Bowles suggests, salient to bear in mind how little the intentions and purposes sustaining the Bemboka picture show had to do with the films themselves.

A history that addresses itself to the place that cinema exhibition attendance came to occupy in specific communities cannot, however, confine itself to the idiosyncrasies of the local microhistorical narrative. Films might seem to arrive at the local theatre out of the blue, and it is certainly the case that audiences were shielded from many of the business dealings that constitute the contractual history of the distribution industry. Ethnographies of cinemagoing provide only a very weak account of how distribution might have operated, often based on guesswork and patchy observation. Nevertheless, every screening was the successful outcome of negotiations exchanged by mail, telegraph or telephone, and a sequence of physical journeys by air, sea, road and rail, in order to enable the audience's cultural encounter with a film's content through the delivery of a film print. This is a logistical and strategic history that expresses itself archivally in multiple discursive forms of involuntary testimony: theatre records, newspaper reviews, the trade press and business correspondence.

Much of the existing literature on the history of exhibition in the United States has tended to separate exhibition from production-distribution, or otherwise reinforce the perception that it is the junior partner in the industry. Histories of both the conversion to sound and the Paramount case, which ended with the divorcement of the major companies' theatre chains from their production and distribution operations, are most frequently written from perspectives that emphasise the activities of the production studios and disregard the role of exhibitors in precipitating or resisting these events, or the consequences of these events for exhibitors or audiences (Conant, 1960; Izod, 1988; White, 1988b; Crafton, 1997; Gomery, 2005). Throughout its history, however, the US cinema industry has been fundamentally structured by the continually hostile relationship between the major companies and the independent exhibition sector. This tension was in part an inevitable commercial opposition between wholesaler and retailer over the division of profitability and risk, and over the exercise of economic control. This conflict was intensified by the particular nature of the business, where products were leased rather than sold, and where the wholesale price was determined more by the location and condition of the theatre than by the quality of the picture. From 1915 onwards, as the major companies sought to concentrate audiences in the most profitable tiers of the exhibition chain, the more or less continuous restructuring of the exhibition industry repeatedly exacerbated the tensions in this relationship. One perennially divisive issue revolved around the extent to which production and distribution companies could transfer some of the financial risks of production to exhibitors. In the early 1920s production companies sought to do this through advance booking payments; after this practice was abandoned, studios adopted the mechanisms of block booking and clearance as means of both ensuring the circulation of all their product and regulating exhibitors' access to pictures. Exhibitor resistance to these practices and the control they gave the major companies over the profitability of exhibition was central to the US government's antitrust suit in the Paramount case.

Extending the history of distribution practice beyond the Paramount decision, Deron Overpeck in Chapter 10 examines the relationship between US exhibitors and the major studios in the 1970s, when the growth of pay cable television stations threatened to reduce the supply of both films and audiences to US movie theatres. In the post-Paramount period, the principal instrument by which producers passed on risk to exhibitors was through the practice of blind bidding, in which exhibitors paid in advance for the licence to show a film in their theatres, effectively obliging them to invest in the movie's production and share in its risk. Blind bidding became a critical part of studio business planning after 1948, providing the studios with an advance income stream that minimised their dependence on bank loans to finance production. It remained a cause of bitter dispute between studios and exhibitors for more than two decades after the Paramount case was settled. From the mid-1970s, the exhibitors' trade organisation, the National Association of Theater Owners (NATO), campaigned vigorously for the abolition of blind bidding, initially asking the Department of Justice to pursue an antitrust case, and then turning to individual state legislatures to prohibit it. Despite the studios' fervent resistance, by October 1979 16 states had outlawed blind bidding; by 1984, when the distributors effectively conceded defeat after the last appeals of the studios' various lawsuits were rejected, 24 states had enacted anti-blind-bidding legislation.

As Overpeck argues, the battle over blind bidding stands as one instance in which exhibitors successfully fought back against studio domination. It was not, of course, the only such instance: exhibitor campaigns were the key component in the elimination of previous anti-competitive behaviour by the major companies, including advance booking and the Paramount case. By improving exhibitors' cash flow, the exhibitors' success facilitated the renewal of the country's theatre stock in the 1980s, but as on previous occasions, the exhibitors' victory also had perverse consequences. The President of the Motion Picture Association of America (MPAA), Jack Valenti, had warned in 1979 that without the financial guarantees provided by blind bidding, the studios would become more conservative in their production policies, producing 'fewer big budget blockbusters, fewer imaginative films, and more and more sequels and remakes'.[14] Overpeck argues that in removing the financial safety net that encouraged studios to support more challenging film-making, the exhibitors' defeat of blind bidding contributed significantly to the growth of high concept film-making in the 1980s. But he also concludes that, since the expansion of the exhibition sector in that decade came via movies such as *Raiders of the Lost Ark* (1982), *Flashdance* (1983) and *Top Gun* (1986), exhibitors were more likely to welcome the shift to adaptations and other popcorn fare than they were to lament the decline in Hollywood's aesthetic ambition.

Complementing Overpeck's business history, Deb Verhoeven's more sociological approach, in Chapter 14, uses the example of the circulation of Greek films for Greek diasporic audiences in Australia, to examine the interplay between the space and time of film distribution. The business of film distribution, she argues, is founded on the establishment of temporal hierarchies: it relies equally on the continuous supply of new products and on the predictable obsolescence that moves them through the supply chain. In achieving its commercial purpose of maximising the financial return from a limited number of prints being exposed to the largest number of people over a defined period of time, a system of distribution uses its temporal regulation of the exhibition market to construct hierarchies of access that are both spatial and social. Temporal differences are also distances. On a global scale, the greater the distance from a film's domestic market, the longer the delay in its arrival. Within a region, access spreads from the metropolitan centre to the suburban hinterlands, with the product losing value as it passes through time and space. The print bears the signs of its physical journey in 'the uneasy splices, the perceptible hiss or mismatched dialogue of a damaged soundtrack, the palimpsest of green, yellow and white lines that run amok over the drama', and these visible scars position and address its audiences, informing them of their place in a socioeconomic hierarchy entirely unrelated to the content on the screen.[15]

In her account of Greek cinema in Australia, Verhoeven stresses the possibility of other, qualitatively different, temporalities of distribution that resulted, at least in part, from the distinctive social function that Greek cinema had for its diasporic community, to 'bring our country to us'. Exhibitors understood their audiences to be using cinema to recover past experiences in another country, and constructed their programming policies accordingly. As a result, distributors felt little obligation to rush new films to market, and accommodated their audiences' preferences for film revivals, in the process ensuring that successive waves of migrants arriving in Australia would have access to common cinematic memories of their homeland. Along with several other authors in this collection, Verhoeven suggests that a consideration of this diasporic audience encourages us to redefine our understanding of 'national cinemas' as politically, linguistically or geographically bounded entities. Australia's Greek diasporic cinemas, she argues, did not operate in 'opposition' to Hollywood – indeed, they conventionally played subtitled Hollywood movies as the second item in their double bills. Rather, they suggest a way of thinking about the globalisation of cinema, and the constitution of its audiences as communities of belonging, that is, not simply contained by an account of cultural imperialism.

In his discussion of the spread of cinema exhibition and the beginnings of everyday moviegoing in Ontario in the early twentieth century (Chapter 15), Paul Moore argues that the region is a neglected transitional scale between the locality and the mass market for cinema, just as it also constitutes a site at which microhistorical and macrohistorical levels of enquiry intersect (Peltonen, 2001, p. 348). Moore demonstrates that the emergence of mainstream cinema was not simply an urban phenomenon but a metropolitan one, in that it almost immediately included the surrounding region in the creation of a mass market. What made cinema modern, he suggests, was not so much its apparatus, its commerciality or its sensationalism as its creation of a form of consumption that connected all places in a region, not to each other so much as to the mass market of modern metropolitanism, most frequently expressed in local newspapers' claims that the arrival of cinema in an Ontario town was proof that its town was 'up-to-date'.

Moore's extensive study of the newspaper coverage of early cinema in Ontario reveals that the daily newspapers of small cities and towns recorded their local cinema history with far more accuracy and detail than the press in larger urban locations where nickel shows – the entertainment equivalent of corner stores – opened almost anonymously, without advertising, reporting or building permits. Addressing a diverse, dispersed and fractious readership, major metropolitan daily papers did not treat cinema with the same promotional zeal until years later, when the movies had become a much more culturally homogenised mass culture. Cinema was much more likely to make an appearance in the metropolitan press when it was 'newsworthy'; as a result, much of the metropolitan coverage was negative, dwelling on fires, accidents or moral dangers. The primary function of a small city daily, on the other hand, was to advertise its local business to its readership, and in this setting, picture shows were 'adworthy' from their first appearance. The advertising columns of these papers provide some of the most comprehensive records available for documenting the history of early cinema.

From this material, Moore develops both a methodology for the use of newspaper coverage of early cinema, and an analysis of the variable relationships between cinema and locality that were embedded in and dependent on the social purpose and scope of the town's newspaper. As he points out, looking for information in the wrong place – for advertising in village weekly papers, for example – can easily mislead the researcher into believing that cinema was absent from locations in which it actually flourished. The mass market for movies was, he suggests, created by the independent activity of thousands of small entrepreneurs who responded to the opportunities presented by the mass production of celluloid entertainment. By creating a radically decentralised exhibition system, these showmen integrated their activities into the local norms of their communities, fitting cinema into existing social and cultural routines. As a result, the appearance of cinema 'did not immediately change how local publics congregated, how local businesses promoted themselves, or how local news was communicated'. But as a more elaborated distribution system of runs and clearances established itself in the 1910s, this pattern of information and promotion was replaced by one more firmly determined by production-distribution companies and focused on movie stars and film titles. The disciplines of a more centralised distribution system gradually eroded the distinctive character of disparate exhibition venues, stripping away their cultural specificity in favour of a much more highly concentrated economic model for cinema's mass market. It was on the foundations provided by this model, Moore argues, that the classical Hollywood system of production was established.

Like Moore, Kathryn Fuller-Seeley, in Chapter 16, examines the appearance of early cinema in a non-metropolitan venue, Cooperstown, a village of 2500 in rural upstate New York, focusing on the village's Centennial Celebration in August 1907. Using accounts of this event, Fuller-Seeley discusses the recognition of films as suitable entertainment for provincial viewers. Unlike the World's Fairs being held in major cities in this era, the Cooperstown Centennial did not celebrate new inventions, manufacturing progress or developments in consumer culture. Instead, it commemorated the town's history, literary heritage and mythical pioneering past. The Cooperstown event prominently featured a motion picture show presented by the Cook and Harris High Class Moving Pictures Company, which had as its centrepiece an Edison historical drama, *Daniel Boone: or Pioneer Days in America*. The Cooks' two-hour show, which was advertised as '100% moral' and containing 'Nothing to offend', also included patriotic actualities, romantic melodramas, light comedies and songs. According to local newspaper reports, it proved to be 'one of the most popular of all the attractions' at the celebration, entirely in keeping with the 'dignified and commendable manner' in which the week's events were conducted.[16] Whatever concerns were being raised about the physical and moral safety of the new nickelodeon entertainment in the cities, the Cooperstown event demonstrated that moving pictures could be acknowledged as an acceptable accompaniment to the celebration's more traditional spectacles of parades and concerts, as well as being a source of historical representation, education and amusement fit for provincial families, women, and children.[17]

Although microhistorical enquiry frequently considers cases that seem marginal or have been overlooked, it is not perforce confined to accounts of the suppressed and the precarious (Peltonen, 2001, pp. 347–359). One consistent if unplanned aspect of this kind of microhistorical enquiry is that its precise objects rarely emerge as an interest shared by more than one scholar. Two essays in this collection, however, examine different aspects of the exhibition history of one cinema, the Rialto, in New York's Times Square, by focusing on the discursive constructions of its audiences in press reports and critical commentaries on the cinema and the films it screened. Tim Snelson and Mark Jancovich (Chapter 11) trace the career of its notorious manager, Arthur Mayer, who took control of the Rialto at the height of the Depression, converting it from a failing movie palace into an upmarket grind-house cinema playing 'mystery, mayhem and murder': sensationalist movies to a surprisingly upmarket, bourgeois audience 'slumming' it. Rebuilt in 1935 in Art Moderne style, the Rialto was far from the 'fleapit' it represented itself as being, and Snelson and Jancovich argue that the theatre's significance lay in the effectiveness with which it branded the films it showed from the late 1930s to the 1950s with its own distinctive identity. Positioning itself as the 'cinematic chamber of horrors' in New York's imagination in the 1930s and 1940s, the Rialto provides a prime illustration of the claim that different cinemas not only had meanings that exceeded their function as places to show films, but could also transform the meanings of the films shown within them.

With the complicity of the New York press, Mayer self-consciously defined the Rialto as an oppositional, even offensive, space, in revolt against mainstream Hollywood's 'safe', 'censored', bourgeois and feminised sensibility. Snelson and Jancovich argue, however, that the theatre's image as luridly lowbrow, the last, disreputable 'refuge of the oppressed sex', was heavily ironic: the Rialto and its policy of 'no hits, no runs, just terrors' were consciously marketed to middle-class audiences searching for an alternative to middlebrow culture. Even the misogyny of the theatre's publicity was attached to a discourse of connoisseurship and sophistication in subcultural capital that circulated widely in press discussions of Mayer and his cinema. Focusing on the discursive construction of the Rialto's audience in Mayer's promotional strategies and in the observations of other commentators, Snelson and Jancovich argue that the Rialto's exhibition practices would become central to the emergence of cult film, particularly in the ways in which it constructed a culture of alternative film consumption through discourses of transgression, urbanity, masculinity and active spectatorship.[18]

Peter Stanfield (Chapter 12) uses the Rialto as his entry-point for a consideration of the cultural discourses surrounding underground film and its audiences, in which he tracks the move from the 'underground cinema' identified by the critic and painter Manny Farber to that defined by film critic, publisher and filmmaker Jonas Mekas. In his 1957 essay 'Underground Films: A Bit of Male Truth', Farber used the term 'underground' to describe the work of American film-makers who 'tunnelled' inside the action movies at which they excelled. But for Farber, going underground also implied a climb down the social and cultural ladder, to discover a more vital and essential film-making than that offered in first-run theatres. The hard-bitten action movies in which he discovered 'expedience and tough-guy insight' found their natural home in the murky, congested 'grind-house' theatres in big cities, where they were screened in what Farber called 'a nightmarish atmosphere of shabby transience' (Farber, 1957, p. 489).

Farber's authentication of his moviegoing experiences 'as a steady customer in male-audience houses', and his acts of discrimination between Hollywood's commercial products, was a form of slumming (Farber, 1953, p. 405). He provided an intellectual defence for the bourgeois patrons of the Rialto. Farber's search for an authentic cinemagoing experience was shared with a group of critics who were writing during the 1930s: Mayer Levin, Otis Ferguson and James Agee, who identified the 'poor, metropolitan, and deeply experienced ... West Times Square audience' as 'probably ... the finest movie audience in the country', validating a male proletarian audience's taste over and above the acts of distinction performed by an educated elite (Agee, 2005, p. 105). Farber's 'Underground Films' essay was an elegy for the 'literate audience for the masculine picture-making', able to discriminate between 'perceptive trash and Thalberg pepsin-flavored sloshing', which had 'oozed away ... during the mid-1940s when the movie market was flooded with fake underground films – plush thrillers with neo-Chandler scripts and a romantic style that seemed to pour the gore, histrionics, décor out of a giant catsup bottle' – precisely those *films noir* subsequently celebrated for their *zeitgeistigkeit* (Farber, 1957, p. 496).

Although Jonas Mekas also celebrated the films and filmgoing experience of the fleatraps of 42nd Street, he played a key role in shifting the meaning of the underground film experience, to describe American avant-garde film practice, 'a cinema that is anti-bourgeois, anti-patriotic, and anti-religious, as well as anti-Hollywood', and more likely to be screened in Greenwich Village or the Lower East Side than 42nd Street (Tyler, 1994, p. v). Critics championing action films or the avant-garde might argue that one contested Hollywood from within while the other did so from without, but Stanfield also invokes Pauline Kael's critique of the 'peculiar emphasis' placed by both groups of critics on 'virility', as well as their common resort to 'the language of the hipster' (Kael, 1963, pp. 12–26). Exhibitors' motives were equally ambiguous. As early as 1947, Arthur Mayer changed the Rialto's programming policy to show imported films, complaining that the studios had largely abandoned the opportunities for technical and aesthetic experiment provided by B-feature production (Mayer, 1947–48). *Variety*, however, explained that Mayer hoped 'to latch on to foreign pix which are steeped in a reminiscent flavor of action and sex so that the drop-ins continue to haunt his theatre'.[19] *Rome Open City*, which Mayer distributed in the United States with his partner Joseph Burstyn, was advertised in Chicago as featuring a 'Savage Orgy of Lust', and double-billed with *Romance of the Rio Grande*, a five-year-old Western starring Cesar Romero.[20] Barbara Wilinsky's meticulous history of the emergence of art house cinema in postwar America essentially confirms Mayer's observation in his 1953 autobiography that the most successful European imports were 'pictures whose artistic and ideological merits were aided and abetted at the box office by their frank sex content' (Mayer, 1953, p. 233; Wilinsky, 2001, p. 37). The postwar American film culture that Wilinsky describes relied to a material extent on the disreputable venues that played both sets of underground cinema, and where audiences in the 1950s and 1960s could see European art cinema interspersed with the 'lowest action trash' that even Kael found 'preferable to wholesome family entertainment' (Kael, 1970, pp. 115–129).

These discursive identifications of a disreputable audience suggest further avenues of inquiry. Farber's 'Termite Art' and the 'subversive gestures' that Kael found in trash were not created solely to play in underground, male-audience cinemas; elsewhere they might perhaps occupy the bottom half of double bills, satisfying the 'masculine escapist urge: adventure, horror, blood', of suburban males-in-revolt, who might only read about the lurid pleasures of the Rialto in their newspapers. Can we attach an economic or demographic identity to the audience described by Ferguson and Farber as resisting the dominant post-Production Code culture of wholesome middlebrow entertainment respectability? To what extent was the 'male revolt' that Arthur Mayer advertised and the *New York Times* publicised a discursive invocation of a more broadly dispersed phenomenon? Was Farber right about this audience's demise, or does it form part of the 'gray flannel rebellion' against 'conformity' that Barbara Ehrenreich describes in *The Hearts of Men* (Ehrenreich, 1983, p. 40; Fraterrigo, 2009, pp. 28–36)?

In asking these questions we are explicitly following the line of historical enquiry suggested by the microhistorical detail, which then requires the tools of more complex large-scale analysis to understand how and why audience behaviour might be both locally idiosyncratic and at the same time attached by complex cultural practices to other sites, other imagined audiences and other imagined mores. To understand what audiences have chosen to do in terms of cultural and economic relations across sites as well as in their relationships within venues, we need different tools and different kinds of data. Surviving box office records have, for instance, attracted the attention of economic historians undertaking large-scale analysis. In this field John Sedgwick's pioneering development of tools with which we can gauge film popularity based on cinema attendance has drawn attention to the opportunities afforded to cultural history by statistical instruments capable of detecting significant variation across large datasets.

Sedgwick's chapter in this collection (Chapter 7) extends his earlier work on the POPSTAT Index of Film Popularity to examine the multiple markets for cinema products and the distinctions among the products supplied to those markets (Sedgwick, 2000). Examining first-run and suburban filmgoing in Sydney, Australia, in the mid-1930s, Sedgwick identifies distinctive patterns of film tastes among the geographically specific audiences attending different types of cinemas, and establishes the extent to which cinemagoing preferences in the suburbs differed markedly from those of city centres. From this he demonstrates that the city centre market was designed to absorb the enormously variable popularity of different movies. Sedgwick's data suggest that 12% of the movies screened in metropolitan Sydney earned half the total box-office revenue generated by those cinemas in 1934. This pattern, in which a very small number of hit films earned disproportionate amounts of first-run box-office, was also common to first-run exhibition in the United States and Great Britain, and provides the underlying economic explanation for the industry's reputation as a high-risk environment (Sedgwick and Pokorny, 2005, pp. 15–16).

The suburban market operated quite differently, however. The overwhelming majority of programmes screened in Sydney's suburban cinemas in 1934 were double bills, with a twice-weekly change of programme. While the first-run cinemas allocated screen time according to a movie's popularity, these suburban theatres, screening 200 movies a year, sought to maintain admission levels regardless of any individual movie's popularity. In these conditions of circulation, the difference between one movie's earnings and another's was far less variable than in the metropolitan cinemas. Because a popular movie would have already received extended exhibition in the first-run market, middle-ranking movies received much greater exposure in the suburban market than in first-run cinemas. First-run exhibition aimed to recruit as large an audience as possible to pay the highest prices to watch a single attraction for as long as possible. The circulation of movies through the suburban market, on the other hand, much more closely resembled a long tail, in which retail business was generated by selling relatively small quantities (seats in individual theatres) at relatively low prices on a regular basis (Sedgwick and Pokorny, 2010). This pattern of retail activity emphasised a schedule of regular changes as the mechanism by which audiences were continually attracted back to the cinema, and by which distributors ensured the circulation of all their stock.

In Chapter 6, Clara Pafort-Overduin also considers patterns of film distribution in the mid-1930s: in this case in The Netherlands, where her enquiry concerns the viability of a Dutch film production industry and the appeal of Dutch films to a Dutch audience. The received history of Dutch national cinema bears a striking similarity to that of other small national cinemas: a story in which the principal villains are an improbable combination of invasive American capitalists and neglectful national audiences. Analysing the evidence of demand available from the remarkable Cinema in Context database, Pafort-Overduin's research uncovers a more complex narrative, in which domestic productions were far more popular with audiences than was indicated by the hostility of the Dutch film press to 'low class' productions.[21] As she observes, a film's critical failure did not by any means result in a failure at the box office.

Although Pafort-Overduin describes the extent to which US and German product dominated the supply of film to the Dutch market, she also points out that two-thirds of these films circulated with only one copy. While Dutch films comprised only 1% of the total number of films in circulation, they occupied a much higher proportion of the total number of screenings, with five of the ten most frequently screened movies in the period being domestic productions. One in five Dutch productions secured a place in the top 20 most screened films, compared with less than 1% of American, German or French films. The successful Dutch films – optimistic comedies with music, featuring local theatre or vaudeville stars – regularly outperformed German films of the same type and Hollywood's most extravagant productions.

Despite the strong demand for domestic films, the Dutch film production industry nevertheless remained economically extremely fragile and ultimately unsustainable, as its high degree of fragmentation made it impossible to develop a continuous mode of production. With no vertically integrated spine to the industry, producers had to raise new finance for every production, and the small size of the market set producers the near-impossible requirement that every film be profitable. Pafort-Overduin's conclusions align with those of other scholars looking at the popularity of national films from the perspective of distribution and exhibition, and it seems clear that a closer attention to demand, measured by the frequency of a movie's screenings, will provide us with a significantly more accurate analysis of the market relationship between Hollywood and domestic productions. This, in turn, may well modify our view of the nature and extent of Hollywood's cultural dominance of its foreign markets.[22]

Like Pafort-Overduin, Mike Walsh (Chapter 8) provides a critique of the idea of a 'national cinema' as equating with its production sector. He argues that such a framework allows distribution and exhibition to occupy roles only as either 'victims or ... *compradors* in the hegemonic dominance of Hollywood'. His analysis of Australian distribution and exhibition in the 1920s and 1930s calls into question some long-standing assumptions about the practices that underpinned the circulation of Hollywood movies. Against the conventional wisdom that blames the domestic production industry's repeated failures on the industrial dominance of the major American companies, Walsh argues that until the late 1960s, Australian governments made a clear decision to import and tax entertainment films rather than subsidise a production industry. This policy ensured that the Australian film industry was dominated by local corporations that chose to invest in exhibition and exploit the availability of low-cost high-quality foreign imports. The demand that these decisions generated provided a stable market in which American distributors competed with each other for access to Australian screens.

Distributors did not follow a single pattern either in their negotiations with exhibition circuits or in the ways in which they moved a small number of prints around a large territory such as Australia. Walsh demonstrates that distributors were as likely to collude with exhibitors – particularly the dominant Union Theatres chain – to gain advantage over their rivals as they were to conspire together against local interests in either production or exhibition. Even local exhibitors were not without effective bargaining power. While first-run exhibitors demanded long 'clearance' windows before distributors made films available for suburban theatres, distributors were anxious to keep the prints of each picture working as hard as possible. This aligned their interests with those of suburban cinemas like the independently owned Colonel Light Gardens cinema (CLG), in a suburb of Adelaide, South Australia, which was anxious to show movies as soon as possible after their first run, so that locals would wait to see them in their neighbourhood rather than journey 'up to Adelaide'. The major threat to the CLG's business in the 1930s did not, however, come from competition with the city cinemas, but from the introduction of Saturday night harness racing at a nearby racetrack, drawing large crowds and undermining the theatre's profits.

Although the Colonel Light Gardens cinema showed single-feature programmes rather than the double bills that were standard in the Sydney market, its screening pattern confirms Sedgwick's emphasis on the long tail in subsequent runs. Despite only screening three days a week, the CLG showed 225 films in 1936 – slightly more than half the total number of films released in the country that year. Even with films usually playing to quarter-capacity houses, the CLG's management could bargain effectively with distributors. The theatre was not, as nationalist legends conventionally report, tied into undifferentiated block-booked contracts and forced to take whatever was 'dumped' on it. Rather, the CLG had contracts with virtually all the US distributors, and these contracts left room for considerable negotiation over price and other terms. Walsh's fine-grained analysis reveals the oversimplifications of generalised discussions of film policy. As he concludes, only after we have discarded the notion that American distributors were to blame for the repeated failures of the Australian production industry can we write a history of Australian cinema in which Australians – industry personnel and audiences alike – occupy positions of agency. As historians elsewhere also shift the focus of their investigations from production to exhibition, they may reach similar conclusions about other national cinemas.

Given the long-standing debates about Hollywood's role as an instrument of US cultural imperialism, surprisingly little research has been conducted on the actual success of Hollywood films in particular countries, especially in those countries where the majority of the world's population lives and the majority of worldwide ticket sales take place. While Hollywood has supplied a substantial share of films released in industrialised countries since the 1910s, there is considerable evidence that in most of these countries American imports have only come to dominate annual box office charts since the 1970s. Peter Krämer points out that since then, more than three-quarters of Hollywood's international theatrical rental income has come from only eight countries: Japan, Canada, Australia and the five most populous countries of Western Europe. Together, these markets constitute less than 10% of the world's population, and account for only a small fraction of worldwide paid cinema admissions. They have much lower rates of cinema attendance than markets such as India, Singapore and Hong Kong, in which Hollywood product has had only a minor share. Following Joseph Garncarz, Krämer argues that the claims for Hollywood's international success have traditionally relied on figures relating to supply – that is, to Hollywood's share of all films released in a particular country – rather than to demand, expressed as Hollywood's share of total ticket sales in that country (Garncarz, 1994, p. 96). Drawing attention to the extent to which a statistical emphasis on the dollar value of ticket sales distorts our understanding of world cinema by excluding most of the world's population and most of the world's cinema consumption, Krämer argues that Hollywood's often dominant share of film supply in countries around the world has rarely translated into an equivalent share of ticket sales. His speculative analysis of the broad categories of movie that have proved most successful in different markets suggests that the similarities and differences between the hit films in different countries warrants a more extensive examination of the patterns of relative popularity across a range of international markets, and indicates a framework in which we might reconsider Hollywood's role in the processes of international cultural exchange.

Together, these analyses begin to identify a specific role for much of Hollywood production circulating in international markets, as something akin to a form of commercial ballast, the function of which was to occupy a sector of the market with a steady supply of product.[23] While both risk and profitability were concentrated on the performance of a small number of high-budget movies in first-run cinemas, the volume production of Hollywood's studio system serviced the outer tiers of the cinematic institution and secured their economic stability. Because of its economies of scale, which were themselves a consequence of the size of its domestic market, the American cinema could service the large but relatively unprofitable lower runs of the exhibition system more effectively than its domestic rivals.

In its focus on titles and genres, the quantitative analysis of box office as an index of consumer behaviour inevitably underplays the significance of the multiple contextual factors that influence spectators' decision-making. Assertions based on distribution and demand for particular titles must be qualified by remembering that the act of choosing to buy a theatre ticket is a practice that is always framed by complex physical and discursive constraints, reverberating between the micrological and the macrological realms. The socio-spatial dimension to this kind of everyday decision-making behaviour is familiar to geographers and anthropologists, but has only recently been appreciated as a significant factor in the diverse and often perverse stories of survival, closure or transition within cinema exhibition histories. In short, because the effect of film-centred film history has been to overlook local irregularities at the microhistorical level in cinema markets (and, indeed, mostly to overlook cinema markets altogether), this has driven an historical account that has significantly elevated the temporal over the spatial or ecological. As a result, while the ideological interpretation of film texts is an established standard in the repertoire of film studies, consideration of the ideological segmentation within the market – the orientation of individual venues to particular populations at particular times – has been slower to emerge. Moviegoing may have been claimed as classless, at least in the sense that it was demonstrably a social phenomenon that unsettled the common patterns of leisure segregation by class, particularly in cities, but like all forms of consumption it also acted as a source of social fragmentation, providing new opportunities for discrimination, exclusion and distinction. Cinema attendance was locally specific. For much of its history it involved the cultivation of highly parochial habits of loyalty exercised within a very small territory of choice, in ways that were nevertheless critical to the survival of the industry as a whole. The sociality of this experience was at no stage meaningfully separate from other locally prevailing patterns of social segmentation, and the cultural boundaries that these conventions of social geography constructed were more than strong enough to determine the parameters of a leisure activity such as cinemagoing, regardless of the choice of film title on any particular occasion.

As part of a large-scale investigation into the social role of film exhibition and consumption in Flanders from 1895 to 2004, Daniel Biltereyst, Philippe Meers and Lies Van de Vijver (Chapter 5) have explored the extent to which Belgium's 'pillarized' social organisation affected the structures of film exhibition and the experience of cinema, focusing on the industrial city of Ghent in the period after World War II. Pillarisation describes the form of social and political organisation that emerged in several European countries in the nineteenth century as a response to industrialisation. In pillarised societies, religious or ideological divisions were embedded in parallel institutional structures performing similar social and political tasks. Overlapping with more traditional class conflicts, pillars formed 'vertical' social segregations, with each pillar maintaining a network of separate social institutions – banks, trade unions, newspapers, schools, hospitals – and individuals might live their lives almost entirely within the institutional framework of their pillar. Belgium was a particularly pillarised society, with Catholic, socialist and liberal pillars competing for the allegiance of the population through leisure and entertainment activities as well as by conventional political and economic means.

Belgium's dense provision of cinemas was in part a consequence of pillarisation, as commercial exhibitors in small towns found themselves in competition with Catholic venues. In the major cities, however, the ideological orientation of most cinemas was much less explicit, and other forms of social, cultural and commercial distinction also influenced audience behaviour. Venues that explicitly targeted a specific audience segment were generally regarded as operating at the margin of entertainment cinema, while Ghent's most prominent socialist cinema, the Vooruit, operated as a low-price commercial cinema, attracting a broader audience.

Arguing for what they call a 'triangulation of data, theory and method', Biltereyst, Meers and Van de Vijver explore ways in which a range of methodologies – longitudinal databases that track programming and exhibition patterns, ethnographic and oral history research into audience behaviour and memory, archival research in corporate records and local and trade press – can be integrated in the production of a social geography of cinema. The substantial oral history component of their research, in which respondents discussed the social composition and behaviour of different cinemas' audiences, allows them to layer a subjective component, expressed in terms of audience manners, dress codes and language as well as venues' programming styles, onto their map of cinema in Ghent. This evidence describes how the choice of venue reflected people's sense of social and cultural distinction, the strength of their attachment to community and their awareness of geographical stratification. Regular attendance at a neighbourhood cinema was an act of belonging, to family or community, while seeking a 'better' film experience in the burgundy velvet seats of Ghent's most prestigious cinema was an act of social aspiration expressed through the desire for conspicuous comfort or higher projection quality.

Along with the work of several other contributors to this collection, the research of Biltereyst, Meers and Van de Vijver demonstrates the centrality of databases to research in new cinema history as well as the utility of the empirical data they synthesise. Jeffrey Klenotic has pioneered the use of a geospatial component in the compilation of exhibition databases, and in Chapter 3 he reflects on some of the possible uses of Geographical Information Systems (GIS) for film historians exploring the spatial and geographic dimensions of movie distribution, exhibition and audiences. Klenotic envisages GIS as a research tool rather than as an instrument for making maps: mapping the location of cinema is only a starting point for the spatial analysis of cinema, not the end product. GIS, he argues, is a form of *bricolage*, in which knowledge is constructed through a trial-and-error research process of rearranging layers of spatial and temporal information 'to facilitate the difficult task of seeing, representing and theorizing the simultaneous multiplicity of social and historical experience in spatial terms and from a variety of partial perspectives'. It allows for the interaction of quantitative and qualitative methods, and provides a platform on which marginalised voices and competing historical perspectives can be presented, compared and tested. As well as its utility as a tool with which we can historicise space, this open, multiple and fluid approach to using GIS makes it, he argues, 'good to think with'.[24]

Klenotic's goal is to generate a 'landscape of inquiry' that maps the networks of interrelationships forming the cinema culture of a particular place and time, in order to investigate 'what these networks meant to people and the role moviegoing played in shaping those meanings'. He describes, for example, how he has built on the work of Harlan Paul Douglass in the 1920s and 1930s to recreate a thematic mapping of the social and spatial relationships between people and places in Springfield, Massachusetts, in order to examine the immediate social, cultural and economic context of individual acts of cinemagoing. In this landscape, a critical inquiry concerned the extent to which the major companies' economic consolidation and vertical integration of exhibition venues had produced a standardised experience of moviegoing. Did the socioeconomic variations embedded in the geographic locations of specific theatres continue to influence their significance as sites for cultural assimilation, negotiation or resistance? Klenotic argues that the iterative process of thematic mapping that GIS enables makes it possible to deconstruct Douglass's assumptions in the formulation of his key concept of 'social quality', and thus to relate Douglass's understanding of the social geography of Springfield to both quantitative demographic data and the qualitative information provided by moviegoers' oral histories. Although the Franklin Theater in

Springfield's North End was within easy walking distance for many city residents, most of them travelled much farther afield to theatres in other parts of the city, because the Franklin was in a neighbourhood with a 'bad' reputation for its low 'social quality'.[25]

Klenotic advocates the use of a framework he identifies as 'grounded visualization'. This is a critical, empirical and interpretive approach that integrates qualitative and quantitative sources of information and draws upon the resources of grounded theory, ethnography and GIS visualisation. Grounded theories of historical explanation begin with the evidence, and induce theoretical explanations from the patterns and themes disclosed by its analysis. A spatial history of cinema must map both the routes by which films circulated as commodities and the geographic constraints and influences on the diverse set of social experiences and cultural practices constituted by going to the movies. In such a map, movie theatres are themselves configured as the nodal points at which cinema takes on material form, to constitute a 'network of time-space relations with socially embedded and physically embodied audiences'.

Historical engagements with the circumstances of individual cinemas such as Klenotic's analysis provides suggest the rich possibilities that an historical geography of cinema can provide, by comparison with a reliance on such apparently ahistorical and non-geographical generalisations as 'the city' and 'the urban sensibility' (Lury and Massey, 1999, pp. 230–1). A spatial analysis of cinema can help us understand the shifting forms of exhibition and moviegoing, and how the location of emerging, disappearing or residually surviving forms of exhibition have been related to the flow of other resources within and across the geography of ruralities, small towns, cities and metropolises.

The contributors to this collection share a number of propositions that are forcefully articulated by Robert Allen in Chapter 2. Beginning with a description of theatrical moviegoing from the perspective of a contemporary teenager, unenthusiastically constrained by 'paying nearly the equivalent of buying a DVD to see a film once in a dark room without wireless internet connectivity with strangers at a time determined by someone else's schedule', Allen argues that the present generation of teenagers and young adults – always the most frequent and reliable moviegoers – no longer experience theatrical moviegoing as more 'authentic' than any other way of consuming cinema. For the first two generations of movie audiences in the first world, the experience of cinema was available only as a social activity, while for their children, the baby boom generation, 'the big screen' and the regular 'social convergence under the sign of cinema' remained the preferred mode of consumption. Allen argues that the present generation, however, 'understands cinema as a textually disintegrated phenomenon experienced through multiple … sites and modalities'. For them, the sociality of the experience of cinema is merely an option, and not necessarily a desirable one; they now experience cinema from the other, post-moviegoing side of what Allen considers to be 'an epochal divide'.

Allen's central proposition is that the subject of what we are calling the new cinema history is the experience of cinema. That experience, for most of the history of cinema, has been 'social, eventful and heterogeneous', so that the history of the experience of cinema is ineluctably a social history. As Klenotic argues, this social history is also a spatial history: each event of cinema was, as Allen suggests, a unique convergence of multiple individual trajectories upon a particular social site, and as such, it was both an unpredictable and unreproducible conjunction of undocumented purposes and meanings.

If the individual significances of these events are largely irrecoverable, some broader purposes and meanings are more susceptible to representation. Allen's mapping of the sites of North Carolina movie theatres reveals that in town after town, the emergence of cinema was a phenomenon of the formation and growth of urban central business districts. Rather than providing the alternative public sphere suggested by some accounts of cinema as vernacular modernism, cinemagoing was 'part of the experience of the spaces of downtown social, cultural, commercial and consumer life' (Hansen, 1991, 2000). Throughout the 1920s and beyond, the majority of movie theatres in the United States were in small towns where the community's only cinema was likely also to be its largest secular meeting space, functioning as a multipurpose venue, tightly woven into not only the community's social and cultural life but also its civic life. Exhibitors were embedded in their communities, boosting the town and its retail enterprise as members of the Chamber of Commerce and cooperating with the churches, the Women's Club and the PTA (Gomery, 1992, p. 216). Just as oral histories of cinema have consistently alerted us to the social significance of the routines and rituals of cinemagoing – 'who sat where each week, and with whom, and what they wore' – the picture show also provided an occasion at which existing social, economic and religious distinctions could be projected onto the informal social segregation of cinema seating arrangements (Huggett and Bowles, 2004; Allen, 2007; McKenna, 2007).

Finally, do we need another 'new' history? Apart from editorial hubris, what justifies the claim to novelty of the work presented here? Like many rhetorical claims to the new, we are in fact advocating an historical return to the prevailing concerns of some of the earliest studies of cinema as an object of sociological and psychological enquiry, rather than the object of aesthetic, critical and interpretive enquiry that has ensued from the construction of film studies as an academic discipline in the humanities. These earlier studies, from Hugo Münsterberg and Emilie Altenloh to the Payne Fund research, concerned themselves with what Frankfurt School theorist Leo Löwenthal called 'the underlying social and psychological function' of cinema as a component in the modern urban environment; their methods were those of the 'human sciences', and their objects of enquiry were people, rather than artefacts.[26] This research tradition has remained much stronger in television studies, where questions of industrial organisation and product circulation, qualitative approaches to audience research and a concern with culturally inscribed conditions of reception have persisted in offering a counterpoint to textual interpretation.[27] In some respects, at least, the focus of the new cinema history represents an application to cinema of questions already familiar to the broader field of media studies.

From another perspective, an overview of the Euro-American historiography that has influenced the new cinema history would register the extent to which historians have, in Krzysztof Pomian's phrase, 'shifted their gaze from the extraordinary to the everyday', from history's exceptional events to the large mass of its commonplaces (Pomian, 1988, pp. 115–116). For more than the last half-century, the questions that we ask about the past, about experience and about culture have become more democratic as they have diversified. This broad development has occurred in waves, with each oscillation responding to its predecessor by seeking to rebalance the scales between a social history that, in Braudel's words, studies 'the deep currents in the lives of men', and the more immediate and specific engagement provided by 'for one man in poring over the fate of another' (Braudel, 1980, p. 20).

Braudel's dismissal of *'l'histoire événementielle'* sought to correct what he saw as an excessive tendency among his immediate predecessors to allow themselves 'to be borne along by the documents, one after another', following a narrative of events step by step (Braudel, 1980, pp. 28–9). The founders of the *Annales* began as heretics, publishing manifestos for a 'new kind of history' that required collaborative, interdisciplinary analysis of structures and *mentalités*.[28] After their heresy achieved orthodoxy, its quantitative, serial approach, once valorised as a 'history without names', was criticised by others as a 'history without people' (Comte and Andreski, 1974, p. 203; Le Roy Ladurie, 1979, p. 285). As 'la nouvelle histoire' begat 'new social history', the latter in turn engendered 'history from below' in reaction to the anonymity of quantitative data, in which, as E.P. Thompson wrote, 'working people are seen as a labour force, as migrants, or as the data for a statistical series' (Thompson, 1963, p. 12). Thompson sought to restore the agency of such people, by recognising 'the degree to which they contributed by conscious efforts to the making of history' (Thompson, 1963, p. 13). If his methodology dismissed the quanta of serial history as 'the mumbo jumbo of those latter-day astrologers … who for 200 years have been trying to persuade us that nothing is real that cannot be counted', his insistence that historians understand 'how past generations experienced their own existence' was entirely in keeping with what Peter Burke has identified as the philosophical foundation of the new structural history identified with the *Annales*: 'the idea that reality is socially or culturally constituted' (Thompson, 1972, pp. 48–49; Burke, 2001, p. 3).

In seeking to examine the social experience of cinema, the new cinema history can claim a close affinity with the new histories described by Burke as studying topics not previously thought to possess a history: childhood, death, madness, climate, cleanliness, reading. Like many of these other versions of the socio-cultural history of experience, the new cinema history raises problems of definition, evidence, method and explanation, problems that are explored but not necessarily resolved in the chapters that follow. Some film historians will, no doubt, continue to dismiss this history as gossip-column trivia in the same way that *Alltagsgeschichte*, the history of everyday life, was once dismissed as trivial. But if, as Burke suggests, the challenge for social historians is 'to relate everyday life to great events like the Reformation or the French Revolution, or to long-term trends like westernization or the rise of capitalism', then the new cinema history provides an exemplary instance of what Max Weber called *Veralltäglichung*: 'routinization', or more literally, 'becoming like everyday'.

Moviegoing, as Robert Allen reminds us, was an everyday encounter with the extraordinary – in Weber's terms, an *alltägliches* encounter with the *ausseralltäglich* (Swedberg, 2005, p. 93). Despite the extraordinary content of the events that cinema presented to its audiences – 'Each Day a Rendezvous with Peril! Each Night a Meeting with Romance!' – their everyday occurrence rendered these encounters customary; like the leopards breaking into the temple in Kafka's parable, when the extraordinary events of the movies were repeated so often that they could be reckoned on in advance, they became part of the ritual, or of what Juri Lotman (1984) called 'the poetics of the everyday'.[29] As Paul Moore demonstrates, these rendezvous were seldom newsworthy; when they were, as in the 1940 Elizabeth City, NC, riot that Allen describes, it was more often for events unconnected to their extraordinary content, which also went largely unrecorded in the memories of their audiences.

The methodological challenges of writing histories of the experience of cinema remain: at one level, that of Annette Kuhn's first type of fragmented cinema memory, we seek to capture (or at least record) something as insubstantial as dreams; at another, equally irrecoverable, we pursue the heterogeneous purposes of the unidentified participants in a myriad of undocumented events. As Allen argues, an historical perspective that seeks to engage with the social experience of cinema rapidly makes it apparent that this experience cannot be reduced to 'some reified notion of spectatorship', any more than the abstraction of 'the movie audience' can serve as an object of empirical historical inquiry. This perspective also makes clear how arbitrary it is to select the film text as a representation of the cinematic event of which it is a constituent part, and how important it is to qualify the analysis of any individual film's meaning within the limits of what we can recover about the times and places where it circulated; to accept, in other words, the modest scope of the textual microstudy for what it is.

As part of a public relations campaign promoting movie attendance for 'Motion Pictures' Greatest Year' in 1938, the American film industry ran a full-page advertisement in 2000 newspapers in the United States and Canada. Under the headline 'The Average Movie-Goer Speaks His Mind', a family patriarch declared that despite occasional family disagreements about the merits of individual movies,

> Taking them all together, I figure that the 'movies' give more pleasure to more people at a lot less cost than most anything the mind of man was ever responsible for – and have done the human race more downright good than all the medicines concocted since creation.[30]

Histories that seek to argue that by improving the general quality and availability of entertainment at a low admission cost, cinema contributed positively to the stock of social well-being in the same way that low-cost electric street lighting did by markedly improving the quality of illumination, must go some distance beyond the confines of the film text or the screen itself (Sedgwick *et al.*, personal communication, 2004). As the findings of the research contained in this collection make clear, these histories are likely to pay more attention to questions of circulation than questions of production, questions of agency and brokerage rather than questions of authorship, to consider cinema as experience rather than film as apparatus, and to examine the heterogeneity and social construction of cinema audiences rather than the textual construction of spectatorship.

We are, however, not proposing to replace one master narrative of cinema history with another; as the variety of the case studies presented here makes clear, the new cinema history is a quilt of many methods and many localities. Many of its methods, particularly those involving computation, mapping and other forms of data visualisation, are collaborative, and its project is inherently interdisciplinary. As a practice of historical enquiry it is decentred, exploratory and open, requiring that the subjectivities of oral history converse with the quantitative data of economic history and the resources of the archive to answer the apparently simple question 'What was cinema?' We do, however, recognise the extent to which a pursuit of the new cinema history will require some considerable practical reskilling for many film historians, in learning to recognise new kinds of relevant data in the archives, involving distance, demography, topography and environment; in learning to represent research in terms of spatial databases and maps as well as conventional historical narratives; and in embedding within our histories the understanding that social subjectivity is always shaped by the particularities of place as much as epoch. Part of the intellectual challenge that humanities scholarship in general faces in the next decade is the development not just of the research capacity to integrate quantitative information within qualitative analysis, but also to devise curriculum strategies and models that enable our students to traverse the methodological boundaries that currently Balkanise our fields of study. In engaging the historical and historiographical challenges I have been describing, the new cinema history has much to offer this larger project.

Notes

1 No introductory essay is, or should be, an island. The ideas expressed here have been honed and shaped by discussions with my co-editors, Daniel Biltereyst and Philippe Meers, with the contributors to this collection, particularly Robert Allen and Jeff Klenotic, and as always with Ruth Vasey. Most influentially, Kate Bowles and I have been trading ideas, phrases and paragraphs on the new cinema history for the best part of a decade. This chapter owes its best turns of phrase, as well as the absence of locomotives, to Kate.

2 This work builds on a tradition of social enquiry into cinema that includes Margaret Thorp, *America at the Movies* (London: Faber and Faber, 1946), Garth Jowett, *Film: The Democratic Art: A Social History of American Film* (Boston: Little, Brown & Company, 1976) and Douglas Gomery, *Shared Pleasures: A History of Movie Presentation in the United States* (London: British Film Institute, 1992). Recent key works in the field include Jackie Stacey, *Star Gazing: Hollywood Cinema and Female Spectatorship* (London: Routledge, 1994); Gregory A. Waller,

Main Street Amusements: Movies and Commercial Entertainment in a Southern City, 1896–1930 (Washington: Smithsonian Institution Press, 1995); Kathryn H. Fuller, *At the Picture Show: Small-town Audiences and the Creation of Movie Fan Culture* (Charlottesville/London: University Press of Virginia, 1996); Martin Barker and Kate Brooks, *Knowing Audiences: Judge Dredd, Its Friends, Fans and Foes* (Luton: University of Luton Press, 1998); *American Movie Audiences: From the Turn of the Century to the Early Sound Era,* eds Melvyn Stokes and Richard Maltby (London: British Film Institute, 1999); *Identifying Hollywood's Audiences: Cultural Identity and the Movies*, eds Melvyn Stokes and Richard Maltby (London: British Film Institute, 1999); John Sedgwick, *Popular Filmgoing in 1930s Britain: A Choice of Pleasures* (Exeter: University of Exeter Press, 2000); *Hollywood Spectatorship: Changing Perceptions of Cinema Audiences*, eds Melvyn Stokes and Richard Maltby (London: British Film Institute, 2001); Annette Kuhn, *An Everyday Magic: Cinema and Cultural Memory* (London: I.B. Tauris, 2002); *Moviegoing in America: A Sourcebook in the History of Film Exhibition*, ed. Gregory A. Waller (Oxford: Blackwell, 2002); *Hollywood Abroad: Audiences and Cultural Exchange,* eds Richard Maltby and Melvyn Stokes (London: BFI Publishing, 2004); Jacqueline Najuma Stewart, *Migrating to the Movies: Cinema and Black Urban Modernity* (Berkeley: University of California Press, 2005); Martin Barker and Ernest Mathijs, eds, *Watching the Lord of the Rings: Tolkien's World Audiences* (New York: Peter Lang, 2007); *Going to the Movies: Hollywood and the Social Experience of Cinema*, eds Richard Maltby, Melvyn Stokes and Robert C. Allen (Exeter: University of Exeter Press, 2007); and Daniel Biltereyst, Richard Maltby and Philippe Meers, *Cinema, Audiences and Modernity: New Perspectives on European Cinema History* (London: Routledge, 2011).

3 Much of the information produced by these projects is available on their websites, as are a range of tools for the presentation and analysis of their data. The HOMER (History of Moviegoing, Exhibition and Reception) website maintains a list of web pages examining the social history of cinemagoing: http://icarg.wordpress.com/links/. For examples, see *Going to the Show*, documenting moviegoing in North Carolina from 1896 to 1930 (http://docsouth.unc.edu/gtts/); *Cinema in Context*, an encyclopaedia of film culture in The Netherlands from 1896 (http://www.cinemacontext.nl/); *The London Project*, examining the film business in London from 1894 to 1914 (http://londonfilm.bbk.ac.uk/); *The Siegen Cinema Databases*, documenting film exhibition in Germany from 1896 to 1926 (http://fk615.221b.de/siegen/start/show/index.php?language=en); *The Williamsburg Project*, a portrait of moviegoing in Williamsburg, VA, from 1900 to the present (http://moviegoing.wm.edu/wtp); *Film Culture in Brno (1945–1970)*, documenting filmgoing in Czechoslovakia (http://www.phil.muni.cz/dedur/index.php?&lang=1). For a discussion of methodological issues involved in the production and analysis of these data, see Michael Ross, Joseph Garncarz, Manfred Grauer, Bernd Freisleben (eds), *Digital Tools in Media Studies: Analysis and Research. An Overview* (Bielefeld: Transcript Verlag, 2009).

4 Among other reasons given for the decision was the comment that 'the dominant approach of reviewers has been to assess the historical accuracy of a film, paying little attention to the specificity of film as a language or mode of representation (something which those with a deep interest in film are quick to point out). When historians review films, they usually write about what they know about – accuracy, verisimilitude, and pedagogical usefulness. These are not inconsiderable as commentary, but it is a far cry from what we expect from them in a book review.' Robert A. Schneider, On film reviews in the *AHR*, *Perspectives*, May 2006, online at http://www.historians.org/perspectives/issues/2006/0605/0605aha2.cfm (accessed 1 February 2010).

5 'The historical and social reading of film … has permitted us to reach nonvisible zones in the past of societies – to reveal self-censorship or *lapses* (which remain in the unconscious of participants and witnesses) at work within a society or an artistic creation … These lapses of a creator, of an ideology, or a society constitute privileged significant signs that can characterise any level of film, as well as its relationship with society. Discovering them, seeing how they agree or disagree with ideology, helps to discover what is latent behind what is

apparent, helps to see the nonvisible by means of the visible.' Marc Ferro, *Cinema and History*, trans. Naomi Greene (Detroit: Wayne State University Press, 1988, pp. 30–31). The cardinal example of an analysis of the unconscious of a filmic text is 'John Ford's *Young Mr Lincoln*', a collective text by the editors of *Cahiers du Cinéma*, trans. Helen Lackner and Diana Matias (1972) *Screen*, 13 (3), 5–44: see in particular pp. 30, 36, 41.

6 Belton. For a critique see Janet Staiger (2004) The future of the past. *Cinema Journal*, 44 (1), 128–129.

7 The critical literature on film noir is very extensive. The best guide remains James Naremore, *More Than Night: Film Noir in Its Contexts* (Berkeley, CA: University of California Press, 1998).

8 Roland Barthes famously writes of leaving the movie theatre as 'coming out of hypnosis'. In the same 1975 issue of *Communications*, Christian Metz writes that 'spectators, on leaving, brutally expelled from the black interior of the cinema into the vivid and unkind light of the lobby, sometimes have the bewildered face ... of people just waking up. Leaving the cinema is a bit like getting out of bed: not always easy.' Roland Barthes (1975) Leaving the movie theatre. *Communications*, 23, 345. Christian Metz (1975) Le film de fiction et son spectateur. *Communications*, 23, 119.

9 While subsequently regretting that my concern did not extend to the horses' Indian riders, who were shot in equal profusion by John Wayne and Stuart Whitman, the fact that *The Commancheros* was directed by Michael Curtiz, notorious for his disregard for equine casualties, may give my 9-year-old self's selective concern some justification.

10 *Son of Captain Blood* was an Italian production starring Sean Flynn, the son of Errol Flynn, who subsequently became a war photographer and died in Cambodia in 1970. *Dr. Syn, Alias the Scarecrow* was a Disney production starring Patrick McGoohan, originally conceived as a three-part television series but re-edited for British and European theatrical release.

11 Ulysses Santamaria and Anne M. Bailey have argued that Braudel's distinctions between the long term, the conjuncture and the event are theoretically inconsistent, and provide a 'bricolage' of durations rather than a dialectic. See Santamaria and Bailey (1984), pp. 78–83.

12 For a study of contemporary Indian audiences, see Adrian Athique and Douglas Hill, *The Multiplex in India: a Cultural Economy of Urban Leisure* (New York: Routledge, 2010).

13 The American film industry's development of a comparable typology of audiences is examined in Richard Maltby, 'Sticks, hicks and flaps: classical Hollywood's generic conception of its audiences', in *Identifying Hollywood's Audiences: Cultural Identity and the Movies* (eds Melvyn Stokes and Richard Maltby), British Film Institute, London, 1999, pp. 23–41.

14 'Friedberg's discount excludes blind bid films', *Boxoffice*, 29 October 1979, p. 1.

15 These observations echo Manny Farber writing of 'murky, congested theaters, looking like glorified tattoo parlors on the outside ... showing prints that seem overgrown with jungle moss, sound tracks infected with hiccups,' where 'the screen image is often out of plumb, the house lights are half left on during the picture, the broken seats are only a minor annoyance in the unpredictable terrain.' See Farber (1957), pp. 489, 492.

16 'Cooperstown celebrates centennial', *Otsego Farmer*, 9 August 1907; *Cooperstown Freeman's Journal*, 15 August 1907.

17 'Cooperstown historically', *Utica Daily Press*, Tuesday 6 August 1907, p. 8.

18 Mayer occupied a complex position in the industry. Formerly head of Paramount's publicity department, he began distributing foreign films in the United States in partnership with Joseph Burstyn in the 1930s. Their company was responsible for distributing most of the Italian neo-realist films to play in the United States in the 1940s, including *The Miracle* (1950), the film involved in the legal challenge to the constitutionality of New York's state censorship. During World War II, Mayer served as Assistant Coordinator of the War Activities Committee of the Motion Picture Industry, and he subsequently supervised the Motion Picture Association's experimental educational project, Pilot Films. In 1964, aged 77, he began a teaching career, and taught film courses

at Stanford, USC and Dartmouth College. He died in 1986.

19 'Rialto, Broadway horror showcase, may switch to class lingos', *Variety*, 29 October 1947, p. 5.

20 Advertisement for *Open City*, *Chicago Tribune*, 13 October 1946, part 6, 19. Reproduced in Wilinsky (2001), p. 126.

21 The Cinema in Context database documents film distribution and exhibition in The Netherlands from 1896 to the present, through four data collections on films, cinemas, people and companies, derived from carefully researched data on nearly all films exhibited in Dutch cinemas before 1960. Produced by a research team under the direction of Karel Dibbets of the University of Amsterdam, the collection is available at http://www.cinemacontext.nl/.

22 This issue is also discussed, for example, in *Hollywood in Europe. Experiences of a Cultural Hegemony*, eds David W. Ellwood and Rob Kroes (Amsterdam: VU University Press, 1994); *Hollywood Abroad. Audiences and Cultural Exchange*, eds M. Stokes and R. Maltby (London: BFI, 2004); *Hollywood and Europe: Economics, Culture, National Identity 1945–1995*, ed. Geoffrey Nowell-Smith (London: British Film Institute, 1998); *European Cinema. Face to Face with Hollywood*, ed. Thomas Elsaesser, (Amsterdam: Amsterdam University Press, 2005).

23 Writing in 1944, George Orwell invoked an idea of cultural ballast in decrying the process of Americanisation that he attributed, in part, to the influence of what he called 'Yank Mags', which were imported into Britain literally as ballast in the holds of ships. According to Orwell, this mode of transport 'accounted for their low price and crumpled appearance'. Since the war, he added, 'the ships have been ballasted with something more useful, probably gravel'. George Orwell, 'Raffles and Miss Blandish', in *Decline of the English Murder and Other Essays* (Harmondsworth: Penguin, 1965, p. 72).

24 The phrase comes from Claude Lévi-Strauss, *Totemism* (Boston: Beacon Press, p. 89). Robert Darnton and Marjorie Garber explore the idea in ways that are relevant to this book's project. Robert Darnton, *The Great Cat Massacre and Other Episodes in French Cultural History* (New York, NY: Basic Books, 1999, pp. 3–7); Marjorie Garber, 'Good to think with', *Profession* (New York: MLA, 2008, pp. 11–20).

25 For a full history of the Franklin Theater in its social and cultural context, see Jeffrey Klenotic, ' "Four hours of hootin' and hollerin": moviegoing and everyday life outside the movie palace', in *Going to the Movies*, eds. R. Maltby, M. Stokes and R.C. Allen, pp. 130–154.

26 Leo Löwenthal, quoted in Lee Grieveson, 'Cinema studies and the conduct of conduct', in Lee Grieveson and Haidee Wasson (eds), *Inventing Film Studies* (Durham, NC: Duke University Press, 2008, p. 25). The history of the 'disciplinarization' of film studies, and in particular its establishment as a critically based humanities subject and its divorce from earlier connections to the social sciences and communication studies, is traced in several essays in *Inventing Film Studies*, and in particular in Lee Grieveson and Haidee Wasson's Introduction, 'The Academy and motion pictures'. See also Dana B. Polan, *Scenes of Instruction: The Beginnings of the U.S. Study of Film* (Berkeley: University of California Press, 2007). See also: Emilie Altenloh (2001) A sociology of the cinema: the audience, *Screen* 42 (3), 249–293; Hugo Münsterberg (1970) *The Film: A Psychological Study: The Silent Photoplay in 1916,* New York: Dover; Garth Jowett, I.C. Jarvie and Kathryn Fuller-Seeley (1996) *Children and the Movies: Media Influence and the Payne Fund Controversy,* Cambridge: Cambridge University Press; Robert S. Lynd and Helen M. Lynd (1965) *Middletown in Transition: A Study in Cultural Conflicts,* New York: The Harvest Book (originally 1937).

27 See, for example, David Morley, *The "Nationwide" Audience* (London: British Film Institute, 1980); Tamar Liebes and Elihu Katz, *The Export of Meaning: Cross-Cultural Readings of Dallas* (New York: Oxford University Press, 1990); Ien Ang, *Desperately Seeking the Audience* (London: Routledge, 1991); Henry Jenkins, *Textual Poachers: Television Fans & Participatory Culture* (New York: Routledge, 1992); Roger Silverstone and Erich Hirsch, *Consuming Technologies: Media and Information in Domestic Spaces* (London: Routledge,

1992); Lynn Spigel, *Make Room for TV: Television and the Family Ideal in Postwar America* (Chicago: University of Chicago Press, 1992); John Corner, *Television Form and Public Address* (London: Edward Arnold, 1995); Ellen Seiter, *Television and New Media Audiences* (Oxford: Clarendon Press, 1999); Anna McCarthy, *Ambient Television: Visual Culture and Public Space* (Durham: Duke University Press, 2001); *Media Industries: History, Theory, and Method*, eds Jennifer Holt and Alisa Perren (Oxford: Wiley-Blackwell, 2009); *Convergence Media History*, eds Janet Staiger and Sabine Hake (New York: Routledge, 2009); Robert C. Allen and Annette Hill, eds, *The Television Studies Reader* (London: Routledge, 2003).

28 Lucien Febvre, the co-founder of the *Annales d'histoire économique et sociale*, declared in his inaugural lecture in 1933 that 'it is necessary to be a heretic'. Lucien Febvre, *Combats pour L'histoire* (Paris: Librairie Armand Colin, 1953, p. 16). Quoted in Peter Burke, *The French Historical Revolution: The Annales School, 1929–89* (Cambridge: Polity, 1990, p. 31).

29 Poster for *Only Angels Have* Wings (Columbia Pictures, 1939), reproduced in Rick Altman, *Film/Genre* (London: British Film Institute, 1999, p. 5); Franz Kafka, 'Leopards in the temple', *Parables and Paradoxes* (New York: Schocken, 1961, p. 93).

30 'The average movie-goer speaks his mind', *New York World Telegram*, 31 August 1938; *The Daily News*, Luddington, Michigan, 1 September 1938. I am grateful to Catherine Jurca for drawing this advertisement to my attention: see Catherine Jurca (2008) Motion pictures' greatest year (1938): Public relations and the motion picture industry. *Film History*, 20 (3), 344–356.

References

Abel R. (2004) History can work for you, you know how to use it. *Cinema Journal*, 44 (1), 107–112.

Abel, R. (2006) *Americanizing the Movies And "Movie-Mad" Audiences, 1910–1914*, University of California Press, Berkeley.

Agee, J. (2005) *Agee On Film: Reviews and Comments*, Library of America, New York.

Allen, R.C. (2006) Relocating American film history. *Cultural Studies*, 20 (1), 48–88.

Allen, R.C. (2007) Race, religion and rusticity: relocating US film history, in *Going to the Movies: Hollywood and the Social Experience of Cinema* (eds R. Maltby, M. Stokes and R.C. Allen), University of Exeter Press, pp. 25–44.

Allen, R.C. and Gomery, D. (1985) *Film History: Theory and Practice*, Alfred A. Knopf, New York .

Asheim, L. (1947) The film and the zeitgeist. *Hollywood Quarterly*, 2 (4), 414–416.

Barry, I. (1939) Preface, in *The Rise of the American Film: A Critical History* (L. Jacobs), Harcourt, Brace & Co., New York, pp. vii–xi.

Barthes, R. (1986) Leaving the movie theatre, in *The Rustle of Language* (trans. R. Howard), Blackwell, London, pp. 345–349.

Bloch, M. (1953) *The Historian's Craft: Reflections on the Nature and Uses of History and the Techniques and Methods of Those Who Write It* (trans. P. Putnam), Knopf, New York.

Bordwell, D. (2005) Film and the Historical Return, http://www.davidbordwell.net/essays/return.php (accessed 5 April 2010).

Bowles, K. (2009) Limit of maps? Locality and cinema-going in Australia. *Media International Australia*,131 (May), 83–94.

Bowles, K., Maltby, R., Verhoeven, D. and Walsh, M. (2011) *The New Cinema History: A Guide*, Wiley-Blackwell, Oxford.

Braudel, F. (1967) *Capitalism and Material Life, 1400–1800* (trans. Miriam Kochan), Weidenfeld and Nicholson, London.

Braudel, F. (1980) *On History*, University of Chicago Press.

Burgin, V. (2004) *The Remembered Film*, Reaktion, London.

Burke, P. (2001) *New Perspectives on Historical Writing*, 2nd edn, Pennsylvania State University Press, University Park, PA.

Chapman, J., Glancy, M. and Harper, S. (2007) Introduction, in *The New Film History: Sources, Methods,*

Approaches (eds J. Chapman, M. Glancy and S. Harper), Palgrave Macmillan, Basingstoke, pp. 1–12.

Comte, A. and Andreski, S. (1974) *The Essential Comte; Selected from Cours De Philosophie Positive*, Croom Helm, London.

Conant, M. (1960) *Antitrust in the Motion Picture Industry*, University of California Press, Berkeley.

Crafton, D. (1997) *The Talkies: American Cinema's Transition to Sound, 1926–1931*, Charles Scribners' Sons, New York.

Dibbets, K. (2007) Culture in context: databases and the contextualization of cultural events. Paper presented at "The Glow in Their Eyes": Global Perspective on Film Cultures, Film Exhibition and Cinemagoing Conference, Ghent University, December 2007.

Ehrenreich, B. (1983) *The Hearts of Men: American Dreams and the Flight from Commitment*, Pluto, London.

Farber, M. (1953) Times Square moviegoers. *The Nation* (4 July). Reprinted in Bromley C. (ed.) (2000) *Cinema Nation: The Best Writing on Film from The Nation, 1913–2000*, Thunder Mouth Press, New York.

Farber, M. (1957) Underground films: a bit of male truth. *Commentary*, November. Reprinted in Polito, R. (ed.) (2009) *Farber on Film: The Complete Writings of Manny Farber*, Library of America, New York.

Fraterrigo, E. (2009) *Playboy and the Making of the Good Life in Modern America*, Oxford University Press, New York.

Garncarz, J. (1994) Hollywood in Germany: the role of American films in Germany, 1925–1990, in *Hollywood in Europe: Experiences of a Cultural Hegemony* (eds D.W. Ellwood and R. Kroes), VU University Press, Amsterdam, pp. 94–135.

Gomery, D. (1992) *Shared Pleasures: A History of Movie Presentation in the United States*, British Film Institute, London.

Gomery, D. (2005) *The Coming of Sound*, Routledge, London.

Gould, S.J. (1996) *Jurassic Park*, in *Past Imperfect: History According to the* Movies (ed. M.C. Carnes), Cassell, London, pp. 31–35.

Guynn, W. (2006) *Writing History in Film*, Routledge, London.

Hansen, M. (1991) *Babel & Babylon: Spectatorship in American Silent Film*, Harvard University Press, Cambridge, MA.

Hansen, M. (2000) The mass production of the senses: classical cinema as vernacular modernism, in *Reinventing Film Studies* (eds L. Williams and C. Gledhill), Arnold, London, pp. 322–350.

Houseman, J. (1947) Today's hero: a review. *Hollywood Quarterly*, 2 (2), 161–163.

Huggett, N. and Bowles, K. (2004) Cowboys, jaffas and pies: researching cinema in the Illawarra, in *Hollywood Abroad. Audiences and Cultural Exchange* (eds M. Stokes and R. Maltby), BFI, London, pp. 64–77.

Izod, J. (1988) *Hollywood and the Box Office, 1895–1986*, Columbia University Press, New York.

Jarvie, I.C. (1978) Seeing through movies. *Philosophy of the Social Sciences* 8 (4), 374–397.

Kael, P. (1963) Circles and squares. *Film Quarterly*, 16 (3), 12–26.

Kael, P. (1970) *Going Steady*, Temple Smith, London.

Keil, C. (2004) 'To here from modernity': style, historiography, and transitional cinema, in *American Cinema's Transitional Era: Audiences, Institutions, Practices* (eds C. Keil and S. Stamp), University of California Press, Berkeley, pp. 51–65.

Klinger, B. (1997) Film history terminable and interminable: recovering the past in reception studies. *Screen*, 38 (2), 107–128.

Kracauer, S. (1947) *From Caligari to Hitler: A Psychological History of the German Film*, Princeton University Press, pp. 6, 8.

Kuhn, A. (1995) *Family Secrets: Acts of Memory and Imagination*, Verso, London.

Lagny, M. (1994) Film history: or history expropriated. *Film History* 6 (1), 26–44.

Landy, M. (2001) Introduction, in *The Historical Film: History and Memory in New Media*, Rutgers University Press, Brunswick, NJ, pp. 1–22.

Le Roy Ladurie, E. (1979) *The Territory of the Historian*, Harvester Press, Hassocks.

Liang, L. (2005) Cinematic citizenship and the illegal city. *Inter-Asia Cultural Studies*, 6 (3), 336–385.

Lotman, J. (1984) The poetics of everyday behaviour in Russian eighteenth-century culture, in *The Semiotics of Russian Culture* (eds J. Lotman, B.A. Uspenskij and A. Shukman, University of Michigan Press, Ann Arbor, pp. 231–256.

Lury, K. and Massey, D. (1999) Making connections. *Screen*, 40 (3), 229–238.

Mayer, A. (1947–48) An exhibitor begs for 'B's.' *Hollywood Quarterly*, 3 (2), 172–177.

Mayer, A. (1953) *Merely Colossal: The Story of the Movies from the Long Chase to the Chaise Longue*, Simon & Schuster, New York.

McKenna, C.J. (2007) Tri-racial theaters in Robeson County, North Carolina, 1896–1940, in *Going to the Movies: Hollywood and the Social Experience of Cinema* (eds R. Maltby, M. Stokes and R.C. Allen), University of Exeter Press, pp. 45–59.

Miskell, P. (2004) Historians and film, in *Making History: An Introduction to the History and Practices of a Discipline* (eds P. Lambert and P. Scholfield), Routledge, London, pp. 245–256.

Mitry, J. (1973) De quelques problèmes d'histoire et d'esthétique de cinéma. *Cahiers de la cinémathèque* 10–11 (Summer–Autumn), 112–141. Translated and quoted in Abel, R. (1994) 'Don't Know Much about History,' or the (In)vested Interests of Doing Cinema History. *Film History*, 6 (1), 110–115.

Musser, C. (2004) Historiographic method and the study of early cinema. *Cinema Journal*, 44 (1), 101–107.

Nash Smith, H. (1950) in *Virgin Land: The American West as Symbol and Myth*, Harvard University Press, Cambridge, MA.

O'Connor, J.E. (1990) *Image as Artifact: The Historical Analysis of Film and Television*, Robert E. Kreiger Publishing.

Passmore, K. (2003) Poststructuralism and history, in *Writing History: Theory & Practice* (eds S. Berger, H. Feldner and K. Passmore), Arnold, London, pp. 118–140.

Peltonen, M. (2001) Clues, margins and monads: the micro-macro link in historical research, *History and Theory*, 40, 347–359.

Phillips, C. and Phillips, W.D. (1996) Columbus and 1492, in *Past Imperfect: History According to the* Movies (ed. M.C. Carnes), Cassell, London, pp. 60–65.

Pomian, K. (1988) L'histoire des structures, in *La Nouvelle Histoire* (ed. J. Le Goff), Complexe, Paris, pp. 109–136.

Ray, R.B. (1985) *A Certain Tendency of the Hollywood Cinema, 1930–1980*, Princeton University Press, Princeton, NJ.

Rosenstone, R. (1995) *Visions of the Past: The Challenge of Film to Our Idea of History*, Harvard University Press, Cambridge, MA.

Santamaria, U. and Bailey, A.M. (1984) A note on Braudel's structure as duration. *History and Theory*, 23 (1), 78–83.

Sedgwick, J. (2000) *Popular Filmgoing in 1930s Britain: A Choice of Pleasures*, University of Exeter Press.

Sedgwick, J. and Pokorny, M. (2005) The characteristics of film as a commodity, in *An Economic History of Film* (eds J. Sedgwick and M. Pokorny), Routledge, London, pp. 6–23.

Sedgwick, J. and Pokorny, M. (2010) Consumers as risk takers: evidence from the film industry during the 1930s. *Business History*, 52 (1), 74–99.

Staiger, J. (1992) *Interpreting Films: Studies in the Historical Reception of American Cinema*, Princeton University Press, Princeton, NJ.

Stone, L. (1992) History and postmodernism. *Past and Present*, 135 (May), 189–204.

Swedberg, R. (2005) *The Max Weber Dictionary: Key Words and Central Concepts*, Stanford University Press, Stanford, CA.

Thompson, E.P. (1963) *The Making of the English Working Class*, Gollanz, London.

Thompson, E.P. (1972) Anthropology and the discipline of historical context. *Midland History*, 1 (3), 45–55.

Tyler, P. (1994) *Underground Film*, Da Capo Press, New York.

White, H. (1973) *Metahistory: The Historical Imagination in Nineteenth-Century Europe*, Johns Hopkins University Press, Baltimore, MD.

White, H. (1988a) Historiography and historiophoty. *American Historical Review*, 93 (5), 1193–1199.

White, T. (1988b) Life after divorce: the corporate strategy of Paramount Pictures Corporation in the 1950s. *Film History*, 2 (2), 99–119.

Wilinsky, B. (2001) *Sure Seaters: The Emergence of Art House Cinema*, University of Minnesota Press, Minneapolis.

Willemen, P. (1986) For Information: *Cinéaction*, *Framework* 32/33, 227.

Wolfenstein M. and Leites, N. (1950) *Movies: A Psychological Study*, Free Press, Glencoe, IL.

2

Reimagining the History of the Experience of Cinema in a Post-Moviegoing Age

Robert C. Allen

In January 2008 two economists gave a paper at the American Economic Association that received considerable attention in the *New York Times*, National Public Radio and a number of other media outlets. Under the headline, 'Economists Say Movie Violence Might Temper the Real Thing', the *New York Times* lead read: 'Are movies like "Hannibal" and the remake of "Halloween," which serve up murder and mutilation as routine fare, actually making the nation safer?' (Goodman, 2008).

Followers of the 'freakonomics' trend of searching for correlations among huge data sets and then making causal and/or policy arguments based upon them, the authors discovered that over the past decade on weekends when violent R-rated movies were in wide release, the level of reported acts of violent crime in cities across the United States was lower than on weekends when violent films were not available. Contrary to the headline's suggestion, however, the researchers did not attribute this correlation to the cathartic effect of fictionalised media violence, but rather to the following alternative causal chain: young men between the ages of 16 and 25 are disproportionately responsible for acts of criminal violence in the United States. This demographic segment is also the target audience for R-rated violent films. Violent crime rates go up on the weekends, in part because more young men get drunk on the weekends. If young men go to the movies, they do so instead of going to bars and clubs where alcohol is sold. Therefore, by luring millions of young men into movie theatres for a few hours on Friday and Saturday night, as one of the study's authors put it, 'You're taking a lot of violent people off the streets and putting them inside movie theaters'.

Buried in accounts of this study was the fact that watching relatively non-violent films targeting the same young male demographic was nearly as 'effective' in reducing crime rates as slasher films. In fact, one of the authors suggested that a key implication of their study was that 'We need more Adam Sandler movies'. Moviegoing should be encouraged among teenaged males, but not for reasons that

Explorations in New Cinema History: Approaches and Case Studies, First Edition.
Edited by Richard Maltby, Daniel Biltereyst and Philippe Meers.

are likely to be touted by Hollywood: 'If you can incapacitate a large group of potentially violent people, that's a good thing.'

There are a number of interesting issues that arise from this study and how it was framed in the press, but the one most pertinent to this essay is the confusion over the source of the empirical 'effect' purportedly discovered by the investigators. Their argument was not that crime-dampening properties resided necessarily in particular films or even in the act of viewing them, but rather in particular modalities of experiencing cinema: theatrical moviegoing undertaken by particular social groups at particular times on particular days of the week. Removed from this social and experiential context, any given film viewed under different circumstances (on an iPod, on DVD, downloaded from a P2P internet site) presumably would lose its power to affect behaviour. The logic underpinning the study's findings also suggests that any attraction, cinematic or non-cinematic, sufficient to lure large numbers of young men into movie theatres on Friday or Saturday evenings – mud wrestling, telecasts of rock concerts or sporting events, in addition to or instead of Adam Sandler movies – could provide the predicate for a similar social outcome.[1] This is, however, hardly the first time that the social importance of movies has been trumpeted at the expense of the social practice of moviegoing, or that the cinematic text has obscured its social context.

Re-Viewing Cinema History in the Post-Moviegoing Epoch

In 1999 I argued that the assumptions made by a generation of film studies scholars about Hollywood cinema as a cultural industry and about the normative modes by which its products were experienced were no longer valid (Allen, 1999). There were a number of 'drivers' of this transformation, but one of the most consequential was the extraordinarily rapid diffusion of the video cassette recorder and player in the early 1980s. Although marketed initially as a tool for recording television programmes and timeshifting their viewing, Hollywood had realised by the late 1980s that releasing video cassette copies of theatrical feature films for consumer sale and rental could give some films an indefinitely extended shelf life and bring in hundreds of millions of dollars of annual revenue. By the early 1990s, Hollywood was making more money from selling people movies to keep and watch wherever, whenever and however they pleased than it did from selling people tickets to see a film once in a place that had become a concession stand with small, dark rooms attached to it. For the last 20 years, watching movies in a movie theatre has been irreversibly declining as a normative mode of the experience of cinema in the United States, and in the meantime an entire generation has grown up with their earliest, most formative and most common experiences of movies occurring in places that Hollywood dismissively referred to as 'non-theatrical' exhibition sites: bedrooms, living rooms, kitchens, automobiles.

Not only has the principal site of the experience of cinema in the United States been relocated from 15 000 theatres to hundreds of millions of domiciles, the character of the experience of cinema has undergone a profound generational change. In my 1999 essay, I argued that these changes were led by what until the video era Hollywood had marginalised as the 'children's' film – a genre that was transmogrified into the multigenerational 'family' film in the early 1990s. Any parent of young children in 1990s – and, significantly, there were more young children around in the 1990s than at any time since the 1950s – was well positioned to study the effects of the relocation of the principal site of cinematic encounter from the theatrical to domestic space upon what were becoming generationally normative reception patterns.

Our daughter, Madeline, was born in 1994. Her earliest and formative experiences of cinema occurred not in a movie theatre, but in front of a television set connected to a VCR. For her, cinema was experienced through a range of engagement strategies, including but not limited to: rapt, attentive viewing; successive obsessive attachments to one particular film and/or one particular scene in that film; distracted viewing; sleeping; humming, singing or speaking along with the film's soundtrack; acting out scenes from the film; dressing up like characters in the film; attempting to dress up others in the same room as characters in the film; performing scenes from the film; playing computer games based upon the film; playing with plush toy simulacra of characters in the film; eating breakfast cereal simulacra of characters in the film; wearing pyjamas depicting characters from the film; drawing characters from the film; manipulating the remote control to zip through disturbing or boring scenes, songs or dialogue sequences; replaying the same scene, song or dialogue sequence multiple times; increasing the volume in conjunction with replaying the same scene; pausing display of the film; and making narrative, causal and moral queries and commentary regarding the film to whomever happened to be in the same room. The presence of another subject from the same generational cohort made the contextual dynamics of any given instance of cinematic engagement even more complex, variable and unpredictable.

The students now taking cinema studies classes in the United States are, figuratively speaking, Madeline's older demographic sisters and brothers, all members of the 76-million-strong Echo Boom generation born between 1977 and 1995– the second largest generational bulge in American history next to the post-World War II Baby Boom. The residual attractions of screenings of slasher films to crime-disposed teenage boys notwithstanding, my own prediction would be that theatrical moviegoing – which has for them never been more 'authentic' than any other way of experiencing cinema – will continue to decline in importance for her generation if it continues to involve having to wear pants and shoes, travelling to some other place, paying nearly the equivalent of buying a DVD to see a film once in a dark room without wireless internet connectivity with strangers at a time determined by someone else's schedule, seated upright in chairs bolted to the floor, limited in the range of comestible accompaniments to criminally overpriced popcorn, candy and soft drinks, discouraged from talking, singing along, and walking around, unable to pause, replay or fast-forward, deprived of director's commentary track, and absent alternative endings, outtakes, deleted scenes, bloopers, interviews with actors, directors and screenwriter, and 'the making of' featurette.

My daughter's generation understands cinema as a textually disintegrated phenomenon experienced through multiple and unpredictably proliferating sites and modalities. For her, the experience of cinema has always been decentred and fissiparous. The question I am interested in asking is how does her experience of cinema compare with that of her grandmother and great-grandmother? To address this question, I think that we have to see her experience of cinema as situated on the other side of an epochal divide, which we might call the moviegoing epoch and the post-moviegoing epoch. In other words, I am interested in asking the question 'What *was* cinema?' in relation to the century-long epoch of theatrical and extra-theatrical moviegoing in America and elsewhere – from the advent of projected motion pictures in the mid-1890s to the mass adoption of the video cassette player in the 1980s. What distinguished the experience of cinema from other aspects of everyday life and how was the experience of cinema related to other experiences? How did the experience of cinema change during this century? How were patterns of the experience of cinema formed at any given moment, and how and why did the meanings, value, relevance and consequences of that experience vary?

More and more movie theatres serve as haunted houses, not just because of the unnatural acts of mayhem they flash on the walls to lure in young men, but because they are the places where on Friday nights Hollywood studios summon the ghost of a bygone epoch in an attempt to suffuse its products with an aura of cinematic glamour strong enough to survive for a few months in the decidedly unglamorous domestic settings where they will eventually be housed. As theatrical moviegoing becomes a thing more remembered than experienced, we will be reminded that one of the most striking features of the experience of cinema for a hundred years was its sociality. For a century following the demonstration of Edison's Vitascope projector at Koster and Bial's Music Hall in New York on 23 April 1896, the experience of cinema in America and around the world involved groups of people converging upon particular places to experience together something understood to be cinema. As it emerged as a cultural industry, cinema depended upon the regular repetition of this social convergence under the sign of cinema, day after day, week after week, year after year, in hundreds of thousands of places by uncountable billions of people.

Because their first experiences with movies were as video cassettes or DVDs experienced at home, and because theatrical moviegoing remained only one of the many different ways they continued to experience movies as they grew up, our current generation of students is also the first generation of moviegoers in a century for whom the sociality of the experience of cinema is an option rather than an ineluctable and hence assumed dimension of that experience. It is worth pausing to remind ourselves of the magnitude of the social experience that was theatrical moviegoing. Making conservative assumptions about the number of commercial exhibition sites in the United States between 1896 and 1990 and the average number of screenings per week, my back-of-an-envelope calculation produces roughly a billion unique social convergences occurring in movie theatres – not to mention the tens of millions of screenings in tents, amusement parks, church fellowship halls, fraternal lodges, high school auditoria, vacant lots and other so-called 'extra-theatrical' venues.

This book, and other recent collections of research notwithstanding, the full magnitude and implications of the sociality of the experience of cinema over the first century of film history remain inadequately reflected in the ways that film studies courses are taught and experienced by students. This line of enquiry does not register as being central to the field of film studies as a whole. The programme for the 2008 meeting of the Society for Cinema and Media Studies, for example, featured more than 300 panels comprising papers by nearly 1000 scholars, on topics ranging from Aging American Actors and Second Life to *Battlestar Galactica* and the films of Sylvester Stallone. My rough-and-ready 'content analysis' of the panel topics and paper titles in the 85-page conference programme uncovered only three panels that seemed likely even to raise the sociality of the cinema as an issue, and all three of those were devoted to the much more circumscribed topic of film exhibition. Roughly two-thirds of the 1000 papers, I would estimate, were 'readings' of individual films or television programmes.

There are a number of reasons for this, including film studies' academic alignment with literary studies, and a normative pedagogic practice organised around the viewing, analysis and discussion of selected texts. The easy availability of copies of individual films provides a reassuring material basis for organising film studies pedagogy and, to a considerable extent, its critical and historiographic practice. The materiality of individual films now *seems* stronger than ever: arrayed as DVDs on bookcase shelves or gathering dust as video cassettes. Movies have become things that we own, hold and control. The availability of films as personal property and as experience-on-demand (through services such as Netflix) do not, however, produce textual or experiential stability. For example, the combination of Blu-ray DVD technology and display platforms with integrated internet connectivity makes it possible to view a 'film' as a part of a virtual gathering of friends and family around the world, and to communicate with each other in real time. Leading the way here, as it did in the early 1990s with the marketing of its animated films on video, is Disney, which is rereleasing some of its 'classic' animated films on Blu-ray, to the generation of girls slightly younger than my daughter.[2] This model of the social experience of cinema is based much more on the practices of social networking through Facebook or Twitter than on the experience of sitting in a dark room full of strangers at the mall. I can easily imagine in the not-too-distant future receiving a paper from a student on Disney's *Snow White* in which she says: 'For, me the most memorable scene is the one when that girl in Omaha said she had an uncle who looked just like Dopey.'

For nearly 20 years, Hollywood's profitability has depended upon people engaging with its products outside of US movie theatres, as both revenue and profits from the domestic box office shrank in relation to what the industry used to call 'ancillary' markets: video rental and sale, broadcast and cable television sales, licensed products and video games. The theatrical release of a Hollywood film is now the tail that wags the marketing dog. Studios insist that even though very few films stand any chance of returning the cost of their production from the domestic box office, the publicity, reviews and audience interest generated by theatrical release are still crucial to the film's eventual performance in all markets and formats. As a consequence, Hollywood continues, however disingenuously, to tout theatrical moviegoing as the most authentic mode of cinematic experience (especially around the time of the Academy Awards each year). The spoken or unspoken corollary is that seeing a film 'on the big screen' in a movie theatre is still the only way to experience it as it was 'intended' by its makers.

For the generation of aspiring film-makers weaned in front of the VCR and introduced to 'film' production via the family's digital video camera, however, theatrical release is as much a bottleneck as a marketing platform. The proliferation of relatively inexpensive and user-friendly digital 'film' production and editing technologies has resulted in a huge increase in the number of so-called 'independent' feature-length fiction and documentary films produced each year in the United States. Even if an independent film is one of the relatively few selected for festival screening and manages to secure a theatrical distribution deal, pushing past Hollywood blockbusters to get a theatrical screening slot remains a huge challenge. In 2009, IFC Entertainment innovated an independent film marketing strategy that enables independent film-makers to go directly from festival screening to home-viewer end-user: simultaneously debuting the film on its on-demand cable and satellite channel. Joe Swanberg's *Alexander the Last* premiered on the IFC Festival cable channel the same day as its debut theatrical screening at the South by Southwest Film Festival in Austin, Texas. *New York Times* media writer David Carr predicted, 'There may come a day when much of the film business is a digital-in/digital-out affair, with all manner of "films" showing up on all manner of devices, and a consumer algorithm – think Netflix – driving what people end up seeing.' Director Swanberg told Carr, 'I don't care what kind of screen they watch it on. … New films are having a hard time finding an audience, and as a filmmaker I don't really care how the audiences access the work.' He added that he could imagine his films one day having their premieres on iTunes (Carr, 2009).

Representing the Experience of Cinema in the Moviegoing Epoch: 'Going to the Show'

I am engaged in a research and digital publication project that takes as its subject the social experience of cinema in the state of North Carolina between 1896 and 1930. Called 'Going to the Show' after my mother's term for moviegoing when she was growing up in North Carolina in the 1920s and 1930s, this project is being undertaken in collaboration with two units of the special collections library at the University of North Carolina at Chapel Hill (UNC): the North Carolina Collection, and Documenting the American South, a digital library laboratory that creates, develops and maintains online digital collections regarding the history of the American South drawn primarily from the outstanding archival holdings of the UNC library.

"Going to the Show" grew out of my use of archival materials from the UNC Library over the last 29 years in teaching and writing about the history of film exhibition and moviegoing. It was also inspired by the example of a number of my colleagues in the United States, Europe and Australia who are using digital technologies in a variety of innovative ways to collect, organise and display data and materials that illuminate the historical experience of cinema. "Going to the Show" is a historiographic experiment on several levels. It asks how experiences of moviegoing have been represented and what traces of those representations survive? How might those traces themselves be represented and manipulated in an interactive digital library? What aspects of the experience of cinema are highlighted in these representations, and what aspects are obscured or remain unrepresentable regardless of how much or what kind of 'data' my colleagues and I might be able to deploy?

"Going to the Show" is also a contribution to long-standing debates and discussions over the character of the experience of cinema in the United States in the first decades of commercial exhibition. It asks what historiographic benefits might be realised by shifting our perspective on the early history of moviegoing in the United States in three respects. Firstly, most studies of 'local' movie exhibition in the United States take the city as their basic unit of analysis: New York, Chicago, Lexington, Des Moines. How does our view of early movie culture change when we redefine 'local' in relation to another unit of political and geographic organisation: the American state? Secondly, what happens to our understanding of the role of movies and moviegoing in 'local' communities when, in the state chosen for study, patterns of urban development result in hundreds of small towns but nothing resembling a metropolis? Thirdly, how does another unit of geographic, social and political organisation – the region – affect the first two factors? Although regions can easily be assigned a homogeneity they never possessed, there is a strong case for looking at regional differences in the experience of moviegoing in the United States, particularly when the region in question is the American South and particularly when the period under examination is that known as Jim Crow: the half century of racial apartheid in force throughout the Southern United States from the 1890s through the 1950s. The archival resources of the UNC North Carolina Collection made it possible to reframe the historical study of the social experience of moviegoing in this way.

I also wanted to explore both the evidentiary and historiographic opportunities and limitations inherent in such an undertaking: what materials could be deployed in what ways for what purposes? What aspects of early movie culture remain obscured or invisible because they did not leave traces that were or could have been preserved? Finally, I was interested to see how the digital library expertise that my colleagues in the digital publishing unit of our special collections library had applied primarily to literary and oral texts – slave narratives, diaries, fiction, oral history interviews – might be exploited in organising and displaying other kinds of historical materials, particularly spatial data.

Having used the North Carolina Collection many times, I knew that 'permanent' commercial sites of film exhibition in the state were documented primarily through city directories, preserved copies of local newspapers on microfilm, and Sanborn Fire Insurance Maps. Between 1867 and 1977 the Sanborn Map Company of Pelham, New York, produced large-scale (usually 50 feet to the inch) colour maps of commercial and industrial districts of some 17 000 towns and cities in North America to assist fire insurance companies in setting rates and terms. Each set of maps represented each built structure in those districts, recording its use, dimensions, height, building material and other relevant features. The intervals between new map editions for a given town or city in the early decades of the twentieth century varied according to the pace and scale of urban growth – from a few years to more than five. In all, Sanborn produced 50 000 editions comprising some 700 000 individual map pages.[3] Sanborn maps are widely recognised by urban historians and historical geographers as unique and invaluable resources. The North Carolina Collection holds original, unaltered and unbound copies of every known set of Sanborn maps produced for every town and city in the state that was mapped by Sanborn between 1896 and 1930. Movie theatres appear on Sanborn maps from 1908, along with the other businesses along Main Street in the more than 100 towns and cities that were mapped in North Carolina; they were of special interest to Sanborn, since the extremely flammable nature of film stock and its use only inches away from what was in effect an open flame made movie theatres potential fire traps for decades. The Sanborn maps show us how big each theatre was, what it was constructed from, whether or not it had a balcony or stage, and (by comparing successive map sets of the same area) whether it was renovated or expanded and how long it stayed in business.

Poring over thousands of map pages over the past few years, thinking about how they represent the experience of moviegoing, and about how the maps might be represented in 'Going to the Show', drove home for me the need to rethink not only the sociality but also the spatiality of the experience of cinema. What the Sanborn maps enable us to see, in ways that other representations of the social experience of moviegoing do not, is that the space of the experience of cinema in towns and cities across North Carolina, and, I suspect, in many other places as well, was not bounded by the places in which movies were shown. The maps show clearly that the emergence of movie culture in North Carolina is inextricably linked to the rise and development of urban central business districts.

We will represent the Sanborn maps in 'Going to the Show' in a way that they were never intended to be: with individual map pages digitally stitched together so that they form a composite overview of a town's central business district. The resulting map mosaic is then georeferenced so that we can use Geographic Information System (GIS) technology to layer information on them, compare successive map iterations, and show contemporary views of a given town's central business district (CBD) using Google Earth. With the notable exception of

African-American theatres located in black neighbourhoods, the first generation of movie theatres in almost every one of more than 200 communities we have documented were located in the middle of the CBD, or what most people simply referred to as 'downtown' – whether that 'downtown' consisted of a 10–12 square block area as in Wilmington, the state's largest city at the turn of the century, or as was more typically the case, a block or two of civic, social, religious and commercial structures facing each other along Main Street or grouped around a central square. The turn of the century was a time of enormous urban growth and change in North Carolina: new towns sprang up around cotton mills and furniture and tobacco factories; older towns grew and wooden buildings along Main Street were replaced with more substantial and imposing buildings faced with stone or brick. Rapid urbanisation in North Carolina did not produce big cities but rather hundreds of small towns. Downtown commercial real estate development followed the same pattern from town to town: the erection of zero-lot-line (that is to say adjacent) buildings with 25–50-foot frontage, 100–150 feet deep, and two to four stories tall.

The ground floor would be used for retail, and the upper floor or floors might be divided into commercial or professional offices or leased to fraternal organisations, of which there were dozens in nearly every town. Small businesses – hardware stores, drug stores, cigar stores, grocery stores, millinery shops – all vied to rent an affordable retail space in one of these buildings that was as close as possible to the centre of downtown, and viewed by as many passers-by as possible. Retail businesses might change locations when, at the annual lease renewal time (in Wilmington it was the end of October each year), a more central spot came open. No one would have thought it odd that one November a hardware store was transformed into a cigar store, or vice versa, and no one would have expected that someone starting a new retail business would have built a new structure to accommodate it. In the first place, few new retail businesses had the capital to do so, and it would have been much more advantageous to rent space in an existing building at the centre of downtown than to build on available land elsewhere.

For most white people living in towns or cities of any size in North Carolina and those living in the countryside around these towns and cities in the first three decades of cinema history, going to the movies was a part of the experience of the spaces of downtown social, cultural, commercial and consumer life. Understanding what went on inside the theatre requires understanding what went on outside. The devastation of downtowns of many American towns and cities in the postwar period has obscured their social, cultural and economic density and heterogeneity in the first half of the century. Movie theatres depended upon this density and this heterogeneity: so far as I can tell, for years in North Carolina cities and towns people did not go downtown because they wanted to go to the movies so much as they might have gone to the movies because they were downtown. When they went to the movies, they also went to the drug store or the coffee shop or the cigar store or the bank.

The Sanborn maps reveal a social geography of early moviegoing in North Carolina that bears very little resemblance to that depicted as being characteristic of the 'nickelodeon period' based on representations of moviegoing in New York City. Moviegoing was a part of the experience of downtown, not a feature of working-class neighbourhoods. The idea that early white movie theatres anywhere in North Carolina might have represented an alternative working-class social or cultural sphere beyond or beneath the gaze of bourgeois authority would have been as risible as the notion that a main street coffee shop or hardware store might have served the same role.

Offering geographic snapshots of hundreds of towns over three decades at the beginning of the twentieth century, the Sanborn maps show that in most towns there was only one movie theatre in operation at any given time. This is confirmed by a 1938 *Motion Picture Herald* survey of film exhibition in the United States, which found 365 theatres in 196 towns in North Carolina, 40% of them in towns of fewer than 2500 people and two-thirds of them with fewer than 500 seats. In all but 24 of these nearly 200 towns, there was but a single movie theatre, and only nine cities had more than three theatres.[4] Douglas Gomery estimates that of the 25 000 movie theatres in operation in the United States in the mid-1920s, three-quarters of them were in small towns.

Given the fact that in 1920 most Americans still lived in small towns or outside an urban settlement of any size, the normative experience of cinema did not involve choosing which film to see, but rather whether or not to 'go to the show' and see whatever there was to be seen. By the 1920s, in many small towns the movie theatre appears on the Sanborn maps as the largest secular meeting space in town. Both the Sanborn maps and contemporaneous newspaper articles and advertisements suggest not how removed or obscured movie theatres were from what some might call hegemonic culture or how alternative or autonomous they were as public spaces, but rather how tightly woven they were, or aspired to be, into not just the town's social and cultural life but its civic life as well.

For most African Americans in the first three decades of the twentieth century, moviegoing was a part of the experience of Southern small-town urban modernity, not Northern or Midwestern metropolitan modernity. That experience was profoundly shaped by the rigorous and systematic organisation of space in every Southern town of any size, particularly the space of downtown, which was for African Americans a bewilderingly complex and dense social landscape made up of places where you could or could not sit, stand, eat, enter, drink, relieve yourself, walk or buy. In many towns black women could purchase clothing but they could not try them on or return them if they did not fit. I know of no movie theatres anywhere in North Carolina at any point during the time span of my project where blacks and whites occupied the same seating areas. The most common 'accommodation' of African Americans in those theatres that did admit blacks at all was a separate balcony. But because early movie theatres were almost always converted one-storey ground-floor retail spaces, the interior space of the theatre would not have allowed for a balcony. We really do not know what proportion of Southern theatres excluded blacks or whether this strategy tended to be employed more in larger or smaller towns, but it seems to have been a common practice that long outlived architectural exigencies. The first theatre to admit blacks in Durham, North Carolina, was not built until the late 1920s, and was the only segregated white theatre in town until the desegregation of all theatres in the early 1960s.

There has been no systematic, comprehensive mapping of black theatres anywhere, including in the South, by film historians, and black moviegoing was largely ignored by the Hollywood film industry. A 1937 *Motion Picture Herald* survey found that only 1.5% (232) of the nation's 17 000 movie theatres were black theatres.[5] 'Going to the Show' will include in its database every African American movie venue operating in North Carolina for which we can find documentation through the 1950s. Sanborn maps and city directory listings show that these theatres were features of black commercial development in black neighbourhoods away from downtown. Complicating the argument that black theatres might have represented an alternative public sphere for African-American moviegoers, particularly in the South, is the likelihood that many, if not most 'black' theatres were owned and managed by whites.[6]

The Eventfulness of the Experience of Cinema

For a century, cinema was experienced as an event, and, unless you were a wealthy recluse or the owner of your own movie theatre, it was a social event. What makes events eventful is that they are unique convergences of multiple individual trajectories upon particular social sites. Events are necessarily unpredictable and unreproducible. Historical events are, if you like, invisible to us, and they resist being represented either in words or images; and yet, events are the stuff of history. The largely unspoken and unexamined assumption of most film studies scholarship has been that the experience of cinema could be made uneventful, inconsequential and reproducible by reducing it to the abstracted, individual act of textual engagement: the only events that mattered were taking place on the screen. Where film studies has ventured into a consideration of the historical eventfulness of the experience of cinema, it has tended to focus on certain limited instances, audiences or time periods – the immigrant experience of the nickelodeon in 1907; or the experience of African-American movie theatres in Chicago in the 1920s, for example – implicitly or explicitly consigning the other 99.9% of the billion or so theatrical experiences of cinema in the United States to the experiential black hole of 'bourgeois cinema' where, presumably either nothing 'happened' or whatever happened happened to everyone in the same way.

But I can find no theoretical or empirical grounds for believing this was the case. Rather, for a 100 years the experience of cinema was social, eventful and heterogeneous. Movie theatres were spaces where, to use geographer Doreen Massey's phrase, 'distinct trajectories coexist[ed]' (Massey, 2005, pp. 9, 140). As social sites, movie theatres were, to use another of Massey's felicitous terms, 'thrown together', and every cinematic event represented 'the unavoidable challenge of negotiating a here-and-now'. The unprecedented scale of the theatrical experience of cinema, its undocumented, unpredictable, and ultimately unreproducible and unrepresentable heterogeneity and potential eventfulness mean on the one hand that the experience of cinema cannot be reduced to some reified notion of spectatorship and, on the other, that 'the movie audience' cannot serve as an object of empirical historical inquiry.

So, the question for me is not whether the inherent eventfulness of the experience of cinema should matter to us – of course it should and must – but rather what was the nature of that eventfulness? It is clear that Hollywood depended upon the routinisation of moviegoing as a social practice, and, seen in this light, the regularised and frequent change of cinema programmes was key to the strategy of encouraging habitual moviegoing. Conceptually, then, as a social practice moviegoing might be taken up as a part of the historical study of the everyday. This would certainly chime with the emergence of the ordinary, everyday and purposeless from the background of the mundane in certain strands of cultural studies and sociology.[7] This direction is also suggested in Annette Kuhn's memory work with interviewees who experienced cinema in Britain in the 1930s and 1940s, and who remembered cinema primarily as a social practice in relation to the patterns and rhythms of daily and weekly life, rather than as a distinct succession of individual viewing experiences or films (Kuhn, 2002).

For tens of millions of Americans in tens of thousands of towns, moviegoing became woven into the experience of urbanity, along with shopping in department stores and getting a soda at the drugstore. This is, in fact, an important social and cultural phenomenon that is quite difficult to document and represent. My students who are going through miles of microfilm looking for any notice of early moviegoing in local newspapers are surprised, and frankly disappointed by how quickly moviegoing became unremarkable and unremarked upon in the local press. Many theatres, particularly those in small towns, did not even bother to advertise on a regular basis until the 1910s.[8]

But emphasising the ordinariness of the experience of moviegoing runs the risk of obscuring the character of cinema's eventfulness, of taking it out from the shadow of the screen only to push it back against the distant horizon of the quotidian. The eventfulness of cinema in the era of moviegoing was always poised between the everyday and the extraordinary. The first challenge for any early storefront theatre proprietor was to make what only a few weeks before had been an ordinary hardware store into the Bijou, Rialto, Grand or Royal. Because moviegoing was primarily an urban phenomenon and because North Carolina (like most of the United States as a whole) was so rural in the early decades of the twentieth century, moviegoing itself was for millions of Americans extraordinary – something done only once a month or once a season.

Much has been made in cinema studies of the inherent playfulness of cinema. It depends upon the willing suspension of disbelief and upon several levels of illusion – from the illusion that we are watching objects in motion to the correspondence between the fate of the character on the screen and that of the actor playing the role. For 30 years, film theory has told us that the illusion of cinema also depends upon the viewer becoming the cinematic spectator by accepting his or her role as desirous and complicit seer. But for a 100 years the psychic role-playing required for someone to laugh or cry at shadows was enveloped in another, prior role assumption – that of moviegoer. Although cinema studies has invested a great deal in conceptualising what was involved aesthetically, ideologically and sexually in playing the role of spectator, it has left largely unexplored what it might have meant to play the role of moviegoer at particular times and in particular places. For example, in the United States, Catholic objections to cinema have centred around the dubious morality of particular films. However, for conservative Southern Protestants like my grandfather, moviegoing, like dancing and gambling, was a morally problematic participatory event.

For African Americans in every town in the South at every time prior to the mid-1960s, playing the role of a moviegoer involved a complex and unpredictable social negotiation that took place outside the theatre as well as inside, before a ticket was purchased as well as while the movies on the programme were shown. One of the few exceptions to the segregated seating policies enforced in every white theatre that did admit African Americans was for African-American women who were looking after white children. They were the only African Americans allowed to sit in the 'white' section of the theatre. A librarian in Salisbury, North Carolina, told me that African American college students would sometimes wait outside the theatre for an unaccompanied white child whom they might pretend to 'mind' so that they could avoid sitting in the balcony.

Letting the experience of cinema slip comfortably back into the soft embrace of the everyday also distracts us from attending to the work and force involved in fostering and sustaining the ordinary, unremarkable and the routine. Among the materials we will georeference and layer over Sanborn maps are original architectural drawings for 34 movie theatres designed by Erle Stillwell between the 1920s and the 1950s. These drawings reveal more starkly than any other representational source I know how important it was to white theatre owners and managers that African Americans were physically and visually separated from white moviegoers via separate and inferior box offices, entrances, halls and stairways, seating and amenities. The drawings also make clear that where such accommodations were omitted in the plans (e.g. no provision for a balcony), it was not because the owner anticipated the day when blacks might be treated in the same way as whites, but rather that the exclusion of blacks was guaranteed so long as Jim Crow prevailed (Mitchell, 2006). These drawings will serve as reminders of what was involved and what was at stake in enforcing the ordinariness of the experience of cinema in the South from before the first movie theatres opened around 1906 until the desegregation of white theatres in the early 1960s.

Every cinematic event, no matter how unremarkable or unremarked upon in the historical record, represented the playing out of the actualised against the horizon of the possible. Because of the pervasive, unyielding, yet now largely invisible presence of Jim Crow, all 1300 of the cinema venues we have catalogued are haunted spaces, haunted, to use Nigel Thrift's phrase, by 'the unactualized possible without which they cannot be sensed and described' (Thrift, 2007, p. 121).

Sometimes, the possible was actualised. The spell of the routine and the everyday was broken. These eruptions of the possible are themselves historiographically 'messy' and, as we might have once said, 'overdetermined'. For example, here is an article I found by entering the terms 'moving pictures and riot' in the search engine for a database of small-town newspapers. It is from the *Fort Wayne (Indiana) News* of 29 February 1911.[9]

> Fort Worth, Tex, Feb. 28 – Police today made no arrests in connection with race riots in the business section of Fort Worth last night ... A mob of 1,000 attacked a moving picture show on lower Main Street because it was conducted for negroes only. Whites resented its being established on the city's principal street. After smashing down doors and windows of this building, the mob proceded [sic] to attack a large number of negro saloons and dwellings, causing much damage. A score of negroes found on the streets were beaten and police did not interfere. ... No lynchings were attempted.[10]

A subsequent article reveals that the theatre was owned and operated by a white man.

The same search also produced a series of articles from the Elizabeth City (NC) *Daily Advance* over a several-week period in September 1940, the first of which was headlined 'All Quiet Today After Negro Riot at Gaiety'.[11] The previous evening, local police and firemen, state highway patrol officers, and sailors from the local coast guard station were called to protect a black theatre when a 'sullen mob of Negroes' gathered in front to protest the firing of the African-American manager of the theatre by its white owner. The authorities came equipped with pistols, rifles, hand grenades, fire hoses and submachine guns. They were aided by white citizens who 'volunteered automatically' to protect downtown property. A few rocks and an empty soda bottle were thrown by the 'mob' before it was chased away and eight black men arrested. 'Ironically', the article noted, 'the picture at the theatre for the night was *Torrid Zone*.' It starred Jimmy Cagney and Ann Sheridan. Despite no direct testimony that they had done anything illegal, three of those arrested were convicted of assault and creating a public disturbance and sentenced to two years at hard labour.[12]

The surviving versions of films from the moviegoing epoch that we show in our film history classes are historical artifacts of limited value in representing the complexity, dynamics and importance of any particular cinematic event or the historical experience of cinema more generally. They are souvenirs of events of which they were a part, but by no means the only or even the most important part. What would a reading of *Torrid Zone* tell you about the cinematic event of which it was a part or the experience of cinema in Elizabeth City, North Carolina, in the 1940s?

For 100 years, individual films were among the most ephemeral aspects of the experience of cinema. Any particular film was but one part of an event that also involved other people, performances (cinematic and non-cinematic), things (furniture and architecture), spaces, technologies and experiences: tastes, smells, sounds and sights. The economic logic developed for theatrical exhibition depended upon any given film being a part of the experience of cinema only for a single, very brief period of time, after which it became a part of the memory of an experience of cinema. In many towns in the United States well into the sound era, any particular Hollywood film was a part of that experience of cinema in that place for no more than 72 hours. Early movie theatres in the United States changed their programmes of short films as frequently as possible – every other day or even daily – and many in North Carolina (particularly those in one-theatre towns) did not regularly pay for newspaper ads to advertise their daily programmes until the advent of the feature film in the 1910s. Once a film was seen, it became even more ephemeral as a part of memory, competing for space with all the hundreds or thousands of other films someone might have seen in a lifetime, in most cases without the possibility of memories being confirmed or refreshed by a subsequent viewing.

The experience of cinema is open-ended in several senses. Spatially, the relationships that constitute the experience of cinema are not bounded by the borders of the screen, the theoretical space between spectator and image, the physical space between viewers, or the spaces between them and the places in which movies are shown. These relationships extend from the intimate to the global. Temporally, the experience of cinema does not begin when the lights go down or even when a ticket is purchased, and it does not end when the credits roll or we step back into the 'real' world outside the exhibition space. The experience of cinema is, for the most part, memories of experiences of cinema, and for a 100 years what was remembered as the experience of cinema was the experience of public moviegoing. The experience of cinema is open-ended with respect to determination and effectivity as well. The relations that constitute the experience of cinema are not fixed; the character of its heterogeneity cannot be predicted or assumed. The experience of cinema is a product of relations but, as Doreen Massey says about space more generally, 'these are not the relations of a coherent, closed system within which, as they say, everything is (already) related to everything else' (Massey, 2005, p. 11).

The heterogeneity and open-endedness of the experience of cinema require an open-ended and open-source historiography. For example, memories of moviegoing are the primary resources for documenting and understanding the African-American experience of moviegoing under Jim Crow. Oral histories, which we hope to add to 'Going to the Show' in a later phase of the project, exponentially increase the number and variety of available film histories; they implicitly contest both the empiricist objectification of film history and the epistemological authority of the interpretive analyst. They explode any notion of a master narrative of cinema history into what Della Pollock has called 'a somewhat humbler quilt of many voices and local hopes' (Pollock, 1998, p. 21).

Because of the enormity and diversity of the historical experience of cinema, studying and representing it is almost by necessity an interdisciplinary, collaborative undertaking. Illuminating the relational, heterogeneous and open character of the historical experience of cinema will require the development of new representational strategies, as well as coming to terms with the intractably unrepresentable nature of historical experience. Massey suggests thinking of spatial representation not in terms of mimetic outcome but rather as activity, practice and experimentation (Massey, 2005, pp. 26–28).

When the object of cinema studies is recast as the experience of cinema, the film from the past that is available to the film historian can be seen as itself a representation, with mimetic limitations that are different in kind but no less conceptually and historiographically consequential than those of the map or the photograph that we rely upon to represent the location of long-gone picture palaces. As Michel de Certeau has put it, whatever else texts might signify, they signify and are always marked by the history of their own performance and 'the operations whose object they have been'. They are 'tools manipulated by users' (Certeau, 1984, p. 21). If space is the simultaneity of stories-so-far, any surviving filmic text is, if you like, an imagined simultaneity of all its spatialisations-so-far.

Digital technologies and the applications being developed for their use in social and cultural history have far-reaching implications for the kinds of questions we can ask, the kinds and amount of data we can gather, represent and make accessible. The sophistication, complexity, dynamism and infrastructure cost associated with these technologies also shape the way historians work, who they work with, what kind of knowledge they can claim, and how they share their work. At this point in my work on 'Going to the Show', I am struck by the enormity and complexity of the challenge of asking 'What was cinema?' about any place at any moment in the past. For me the kind of decentred, centrifugal cinema history I am proposing also suggests a humble, open and flexible theoretical stance, and despite having accumulated more data about moviegoing for an entire state than anyone else (so far as I know), my epistemological goals are and, I think, will necessarily remain modest. Reconceiving cinema as experience would, I think, open up multiple new research and teaching pathways and connect the study of cinema to other and different intellectual networks – uncertain, untethered pathways and networks that might carry teachers and students to places where movies as we think we understand them are no longer the only or even the most prominent features of the experiential landscape.

Notes

1 The civic benefits of moviegoing among young men, irrespective of what films they might actually see, were recognised a century ago. As Terry Lindvall has noted, theatre managers and local clergy in Norfolk, Virginia, a seaport and important naval centre, formed an alliance to encourage sailors on shore leave to frequent movie theatres in the belief that the more time they spent there the less time they would spend in saloons and brothels. See Lindvall T. (2007) Sundays in Norfolk: toward a Protestant utopia through film exhibition in Norfolk, Virginia, 1906–1926, in *Going to the Movies: Hollywood and the Social Experience of Cinema* (eds R. Maltby, M. Stokes and R.C. Allen), University of Exeter Press, pp. 76–93.

2 See http://www.disneybdlivenetwork.com/.

3 See *Fire Insurance Maps in the Library of Congress: Plan of North American Cities and Towns Produced by the Sanborn Map Company* (Washington, Library of Congress, 1981). Most of the Sanborn maps published between 1867 and 1950 in the Library of Congress's collection were microfilmed and marketed by a commercial publisher in the 1980s. The large scale of the map pages required an 18× reduction when microfilmed, and cost considerations drove a decision to reproduce the maps in black and white rather than colour. Despite this cost-consciousness, the retail price of state-wide map sets ranged from $110 (Alaska) to more than $15 000 (New York), with the complete collection priced at $195 000. More recently Sanborn maps have been made available electronically to institutions on a state-by-state basis, but the displayed map pages are taken from the black-and-white microfilms rather than from colour originals. See Stuart Blumin's review of *The Sanborn Fire Insurance Maps 1867–1950* (Alexandria, VA: Chadwyck-Healey, 1982–86) in *Journal of American History,* 73 (4) (March 1987), pp. 1089–90.

4 *Motion Picture Herald*, 28 May 1938, quoted in Martin Johnson (2005) 'See[ing] yourself as others see you', in The Films of H. Lee Waters. MA thesis, University of North Carolina at Chapel Hill, pp. 24–25.

5 For further statistical analysis of the provision of theatres for black moviegoers, see Chapter 13.

6 See Douglas Gomery, *Shared Pleasures: A History of Movie Presentation in the United States* (Madison: University of Wisconsin Press, 1992), pp. 155–170. Stewart acknowledges that most of the black theatres in Chicago were owned by whites (p. 162). In her *Film History* article, Charlene Regester discusses several notable exceptions to this generalisation, in particular the theatres owned by the black exhibitor Frederick King Watkins in the 1910s and 1920s.

7 See, for example, Michael E. Gardiner, *Critiques of Everyday Life* (London: Routledge, 2000).

8 For a discussion of early representations of cinema in local newspapers, see Chapter 15.

9 See www.newspaperarchive.com.

10 A Mob in Fort Worth Starts Wild Race Riot, *News* Fort Wayne (Indiana) 28 Feb. 1911, p. 1.

11 All Quiet Today After Negro Riot at Gaiety, *Daily Advance*, Elizabeth City, NC, 10 Sept 1940, pp. 1–2; Trial of Negroes Is Set for Friday, *Daily Advance*, Elizabeth City, NC, 11 Sept. 1940, p. 1.

12 Three Negroes Sentenced to Roads for Two Years, *Daily Advance*, Elizabeth City, NC, 14 Sept. 1940, pp. 1–2.

References

Allen, R.C. (1999) Home alone together: Hollywood and the 'family film', in *Identifying Hollywood's Audiences: Cultural Identity and the Movies* (eds M. Stokes and R. Maltby), British Film Institute, London, pp. 109–134.

Carr, D. (2009) A Red Carpet That Leads to All Homes. *New York Times* (16 Mar), pp. B1, B7.

Certeau, M. de (1984) *The Practice of Everyday Life* (trans. S. Rendell), University of California Press, Berkeley.

Goodman, P.S. (2008) Economists Say Movie Violence Might Temper the Real Thing. *New York Times* (7 Jan.), http://www.nytimes.com/2008/01/07/business/media/07violence.html (accessed 5 May 2010).

Kuhn, A. (2002) *Dreaming of Fred and Ginger: Cinema and Cultural Memory,* New York University Press, New York.

Massey, D. (2005) *For Space,* Sage, London.

Mitchell, W. (2006) *Buildings as History: the Architecture of Erle Stillwell,* Friends of the Henderson County Public Library, Hendersonville, NC.

Pollock, D. (1998) Introduction, in *Exceptional Spaces: Essays in Performance and History,* University of North Carolina Press, Chapel Hill.

Thrift, N. (2007) *Non-Representational Theory: Space, Politics, Affect,* Routledge, London.

3

Putting Cinema History on the Map

Using GIS to Explore the Spatiality of Cinema

Jeffrey Klenotic

In GIS the map is no longer an end product; it is now a research tool.

Gregory and Ell (2007, p. 10)

Several years ago in the midst of a daunting New Hampshire winter, I found myself driving along treacherous snow-covered roads to sit in a week-long workshop designed to introduce scholars from diverse disciplines to Geographic Information System (GIS) technology.[1] At the time, the relevance of the workshop for my research was not clear. GIS had barely begun to catch the eye of historians, let alone film historians, so like most scholars working outside the earth and ocean sciences I had only vague ideas of what GIS represented.[2] My fogginess about the subject was clouded further, when, turning to Google, a search of the phrase 'GIS and film history' generated only a profusion of websites relating to the portrayal of World War II US soldiers in Hollywood films. Although I knew little more than that GIS had 'something to do with maps', my long-standing research on the social history of movie audiences had a considerable geographic dimension that demanded fuller exploration. The lure of somehow being able to actually map the mountains of information I had collected over the years provided just enough motivation to keep my tyres skidding in a forward direction.

Having now travelled quite a distance down this road, I have found that GIS has indeed made a significant difference to the methods and resources I bring to bear on my research, in ways almost entirely unimaginable to me at the outset. GIS has enabled me to think more carefully about cinema history as a history of spatial relations, and it has helped me to rethink the modalities in which historical evidence can be examined, assembled, interpreted, stored and presented to the public; modalities that are impossible to describe and explain in writing alone. These changes have occurred despite the fact that my knowledge about the technology

Explorations in New Cinema History: Approaches and Case Studies, First Edition.
Edited by Richard Maltby, Daniel Biltereyst and Philippe Meers.

remains only at a moderate level. Although the more esoteric capabilities of GIS have a steep learning curve, there is no need to be an 'expert' to begin deriving benefits from using it as part of the process of historical inquiry. Most researchers can begin exploring the spatial dimensions of their objects of study after only a few days of GIS training, and can do so with intriguing results. As historical GIS scholar Anne Kelly Knowles has observed:

> One of the technology's most appealing advantages is that, once spatial and attribute data is [sic] correctly entered into the system, a GIS can almost instantly generate maps in answer to queries, and can do so as easily for a very large data set as for a very small one. The ease of mapping in GIS removes the technical obstacles that formerly limited most scholars to mapping only their final results, and even then only with the help of skilled cartographers. While compelling, handsome, thoroughly convincing cartography remains a fine art, GIS has made it possible for those without cartographic training to explore the geographical patterns in data through on-screen visualization. (Knowles, 2002, p. xv)

Beyond the technology's immediate practical advantages, a strong case can be made philosophically and empirically for the value of partial, self-taught, bottom-up applications of GIS: what might be termed 'little g' GIS as opposed to 'big G' GIS.[3] Despite (or because of) their relatively modest scope and piecemeal nature, these 'little g' GIS applications can dynamically alter how one assesses received historical knowledge, analyses historical evidence and learns through the research process itself.[4] These outcomes are possible, in large part, because GIS provides an open-ended platform on which diverse, competing and often marginalised voices and historical perspectives can be presented, and also because the technology can be used in creative yet systematic and rigorous ways that challenge and overcome the divide between qualitative and quantitative methodologies.

The distinction between 'little g' and 'big G' approaches to GIS is intended to recognise and encourage the appropriation of geospatial tools by researchers and users who have widely varied interests and competencies with the technology. In its earliest manifestations within hard science and quantitative social science disciplines, GIS was almost exclusively viewed as a top-down, technology-driven platform for advanced geostatistical analyses of large data sets with the goal of accurately representing the natural and social world for the purpose of generating predictions about it. The positivist underpinnings of this perspective were subsequently critiqued on epistemological and sociological grounds from within human geography, feminist theory and social theory.[5] As LaDona Knigge and Meghan Cope explain, 'Early critiques of GIS by social theorists raised significant issues concerning how technologies are used in ways that rigidify power structures while simultaneously masking – through the legitimizing strength of "science" and gee-whiz displays – the possibility of multiple versions of reality or "truth", socially constructed knowledges, and other sources of subjectivity that are inherent in all social research' (Knigge and Cope, 2006, p. 2022; see also Matthews *et al.*, 2005, pp. 75–90). In this context, 'little g' GIS emerged not as a diminished or less valid application of GIS, but instead offered a multiple and open approach to the technology that sought to be critical, reflexive, inclusive and participatory. It was and is an approach aimed at levelling the playing field in the social struggle to shape space, determine spatial practices and represent spatial relations by expanding the range of GIS users both in the academy and in the community, often with the outcome of bringing these two groups closer together.[6]

The GIS technology is, of course, no methodological magic bullet, no cure-all for long-standing problems of historical enquiry, such as how to locate documents, records and data and assess their complex discursive mediations of experience. Nonetheless, the technology has vast potential for historical analysis and visualisation, and has an instrumental role to play as an heuristic. In short, it is good to think with. Like other initiatives in Digital Humanities, historical GIS both enables us and requires us to 'participate more actively in constructing knowledge *in and through* our objects of study' (McPherson, 2009, p. 120). From this perspective, GIS is not just a tool by which to historicise space, drawing ever more contextually layered and geographically detailed maps. Instead, it is an open and dynamic form of *bricolage*, one that is subject to constant rearranging as an embedded part of a trial-and-error research process designed to facilitate the difficult task of seeing, representing and theorising the simultaneous multiplicity of social and historical experience in spatial terms and from a variety of partial perspectives.[7] This open, multiple and fluid approach to GIS meshes with a view of cinema history as a study aligned with people's history, resulting in a bottom-up history of people, places and the manifold relations and flows between them. It also considers how these spatial patterns have been routed at any given moment and how they changed over time in relation to cinema and to broader social, economic, cultural and geographic forces.[8]

In the remainder of this chapter, I briefly examine some of the ways in which cinema studies and geography have crossed paths in the analysis of films, and then suggest possible uses of GIS that may be of value to film historians exploring the spatial and geographic dimensions of audiences, moviegoing, exhibition and distribution. Examples from my ongoing work on the history of moviegoing and exhibition in Springfield, Massachusetts, and in New Hampshire will help to illustrate these latter methods. The discussion of methods will be partly informed by a GIS perspective that Knigge and Cope have called 'grounded visualization'. This is a critical, empirical and interpretive approach that integrates qualitative and quantitative sources of information and draws upon the resources of grounded theory, ethnography and GIS visualisation. The platform for grounded visualisation is built on an open, non-linear and often 'messy' research process that is 'exploratory', 'iterative and recursive', capable of simultaneously considering both 'particular instances and general patterns', and amenable to 'multiple views and perspectives for building knowledge' (Knigge and Cope, 2006, p. 2022).

If GIS and grounded visualisation can be adapted to fit the challenges of historical inquiry, they may provide a promising framework for a geo-ethno-historical approach to cinema's spatiality that recognises – in theory, in the research process, and in the representation of history itself – the simultaneous multiplicity of the spatial history of the social experience of moviegoing in relation to the spatial distribution of cinema as a commodity.[9] This use of GIS to explore cinema's socio-spatiality may be capable of creating empirically informed, theoretically grounded knowledge that is rigorous, yet resists grand narrative and remains open to revision and to multiple perspectives and interpretations. Moreover, if the methods of GIS and grounded visualisation are placed within a larger understanding of mapping not as a cartographic endpoint – the final output of spatial exploration – but as part of a 'landscape of inquiry' in which foreground and background are constantly adjusted and readjusted, then we may have the basis for a spatialised historiography of cinema that aspires in principle and in practice to recognise that space never stands still, but is instead 'always under construction'.[10] As Rob Kitchin and Martin Dodge put it, 'Maps are of-the-moment, brought into being through practices (embodied, social, technical), *always* remade every time they are engaged with; mapping is a process of constant reterritorialization ... *Maps are practices* – they are always *mappings*' (Kitchin and Dodge, 2007, p. 335).

Film History Takes a Spatial Turn

One consequence of film studies' focus on text and textual interpretation has been the suppression or marginalising of the spatiality of the experience of cinema. However, new histories of movie exhibition, movie audiences and the social experience of moviegoing along with the deployment of new technologies for reimagining and representing these histories suggest the need to reconstitute the object of film studies in relational, social and fundamentally spatial terms (Allen, 2006, p. 15).

Where does film studies go after it takes a 'spatial turn' and how might the practice of cinema history, specifically, be done differently as a result of the journey? This is not necessarily a new question, but it remains one with great power to inspire methodological and theoretical reflection if fresh perspectives are introduced into the conversation. Before exploring that possibility, however, it is important to consider some of the answers that have already been given regarding what a spatialised cinema history might look like. Indeed, over the last 15 years, the spatial turn has taken cinema studies in a direction that has increasingly crossed paths with cultural geography. As a result, there has been significant cross-fertilisation in both fields, particularly in proximity to mutually shared interests in concepts of space and place. These concepts have been most prominently foregrounded and explicated through investigations of the interplay between filmic representation, landscape, architecture, memory and mobility. In this work, scholars have sought to excavate the psychogeography of place and space as produced within historical processes of urbanisation, modernity and globalisation in the twentieth and twenty-first centuries.[11]

The connections between cinema and geography were first highlighted in 1999, in a special issue of *Screen* devoted to 'Space/place, city and film'. To introduce the issue, film and television studies scholar Karen Lury participated in a pathbreaking dialogue with geographer Doreen Massey in which the former framed the spatial turn and its significance for cinema studies by noting the 'ways in which space, place, the city and mobility as structuring metaphors can underpin new readings and understandings of different film texts and television as a medium'. Lury went on to delineate two major outcomes of the subfield that was then forming at the confluence of cinema studies and cultural geography: 'Firstly, representation: an expanding body of literature … uses historical and critical material related to the "city" and discusses the way in which certain films have represented the modern or postmodern city. … [S]uch work has also attempted to understand the representation of the city by cinema as a fundamental part of the construction of actual cities themselves, and the lived experience of individuals who inhabit these particular places' (Lury and Massey, 1999, p. 230).

Intellectual influences on the emergent subfield of film geography flowed from many directions, but a key wellspring was critical theorist Henri Lefebvre's elaboration of the ways in which spatial practices and relations, like social practices and relations, must be continually produced and reproduced (Lefebvre, 1991, pp. 46, 67–79).[12] In his seminal work, *The Production of Space*, Lefebvre developed a triad of interrelated spatial concepts that covered the realms of lived space, conceived or planned space, and perceived space. These concepts included: '*Spatial practice*, which embraces production and reproduction and the particular locations and spatial sets characteristic of each social formation'; '*Representations of space*, which are tied to the relations of production and the order which those impose'; and '*Representational spaces*, embodying complex symbolisms … linked to the clandestine or underground side of social life, as also to art' (Lefebvre, 1991, p. 33; emphasis added). Film texts, then, might be understood as metaphorically productive 'representational spaces' that work as perceptual tools with which 'spatial practices' can be mediated in the common sense and lived experience of individual members of society, as well as in the designs of planners and other creators of dominant 'representations of space'.

Lefebvre maintained that from the standpoint of social and spatial hegemony, the 'lived, conceived and perceived realms should be interconnected, so that the "subject", the individual member of a given social group, may move from one to another without confusion', but he was equally certain that 'whether they constitute a coherent whole is another matter. They probably do so only in favourable circumstances.' This caveat suggests that the question of spatial hegemony is ultimately an empirical one, and for this reason he maintained that 'the specific spatial competence and performance of every society member can only be evaluated empirically' (Lefebvre, 1991, pp. 38, 40).

Lefebvre's conceptual triad provides a rich theoretical framework on which to build critical, empirical, interpretive and historical investigations of cinema that combine analyses of spatial practices and representational spaces, as well as representations of space. However, the journey into film geography has yet to take a potentially fruitful audience turn and so it has thus far bypassed the opportunity to pursue the fully embodied critical geography of cinema history in relation to social and spatial practices that lies redolent in Lefebvre's work.[13] Instead, film studies and cultural geography have crossed paths to head out in promising new directions, only to circle back to more familiar territories of textual analysis and spectatorship. To date, film geography has tended to assume a relatively tight homology between the various tools by which representational space is produced within a society, as well as between the realms of representational space (perception) and spatial practices (lived experience). While film geography does create space for the possibility of contradiction or disjuncture within or between spatial realms, it often does so largely in theory, without exiting the text or the architext in search of evidence as to the particular spatial imaginations, practices and performances of film audiences.

Nonetheless, the audience turn remains open and should we wish to venture to take it we may find that it branches out into promising new directions of research. Tracks for one such direction were laid down by Doreen Massey in the *Screen* dialogue mentioned earlier, where she observed:

> [T]here is a deep historical connection between the development of cinema and a particular form and type of urbanization. That last bit is important: there were cities way before cinema, and cinema developed in particular cities. And they inevitably reflected that particularity. There is, in other words, a historical geography of this intimate connection which we should always recognize … I start feeling itchy when arguments about the relation city/cinema evoke such generalizations – apparently ahistorical and nongeographical – as 'the city' and 'the urban sensibility' … let us be careful not to essentialize what was a genuine and deep, but historically and geographically grounded, connection into a narrative which separates 'cities' off within what, I believe, is an immensely rich field of enquiry: that of the relation between film and spatiality in general. (Lury and Massey, 1999, pp. 230–231)

Massey's concern for greater specificity about film's relation to spatiality *in general* invites us to readjust our view of the landscape of cinema history to consider carefully the historically shifting yet geographically grounded relationships between space and particular places. As Ian Gregory has observed, 'If geography is thought of as the study of places and the relationships between them, then space must be important, as it enables and limits the interaction between people and places. Almost everything that interests a historian – goods and services, capital and labor, ideas and innovations, fashions and epidemics – moves from one place to another; thus space enables and constrains their spread (Gregory, 2008, pp. 126–127) (Figure 3.1). For cinema history, this means shifting our focus from cinema and the city to a broad examination of the precise locations of cinema within a simultaneous multiplicity of sites (regions, cities of diverse sizes and types, rural villages, small towns, farming communities and so on), including a consideration of cinema's connections to the socio-spatial practices, flows and blockages within and between these sites. Such a recalibration of the landscape of enquiry opens the door to an exploration of the historical geography of cinema as it has unevenly developed and been differentially experienced by audience members situated across a range of intersecting social, cultural, emotional and economic networks routed along particular geographic lines and territories. By exploring these networks and experiences we may be able to draw out the spatial perceptions, competencies, practices and relationships of cinema audiences in relation to the surrounding social, cultural and physical geography and to the multiple locations they chose to attend (or not).

The project that Massey envisioned has made slow but steady inroads within film historiography, and as Robert Allen recently argued, 'the local places of moviegoing [now] need to be re-presented ... as internally heterogeneous nodal points in a social, economic and cultural cartography of cinema: intersections of overlapping trajectories, networks, trails, and pathways, whose identities are constructed through the connections and collisions that occur there' (Allen, 2006, p. 24).[14] But given the complexity of representing the simultaneous multiplicity of historical geographic experience, how do we go about doing this? Moreover, what kinds of spatial and social information – beyond the places of moviegoing and the flows and vectors of people within and between them – do we need to include as part of 'a social, cultural and economic cartography of cinema'? One answer has been offered by Richard Maltby and Melvyn Stokes: 'To begin with, we will need detailed maps of cinema exhibition, amplified by evidence about the nature and frequency of attendance. This data then needs [sic] to be combined with broader demographic information derived from census data and other surveys to amplify our understanding

(a)

Figure 3.1 (a) Postcard of the Gem and Albert Theatres, Berlin, New Hampshire, in 1912. The message on the back (b), written in French and reflecting the cultural flow between French Canada and New Hampshire, describes the Gem as 'the largest church of the New England states'.

(b)

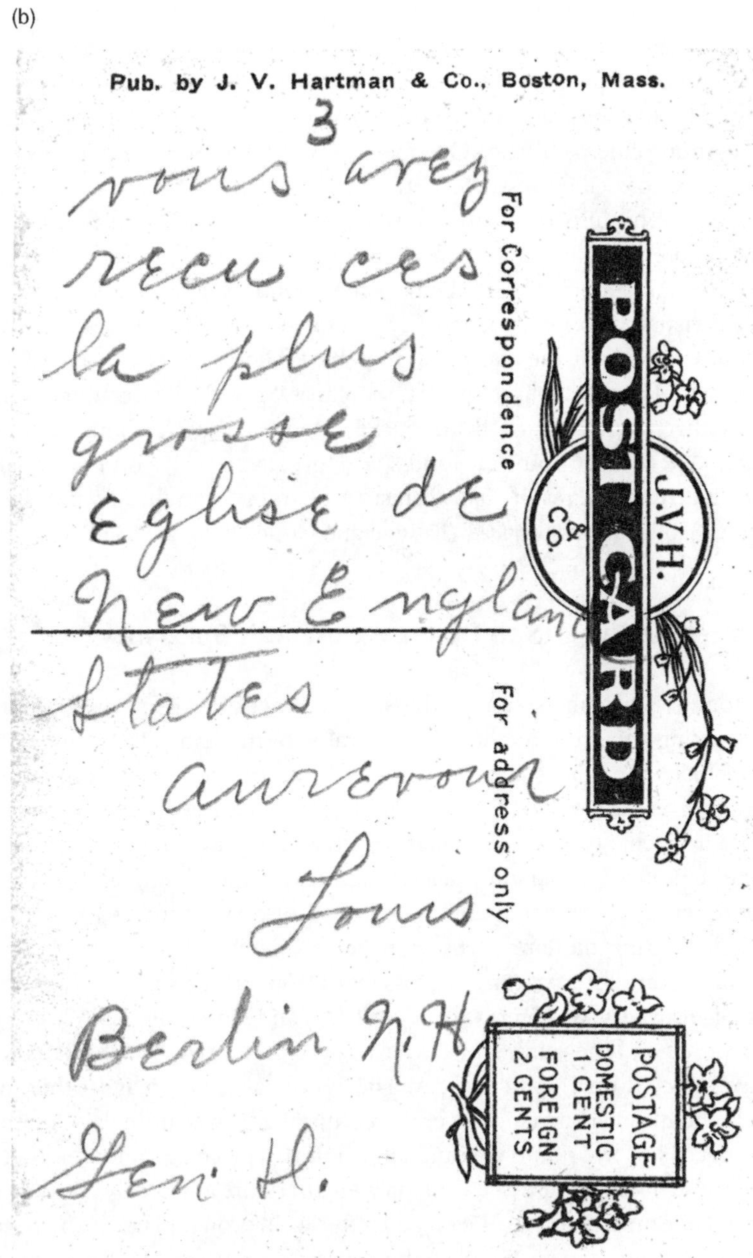

Figure 3.1 (Cont'd).

of cinema's audiences. … Just as vital as this demographic history, however, is the inclusion of experience that will ground quantitative generalisations in the concrete particulars of micro-historical case studies of local situations' (Maltby and Stokes, 2007, p. 21).

It is at this confluence of qualitative and quantitative methods and diverse informational resources that GIS and grounded visualisation can be put to use as part of the process of enquiry for mapping, exploring and visualising not only cinema's spatiality, but also its sociality. In addition to offering powerful tools for researching and representing cinema history, GIS opens new opportunities for interdisciplinary engagement across cinema studies, ethnography, oral history, architecture, economics, geography, historical geography, historical GIS and other fields and disciplines with potentially mutual interests in the socio-spatial history of cinema and everyday life. As geographers LaDona Knigge and Meghan Cope have argued: 'Grounded visualization is a particularly *geographical* set of analyses that could be used broadly outside of the discipline, thereby expanding the relevance and capabilities of spatial perspectives to other researchers. Specifically, grounded visualization is sensitive to *scale* issues, from local to global and back again; can integrate mobility and *flows* over both time and space; greatly depends on both qualitative and quantitative measures of *context* (historical and geographical); and, finally … enables rich explorations of *place*' (Knigge and Cope, 2006, p. 2035).

Using GIS to Explore Cinema's Spatiality

Film historians who take seriously the spatial dimensions of their research need little convincing about the methodological value of mapping. There are many reasons to include mapping as an integral part of one's methodology, but among the most common is the need to take geographical information from historical records and locate it on the ground. For instance, after toiling through archives in search of elusive references to persons, places or phenomena relating to one's research question – perhaps a question about the social history of moviegoing in a New England city during the late 1920s – one may discover that some such persons touched down on Eastern Avenue across from Winchester Square where the phenomena of films (*The Girl From Gay Paree* (1927) and *Fury of the Wild* (1929)), local amateur shows and the raffling of two live turkeys and two live chickens were all scheduled to occur on a particular day. The historical record may further indicate that while the film performances were to continue for two more days, neither live amateur talent nor live poultry would appear at this place again for another seven days, and those seeking these phenomena were therefore advised by the Winchester Amusement Company to travel instead to the well-known place at the corner of Liberty and Carew Streets. Faced with such rich yet furtive evidence about the already ephemeral practice of moviegoing, one can begin to assess, assemble and interpret this information by asking, simply, where were these places and how much distance lay between them? Mapping thus becomes a tool for visualising the geographic dimensions of historical documents by pinpointing locations to clarify patterns of spatial dispersion within one's object of study.[15]

Traditionally, historians have plotted locations on the ground using surviving maps from the period in question. Archives are culled for street surveys and neighbourhood atlases created under various auspices at different times to serve a range of commercial, political, legal and civic purposes. These materials may then be reproduced using a document scanner, with computer mark-up tools subsequently applied to denote or highlight locations of interest. In GIS, such procedures remain intrinsic to the process of spatial inquiry, but what is new is the degree to which these methods can be dynamically enhanced and extended. Period-specific maps, such as administrative town boundaries, topographical and geological surveys or transportation routes, can be enhanced with new stores of data and visually symbolised with extraordinary cartographic power. Moreover, once historical maps have been incorporated into GIS either in the form of scanned image documents (raster data) or GIS feature shapefiles (vector data), then the spatial information contained in those maps can be georeferenced with precise *x,y* coordinates. Among its many benefits, georeferencing enables data from diverse sources to be spatially overlaid using a common coordinate system.[16] Greater or lesser degrees of transparency can then be applied to display potentially significant spatial relationships between different phenomena, such as the total number of theatres per town in relation to major railroad lines, or to reveal changes in proximity, location and landscape over time (Figure 3.2). Georeferencing also means that maps from different periods, social perspectives or geographic vantage points can be overlaid and compared, leading to a richer understanding of the political, ideological and rhetorical motives behind epistemological claims contained in representations of space, including those made possible by the design of the GIS itself.

The introduction of GIS into the landscape of cinema history enquiry brings to the fore questions about cinema's spatial positioning, dispersion and historical representation; it also affords a means of interactively and iteratively exploring such questions in keen detail. Once features within an object of study have been located on the ground and mapped into GIS shapefiles as points, polygons (areas) or arcs (lines) with specific *x,y* coordinates – such features are called 'spatial data' – then a wide range of informational attributes and descriptive values can be attached to those features. These 'attribute data' are stored in a geodatabase that can be queried from the map surface via an 'identify' tool that researchers can apply to answer the most fundamental of all spatial questions: What is at this location?[17] Information in the geodatabase can be edited or updated as needed and may be numerical, date-based, string-based or text-based.[18] The geodatabase can also include hypertext that links specific locations on the map to sources of external information such as audio or video files, text or image documents, online archival materials, internet websites or even to other GIS map documents. One click on a particular movie venue location, perhaps a vaudeville and movie theatre opened in Springfield, Massachusetts, by Sylvester Poli in 1913, immediately affords access to contextual material such as postcards, oral histories, newspaper articles, historical essays and a map showing how the theatre was positioned within the broader regional theatre chain owned by Poli at that time.

Attribute data from GIS are spatially coded (linked directly to *x,y* coordinates on the map), but the data and the spatial features they point to can be temporally

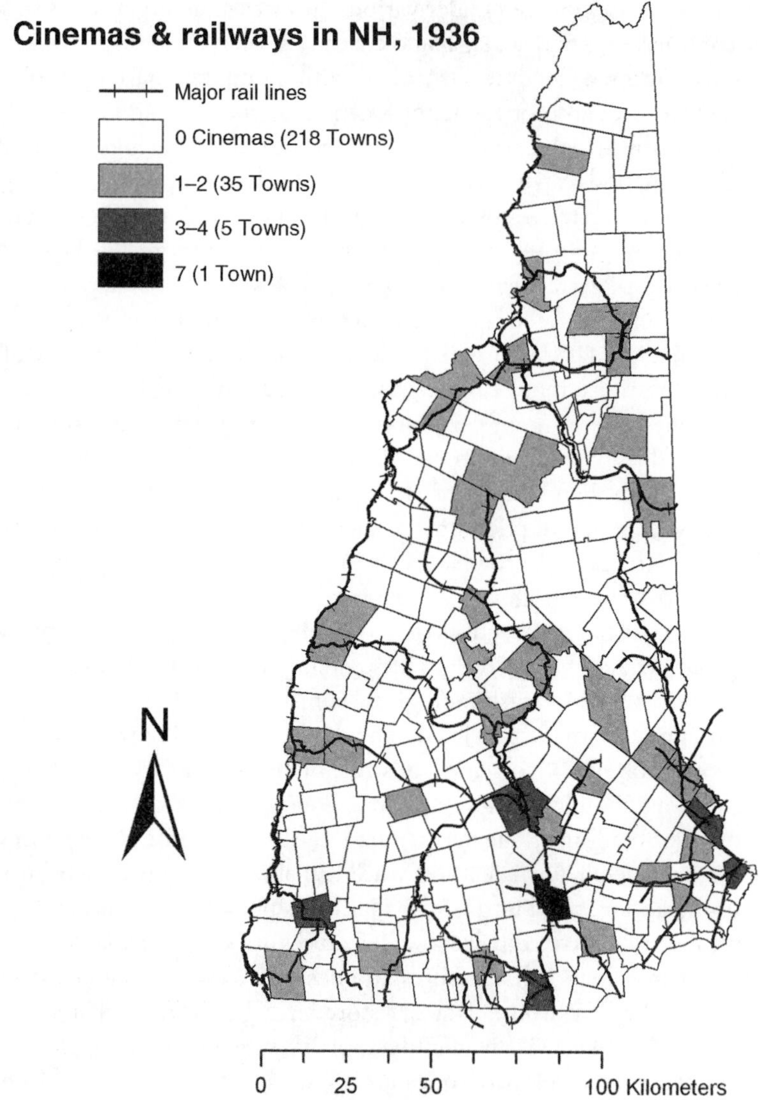

Figure 3.2 Layers of spatial information: cinemas and railways in New Hampshire, 1936.

coded as well. One might, for instance, create a table that records when a venue first exhibited films, changed names or prices, replaced owners or managers, changed programmes or run position, showed films of a certain genre or narrative franchise, featured films with a particular star or national origin, included live entertainment on the bill, ceased to operate as a cinema or was altogether demolished as a structure. Patterns of spatial distribution for each field of time-stamped information could then be iteratively displayed using thematic maps to illustrate data on a daily, weekly, monthly, yearly or any other temporally determined basis.

Thematic maps are mappings where the symbology deployed to depict spatial features is differentiated by size, colour, shape, shade or some other characteristic in order to represent breaks in data values stored in fields within the table. Thematic maps represent horizontal cross-sections of historical geography. As geographer Alan Baker explains:

> An individual cross-section can be justified for its own intrinsic interest, in providing a snapshot of the geography (or aspects of the geography) of a particular place at a specific moment in time. A series of cross-sections can be employed to provide an indication of the changes that have taken place during intervening periods, focusing on the additions to and the subtractions from the geography of an area between one date and another. This method – comparative statics – focuses on changes in the distribution patterns, leaving to be inferred the processes behind the changes. (Baker, 2003, p. 39)

Thematic maps must necessarily be taken as partial and limited representations of space because they ostensibly claim to capture a moment in the history of what Doreen Massey calls 'time-spaces'. Since space is always 'under construction' the simultaneous multiplicity of space cannot be 'frozen' (Massey, 2005, pp. 177–195). Nonetheless, Baker points out that the limitations of a cross-section approach 'do not thereby undermine the continuing relevance and legitimacy of mapping the distributions of individual components, or even of related sets of components, of an area's geography. Such mappings need to be seen, however, as contributions as much to the study of geographical change as to the study of past geographies' (Baker, 2003, p. 40).

To study geographical change is inevitably to study historical change, and thematic maps can be generated using data from a wide variety of historical sources. The United States decennial census provides a vast amount of spatial and attribute data that can be incorporated into GIS to display geographic patterns of population distribution and social demography at a single moment in time or at different times (Figure 3.3).[19] On the county level of census geography, much of this information is available in aggregate form dating back to the origins of cinema and beyond. Aggregate data at the town, tract, enumeration district or block group levels is harder to come by on a regular basis, especially prior to 1970, but with due diligence and a measure of good fortune it can sometimes be tracked down in federal, state or local archives.

Online genealogy services have also emerged as valuable resources for compiling geodatabases that can be used to display themes of socio-spatial information in GIS. For a fee, ancestry.com provides easy access to digitised census records that can be viewed either in their original form or as a list of abbreviated records that can be copied in batches and pasted into a spreadsheet. This spreadsheet can then be imported into GIS for conversion into a geodatabase. The abbreviated records from ancestry.com have been expunged of street addresses that may compromise individual privacy, but the records do include the country or state where a person was born and the name of the town where they lived at the time of the census. These data alone are enough to enable cinema historians to create thematic mappings to illustrate and compare, on a town-by-town basis, specific patterns of in-migration and to explore how these patterns may have factored into the emergence, development and transformation of cinema as a social and economic practice and as a site for cultural assimilation, negotiation or resistance. Data on patterns of in-migration can also lead to empirical mappings of the networks of interrelationships between places, and between people and places. It is vital to know how these

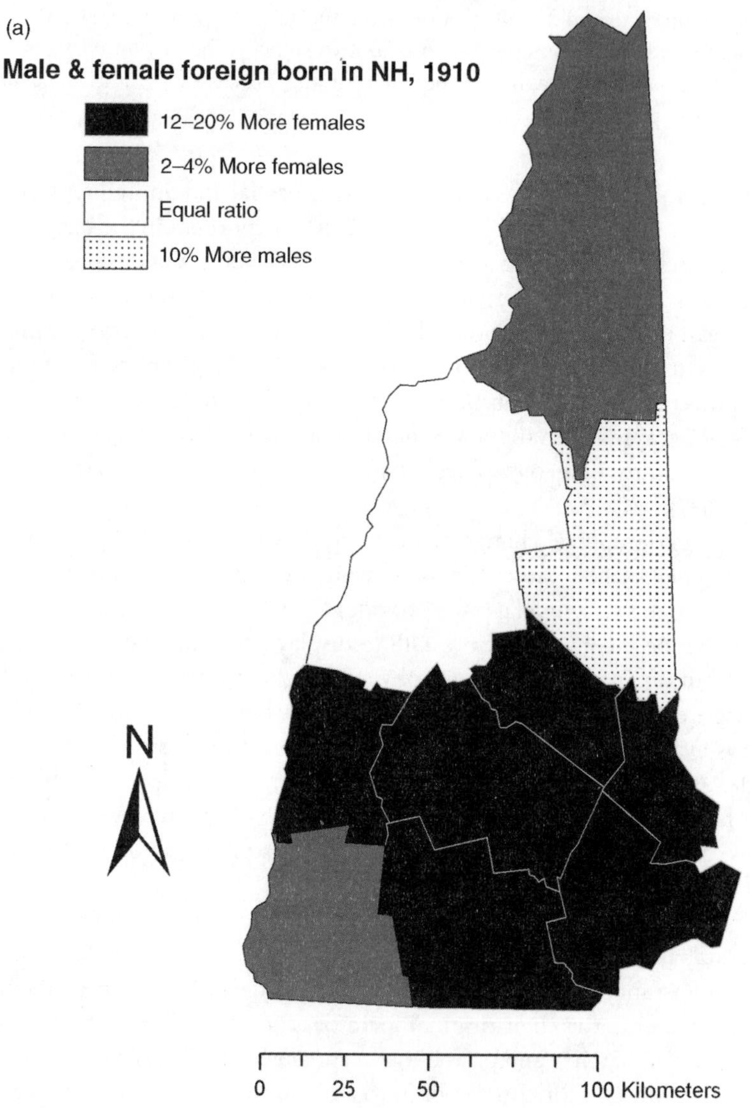

Figure 3.3 (a,b) Thematic maps using census data to visualise contexts for cinema history: New Hampshire population.

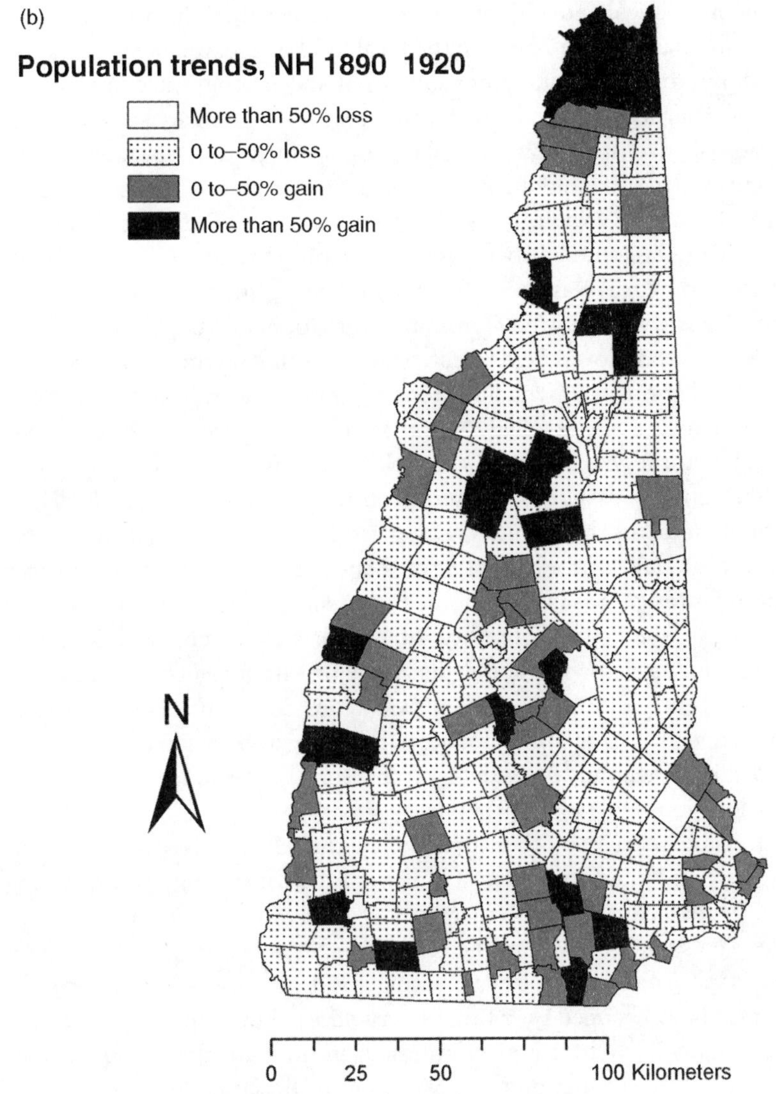

Figure 3.3 (Cont'd).

informal networks of social, cultural, economic and geographic connection may have influenced the flow and direction of cinema culture and moviegoing practices across space and over time. We need to understand what these networks meant to people and the role moviegoing played in shaping those meanings, particularly in relation to the lived experience of mobility and change. We also need to explore the extent to which these networks may have drawn upon, exceeded or undermined not only the representational spaces metaphorically conjured up by cinematic images but also the official maps and formal representations of space contained in political and administrative boundaries that directly sought to shape and regulate spatial movements on the local level of everyday life.

In addition to census data, other sources of social geographic information may also exist for particular periods and locations within a given area of study, although such materials may naturally be available on a much more sporadic and fugitive basis. One example that highlights the role diverse sources of historical geographic data can play in GIS explorations of cinema history is the work of Harlan Paul Douglass. Douglass studied sociology at the University of Chicago and Columbia University and he was Research Director of The Institute of Social and Religious Research (1921–1933) and the Committee for Cooperative Field Research (1944–1950). Douglass employed field research and scientific methods to empirically analyse the social contexts in which Protestant churches were situated. The resulting studies contained many detailed maps that offered nuanced interpretations of the social and cultural geography of select cities, towns and rural areas, including St Louis, Springfield, Pittsburgh and an assortment of small towns and villages from various regions across the country (Douglass, 1919, 1924, 1926, 1948). These maps charted the spatial distribution of Protestant churches in relation to social phenomena as far ranging as rates of home ownership, foreign-born and black populations, poverty, tuberculosis mortality, infant mortality, juvenile delinquency, social congestion, industrialisation and dependence on charity. Such data can readily be incorporated into GIS to compare movie venue locations in relation to church locations, as well as to create thematic maps that provide a contemporaneous context and enrich our understanding of the social experience of moviegoing in different locations and neighborhoods.

When using census or other forms of historical data, researchers need to be both creative and judicious in developing methods for sorting it and adapting it for use in a geodatabase. In particular, special care must be given when attaching attribute data such as that from the census to spatial features on the map because the boundaries of counties, towns, voting wards, enumeration districts or block groups may have changed over time. Every effort should be made to ensure that attribute data collected for a given moment in time attaches to spatial data as it historically existed for that unit of geography at the same time. In practice, however, the vagaries, elisions and biases of the historical record in conjunction with the large number of diverse data layers required to build a GIS may make it difficult or impossible always to achieve perfect synchronisation between the temporality of attribute data and the temporality of corresponding spatial data. Depending on the object of study, slight changes in the political or administrative boundaries of historical geography over time may or may not significantly affect the integrity of one's research. If one wished to use census data to explore how many foreign-born persons may have lived within a 500-metre radius of a cinema venue and how this changed between 1910 and 1920, then GIS could be used to create a 'buffer' that visualised that radius around the venue for both 1910 and 1920. The fact that the town may have had its eastern administrative boundary increased or decreased by one kilometre is unlikely to have much bearing on one's query, assuming the 500-metre buffer was distant from the area of town boundary change. If, however, one's research focused precisely on venues positioned along borderlines or amidst border regions, then the need to accurately synchronise attribute data to changes in political and administrative town boundaries would clearly be critical.

On a philosophical level, if we view maps as the cartographic endpoints of a closed, linear and finite process of spatial enquiry, then the almost inevitable appearance of asynchronous layers of information in the geodatabase may well be considered an insurmountable flaw in the attempt to use GIS to create a universally valid and reliable representation of historical geography that can be used and built upon by researchers in the future. Conversely, if our approach emphasises the open, iterative and reflexive nature of mappings as part of a landscape of inquiry that is always adjusted and readjusted, then we may seek to redefine asynchronous layers of information as an opportunity to explore critically cinema's spatiality and history from a series of partial, dialogical, potentially contradictory viewpoints that are always under construction. The more open and creative GIS becomes as an heuristic *bricolage*, potentially involving community participation far beyond academia, the more difficult and more counterproductive it may become to impose a singular scholarly authority over its representations of space and place. Regardless of how one approaches this larger debate, there likely will be considerable agreement that information on the historical sources and geographic properties of all attribute and spatial data in the GIS should be duly documented in project metadata.[20]

The data in GIS tables can be visualised in still snapshots comprising thematic maps. These snapshots may even take the form of animated maps that can dynamically display the movement of spatial features or changes in attribute data attached to geographic locations. Such techniques reveal patterns in historical geography that may support the development of spatially informed explanations to account for changes in a single attribute or multivariate system of attributes over time. Moreover, the information in GIS data tables can quickly be recast in a wide variety of visually engaging and analytically productive forms, such as charts, tables, scatter plots and graphs. These relatively simple and easily created representations of quantitative data are no substitute for statistical analysis, but they are nonetheless among the most accessible tools that GIS affords and they may be useful for visualising data in multiple formats (Figure 3.4).

Grounded Visualisation

The power of GIS for thematic mapping and other forms of visualisation is clear. Yet how might such techniques be marshalled to integrate data from qualitative and quantitative methods into a unified analytic framework capable of creating new knowledge and advancing new modes of historical understanding and representation that take into account the simultaneous multiplicity of cinema's

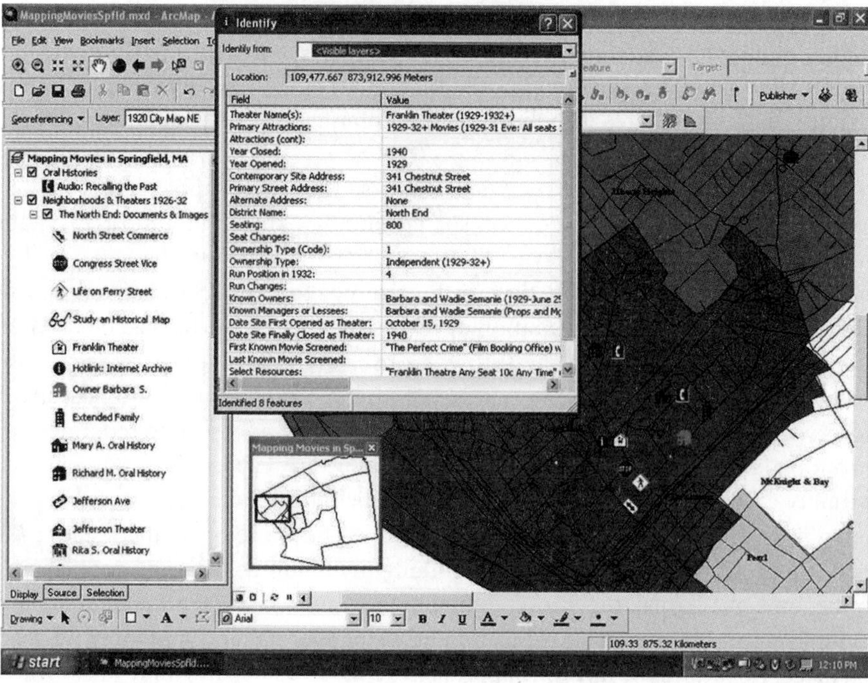

Figure 3.4 Grounded visualisation: GIS data tables underpinning the map surface.

spatiality? One potentially promising answer may be found in the GIS platform of 'grounded visualisation'.

LaDona Knigge and Meghan Cope describe grounded visualisation as an integrated analytical method that fuses the capacities of GIS visualisation for displaying and exploring quantitative spatial and attribute data with the qualitative resources of ethnography and grounded theory. The result is a mixed method of GIS that can 'accommodate and represent multiple interpretations of the world and diverse views of reality' (Knigge and Cope, 2006, p. 2028). Here the situated knowledges of partial perspectives constantly inform each other as they heuristically and dialogically interact within the multilayered representational space of the GIS. Knigge and Cope point out that such partial perspectives may complement each other but just as often they will contradict or compete with each other: 'Displaying quantitative spatial data in a variety of ways may reveal patterns, and statistical analysis may reveal correlations, but it is often the case that explanation (and thus theory building) is grounded in the experiences of real people living through specific conditions and they are in many ways the "experts", even if their explanations seem to be at odds with other sources of data' (Knigge and Cope, 2006, p. 2028). In grounded visualisation the appearance of contradictory perspectives does not make any one perspective, or the simultaneous multiplicity of all perspectives, equally null and void. Rather, this heterogeneity works to create new questions and produce complex explanatory narratives in which different interpretations and constructions of reality may be considered both contradictory and true because they capture social meanings attached to spatial locations situated at different scales of experience.

Grounded visualisations of GIS must therefore be robust in allowing researchers to explore spatial locations, perspectives and relationships from a variety of viewpoints and at differing scales, from the macro to the micro. This exploration would require using the full range of panning, zooming, identification, searching, thematic mapping, hyperlinking and other GIS tools. One strength of this approach would be its capacity to reveal spatial connections between social, cultural and economic practices that may at first glance seem unrelated. As feminist geographer Mei-Po Kwan puts it, 'When complemented by contextual information on the ground and at microscale (e.g., stories about the lived experiences of individuals), GIS visualizations can establish important connections between large-scale phenomena (e.g., urban restructuring or land-cover change) and the everyday lives of individuals' (Kwan, 2002, p. 650). These connections, however, would not be created or controlled by the GIS so much as they would be discovered through active and creative exploration. Knigge and Cope observe that within contemporary thought about cartography, geographic visualisation is increasingly defined as an 'activity that facilitates exploring unknowns in a highly interactive environment, as opposed to the use of maps as a tool to communicate "knowns" to a public audience' (Knigge and Cope, 2006, p. 2026). This has major implications for scholars who wish to develop web-enabled GIS public history projects, but it also has import for researchers using the technology to support more normative forms of academic scholarship and publication. Grounded visualisation affords researchers the opportunity to build a geodatabase from the ground up, using an iterative process that draws upon mixed methods and adds data in an incremental manner. This piecemeal and open-ended approach to GIS promotes continual analysis and reanalysis as the geodatabase expands and develops. In short, 'researchers can recursively explore data in order to identify themes and processes, raise new questions, and begin to build theories' (Knigge and Cope, 2006, p. 2026). Publication, like mapping itself, might then become less the closed product of a finished research process and more the open product of an engagement with the geodatabase and a reflection of a particular stage of a work in progress. The publication itself may then be integrated back into the geodatabase to take a place on the map where it can be read and critiqued from diverse spatial perspectives and assessed in relation to new layers of data that may yet be discovered.

The principle that theories of explanation should be built from the ground up roots grounded visualisation in grounded theory, which Steinberg and Steinberg note is designed to 'generate information, themes and patterns, not to prove theory' (Steinberg and Steinberg, 2006, p. 78). Grounded theory is connected to the heterogeneous particularities of lived experience and everyday life, and it approaches this connection critically, starting 'from the premise that the world is in a constant state of flux, and that individuals are not all equally placed' (Bailey *et al.*, 1999, p. 173). Theoretical explanations for a phenomenon are therefore not deductively imposed in advance but instead emerge inductively as patterns and themes are gradually recognised within and through the object of study. The research process is 'very iterative; the researcher is constantly conducting analyses, looking for themes, and then conducting more analyses. It is a very hands-on approach to sorting through one's data' (Steinberg and Steinberg, 2006, p. 79). Researchers must be open to all forms of data and methodologically flexible if they are to grasp the phenomenon in its full complexity. When the data cease to offer up new themes, concepts, categories or relationships then a point of theoretical saturation has been reached. The adequacy of any emergent explanation is assessed in relation to the empirical phenomena in which it is grounded.

How might grounded visualisation be applied by researchers who wish to use GIS to explore the socio-spatial history of moviegoing? There are numerous possibilities, but a brief discussion drawing upon my ongoing work in Springfield, Massachusetts, may help illustrate the general utility of the approach.[21]

My research on the history of moviegoing in Springfield began long before I was introduced to GIS, and like most film historians my attempt to understand the history of moviegoing and exhibition in this city began with the familiar methods of an exhaustive reading of the city's three daily newspapers, combined with extensive review of city directories, local fire insurance maps, photographs and any other archival materials available through the local historical society. These materials constituted my initial 'run' of data, and through them I was able to develop a list of movie venues operating in this city of 150 000 persons for the period between 1926 and 1932. These theatres were then plotted on a street map from the same period.

The focus of research, however, was not only upon knowing what movie venues existed and where they were located. Rather, following a cultural studies approach to the social history of film, the real interest was to learn about the audiences at these different theatres and to understand what the diverse social experiences of moviegoing meant to them. The question of whether the moviegoing experience had become standardised as a result of vertical integration of exhibition venues by the major Hollywood studios was of special importance. Had economic consolidation and standardisation of exhibition produced a corresponding tendency in the cultural experience of moviegoing? My list of theatres seemed wholly insufficient to get at these more subjective questions of audiences and their social practices and cultural meanings, and so to add an interpretive context I went further back in time to uncover the operation of every movie venue that had ever operated in the city going back to the origins of cinema. These venues were added to the map, which began to wither and tear in its hard-copy inflexibility under the growing weight of an increasing number of data points, all of which seemed to be opening and closing and refusing to stand still in one place for very long. Nevertheless, filling in the backstories for movie venues before 1926 enabled me to understand the specific histories of some of the venues and to begin to grasp their accumulated meanings for local audiences. But most of the theatres did not have much enduring history to speak of, and this spurred me to collect a number of oral histories and to supplement these with a sort of fledgling historical ethnographic approach to the city's neighbourhoods as key geographical contexts for discerning the possible local meanings of moviegoing. This approach was greatly aided by the discovery of Harlan Paul Douglass's *Springfield Church Survey*, which was published in 1926. Douglass's maps and their quantitative data enhanced my understanding of how different parts of the city were perceived from the social and spatial vantage points of elites. Still, my ability to assess, assemble and interpret these increasingly diverse layers of information was limited by the inelasticity and unidimensionality of my mappings, which kept me from fully grasping the subjective themes and spatial patterns of the moviegoing experience.

It was this unwieldy cache of data – a cache that had largely ceased to yield new insights and so had lain dormant for some time – that accompanied me to the snowy workshop where I had my introduction to GIS. I left that workshop with a georeferenced GIS shapefile of Harlan Paul Douglass's 1926 map. This may not seem like much, and in practical terms it wasn't, but to see that map lifted off the frozen pages of time into the interactive space of the present was a moment of revelation. It remained unclear to me what should be done with this map after the instructional workshop had ended, but through a gradual process of exploration I was able to create an attribute table that connected the map to all of the social demographic data Douglass had collected at the time of his research. Through an iterative process of thematic mapping, that quantitative data came alive in my historical imagination in ways it had never done before. I was able to explore the data and grasp its key themes and concepts – such as the concept of 'social quality' – in much more compelling and vivid ways. This enabled me to more clearly see the social and spatial connections between different districts of the city, based on how Douglass's official representation of space had classified these habitats.

Gradually, the geodatabase expanded as it went through successive iterations of new data. Layers of spatial data were eventually created for all the movie venues in the city along with their associated attribute values. These locations were supplemented with a wide range of hyperlinks, particularly to photographs and postcards, but also to archival materials such as newspaper clippings and advertisements. Oral histories were also added to the geodatabase, and it was now possible to map the routes that participants had walked to reach the various venues they attended. Patterns of social and spatial separation as well as points of convergence between these routes became apparent. It also became possible to create a table that charted which venues oral history participants had and had not attended. When this was visualised in a thematic mapping, it formed the basis on which I identified provisional networks of social and spatial relationships between people and places. Moreover, I began to include not just photographs and information pertaining to movie venues, but also to adjacent businesses and neighbourhood landmarks. I wanted to know what the experience of walking down different streets on the way to the movie house might have felt like for different moviegoers. At the same time as my understanding of moviegoing in Springfield was becoming more nuanced, traditional academic publications emerged from my research and these

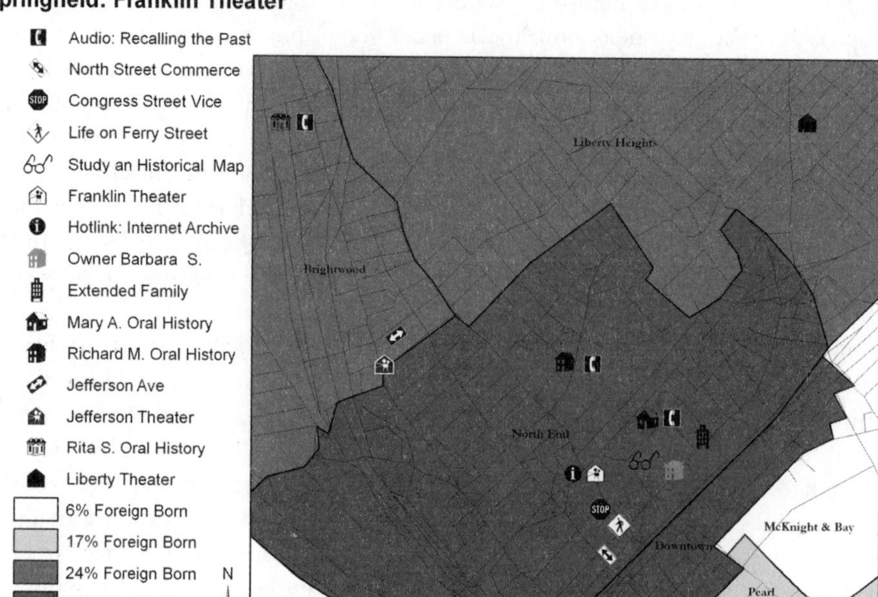

Figure 3.5 Grounded visualisation: the Franklin Theater in its neighbourhood.

were then linked back to the map interface to be assessed for the quality of their fit to the archival data and to the whole set of socio-spatial relations and viewpoints represented within the GIS (Figure 3.5).

The Springfield GIS has not reached the point of theoretical saturation; new bits and layers of information are still regularly being added, leading me continually to reassess the validity of my own prior analyses. The act of interactively exploring the geodatabase from multiple partial perspectives continues to produce fresh insights and enables me to imagine new explanations for patterns in the data. For instance, Ian Gregory has written that 'space can be thought of as a causal variable that represents the costs, in time or money, of two places interacting. This shows how space and time are intrinsically linked, as the cost of crossing space is also likely to be strongly related to the duration of the journey' (Gregory, 2008, p. 127). This is certainly true, although when places are analysed using the rich empirical setting afforded by grounded visualisation we may arrive at new ways of understanding the perceived 'costs' in social and cultural capital of travelling over and through space. To give one example, the Franklin Theater in Springfield's North End was within easy walking distance for many city residents who lived in neighbouring areas.[22] Yet few such persons attended the Franklin, even though they acknowledged travelling much greater distances to attend theatres in other parts of the city. Why? Partly it was a matter of the established socio-spatial networks and relationships some of these people had with others who lived in neighbourhoods beyond the North End. The perceived 'benefits' of maintaining those relationships and cementing them with a visit to the movie theatre, seem to have outweighed the costs, in time or money, of travelling to other parts of the city where they did not know anyone. Just as important were the perceived costs of attending the Franklin, which sat in a part of town with a 'bad' reputation for its low 'social quality'. As one oral history participant commented, 'Brightwood [the home neighbourhood], we thought, was higher class than the North End' so the Franklin Theater 'was restricted for us. It was in a bad section.' Such oral histories of the city's social geography match the 'official' views found in more formal representations of space such as Douglass's 1926 *Church Survey*, which ranked the North End as the ninth worst district in the city for its 'far below average social quality'. North Enders, of course, did not necessarily share this view of their own socio-spatial location, and in fact they were as likely to criticise other parts of town as limited and elitist as they were to accept the definition of their own space as somehow socially and culturally inferior.

Knigge and Cope note that it is difficult to translate a GIS grounded visualisation into the orderly flow of words because the 'actual research process is often messy, nonlinear, and opportunistic, and changes direction with new information' (Knigge and Cope, 2006, p. 2029). This has certainly been the case for my own experience with the method, an experience further shaped by the fact that it has been through the process of developing my own GIS project that I have taught myself how to use GIS technology. Quite literally then, my use and application of the technology represents a partial and highly situated form of grounded knowledge that in many ways embodies the essence of the 'little g' approach to GIS.

Conclusion

One might well reach the end of this chapter unpersuaded by its exhortations proclaiming the value of GIS for film historians. GIS may be fine and good, but at the end of the day, what if anything will mapping the locations of moviegoing tell us about the history of film that we don't already know? The answer, of course, is that we simply cannot know in advance where this spatial information might lead us and how it may call into question what we think we know. Grounded theories of historical explanation start from the bottom up, not the top down, and sites of movie consumption are the precise nodal points where cinema has most directly and consistently touched down to constitute a material network of time-space relations with socially embedded and physically embodied audiences. This is true whether the site has taken the form of the fixed location movie venue or the more portable form of the travelling or amateur exhibitor or today's mobile iPod user.

A good case can therefore be made that using GIS to map cinema's spatial positioning and distribution – aspects of its historical geography – is quite valuable because it enriches the ground from which future historical explanations may emerge. This is especially true in a field like cinema history where relatively little empirical work has been done to connect the cinema's manifold historical development as a diverse set of social experiences and cultural practices to its variable geographic development as a commodity circulated via broader patterns of distribution and retail selling within local, regional, national and international markets.[23] While our knowledge of the history of films, film distribution, film exhibition, film audiences and even of the history of cinema as a social experience slowly grows, we still do not know very much about how all these layers of information actually map onto the historical geography of cinema envisioned as a diverse and continuously changing network of spatio-temporal relations configured within the broader contradictory and uneven developments of capitalism itself. To give just one example, the question of how to explain shifting forms of exhibition and moviegoing (such as the concentrated rise of integrated theatre chains and the scattered decline of independent local ownership) cannot be answered only by examining economic strategies like block booking or corporate practices of creative destruction such as the conversion to talking pictures. We also need to know where the emerging, disappearing or residually surviving forms were located, and how these locations may have been related to broader spatial patterns of economic (dis)investment and population redistribution that perhaps altered the flow of resources within and across the geography of ruralities, small towns, cities and metropolises.

It is, then, crucially important to map and thematically visualise the locations and spatial distributions (inclusions or exclusions) of a given phenomenon over time. If we also approach the application of GIS to cinema history as a research tool rather than as just a means by which to produce a finished map, then the mapping of venue locations gleaned from the historical record will be a necessary starting point for a spatial analysis of cinema rather than the end product. Again, we wish to know not only where and when a particular phenomenon manifested itself on the ground, but also something about the surrounding topography (both built and natural) as well as something about the immediate social, cultural and economic context. Moreover, we clearly want to know how particular geographic locations were and were not articulated to each other both spatially and temporally. For instance, what were the points of origin for people, films and, to recall my earlier example, fowl, at a given location and what transportation routes did these actors travel in order to perform the phenomenon they collectively and individually experienced at each location as it unfolded in time? Were these same routes travelled as the phenomenon dispersed? How did geography and space work to shape patterns of mobility (or immobility) and guide networks of interaction (or separation) between people and places as configured within the broad cultural field established by cinema in different places at a single moment in time or across different times? Conversely, how might cinema and moviegoing have functioned as a 'compass' or 'legend' or 'key' that helped shape how people moved through and perceived space and ascribed meaning to the experience of social hierarchy, mobility or immobility, inclusion or exclusion?

Geographic information systems and grounded visualisation put these sorts of questions about cinema's relation to spatiality in general firmly on the map of cinema history. In turn, cinema history is repositioned as an adjustable but indispensable object of study on a broader map featuring an interdisciplinary and increasingly collaborative landscape of inquiry.

Notes

1 A geographic information system (GIS) is a powerful, integrative, computer-based and web-enabled technology that allows users to create, map, manage, analyse, model and explore spatial information. The spatial dimension may be an exact position on the ground collected via a global positioning system (GPS), or information contained in an address, zip code, town, census block or other geographic entity. Most references to GIS in this chapter derive from a desktop software platform called ArcGIS, which is a licensed product of Environmental Systems Research Institute (ESRI). Geospatial analysis can also be pursued using a variety of other GIS platforms, many of which are open source software. In addition, GIS capabilities for multimedia hyperlinking and basic location mapping are now available in several allied technologies, such as Google Maps, Google Earth and Google Mashups. These platforms can, to a degree, be made interoperable with files produced using GIS software. At the time of this writing, GIS has much more power than such allied technologies for advanced qualitative and quantitative analysis of historical and statistical data, as well as for map cartography. Some of these gains, however, often come with a steeper learning curve and greater need for financial and institutional support.

2 Two key early works in historical GIS were Anne Kelly Knowles (ed.), *Past Time, Past Place: GIS for History* (Redlands, California: ESRI Press, 2002); and Ian N. Gregory, *A Place in History: A Guide to Using GIS in Historical Research* (Oxford: Oxbow Books, 2003). Valuable recent works include Steven J. Steinberg and Sheila L. Steinberg, *GIS: Geographic Information Systems for the Social Sciences: Investigating Space and Place* (Thousand Oaks, California: Sage, 2006), Gregory and Ell (2007); and Anne Kelly Knowles (ed.), *Placing History: How Maps, Spatial Data and GIS Are Changing Historical Scholarship* (Redlands, California: ESRI Press, 2008).

3 I am indebted to geographer Sarah Ellwood whose keynote address for a GIS workshop at the University of Wollongong in March 2008 introduced me to these terms and helped me to think in new ways about the need to widen access to GIS by a broader spectrum of users both inside and outside academia.

4 The case made here for 'little g' GIS is not to deny the value of large-scale efforts, but rather to suggest that projects of increased scope require greater expertise in geography, statistics and GIS, and this may discourage some historians from adopting the technology on any level. One solution to this problem is for researchers interested in large-scale projects to do collaborative GIS. For instance, Ian Gregory and Paul Ell write that 'The historian wanting to use GIS must not only learn the technical skills of GIS, but must also learn the academic skills of a geographer. … This range of skills means that there are many advantages to collaborative research in historical GIS research. This allows individuals to focus on their own particular strengths rather than requiring one individual to be an expert in many fields' (Gregory and Ell, 2007, p. 11). Ultimately, a GIS-enabled spatial history of cinema would provide a compatible platform for a spectrum of small, mid-range and large-scale studies. Some of these studies might complement each other while others might compete with or contradict each other. One of the most exciting aspects of GIS technology for cinema history is precisely its ability to allow users to research a phenomenon by examining the evidence at different scale registers – from the most local of micro data all the way to the broadest scale statistical data in aggregate form.

Historical arguments that hold true at one scale of analysis may or may not hold true at other scales.

5 For social and feminist critiques of GIS, see John Pickles (ed.), *Ground Truth: The Social Implications of Geographic Information Systems* (New York: Guilford, 1995); and Mei-Po Kwan, 'Feminist visualization: re-envisioning GIS as a method in feminist geographic research', *Annals of the Association of American Geographers,* 92 (2002), pp. 645–661. For a review of the epistemological debate about GIS between positivists, realists and social constructionists, and for a discussion of the social embeddedness of GIS and spatial data generally, see Nadine Schuurman, 'Reconciling social constructivism and realism in GIS', *ACME: An International E-Journal for Critical Geographies,* 1 (1) (2002), pp. 75–90; and Nadine Schuurman, *GIS: A Short Introduction* (Oxford, Blackwell, 2004).

6 On community and participatory uses of GIS, see Sarah Ellwood, 'Beyond cooptation or resistance: urban spatial politics, community organizations, and GIS-based spatial narratives', *Annals of the Association of American Geographers,* 96 (2) (2006), pp. 323–341; see also Meghan Cope and Sarah Ellwood (eds), *Qualitative GIS: A Mixed Methods Approach* (London: Sage, 2009).

7 For more on *bricolage* in relation to computer programming, computational objects, and strategic information systems, see Sherry Turkle and Seymour Papert, 'Epistemological pluralism and the revaluation of the concrete', in Idit Harel and Seymour Papert (eds), *Constructionism* (Norwood, NJ: Ablex, 1991), pp. 161–191; C.U. Ciborra, 'From thinking to tinkering: the grassroots of strategic information systems', in Janice I. DeGross *et al*, *Proceedings of the Twelfth International Conference on Information Systems* (University of Minnesota, Minneapolis, 1991), pp. 283–291.

8 A fuller account of what such a 'bottom-up' approach to cinema history might entail can be found in Richard Maltby, 'On the prospect of writing cinema history from below', *Tijdschrift voor Mediageschiedenis,* 9 (2) (2006), pp. 74–96.

9 Perhaps the most pressing challenge that historical inquiry presents for GIS is the need to develop creative, innovative and fluid ways to visualise and analyse historical change over time. For a discussion of time in historical GIS, see Gregory and Ell (2007), pp. 119–144, and Michael F. Goodchild, 'Combining space and time: new potential for temporal GIS', in Knowles (2008, pp. 179–197).

10 James Hay, 'Afterword: the place of the audience: beyond audience studies', in James Hay, Larry Grossberg and E. Wartella, *The Audience and Its Landscape* (Boulder, CO: Westview Press, 1996), pp. 359–378. Hay describes the 'landscape of inquiry' as a 'partial and selective way of fixing social relations and of explaining everyday life, its operation is continually *resituated* yet *territorializing*' (p. 366); Doreen Massey, *For Space* (London: Sage, 2005), p. 9.

11 See, for instance, David B. Clarke (ed.), *The Cinematic City* (London: Routledge, 1997); Karal A. Marling, 'Fantasies in the dark: the cultural geography of the American movie palace', in Paul C. Adams, Steven D. Hoelscher and Karen E. Till (eds), *Textures of Place: Exploring Humanist Geographies* (Minneapolis: University of Minnesota Press, 2001), pp. 8–23; Giuliana Bruno, *Atlas of Emotion: Journeys in Art, Architecture, and Film* (New York: Verso, 2002); Mark Shiel, and Tony Fitzmaurice (eds), *Screening the City* (London: Verso, 2003); Tom Conley, *Cartographic Cinema* (Minneapolis: University of Minnesota Press, 2007); Robert Fish (ed.), *Cinematic Countrysides* (Manchester: Manchester University Press, 2008); Chris Lukinbeal and Stefan Zimmermann (eds), *The Geography of Cinema – A Cinematic World* (Stuttgart: Franz Steiner-Verlag, 2008).

12 For a review of the intellectual influences on film geography and a consideration of its status as a field of inquiry, see Chris Lukinbeal and Stefan Zimmermann, 'Film geography: a new subfield', *Erdkunde,* 60 (4) (2006), pp. 315–326.

13 The suspicion of empirical audience research in cinema studies is discussed in Robert C. Allen, 'Relocating American film history: the "Problem" of the empirical', *Cultural Studies,* 20 (1) (2006), 48–88.

14 For a sampling of what such an approach might look like, see: Jeffrey Klenotic, 'Class markers in the mass movie audience: a case study in the cultural geography of moviegoing, 1926–1932', *The Communication Review,* 2 (4) (1996), pp. 461–495; Mark Jancovich, Lucy Faire and Sarah Stubbings,

The Place of the Audience: Cultural Geographies of Film Consumption (London: British Film Institute, 2003); Kate Bowles, '"Three miles of rough dirt road": towards an audience-centred approach to cinema studies in Australia', *Studies in Australasian Cinema,* 1 (3) (2007), pp. 245–260; Richard Abel, 'Patchwork maps of moviegoing, 1911–1913', in Richard Maltby, Melvyn Stokes and Robert C. Allen (eds), *Going to the Movies: Hollywood and the Social Experience of Cinema* (Exeter: University of Exeter Press, 2007), pp. 94–112.

15 This includes a range of geographic information from locally specific documents as well as information connecting the local to the global, such as the distribution routes for films and possibly even the cartography of geographical settings constructed in the representational spaces of films.

16 An outstanding example of this technique as it applies to raster data can be found in Robert C. Allen's digital humanities project, 'Going to the Show', which documents the history of moviegoing in North Carolina using, among other materials, a wide selection of georeferenced Sanborn fire insurance maps that have been stitched together and overlaid onto Google Earth's contemporary satellite imagery (http://docsouth.unc.edu/gtts/); see also Chapter 2.

17 Geodatabases can also be queried from the other direction, which is to say that one can use a query builder to do more complex SQL searches of information in the geodatabase, with the selected results then being displayed on the map interface. For instance, one might query the geodatabase to find 'venues with fewer than 300 seats located in places with greater than 100 000 persons' and a spatial distribution of the results would then appear on the map, with all venues bearing these particular attributes highlighted.

18 A basic introduction to GIS data collection, as well as to GIS database design and development, is found in Steinberg and Steinberg (2006), pp. 97–123. For an advanced introduction, see Gregory and Ell (2007), pp. 41–62.

19 Sources of census data and census geography include: United States Census Bureau (http://www.census.gov/); National Historical Geographic Information System (http://www.nhgis.org/); Inter-University Consortium for Political and Social Research (http://www.icpsr.umich.edu/ICPSR/); University of Virginia Historical Census Browser (http://fisher.lib.virginia.edu/collections/stats/histcensus/); and Minnesota Population Center's Integrated Public Use Microdata Series (http://usa.ipums.org/usa).

20 Documentation protocols are discussed in Gregory (2008), pp. 59–63.

21 The interactive GIS version of my research in Springfield will be available at: http://mappingmovies.com.

22 For a full history of the Franklin Theater in its social and cultural context, see Jeffrey Klenotic, '"Four hours of hootin' and hollerin'": moviegoing and everyday life outside the movie palace', in *Going to the Movies: Hollywood and the Social Experience of Cinema* (eds R. Maltby, M. Stokes and R.C. Allen), University of Exeter Press, 2007, pp. 130–154.

23 For an example of one such study, see Paul S. Moore, *Now Playing: Early Moviegoing and the Regulation of Fun* (Albany, NY: SUNY Press, 2008); see especially pp. 187–197.

References

Allen, R.C. (2006) The place of space in film historiography. *Tijdschrift voor Mediageschiedenis,* 9 (2), 15–27.

Bailey, C., White, C. and Pain, R. (1999) Evaluating qualitative research: dealing with the tension between 'science' and 'creativity. *Area*, 31 (2), 169–183.

Baker, A.R.H. (2003) *Geography and History: Bridging the Divide,* Cambridge University Press, Cambridge.

Douglass, H.P. (1919) *The Little Town Especially In Its Rural Relationships,* MacMillan, New York.

Douglass, H.P. (1924) *The St. Louis Church Survey: A Religious Investigation With A Social Background,* Doran, New York.

Douglass, H.P. (1926) *The Springfield Church Survey: A Study Of Organized Religion With Its Social Background,* Doran, New York.

Douglass, H.P. (1948) The Metropolitan Pittsburgh Church Study. Unpublished report of the Executive Committee.

Gregory, I.N. (2008) 'A map is just a bad graph': why spatial statistics are important in historical GIS, in *Placing History: How Maps, Spatial Data and GIS Are Changing Historical Scholarship* (ed. Knowles, A.K.), ESRI Press, Redlands, CA, pp. 123–149.

Gregory, I.N. and Ell, P.S. (2007) *Historical GIS: Technologies, Methodologies and Scholarship*, Cambridge University Press, Cambridge.

Kitchin, R. and Dodge, M. (2007) Rethinking maps. *Progress in Human Geography,* 31 (3), 331–344.

Knigge, L. and Cope, M. (2006) Grounded visualization: integrating the analysis of qualitative and quantitative data through grounded theory and visualization. *Environment and Planning A,* 38, 2021–2037.

Knowles, A.K. (2002) Introducing historical GIS, in *Past Time, Past Place: GIS for History* (ed. Knowles, A.K.), ESRI Press, Redlands, CA, pp. xi–xix.

Knowles, A.K. (ed.) (2008) *Placing History: How Maps, Spatial Data and GIS Are Changing Historical Scholarship,* ESRI Press, Redlands, CA.

Kwan, M-P. (2002) Feminist visualization: re-envisioning GIS as a method in feminist geographic research. *Annals of the Association of American Geographers,* 92, 645–661.

Lefebvre, H. (1991) *The Production of Space* (trans. D. Nicholson-Smith), Blackwell, Oxford.

Lury, K. and Massey, D. (1999) Making connections. *Screen,* 40 (3), 229–238.

Maltby, R. and Stokes, M. (2007) Introduction, in *Going to the Movies: Hollywood and the Social Experience of Cinema* (eds R. Maltby, M. Stokes and R.C. Allen), University of Exeter Press, pp. 1–22.

Massey, D. (2005) *For Space,* Sage, London.

Matthews, S.A., Detwiler, J.E. and Burton, L.M. (2005) Geo-ethnography: coupling geographic information analysis techniques with ethnographic methods in Urbun research. *Cartographica,* 40 (4), 75–90.

McPherson, T. (2009) Introduction: media studies and the digital humanities. *Cinema Journal,* 48 (2), 119–123.

Steinberg, S.J. and Steinberg, S.L. (2006) *GIS: Geographic Information Systems for the Social Sciences: Investigating Space and Place,* Sage, Thousand Oaks, CA.

4

What to do with Cinema Memory?

Annette Kuhn

One of the most striking findings to emerge from oral history research into cinemagoing has been the extent to which interviewees' memories of cinema have revolved far more around the social act of cinemagoing than around the films they saw. Memories of individual films have played only a small part in these recorded cinema memories. This discovery raises significant questions not only for the methodology and concerns of research in cinema history, but also for the broad field of film studies, suggesting as it does a sharp divergence between those aspects of the field concerned with the critical and theoretical analysis of the individual film and those that seek to examine cinema as a social and cultural institution. Some historians of cinemagoing have largely eliminated a consideration of individual films from their analysis, while some film scholars in the other camp have dismissed cinema memory as doing no more than providing trivial anecdotes irrelevant to the field's dominant concerns.

My aim in this chapter is to consider the nature of cinema memory, and to examine how it works both as a kind of cultural experience and as a form of discourse. In developing a typology of cinema memory, I am seeking to explore how the personal or the private on the one hand, and the collective or the public on the other, work together and intersect in people's memory of cinema, just as they have done in people's experience of cinema. In the process, I hope not only to refine our understanding of the evidence that cinema memory can provide to cinema historians, but also to suggest ways in which the discursive processes of cinema memory are open to an examination that uses the textual and psychoanalytic procedures familiar to most film scholars.

The first and most extensive source of evidence for my analysis of cinema memory comes from my research project examining 'Cinema Culture in 1930s Britain',[1] the findings from which formed the basis of my book *An Everyday Magic*

Explorations in New Cinema History: Approaches and Case Studies, First Edition.
Edited by Richard Maltby, Daniel Biltereyst and Philippe Meers.

(Kuhn, 2002a). As generalisations inductively derived from empirical data, the propositions that I have developed from this research may be circumscribed by the temporal and geographical frame, of Britain in the 1930s, to which they refer. In this chapter, I use two other works on cinema and memory to test the validity of my propositions in interpreting and conceptualising research on cinemagoing and film reception in other times and places. The first of these is a British Film Institute project called *Screen Dreams*, which involved reminiscence work and interviews conducted several years ago at five cine-clubs for elderly people, mostly in the London area, and dealt with memories of cinemagoing over a much longer period than that covered by my own project.[2] For my second source, I have drawn on the ideas of artist and critic Victor Burgin in his book *The Remembered Film*, which in its consideration of remembered fragments of films and their associations provides a valuable alternative perspective to the emphasis on the social in other projects (Burgin, 2004).

One distinctive element in my 1930s research project was its 'bottom up' approach: its starting point was the experience – and in large part the *remembered* experience – of actual cinemagoers. The memory work part of that project (especially interviews conducted in the 1990s with men and women who were cinemagoers during the 1930s) produced certain repeated themes in their recollections of cinemagoing, and certain ways of narrating those recollections: ways, in other words, of 'doing' cinema memory. An examination of these and other expressions of cinema memory can shed light on how cinema memory works, and particularly on how the private and the public interact in this form of cultural memory.

Cinema memory may simply provide material for solitary reverie or daydream. It may also provide material for stories that we share with others – stories about our lives and the times and places we have inhabited:

> It used to cost tuppence – two pennies old money and we saw a variation of films such as westerns, comedies, not too serious films. Mainly westerns … I did my Saturday morning pictures at the Broadway, at the bottom of Tanners Hill, right opposite Deptford High Street. That was well used by everyone in my area. We mainly were all school kids together … mainly because it was cheap and cheerful and the film suited us … I invariably stood in the queue outside until they let us in with Alec, Gladys, Sid, Keithy – all schoolmates and we're still firm mates. In actual fact *I still see four or five of them now – even at my age and that's nice. We often talk about the old pictures* [emphasis added] (Ted)[3]

Both the reveries and the stories may enter wider, more public, domains in the form of writing, artwork, film-making (in the case of Victor Burgin, and also – perhaps more familiarly – of film director Terence Davies, whose cinemagoing memories are also referred to below); and even, of course, scholarly research. Such reveries, stories and cultural productions may be outwardly different from one another, but they also share certain thematic, discursive, formal or aesthetic attributes. Isolating these shared features will not only enhance our understanding of the cultural instrumentality of cinema memory, but also inform further research on cinema memory, even perhaps bringing an element of predictiveness to such enquiries.

I have identified three forms or modes of cinema memory, which are particularly noticeable in early or childhood cinema memory. The modes are, firstly, remembered scenes or images from films (Type A memories); secondly, situated memories of films (Type B memories); and, finally, memories of cinemagoing (Type C memories). The empirical evidence suggests that these three forms of cinema memory are not separate or distinct from one another, but are more aptly seen as occupying positions along a continuum, with Type A memories at one end and Type C memories at the other. In many actual instances, these memory types merge or share characteristics.

Remembered Scenes/Images

> A dark night, someone is walking down a narrow stream. I see only feet splashing through water, and broken reflections of light from somewhere ahead, where something mysterious and dreadful waits. (Victor Burgin, 2004, p. 16)

> It was ... a silent film about the sea. And these waves were making this ship go, it was a sailing ship. And I was so frightened I got on the floor to hide my face in my mother's lap. (Tessa Amelan)[4]

Type A is the closest of the three modes to the 'remembered film' in Victor Burgin's sense: he calls his own vivid and detailed earliest memory of a film in the first quotation a 'sequence-image', since he is recalling 'a sequence of such brevity that I might almost be describing a still image' (Burgin, 2004, p. 15). In terms of content and tone, both of these examples have markedly distinctive qualities, and the fact that they are very *early* memories is important, suggesting that their vividness may at least in part result from the fact that the child experiencing them had not yet learned to negotiate the transition between the world on the screen and the ordinary world. Very few memories of this sort emerged in my 1930s research (and there are none in the online 'Screen Dreams' material); but in terms of the cultural significance of the finding, their intensity more than compensates for their scarcity.

Remembered scenes or images from films are distinctive in three respects, all of which are observable in the two examples quoted above. Firstly, the descriptions have a vividness and a visual quality that is almost dreamlike. Asking himself how he can be sure that the memory is from a film, Burgin can only assert 'I just know that it is. Besides, the memory is in black and white' (Burgin, 2004, p. 16). These are memories of individual, isolated shots, scenes and images, from films whose titles are more often than not forgotten or unknown. And yet these images are obviously still resonant, in all their intensity, in informants' consciousness decades after the event. It is clear that in the moment of telling in the present the remembered feelings or sensations associated with these memories are in some way being re-experienced.

It is perhaps worth noting that memories of this type may be historically specific in certain respects. For 1930s' cinemagoers at least, such memories seem to be associated particularly, but not exclusively, with recollections of having been frightened at the cinema at a very early age (Kuhn, 2002a, Chapter 4; 2007a). A number of the 1930s' cinemagoers, for example, still recollect with a shudder (and not always accurately in every detail) a particular, very brief moment in the 1933 version of *The Mummy*, which starred Boris Karloff in the title role. Recollecting the moment in the film 'when they opened the lid and it shows him like, you know, he moves his hand', Annie Wright mentions the film by name. Another informant cannot recall the title of the film, but does mention Karloff, and is in all likelihood referring to the same film: 'He [Karloff] had one where he sort of come out the coffin, you seen the hand coming up.'[5]

The allusions to *The Mummy* signal a generationally specific aspect of cinema memory, which could offer interesting material for further research. In the 1930s, 'horrific' films and their effect on children were the focus of intense public concern, and the many references in my 1930s research to being frightened in the cinema indicate that the issues that exercised adults clearly affected young cinemagoers as well (Kuhn, 2007b). Another group of films that 1930s' cinemagoers remember seeing as children all depict World War I, including *Battle of the Somme* (1916), *Seventh Heaven* (1927), *Four Sons* (1928) and *All Quiet on the Western Front* (1930). For this generation (the median year of birth of interviewees is 1922), too, silent cinema has the quality of something barely remembered, if at all: something that coincides with, or predates, their earliest recollected visits to the cinema; something that is on the cusp of their own coming to consciousness. The allusions to World War I films also attest to the fascination with the recent past, especially recent war, that appears to mark everyday historical consciousness. Other generations will, of course, remember different films or media texts in this intense manner; but we might predict that the fascination with the recent past, and with the time of one's own arrival in the world or coming to consciousness, will continue to be apparent in the texts that are recalled most vividly.[6]

A second noteworthy feature of Type A memories is that the remembered scenes or images are characteristically very brief and are always recalled in isolation from the film's plot, which is not recounted and indeed in all likelihood is not remembered. These memories are not as a rule accompanied by details of the circumstances in which the film was seen: it is as if the remembered scene or image stands out in sharp relief against a background that is absent, or vague and lacking in detail; or else it has been displaced from any attachment to the context in which it was originally experienced. Victor Burgin's remembered image is an extreme example of this tendency. He notes that he can remember nothing more about the film than the scene or image he describes: 'There is nothing before, nothing after', he says, 'no other sequence, no plot, no names of characters or actors, and no title.' As to the circumstances in which he saw the film, he implies that he would have been in the cinema with his mother: 'my mother sought distraction at the cinema ... I became her companion there' (Burgin, 2004, p. 16). But this is the adult Victor speaking, and there is no hint of his mother's presence within the telling of the memory itself. On the other hand, Tessa Amelan's remembered image, a frightening one, is associated with a memory of seeking comfort by burying her face in her mother's lap.

Mrs Amelan's story calls attention to a third distinctive aspect of Type A memories: accounts of these remembered scenes or images characteristically re-evoke strong emotions or bodily sensations on the narrator's part. Recollections of hiding or covering one's face, or of cowering under the seat, point to an embodied, and possibly preverbal, response that has become linked in memory to the image or the scene itself. It is as if the remembered image or scene and the body of the person remembering it are fused together in the moment of recollection, and in the feelings that the memory evokes. There is a sense in which the remembered scene or image *enfolds* the subject – who nevertheless figures at the same time as an observer of the film scene and the scene of memory, in much the way that Freud describes the subject of fantasy creating and also placing himself within a *mise-en-scène* – at once directing the fantasy scenario and helplessly caught up in it.[7]

All this lends support to Victor Burgin's observation that the remembered film, as one instance of our everyday encounters with the environment of media, is analogous to such 'interior' processes as inner speech and involuntary association, and that it bears the hallmarks of the primary processes of the 'raw' dream, daydream or fantasy (Burgin, 2004, p. 14). This, along with the investment in the visual, and the fragmentary and non-narrative quality observable in Type A memories, aligns them with the non-verbal or the preverbal, and with the Preconscious and the Unconscious. Referring specifically to his own remembered sequence-image, Burgin notes that this memory, which he associates with a 'particular affect' – a sense of apprehension – becomes somehow diminished when put into words, as if the process of articulation takes the *shine* off the unspoken, unarticulated memory image. As in the telling of a dream, he suggests, forcing the synchrony of the memory 'into the diachrony of narrative' leads him 'to misrepresent, to transform, to diminish it' (Burgin, 2004, p. 15). Elsewhere, Burgin mentions the 'brilliance' that surrounds this kind of memory; a word that captures the feeling of effulgence and vividness apparent also in many of the 1930s' cinemagoers' remembered scenes. It is perhaps the bodily, primary process, preverbal, 'inner speech' quality that still attaches to these now verbalised memories that imbues them also with the directness and simplicity of the child's voice: a quality that is certainly apparent in 1930s' cinemagoers' accounts of their remembered scenes and images.

The Type A cinema memories described by Victor Burgin and by some of the informants in my 1930s research operate on the side of the inner world and the phenomenological. Burgin's rich and resonant descriptions of the experience of the remembered film and of remembering films make especially apparent the connection of these memories to psychical or mental processes, with their marks of interior speech, and of productions of the Unconscious or the Preconscious. Intriguingly, these are among the very attributes of cinema spectatorship explored by Christian Metz and others in work on the psychodynamics and metapsychology of cinema (Metz, 1982). Moreover, looked at discursively – in terms of their rhetoric or address – these Type A memories display many of the formal qualities that distinguish a cultural genre or mode named, in a rather different context, the 'memory text'.[8] These include in particular a non-continuous or non-sequential quality to the narration or telling; a non-specificity as to time; a fragmentary quality; a sense of synchrony, as if remembered events are somehow pulled out of a linear time frame or refuse to be anchored in 'real' historical time. Memory texts, in short, share the generally imagistic quality of unconscious productions like dreams and fantasies (Kuhn, 2002b, pp. 160, 162). Significantly, as we have seen, Burgin notes that his own earliest memory of a film is sufficient ('sharply particular', 'brilliant', he says) within itself, and yet at the same time it is vague as to everything outside itself.

The commonalities of observation and interpretation that emerge here indicate that if Type A memories operate on the side of the phenomenological or the metapsychological and bear the marks of inner world processes, they are by no means to be dismissed as purely subjective, personal or idiosyncratic. There is clearly at some level something shared, and even profoundly cultural, about such 'inner world' productions. At the same time, however, the fragmentary, non-narrative quality of such memories, and Burgin's suggestion that there is 'something private' about them that demands they remain untold may also begin to explain the relative scarcity of recollections of this type in the records of cinema memory (Burgin, 2004, p. 16).

Situated Memories of Films

The cultural is rather more obviously apparent in Type B memories, in which films and scenes or images from films are remembered within a context of events in the subject's own life. This is perhaps equivalent to a type of remembered film that Burgin describes as entirely different in timbre from his enigmatic and mysterious 'sequence-image', in that the former are associated with consciously recollected events in his childhood, recalled 'either in direct relation to a film, or to something that happened shortly after seeing one' (Burgin, 2004, p. 17). Burgin cites no personal examples of such memories, but in my 1930s research, expressions of this type of cinema memory are rather more prominent than examples of Type A. The detail and the nature of the remembered film and the associated life events vary considerably across different instances, as do the weight given to each and the relationship between the two.

> Oh, I remember the first film we went to see [Boris Karloff] in, at the Globe, in, where was it? Old Trafford, I think it was. And it was *The Mummy*. Well there were benches then, you know, not seats. I don't know whether I'd left school. Probably I'd left school. Anyway, I went to see him. I was sat there, dead quiet. And when they opened the lid and it shows him like, you know, and he moves his hand. Well I let out one! I slid along the seat. (Annie Wright)[9]

> I must've been five, and seeing, we came in the middle. Films in those days were continuous. You see. And I remember going in, and it had already, it must've been halfway through. And I remember seeing Janet Gaynor and Charles Farrell, in *Seventh Heaven*. I knew it was called *Seventh Heaven*. I remember them going up this spiral staircase. More than that I don't remember. (Beatrice Cooper)[9]

Annie Wright's story about when she saw *The Mummy* incorporates a vividly remembered image from the film – but this is set within a story of the cinema visit that also contains a considerable amount of scene-setting detail (the name and location of the cinema, a description of its seating arrangements), as well as her own bodily response to the mummy's stirring into life. Beatrice Cooper's brief but vivid recollection of an image in Borzage's *Seventh Heaven* (1927), which she mentions in both her interviews, lacks the kinds of contextual detail observable in Annie Wright's account, while setting the scene in another, rather intriguing, way. Mrs Cooper's allusion to the practice of continuous programming serves to enhance the 'brilliant' quality of her remembered image by making it, in her memory-story, the very first thing that she saw on entering the picture house as a 5-year-old.

Another example of this mode of cinema memory, complete with the scene-setting details, sets out a kind of originary moment of an obsession with cinema that was ultimately to inspire the speaker's own artistic production:

> When I was seven I was taken by my eldest sister to see *Singin' in the Rain*. Sitting in the dark brown, baroque interior of the Odeon, Liverpool, watching Gene Kelly dance with an umbrella, I entered for the first time a world of magic: the cinema. (Terence Davies)[10]

In discursive terms, Type B memories are distinguished by what may be termed an 'anecdotal' rhetoric, a form of address that typically involves a story narrated in the first person singular about a specific, one-off event or occasion, a story in which the informant constructs herself or himself as chief protagonist. The narrator, in other words, figures in the account both as the central character in the personal life events narrated and also as observer of (though not usually as participant in) the scenes or images on the cinema screen (Kuhn, 2002a, p. 10). In my 1930s research, anecdotal address is relatively rare across the entire body of informants' memories; but it is a marked, and perhaps even invariable, feature of Type B cinema memories.

In some narrations of these memories, informants deploy a 'weak' variant of the anecdotal to position themselves as central protagonists of life events or remembered film scenes or images that are in all likelihood (with apologies to *Blade Runner*) *implants*. Implanted memories might originate, for example – with or without acknowledgement on the informant's part – from family stories. Norman MacDonald recounts a story told him by his mother about his unruly behaviour as an infant taken to a screening of *The Kid* (1921). A similar story is told by another of my informants, Leonard Finegold, who writes that in 1938, at the age of three, he was taken to see *Snow White and the Seven Dwarfs* (1937). He recalls 'the (green?) witch/stepmother/queen looking out of a frame. I ran out of the cinema. *My mother said* she didn't catch me for several hundred yards' [emphasis added] (Kuhn, 2002a, p. 39).[11]

Sometimes informants' 'memories' of seeing film scenes or images have almost certainly entered their stories after the event, as a particular image has acquired cultural iconicity in later years. A number of interviewees, for instance, 'remember' iconic moments in the 1933 *King Kong*, and above all they remember the scene in which King Kong sits atop the Empire State Building (Kuhn, 2002a, pp. 77–78). In another very common manifestation of this phenomenon, 'Screen Dreams' informant Ted recollects the serials at children's cinema matinees:

> And sometimes there would be drama and I can always remember the lady being tied down on the track and the hero coming to rescue her, and the music playing. Pearl White I believe.[12]

These memories tend to give themselves away as 'implants' in that in the telling they lack the 'brilliance' of scenes from the truly remembered film.

Describing what he calls a secreted 'memory' of his mother, 'pale and anxious' and pregnant with him, in a bomb shelter during World War II, Victor Burgin also alludes to this 'implant' phenomenon. 'This "memory" of course', he observes, 'is a fantasy with a décor almost certainly derived from a film'.[13] He suggests that 'the tendency for personal history to be mixed with recollections from films and other media productions' is 'almost universal' (Burgin, 2004, p. 68). Investigating the same phenomenon, in which recollections of life events become unconsciously coloured or shaped by scenes in films, oral historian Marie-Claude Taranger has called them 'second-hand' memories. When Taranger conducted life story research with a group of women living in southern France, a number of her informants talked about how, in the absence of nylon stockings during World War II, they improvised by painting seams up the backs of their legs. As Taranger notes, the details of their descriptions of this activity, however, exactly mirror a scene from François Truffaut's 1980 film set in World War II, *Le Dernier Métro* (Taranger, 1991).

Situated memories tend to lack the 'illumination', the shine and intensity, that mark the remembered scenes or images of Type A. These 'anecdotal' memories bear the traces of having been subjected to various forms of secondary revision; and may well also have been embellished over the years through numerous retellings and the retrospective addition of details. Unlike the intense, and apparently idiosyncratic, quality of remembered scenes or images from films, cinema memories of Type B outwardly manifest an active, or at least a potential, *social* currency as stories that have been exchanged, negotiated, re-enlivened, and even embroidered in retellings over the years.

In Type B memories the balance of emphasis in narration between memories of films on the one hand and memories of life events on the other may vary across different instances. Where the balance of emphasis rests mainly on life events, however, these situated memories begin to shade into the third mode.

Memories of Cinemagoing

> Normally when we went to the 'Ionic' [in Golders Green], one of us would pay and then ... go to the toilet and open the emergency exit doors and let our friends in for free. (J.B. Ryall, b. 1922, Bournemouth)[14]

> Used to be shelling the nuts on the floor, and then they'd take an orange, peel would be on the floor. All these were going backwards and forwards. And when you sat next to some children you could smell camphorated oil. You know, they'd have their chests rubbed with camphorated oil. (Ellen Casey)[14]

Memories of this type do not involve 'remembered *films*' at all. They are actually memories of the activity of going to the cinema. Even in recollections of the very earliest cinema visits – as, for example, in Ted's 'Screen Dreams' memory quoted at the beginning of this chapter – the name and the location of the picture house are typically carefully noted, and there is very often also some detail about the journey to it and the routes taken. Informants also frequently recollect their cinemagoing companions, as well as what it was like inside the cinema: the decor, the seating, the behaviour of the staff and the audience, and so on.

In my 1930s research, these Type C memories are more prevalent by far than those in the other two categories; and they are normally recounted entirely separately from memories of actual films. In fact, one of the key conclusions to emerge from my project is that, certainly in the memories of the vast majority of these cinemagoers of the 1930s' generation, the essentially *social* act of 'going to the pictures' is of far greater consequence than the cultural activity of seeing films. This is true also of the 'Screen Dreams' accounts. Significantly, however, this 'social' mode of cinema memory plays little or no part in *The Remembered Film*, since, as its title suggests, Victor Burgin's book is about film rather than cinema, and his central concern lies with the experience of seeing and remembering *films*. In an important argument that helps to illuminate the relative scarcity of Type A and Type B memories, Burgin suggests that the fragmented sequences that constitute their content are 'transient and provisional images, no doubt unconsciously selected for their association with thoughts already in motion ... but no more or less suitable for this purpose than other memories I might have recovered, and destined to be forgotten once used' (Burgin, 2004, p. 16).

Informants' memories of cinemagoing are often discursively marked by the deployment of a 'repetitive' type of narrative rhetoric. In 'repetitive memory discourse' – the stance in fact most frequently adopted by these 1930s' cinemagoers – the narrator implicates himself or herself in the events recollected, but (by contrast with the anecdotal) those events are represented as habitual rather than as singular or one-off. Often the narrator will adopt the first person plural, which brings with it a certain personal distance from the events being narrated, while at the same time imparting a strong sense of collective involvement. 'We used to' is the characteristic introductory turn of phrase here; and it is implicit in both of the stories quoted above. Although Mr Ryall sets the scene in a particular picture house, his story is about what he and his friends habitually did in order to get into the cinema without paying. Mrs Casey's story about the behaviour of children at matinees suggests that she was part of the scene as an observer of all the naughtiness; but in referring to her fellow picturegoers as 'they', she distances herself somewhat from the rowdy behaviour. Mr Ryall's setting the scene for his story by mentioning the name and the location of his picture house is an instance of another frequently observable attribute of memories of cinemagoing, their investment in place: indeed, it is a very striking feature of cinema memory that place operates as both a prompt and a *mise en scène* of memory (Kuhn, 2002a, Chapter 2; 2004).

The overwhelmingly repetitive and collective rhetoric of memory stories of Type C is typically allied with a set of repeated themes and contents, and also with stereotypical turns of phrase in the narration. For example, variations on the theme of 'making do' or evading adult authority, all deploying the same narrative tropes and even turns of phrase – stories of collecting jam jars to pay for admission, children's matinees, stories about getting adults to 'take them in' to 'A' films – come up again and again in my informants' cinemagoing memories (Kuhn, 2002a, Chapter 3). There are examples, too, in the 'Screen Dreams' interviews:

> So you had to go out on Saturday mornings with a bucket and shovel, shovelling up horse manure because we had all the horse traffic around and selling it for a penny a bucket ... All young boys would be doing it because we'd all go to the cinema ... This was the Park Cinema up at Hither Green. (Ronald)[15]

This significant observation draws us onto a little-explored byway in the terrain of oral history studies, where it has been observed that raw oral history interview material, especially from working-class or peasant informants, often features conventional forms of speech and modes of narration in a manner that melds the personal with the collective, or frames the personal within a collective experience. As the Italian historian Sandro Portelli notes,

> The degree of presence of 'formalised materials' like proverbs, songs, formulaic language, stereotypes, can be a measure of the degree of presence of a 'collective viewpoint'. (Portelli, 1981, 99)

The repeated themes and formulaic modes of telling that mark so many of these memories of cinemagoing (and especially memories of early and childhood cinemagoing), allied with the continuing active currency of these much-told stories, may well signal something that is quite distinctive and culturally significant about this form of cultural memory – and not only in relation to one generation or one country. The collective forms and currencies of Type C memories, along with their characteristically formulaic themes and contents, suggest a sliding together of the personal and the collective. It also aligns them on the side of the social (and the cultural), and of the social audience (as against the spectator, as

Table 4.1 Attributes and interrelationships of the three modes of cinema memory.

A	*B*	*C*
Remembered scenes/images	Situated memories of films	Memories of cinemagoing
Sequence-image		*Social cinema scenes*
Phenomenological	Secondary revision	Social audience
Metapsychological	Social currency	Everyday life
Primary process		Place
Inner world/speech		
Pre-Conscious, Unconscious		

Table 4.2 Discursive features of the three modes of cinema memory.

A	*B*	*C*
Remembered scenes/images	Situated memories of films	Memories of cinemagoing
Sequence-image		*Social cinema scenes*
Fragmented narration	Anecdotal	Collective
Memory-text		Repetitive
		Formulaic

constructed in some branches of film theory), and locates them on the terrain of film (and media) as they figure in everyday life. In her study of the cinemagoing habits of postwar immigrants to Britain from South Asia, the sociologist Nirmal Puwar coins the term 'social cinema scenes' to describe the sociality (and the place-related nature) of this noteworthy aspect of cultural memory and cinema memory, and looks at the instrumentality of social cinema scenes in forging collective identities (Puwar, 2007).

The attributes, interrelationships and discursive features of the three modes of cinema memory may be represented as shown in Table 4.1, and their respective discursive features are summarised in Table 4.2.

What can be concluded from this about cinema memory, about the remembered film, and indeed about the remembered visit to the cinema? What are the uses of this knowledge? What else might it be useful or important to know, and how can we go about finding out? Drawing on empirical data, this exploration brings to light a great deal about the discursive, thematic and experiential features of cinema memory, and with it a great deal about what marks out cinema memory as a distinctive subtype of cultural memory.

For example, while cinema memory has qualities that might appear universal, even archetypal, these are expressed through memory-stories and other elements that are historically and generationally situated or specific. At the same time, features of cinema memory that might at first sight seem merely personal or idiosyncratic will usually, on closer inspection, reveal certain shared or collective attributes.

Therefore a deeper understanding of how cinema memory works discursively, rhetorically and experientially can bring to light, concretely, some of the psychical and cultural processes through which the act of remembering film and remembering cinema can bind us into shared subjectivities. This exploration thus demonstrates how in the production and operation of cinema memory private and public, personal and collective, worlds shade into one another, interweave and work together in a range of different ways. Finally, and coming full circle, all this in turn can offer broader insights into the workings of cultural memory in general, especially with regard to the production and sustaining of identities and communities. Because a similar inductive exercise may be productively conducted with any corpus of cinema memory data, it is possible to test the propositions that I have made, and also to adjust them for sensitivity to historical, cultural and geographical variation in the expression of cinema memory. In this way, the research I have described in this chapter can allow us to bring a global perspective to the very local, everyday activity of cinemagoing, and memories of cinemagoing.

Notes

1 'Cinema Culture in 1930s Britain', Economic and Social Research Council (ESRC) Project R000235385 (hereafter CCINTB).

2 'Screen Dreams: Cinema-going in South East London 1920–60', held at the Age Exchange Reminiscence Centre, September–December 2003. The interview transcripts are not at present publicly available, but some quotations from interviews included in an exhibition held in London in 2003 are available online, at http://www.bfi.org.uk/education/teaching/screendreams/ (accessed 16 January 2009). It is perhaps worth noting that these quotations were selected from a large corpus of material for a non-scholarly purpose.

3 'Screen Dreams'.

4 CCINTB T95-158, Tessa Amelan, Manchester (quoted in Kuhn, 2002a, p. 72).

5 CCINTB T95-32, Annie Wright, Manchester, quoted in Kuhn, 2002a, p. 66; CCINTB T95-15, Helen Donaghy, Glasgow, quoted in Kuhn, 2002a, p. 71.

6 For further discussion of this phenomenon, see Kuhn, 2002b, Chapter 7.

7 On enfolding see Laura U. Marks, *The Skin of the Film: Intercultural Cinema, Embodiment, and the Senses* (Durham, NC: Duke University Press, 1999); Sigmund Freud, '"A child is being beaten." A contribution to the origin of sexual perversions', in *The Standard Edition of the Complete Psychological Works of Sigmund Freud XVII*, trans. and ed. J. Strachey (London: Vintage, 2001), pp. 177–204.

8 For a fuller discussion of 'memory texts', see Kuhn, 2002b, Chapter 8.

9 CCINTB T95-32, Annie Wright, Manchester, quoted in Kuhn, 2002a, p. 66; CCINTB T95-96, Beatrice Cooper, Harrow, 20 July 1995.

10 In an exhibition on Terence Davies at BFI Southbank, March 2007.

11 CCINTB 07–08, questionnaire Leonard Finegold.

12 Ted, 'Screen Dreams'.

13 Burgin borrows from Jean Laplanche the idea that memory and fantasy comprise a '"time of the human subject" that the individual "secretes" independently of historical time. Temporal "secretions" very often combine memories and fantasies with material from films and other media sources.' Burgin (2004, p. 15).

14 CCINTB, 95-48-1 letter, J.B. Ryall, Bournemouth; CCINTB T95-37, Ellen Casey, Manchester, quoted in Kuhn, 2002a, p. 59.

15 Ronald, 'Screen Dreams'.

References

Burgin, V. (2004) *The Remembered Film*, Reaktion Books, London.

Kuhn, A. (2002a) *An Everyday Magic: Cinema and Cultural Memory*, I.B. Tauris, London; published in the USA as *Dreaming of Fred and Ginger*, New York University Press, New York, 2002.

Kuhn, A. (2002b) *Family Secrets: Acts of Memory and Imagination*, Verso, London.

Kuhn, A. (2004) Heterotopia, heterochronia: place and time in cinema memory. *Screen*, 45 (2), 106–114.

Kuhn, A. (2007a) *Snow White* in the 1930s. Raphael Samuel Memorial Lecture, Bishopsgate Institute, London, Nov. 2007.

Kuhn, A. (2007b) Children, 'horrific' films and censorship in 1930s Britain, in *Going to the Movies: Hollywood and the Social Experience of Cinema* (eds R. Maltby, M. Stokes and R.C. Allen), Exeter University Press, Exeter, pp. 323–332.

Metz, C. (1982) *The Imaginary Signifier: Psychoanalysis and the Cinema* (trans. C. Britton, A. Williams, B. Brewster and A. Guzzetti), Indiana University Press, Bloomington.

Portelli, A. (1981) The peculiarities of oral history. *History Workshop Journal*, 12, 96–107.

Puwar, N. (2007) Social cinema scenes. *Space and Culture*, 10 (2), 253–70.

Taranger, M-C. (1991) Une mémoire de seconde main? Film, emprunt et référence dans le récit de vie. *Hors-Cadre*, no. 9, pp. 41–60.

Part 2

Distribution, Programming and Audiences

5

Social Class, Experiences of Distinction and Cinema in Postwar Ghent

Daniel Biltereyst, Philippe Meers and Lies Van de Vijver

A wide range of methods, theoretical underpinnings, and temporal and spatial limitations have contributed to the construction of new cinema history (Maltby, 2006, pp. 74–96). Writing what Richard Maltby has called the 'social history of a cultural institution' has involved quantitative approaches to box-office revenues, the use of longitudinal databases in relation to exhibition patterns and programming, reception studies and other types of ethnographic research into film audiences.[1] This history deals with both economic questions about film trade and distribution patterns, and also micro histories of cinemagoing on a local level.[2] As well as examining corporate business strategies, it attempts to deal with bottom-up experiences, using oral history and methodologies drawn from the intellectual history of cultural and memory studies (Kuhn, 2002).

How do all these different levels of empirical evidence converge and integrate? How can cinema's industrial and institutional history be bound together with a socio-cultural history of its audiences? How can we integrate 'detailed historical maps of cinema exhibition, telling us what cinemas were where and when' with 'the inclusion of experience that will ground quantitative generalisations in the concrete particulars of microhistorical studies of local situations' (Maltby, 2006, p. 91)? Without pretending to fulfil this ambitious research agenda, this chapter aims to indicate how structure and experience can be bound together, and to illustrate the usefulness of combining different data, methods and theories. We will argue that a triangulation of data, theory and method not only validates earlier insights, but also enriches our knowledge of significant questions in cinema history.[3]

The question of class distinction and differentiation has been central to recent research debates over historical cinema audiences and film exhibition in the

Explorations in New Cinema History: Approaches and Case Studies, First Edition.
Edited by Richard Maltby, Daniel Biltereyst and Philippe Meers.

United States and the United Kingdom.[4] These debates have examined the position and experiences of working-class audiences, the question of audience formation and class-mixing in film venues in urban and rural environments, and the issue of Hollywood's efforts to add a middle-class taste to the film experience by creating a 'cross-class fantasy' (Ross, 1998). This chapter aims to contribute to the discussion by turning to a continental European case where issues of social class, emancipation and cinema have had a quite different shape and tradition than in the United States or the United Kingdom. We concentrate on the Belgian industrial city of Ghent, and look at working-class audiences' experiences of cinema. Relying on data and insights from a major research project on the history of film exhibition and cinema-going in Flanders, the northern, Dutch-language part of Belgium, and using both top-down and bottom-up approaches, we examine where, how and when Ghent audiences consumed movies after World War II and during the 1950s.[5] Firmly situated within the new cinema history perspective, our 'Enlightened City' project integrates several research strands, including a longitudinal database of film exhibition structures, a large-scale database on film programming in various cities and towns, and an oral history project on cinema experiences.[6] Our analysis in this chapter on class distinction and differentiation within one historical setting is loosely inspired by Pierre Bourdieu's field theory on cultural distinction and the reproduction of inequality (Bourdieu, 1984). Although Bourdieu has been forcefully criticised, his work is still useful in understanding cinema's strategies for attracting audiences from different class fractions and people's social experiences of going to the movies (Jenkins, 2002, p. xiv).

Social Class, Pillars, Cinema

During the nineteenth century, Belgium became one of the most industrialised, urbanised and densely populated countries on the European continent.[7] Although Catholic organisations and the Church traditionally played a key role in Belgian society, especially in rural areas and smaller towns, industrialisation helped to create a powerful left-wing workers' organisation. In major cities such as Antwerp, Brussels, Ghent and Liège, local workers' organisations were active in spheres ranging from trade unions and political parties to banking, health care, education, leisure and culture. The centre of this type of interventionist socialist action was Ghent, which was considered to be 'one of the homes of the industrial revolution on the continent' (Strikwerda, 1999, p. 71). The city had a long tradition of linen and cotton factories, and by 1870 it had become the most proletarianised city in Belgium, with a long-established, native working-class (Robert *et al.*, 2004, p. 93). Living in what is now called the 'historical belt' around the city centre, workers traditionally had a low standard of living, characterised by high mortality, poor housing and low wages. In the nineteenth century, a large network of socialist-inspired organisations (trade unions, political parties and a labour bank), cooperatives (such as a bakery and newspaper) and particular spaces (cafés, *volkshuizen* or people's houses, theatres and other meeting places) emerged to compete with or parallel their capitalist counterparts.

Although most of their actions were strongly rooted in a programme and discourse of counter-hegemonic emancipation, socialists had to live with the reigning liberal laissez-faire principles of free-market competition, profit motive and individual consumer choice. This was clearly the case with cinema, which was extremely popular among workers and which soon entered socialist *volkshuizen*. Beginning with occasional screenings in 1904, Ghent socialists were regularly integrating cinema into their leisure activities by 1908. In 1913, when the socialist movement was at its height, they opened the Vooruit (Forward), a luxurious, multifunctional community 'palace' featuring a large cinema for daily screenings, in the bourgeois centre of Ghent. Although the socialist cinema occasionally included left-wing or socially critical pictures in its programme (Chaplin was an excellent compromise), the Vooruit mainly screened commercial fare from major distributors such as Pathé (Stallaerts, 2007). This 'bourgeois' programming strategy lasted until the closure of the Vooruit in 1980, and occasionally provoked virulent ideological criticism from orthodox socialist leaders.

The appeal of the Belgian socialist movement, which was in theory violently anti-Christian and anti-establishment, prompted Catholics to engage more actively with the problem of labour, the industrial proletariat and the role of faith. On a local level a social democratic Catholic reform movement emerged, creating a competitive network of organisations. The growth of Catholic workers' organisations was strongly stimulated in 1891, when Pope Leo XIII promulgated the Vatican's new ideology of social reform in his landmark encyclical letter *Rerum Novarum*. While socialists were strong in large cities, the Belgian social democratic Catholic movement flourished among lower and lower-middle social strata in rural and smaller towns, and the Catholic union movement also operated successfully in Flemish cities with a substantial Catholic population, including Ghent (Strikwerda, 1997, pp. 219–220).

This open conflict between Catholic and socialist organisations strongly influenced Belgian society from the end of the nineteenth century until the 1970s.[8] The competition between blocks or 'pillars' of ideologically more-or-less coherent organisations created a pattern of social segmentation in which different groups had their own networks of schools, hospitals, trade unions and political parties (Billiet, 1988). This process of 'pillarisation' overlapped with more traditional class conflicts, and both Catholics and socialists developed strategies to attract the masses through leisure, recreational activities, newspapers and other media or entertainment facilities as well as in hard political and socioeconomic terms. Pillarisation was not an exclusively Belgian phenomenon, but the ideological and religious segregation created by pillarisation had a more profound impact across a range of social fields in Belgium than was the case in The Netherlands, where the dominant ideological groups did not, for example, actively enter the field of film exhibition (Lijphart, 1977).

It is hard to estimate how successful Belgian socialists and Catholics were in 'guiding' film audiences, particularly among the lower social classes, in their cinema-going practices (Dibbets, 2006). In the period before the Great War, most Catholic film screenings were held outside commercial exhibition circuits, often in parish halls or theatres linked to Catholic schools or other public institutions (Convents, 1992, pp. 33–34). In the interwar and postwar years, a powerful Catholic film movement emerged. As well as maintaining a film classification board, Catholic Film Action (CFA) published film magazines, had a wide membership of several thousand film fans, and operated small-scale film venues. The CFA also controlled a commercially operating film distribution business and maintained a network of dozens of regular cinemas loosely associated with its distributor (Biltereyst, 2007).

Spaces of Distinction

With the exception of a few case studies on the film market in particular towns or periods, the history of Belgian film exhibition is heavily under-researched, and key questions remain as yet unanswered.[9] How, for instance, can the vividness of the Belgian film scene be explained, and why was the country so highly ranked in international statistics on cinema attendance until the 1960s?[10] What was the impact of pillarisation on the film exhibition and cinemagoing experiences of ordinary film fans? How 'loyal' were people in a particular pillar, class or community in their cinemagoing choices and experiences? How much class mixing took place in pillarised film exhibition or in regular commercial picture houses? Although the phenomena of pillarisation, class and ideological segregation have stimulated wide research efforts, none of these questions focusing on cinemagoing as a significant act of cultural distinction have been studied thoroughly.

To begin to address these issues, the 'Enlightened City' research project built a longitudinal database of Flemish cinemas and other regular film-screening venues, covering the period from World War I onwards. Compiled from a wide variety of sources (official statistics, industry yearbooks, film programmes in newspapers and trade journals, and information in public and private archives), this database contains some 47 500 entries detailing who organised screenings in which venues, where and when, as well as recording any financial, architectural or ideological information that we found on individual venues.

In general, the 'Enlightened City' database confirmed the high number and wide variety of regular film venues operating in Flanders and Brussels until the 1960s (Biltereyst *et al.*, 2007). The database indicated that local film exhibition markets were highly competitive, not only in major cities but also in smaller, even rural towns where commercial exhibitors often had to confront pillarised film screenings, mostly dominated by Catholics. From the 1920s until the 1960s, Catholic, socialist and to a smaller extent Liberal and Flemish-nationalist exhibitors made up between 19% and 35% of all film venues.[11] After World War II, the general growth in the number of Flemish cinemas (from 560 film venues in 1946 to 984 in

Table 5.1 Film exhibition in Ghent, 1952.

	Number of seats	*Location*	*Map location*	*Ideological profile*
Capitole	1663	City centre	Centre 1	
Vooruit	1500	City centre	Centre 1	Socialist
Majestic	920	City centre	Centre 2	
Royal	800	District	Patershol	
Century	791	City centre	Centre 1	
Plaza	750	City centre	Centre 2	Liberal
Pax	700	Suburbs	Gentbrugge	Catholic
Metropole	690	Suburbs	Sint-Amandsberg	
Eldorado	651	City centre	Centre 2	
Rex	645	City centre	Centre 4	
Agora	600	Suburbs	Ledeberg	
Cameo	595	District	Rabot	
Casino	582	City centre	Centre 2	Catholic
Savoy	581	City centre	Centre 2	
City	580	District	Brugsepoort	
Novy	560	District	Brugsepoort	
Ganda	550	District	Brugsepoort	
Nova	550	Suburbs	Sint-Amandsberg	Catholic
Leopold	547	City centre	Centre 3	
Select	547	City centre	Centre 1	
Forum	540	District	Rabot	
Lido	540	Suburbs	Ledeberg	
Ideal	491	District	Brugsepoort	
Rio	460	District	Brugsepoort	
Vox	450	District	Strop	
Nord	436	District	Muide	
Roxy	430	Suburbs	Ledeberg	
Odeon	425	Suburbs	Sint-Amandsberg	
Ritz	374	Suburbs	Gentbrugge	
Vriendenkring	350	Suburbs	Gentbrugge	Catholic
Scaldis	332	District	Muide	
Muide	186	District	Muide	Catholic

1957) was accompanied by a slow increase in the number of cinemas in rural areas (in 1958 nearly 52% of all film venues were located here). Film exhibition was far less influenced by pillarisation in the major cities. In Ghent, where the number of regular film venues grew from 24 just before the German invasion in 1940 to 32 in 1952, the film exhibition market was strongly organised along socio-geographical lines, and as Table 5.1 indicates, pillarisation appeared at first sight to have played a limited role in film exhibition (De Martelaer, 1982, p. 17). Although several regular film venues such as the Cameo (with 595 seats) were associated with the socialist

Figure 5.1 Map showing locations of film exhibition in Ghent, 1952.

movement, only the Vooruit, with the city's second-largest seating capacity (1500 seats) had survived as an openly socialist cinema. Only one commercial cinema, the Plaza (750 seats), was more or less linked to the Liberal party, while five venues were associated with Catholics, and most of these were relatively small (the Casino, 582 seats), located in the suburbs (the Nova, 550, and Pax, 700) and sometimes were parish halls used for screening movies (the Muide, 186).

The Ghent film market was divided between the city centre cinemas, film venues located in the historical belt of mainly working-class city districts, and those in neighbouring towns or suburbs (Figure 5.1; Table 5.1). The city centre had four film exhibition centres with 11 cinemas. Most of the centre's first-run cinemas were operated by major film exhibition companies, particularly Sofexim and Cinex.[12] The biggest film theatres were spread around the former south station in downtown, an area of mixed social class, mainly known for shopping and night life facilities (Centre 1). Besides the Vooruit, three commercial cinemas operated here: the Select (547 seats), Century (791) and Capitole (1663). Opened in 1932, the Capitole was the most prestigious cinema in Ghent, with a superb art déco interior, and its public image appealed to higher-social class audiences. Like most other film palaces, it charged higher entrance fees than the Vooruit or cinemas in the districts and suburbs. It also conducted a policy of price differentiation, maintaining six categories of ticket price, with the most expensive costing three times as much as the cheapest.[13] The Select, which was only one block away, often served as a second-run theatre for movies coming from the Capitole. A second city-centre area for film exhibition was near the main shopping street, Veldstraat, where there were five cinemas: the Majestic (920 seats), the Eldorado (651), the 'liberal' Plaza, and the Catholic Casino and the Savoy (581) (Centre 2). Given its programming strategy (more 'sophisticated' European movies), location and building (a former church), the Savoy catered to higher-class, mainly French-speaking audiences.[14] A third location was the Sint-Pietersplein (a large square, Centre 3), which was associated with students, military barracks and soldiers. Here the Leopold (547 seats) operated as a risqué cinema, specialising in French, controversial, and sometimes soft-core erotic movies. A final city centre cinema was the Rex (645 seats), a splendid art déco film theatre near the central station in a newer part of the city. Although it was in a higher social-class and mainly residential part of Ghent, the Rex tried to attract audiences from different social classes, including passengers and travellers who were attracted by shorter film programmes (e.g. films noir, American B-movies) (Centre 4).

Twelve cinemas were located in the poorer districts of the historical belt around the city centre. Although most of these were smaller second- and even third-run film venues, operated by families or cooperatives, one neighbourhood cinema was the fourth largest theatre in town. The Royal (800 seats) was located in the Patershol district, an old town borough that had become a working-class area in the late nineteenth century, and was characterised by very small, poor housing. In Rabot, another working-class district known for its textile factories, two cinemas operated (the Cameo and Forum, 540 seats), while in the Muide, an older workers' borough in the northern part of the town near the harbour, two smaller film theatres (the Scaldis, 332, and Nord, 436) competed with a regular film programme at the tiny parish hall, the Muide. The oldest historical workers' district, the Brugsepoort in the western part of the city, had five cinemas, including the City (580 seats) and Novy (560).

A third group of film venues was located in the suburbs and the less proletarianised neighbouring towns. In Gentbrugge, there were four neighbourhood cinemas, including the Catholic Pax. Although most of these venues were rather small, some bigger cinemas operated here (Pax, Metropole, 690), along with a number of Catholic venues, including some parish halls regularly screening movies (e.g. the Vriendenkring, 350) (see Figure 5.1).

Despite the city's relatively small population, some 23 cinemas competed in Ghent at the beginning of the 1950s, while nine other regular film venues operated in the rapidly urbanising outskirts of the city.[15] Only two cinemas seated over 1500 people, and most venues had a capacity of between 500 and 750 seats. As in other cities, the most prosperous cinemas were close to 'bright light' centres, shopping and other social activities and mass transport lines. Most film venues, however, were located in poorer people's areas, although these were not insular, homogeneous working-class or socialist-oriented environments. The Capitole promoted itself as a luxurious cinema for the higher social classes and conducted a strategy of spatial segregation through its differentiated price policy, while the Vooruit did almost exactly the opposite by targeting lower social groups. Most major film venues, however, courted patrons from different social classes from around the city, as well as from towns on the outskirts. How did programming strategies target different types of audiences? How did people perceive social distinction in terms of space and programming? Did audiences display their ideological loyalties in their everyday cinema-going practices? How did cinemas target or appeal to different types of audiences?

Distinction on the Screen

The second major research strand in the 'Enlightened City' project investigated cinemas' programming strategies, making use of a database capturing the full programming schemes of regular cinemas in Ghent for a sample of 10 years.[16] With these data, we could analyse programming strategies at a general level, and also conduct a more detailed analysis of individual cinemas or groups of venues. For Ghent in 1952, the database contained information on 1431 film screenings of 654 different films in 32 cinemas.[17] While the average circulation time was a little over 16 days, most pictures (60.3%) left the Ghent market after 1 week, and rapid programme change was the norm for cinemas in the poorer city districts. While the socialist Vooruit also changed its programme each week, the Capitole and other city-centre cinemas often kept successful pictures on their programme for 2 weeks or longer (Table 5.2). In 1952, some 78 movies stayed in the city for at least 5 weeks. Most of these pictures were American: the list was headed by *The Great Caruso* (1951, USA, 16 weeks), the operetta movie *Die Csardasfürstin* (1951, West Germany, 9 weeks), followed by a long list of Hollywood pictures, which were on the programme for 8 weeks (including *Show Boat,* 1951, USA). An analysis of the circulation of these movies clearly underlines the hierarchy among cinemas, whereby bigger city-centre (Capitole, Majestic, Century, Plaza) and district cinemas (Royal) operated as first-run venues, with most second-run cinemas located in the city districts, along with some bigger suburb cinemas (e.g. Metropole).

A further indication of this hierarchy is provided by the movies' year of production (Table 5.3), which shows that city-centre cinemas played much more recent movies than those in the districts and the suburbs. Nearly three-quarters of the pictures screened by the big film venues in the city centre were produced in 1951 or 1952, while neighbourhood cinemas relied much more upon older material. District cinemas, for instance, only had a handful of very recent pictures

Table 5.2 Film programming in the Capitole and Vooruit, 1952 (number of movies, excluding missing data).[21]

		Capitole	*Vooruit*
Number of weeks	1 week	45	52
	2 weeks	5	0
Year of production	1952	18	2
	1951	28	30
	1950	4	12
	1940s	2	4
	1930s	1	1
Origin	USA	29	33
	Europe	18	13
	Other	5	6
Most popular genres	Western	4	8
	War film	5	3
	Musical	7	0
	Comedy	7	4
	Drama	5	6
	Adventure	5	8
Catholic morality codes	All	10	7
	Adults	31	23
	Not advised	6	3
	Forbidden	2	0
Official censorship	Children	32	33
	Adults	20	19

Table 5.3 Film programming in Ghent, 1952 (in percentages).

		Centre	*District*	*Suburbs*
Year of production	1952	20	6	4
	1951	51	46	38
	1950	17	26	25
	1940s	10	17	26
	1930s	2	5	7
Origin	USA	49	79	64
	Europe	31	10	17
	Other	20	11	19
Catholic morality codes	All	26	32	33
	Adults	61	64	63
	Not advised	9	2	3
	Forbidden	4	2	1
Official censorship	Children	57	81	85
	Adults (16 years)	43	19	15

(6% coming from 1952), while exhibitors in suburbs still played a consistent amount of older film material from the 1930s (7%) and the 1940s (26%). Within the city centre, however, huge differences occurred between the competing city-centre palaces Capitole and Vooruit. As well as changing its programme more regularly, the socialist cinema played somewhat older material (e.g. *For Whom the Bell Tolls*, 1943, USA) and programmed a lot of American pictures (e.g. Billy Wilder's *Sunset Boulevard*, 1950, and *Ace in the Hole*, 1951) (Table 5.2). The database reinforces the Capitole's image as a first-run, blockbuster-oriented cinema, screening more musicals and comedies than its lower-class oriented rival.

Our analysis of censorship data suggests that there were no great differences between city-centre cinemas and those in the districts and suburbs. A majority of movies were also given a favourable morality code by the Catholic Film Action, with most recommendations being for 'all' or 'adult' (Table 5.3). This was more explicitly the case for district and neighbourhood cinemas than for the city palaces, where clearly more controversial material was being shown.[18] Classification data from the Belgian film censorship board indicated that 39% of the pictures shown in city-centre palaces were officially prohibited to children and adolescents under 16. Neighbourhood cinemas scheduled more pictures approved for children. Besides the presence of Catholic cinemas here, which were more vigilant in avoiding screening dangerous or controversial material, one might speculate about community-oriented, family-friendly programming strategies aimed at a broader demographic mix in terms of age and gender.

The film palaces in the city centre competed more heavily for filmgoers coming from different parts of the city and its surroundings. Each sought to foster its identity, and even big chains were well aware that while filmgoers might have selected cinemas on the basis of movies and programming, they also looked for a particular experience, atmosphere and the performance of big screen cinema. The technological superiority of most city-centre cinemas was part of their appeal, but some venues also courted an aura of controversy by specialising in more daring material. As well as the soft-core erotic cinema Leopold, which targeted soldiers and male audiences with mainly French pictures forbidden by the CFA (e.g. *Nuits de Paris,* 1951, France), there was the Savoy. This prestigious cinema screened more pictures condemned by the Catholics and given a 16 rating by the censors than any of its competitors. It specialised in suggestive or controversial European pictures such as, in 1952, De Sica's *Miracolo a Milano* (1951, Italy) or Alf Sjöberg's *Fröken Julie* (Sweden, 1951). Although the Capitole scheduled more controversial pictures than the Vooruit (including *A Streetcar Named Desire*, Elia Kazan, 1951, USA, which had received an 16 age restriction), both palaces developed a mixed programme whereby they also tried to attract children and families.

As well as identifying differences in the social geography of cinemas in Ghent, we looked at how cinemas developed various programming strategies in order to attract different types of audiences. One might speculate here about a hierarchy of social and cultural differentiation among cinemas in terms of generic preferences, the average circulation time, or the availability of recent successful or controversial titles. In general, the analysis indicated that smaller neighbourhood and district cinemas operated as second- or even third-run venues, usually scheduling older, but also less controversial material, a pattern we attribute to these venues' more family and community-oriented profile. This was also the case for cinemas located in working-class areas. Catholic cinemas in general were more prudish in what they offered their audiences. The question remains whether this analysis corresponds to audiences' experiences. How did ordinary filmgoers perceive these strategies? How did they experience class distinction and the effects of pillarisation? Did they perceive forms of segregation or distinction along commercial, political or ideological lines? If so, how do they describe the different experiences and practices of going to district, neighbourhood or city-centre cinemas? In order to answer these questions, we integrated a third line in the research project, using oral history methodologies and conducting a large number of in-depth interviews.

Experiences of Distinction

The oral history component of the 'Enlightened City' project explored the social experience of cinemagoing in Flanders from the 1930s to the 1970s; this chapter considers only our findings on the issue of class and ideological distinction in postwar Ghent (Meers et al., 2010). Our respondents were selected and found either in homes for elderly people or within the social circle of acquaintances of the interviewers or by self-selection (responding to advertisements placed in local newspapers). As well as memories from Antwerp and Ghent, we collected a large sample of stories from smaller rural or semi-urbanised villages. As is the case in most qualitative research, statistical representativeness was never the objective of this part of the study. Rather, we sought as much variation by age, class, sex and ideological points of view as possible, in order to grasp a wide variety of routines, ideas and motives concerning cinemagoing. The level of film consumption also varied widely within our group of respondents, from avid daily moviegoers to those who hardly ever visited a movie theatre.

The individual interviews were conducted in 2005 and 2006 in the respondent's home environment by two researchers and trained undergraduate students from the universities of Antwerp and Ghent. The interviews were semi-structured, with the interviewers using thematic spreadsheets to keep the interviews focused, but leaving space for the respondents' own stories and spontaneous memories. Many respondents were highly motivated to talk and had very vivid memories of cinema, often referring to specific moments they remembered. The length of the interviews varied, depending on the storytelling capacities of our respondents, with an average length of around 1 hour. For the Ghent case, 61 interviews were conducted (34 men and 27 women aged between 60 and 83 years).[19] The interviews were transcribed and analysed using Atlas-ti, a software programme suitable for qualitative research. At a first level of analysis, we structured the interviews according to the respondents' age group in order to investigate their stories' evolution. At a second level, we reorganised their memories around a selection of themes, such as choice of movie theatre, frequency, companionship, information about specific films and motives for cinemagoing.

This third part of the project introduces new research questions (bottom-up, audience experiences), methodologies (interviews, qualitative analysis) and traditions (oral history, cultural studies). Our analysis makes use of Bourdieu's work describing the connections between the objective socioeconomic conditions of class on the one hand, and more subjective, internalised or mental structures producing particular lifestyles and cultural tastes on the other. We have concentrated on statements in which respondents discuss their experiences of class and ideological segregation in the postwar Ghent film scene, in order to examine the multilayered character of cultural and social distinction, and to demonstrate how this analysis of individual experiences and collective cultural practices of going to the movies (in sociological terms agency) can add new insights to a structural, political economy analysis of cinema's strategies to attract audiences.[20]

This was clearly the case when interviewees talked about politicised or religiously inspired film screenings. Ideological segregation was an important distinctive feature of the Ghent film scene, but most respondents tended not to overrate its impact on moviegoing practices. Most people seemed not to be well informed about the precise ideological profile of specific cinemas. Respondents knew about the Vooruit as the place for cinema and leisure within the socialist movement, but, except for the cinemas operating within their own pillar, they were usually unsure about other ideologically inspired film venues. While respondents were uncertain about the existence of liberal cinemas, they often considered Catholic cinemas to be very much associated with parochial work and morally prudish movies, somewhat at the margin of the cinema business:

> Socialists had, I think, three cinemas. The big Vooruit, Cameo and a little venue on the Zwijnaardsesteenweg. I think they also screened movies on a less regular basis in other places and organisations. But I am not aware of a real Catholic cinema. I think there were some liberal venues, but I am not sure. (A.V.M., male, b. 1919)

> We knew that the Vooruit was a socialist cinema. I am not sure whether there were other cinemas with a political color. Possibly some at the outskirts of Ghent ... Maybe cinema Plaza at the Korenmarkt. There was a dance-hall and a house for liberals. But I am not sure whether this had any impact on the cinema itself. Let's say that the people going there were not more liberal, but the Vooruit definitely was for the socialists. (W.L., male, b. 1929)

While recognising that some audiences were faithful to particular film venues, respondents strongly questioned the influence of ideological loyalty in relation to cinema and other leisure activities. Interviewees preferred to talk about these cinemas' distinctive profiles in terms of differences in programming styles, degrees of controversy, ethics and audiences' expectations:

> There were two cinemas which were a bit Catholic, I think. They showed movies where there was nothing to see at all. Certain people went to these venues, I know, also because the Church said they should avoid other cinemas which were associated with the devil. The Vooruit was openly socialist and I think the Scaldis also. People didn't know this, but there were many socialists in there … We didn't look at the political orientation of cinemas. We just knew that when you went to a Catholic cinema you didn't have to expect too much. They had beautiful movies, but there was nothing special in it. Priests went to these venues, just to see whether these pictures were decent enough. (G.M., male, b. 1921)

Acknowledging that cinema was not the most productive place for official politics and other forms of ideological work, the oral histories underlined the fact that these movie houses were lucrative entertainment-driven places. Ideological loyalty was countered by the attractiveness of the programme and the movies:

> Even in cinemas like the Vooruit people didn't talk about politics … they did in cafés nearby these venues, but never in cinemas, of course. (C.V.B., male, b. 1915)

> The Vooruit was a socialist cinema. But the other venues were not really politically oriented. At least, we never experienced this. Probably it is true that more socialists went to the Vooruit, but I didn't bother to go there when I really wanted to see a particular movie. But maybe this might not have been the case for everybody. (A.D.V., female, b. 1928)

> The audience didn't look at this. No … if the picture was good, you went there. (V.V.S., male, b. 1928)

Respondents did not really experience ideological segregation as a problem, not only because they had a choice between different styles in terms of particular kinds of movies, genres, ethics, class or political orientation, but also because these venues did not operate as explicit propaganda arms in what they screened:

> I can imagine that the real socialists were more eager to go to their own cinema. But this was less the case in the 1950s and 1960s. And you should not forget that the Vooruit showed all kinds of movies. (S.M., male, b. 1945)

One reason why people went to the Vooruit and other ideologically inspired film venues was financial ('We often went to the Vooruit because it was the cheapest', J.D., male, b. 1935). In many socialist and Catholic film venues, ticket prices were kept considerably lower than in first-run cinemas. This consideration, which was closely linked to social class, also increased the attractiveness of second- and third-run cinemas in the city districts and in the suburbs:

> There were price differences, of course, between cinemas in the districts and those in the city centre. I cannot imagine that blue collar workers could afford to go to city centre film palaces every week. (Y.D., female, b. 1946)

> It was more 'chic'. In the Capitole there was a large balcony where you could sit for a few francs more … Twenty-one francs. And the cinema was beautiful. It was always pleasant to stay there for a movie … I also went to the Vooruit, but that was not so good. It was a very big cinema but the films were regularly interrupted when the film was broken. And then we sat there for a couple minutes … in the dark … Not funny at all, you know … And they didn't have CinemaScope. (A.D., male, b. 1947)

This last comment, which refers to the Capitole's price differentiation policy, indicates how people used very different levels of comparison when describing the different cinema experiences in a city-centre first-run and other cinemas. A key issue here was a multifaceted reference to the aura of luxury around city-centre palaces, described in terms of better infrastructure, architectural beauty, higher projection quality, technical novelty, seating facilities or other features dealing with a superior cinema experience:

> In those cinemas everything was very simple … Wooden chairs and very few lights during the break. It wasn't very comfortable because you were on those chairs for a few hours, you know … I don't know whether there was heating. But anyway, we had our coats on … The Lido was somewhat better: beautiful lighting and the scene was illuminated by spotlights … And then there were the beautiful cinemas in Ghent … the Capitole, Plaza and other cinemas in the centre. These were beautiful, with red seats and a splendid balcony … All very nice … (Y.D., female, b. 1946)

> I adored the Capitole … It was a beautiful cinema. Inside the cinema, it was all red, burgundy velvet, the pillows were all in velvet, which gave you a feeling of luxury. We liked to sit there in the dark with those little tiny lights between the rows. That was my favorite cinema, but it was also the most expensive one … In the other smaller cinemas, with their wooden seats, there was a lot of noise, when people came in … You couldn't hear the movie … a terrible noise, but that was only in the cheap, small cinemas. The large cinema was all velvet, soft … with suspension in the seats, you sat there … really cosy. (A.L., female, b. 1942)

People made a distinction between cinemas on the basis of programming differences such as genre, language, origin, pictures' running time, novelty of the programme and morality, and these differences also influenced their experiences of a hierarchy between first-, second- and third-run cinemas:

> There was a difference according to the type of cinema … In the great cinemas in the centre … in the Majestic, Eldorado, Capitole, Select, there was a better audience, people from the city. In the neighbourhood cinemas you saw a more popular audience. The Agora is an example. They played mostly second- or third-hand films, films that had been previously shown. It was a good opportunity to see them again

if they had been missed. There were mostly people from the neighbourhood. (P.B., male, b. 1947)

I often went to the Savoy and also the Majestic. The Savoy was French … They often gave French-language movies without subtitles at all. It was quite elitist. Chic. (J.D., male, b. 1935)

When describing these differences between the 'better' cinemas and the others, respondents not only discussed location, ticket price, an aura of luxury or programming, but also talked about a variety of other distinctive features, including differences in terms of practical behaviours and lifestyle, taste, language, dress code or ethics. The recurring concept that bound these distinctions together and acted as a central floating signifier was social class:

The city centre cinemas were more for people from higher social classes, you know. These people went to cinemas like the Century and Casino. In fact, you had three types of cinemas … those for ordinary people around the centre, the elite cinemas, and then the Leopold where we even didn't dare to pass. (A.D.G., male, b. 1939)

People going to the Capitole were somewhat more 'chic' … also because it was more expensive. These people never went to the Vooruit or to the Leopold. That was the class difference. (J.D., male, b. 1932)

Class differences were reflected in the clothing and dress codes:

We practically never went to the big cinemas around the former south station, mainly because these were too expensive. We didn't go to cinemas such as the Century and Capitole … People usually dressed up for going to these film theatres. (R.D., male, b. 1946)

Some respondents referred to class-related distinctions in terms of differences of public decency, behaviour, hygiene and even physical cleanness:

This was slightly better in the city cinema, but in neighbourhood cinemas everybody threw everything on the ground. People also brought their sandwiches with them because they were often planning to sit there for three screenings, and they threw it all on the ground. No, it wasn't very clean. (A.A., female, b. 1944)

Others referred to differences in audience mentality, taste and participation:

There was another mentality, another, I would almost say, level of education of the people who live in the centre. And then if you went to the Brugsepoort or to the Muide, people were really more spontaneous, responding to everything. We were more reserved in our reactions, but in neighbourhood cinemas people would react more spontaneously. (C.H., female, b. 1933)

For some the distinction between city-centre and neighbourhood cinemas was also a matter of language, with French-language audiences and vulgar slang as extremes:

> There was the Vooruit and there were people's cinemas for the ordinary workmen. That depended on the neighbourhood. In the centre you had better people … who were usually more bourgeois. Here you had French movies and the people there often talked French. (J.D.M., male, b. 1944)
>
> I didn't go to neighbourhood cinemas. These were for the populace. [Q: What do you mean?] Well, how could I say … People there talked loudly and used language like 'Kiss my balls' and so forth. (M.T., female, b. 1935)

There were other accounts in which neighbourhood cinemas in city districts and the suburbs were compared negatively with those in the city centre, for instance on grounds of public safety, fighting, 'bad' social behaviour and discipline:

> We mostly went to the three cinemas in the centre around the former south station. These were beautiful cinemas and there were never any problems. In neighbourhood cinemas in certain areas people sometimes fought. Yes, that was a different audience, a more simple audience I would say. A word wrong and they could start to fight. That happened, you know, but not in the centre. (A.D., male, b. 1947)
>
> In the large cinemas it was better … There was more discipline … There were more people with a better education, somewhat more the elite, you know … But in the smaller cinemas, and this was also the case in neighbourhoods, you had another audience. So, it depended a bit on the audience where I went. (A.L., female, b. 1942)

It is not difficult to interpret these accounts from a Bourdieuian perspective as utterances of distinction, whereby respondents describe their own position in relation to other social groups and their social practices. The oral histories underlined how important audience composition was as an issue when describing cinemagoing experiences and the atmosphere in cinemas, not only in terms of objective class differences but even more so from the perspective of concrete lifestyle, behaviour, taste or language. People talked about very different audiences, not in a classical class theory sense, but rather in terms of very specific class fractions, professions or generations, although they seldom made reference to either gender or ethnicity. In the way they described the social geography of cinema, people often intermingled various levels of audience compositions:

> The Century played a lot of far west and cowboy pictures, and young people around fourteen, fifteen years sat below … Couples and somewhat older people sat behind them or on the balcony. In the Capitole people came more as a couple, man and wife. (A.D., male, b. 1947)
>
> The audience was very diverse … For example, Tuesday was the day for merchants and independent shop owners. Younger people often went on Fridays … There was

> a real class difference between the cinemas. The working class went to the Vooruit and the middle and more wealthy classes went to the Capitol or Majestic. (G.P., male, b. 1922)

> People did not talk in the cinema. Unless they saw and knew each other. Maybe down there. When I went to the cinema, people on the ground floor were more common and somewhat more vulgar … The balcony was rather chic. Sorry, I can't help it. We were not rich or anything, but the noise makers sat on the ground floor. The same was true for the tram where you had a first and a second class. First class was behind, the second class at the front. (J.V.O., female, b. 1930)

The respondents' mental mapping of cinema was constructed on a multilayered concept of cultural and social distinction, and in part by the aspiration to define and distinguish themselves from other social classes and their daily practices. The experience of cinemagoing was also related to geographical stratification and the feeling of belonging to a community or living in a particular district. From this perspective, it is important to recognise that neighbourhood cinemas were not always defined in a pejorative sense. In their accounts of cinemas in the districts and the suburbs, interviewees often associated these cinemas with a sense of community and familiarity:

> Mostly the same audience … People who were used to go there. I knew almost everyone. This was the case in every neighbourhood. Everybody in the district went to the same cinema. (G.M., male, b. 1921)

> There were a lot of different people in the cinema. Some people had a fixed place … A man who worked with me went with his little sister, his mother and father, and they had a fixed place. One of the parents went early to the cinema in order to keep these places for them. (A.V.M., male, b. 1919)

When they discussed the issue of class-mixing in neighbourhood and city-centre cinemas, people were nuanced, often signalling different levels of distinction by referring to financial issues, dress codes, behaviour and feelings of community. Respondents nevertheless confirmed the predominance of higher social classes in the film palaces, while cinemas in the districts and suburbs were mainly visited by working-class people:

> Yes, there were mainly working people. I do not say that there were no big shots there, but the majority was people who worked in factories or had a low income. If you went to the Century, you saw merchants and independent retailers. You saw that people were very different … In the big cinemas there was a very different audience. Shopkeepers, doctors … Anyway very few working-class people. In the Vooruit, for example, there were also ordinary working people and other people, but you saw that it was still quite different. They sat together. There were working-class people, a bit further you had shopkeepers, and also sons of doctors and lawyers. You saw that there was a difference. (R.D., male, b. 1946)

> In the city centre the audience was mixed. Rich people didn't go to the neighbourhood cinemas, that's true … They went to cinemas in the city, the Majestic and the Capitole. (C.V.B., male, b. 1915)

> There was a very diverse audience. But it is so that people from the belt, the workers from the districts, that they had a bit of a complex, and you know, you could see from how they were dressed that they were from a lower class … And then they actually didn't feel at home in those cinemas … There was a bit of fear, a threshold. (A.V., male, b. 1933)

Visiting cinemas in the city centre also involved a personal social trajectory and a shift in identity, most often defined by respondents in terms of their age, education, social mobility, financial means or by the awakening of cinephilia. As people grew older, became more educated, and climbed the social ladder, they more often went to city-centre cinemas:

> We went to neighbourhood cinemas until the age of fourteen, fifteen, and then we also went to the city … To see better movies … and where the quality of the cinemas was better … more pleasant, if we could get money, at least. (C.V.B., male, b. 1915)

> And when I got older and I became more interested, I became an Anglophile … Music and films … There was the Select, and the Rex. In the Savoy they played the French movies and the slightly more burnt and forbidden pictures. (G.V.V., male, b. 1936)

This analysis has concentrated on the audience's experiences of cinema as a social practice only from the perspective of class distinction and ideological segregation. When considering these responses, it is necessary to take into account historical distance, especially in interpreting critical evaluations of neighbourhood cinemas as areas of poverty, low taste or undisciplined 'bad' public behaviour in the light of the number and success of these venues. Questions might also be raised about statements downplaying the impact of ideological segregation on cinemagoing practices. In this context one might speculate about whether the process of 'depillarisation' of society, which started in the 1960s and soon affected politicised film exhibition in Belgium, also influenced respondents' replies.

The oral history analysis nevertheless underlines the fact that film venues that openly targeted a very specific religious or political audience (predominantly Catholic parish halls with a regular film programme) were conceived as being at the margin of cinema, or at least of cinema understood as a field of entertainment, leisure and pleasure. The Vooruit, one of the three most cited cinemas in the respondents' accounts (the others were the Capitole and the Leopold), was an exception here. Using respondents' accounts in the absence of historical audience surveys, we can agree that while the socialist cinema operated as a low-class commercial cinema, it also attracted a broader audience in terms of class and ideology.

The greatest degree of class-mixing took place in the city-centre film palaces. Although these cinemas were mostly associated in their public image, promotion and architecture with middle and higher social classes, their differentiated price policies and programming strategies succeeded in attracting film fans from other classes who aspired to a 'better' film experience. In the respondents' mental mapping of the field of cinema, the Capitole clearly provided the most intense cinema experience available to them. Respondents from different social classes and ideological backgrounds talked about the Capitole as if it was a film temple, where people were silent or only whispered, and behaved decently. Around this centre, people often located the other city-centre palaces where they found similar traces of luxury, spectacle and superior film experience, although they also made clear distinctions between these cinemas on the basis of their programming, kinds and genres of movies, type of audiences, public image, language, dress codes and atmosphere.

Using a multilevelled concept of distinction, rooted in concrete cinemagoing practices, we could speculate about a second category of venues that were characterised by a more popular experience of cinema (Table 5.4). Here we could locate most neighbourhood cinemas, but also the Vooruit. In their descriptions, respondents brought forward many differences among those cinemas in terms of programming, location in different districts or suburbs, audiences and atmosphere, but in the main, these popular cinemas were associated with an aura of poverty, popular taste and less disciplined public behaviour. Although these cinemas were presented as predominantly oriented to the lower class, people also consistently mentioned ideas of familiarity, community orientation and some forms of class-mixing (everyone from the neighbourhood went there).

In the audiences' mental mapping of the field of cinema, some venues were considered to be marginal, in that they were places where people seldom went (or said they went). These places included Catholic parish halls as well as the soft-core Leopold cinema. Although these two categories might be seen as extremes in terms of public morality, both target explicit audiences (respectively Catholics and 'perverted' men) and were associated with an inferior cinema experience.

Conclusion

Like most other European countries, postwar Belgian society was strongly divided along ideological and religious lines. Pillarisation and class conflicts were strongly intermingled and deeply influenced leisure, media and other cultural industries. The fact that this was certainly the case for film exploitation partly explains the high number of film venues in Belgium at least for more than half a century. Concentrating on the case of the highly proletarianised postwar city of Ghent, this

Table 5.4 Summary: the field of cinema in Ghent.

	Structure	*Programming*	*Audience*
Legitimate cinema			
Capitole City-centre palaces	City centre Price differentiation / more expensive Corporate control Technical superiority High-quality facilities	Premières, blockbusters, novelty Spectacle More adult material Differentiation among cinemas High commercial value	Mixed class / ideology Predominantly middle / upper classes Aura of luxury 'Better cinema' Good taste Discipline, education, decent public behaviour Superior cinema experience Extraordinary Distance
Popular cinema			
Vooruit Neighbourhood cinemas	City centre Districts and suburbs Cheap (fee) Technical mediocrity or inferiority Low-quality facilities	First-run Second / third-run More family / community-oriented material Lower commercial value	Explicit audience (socialists) Mixed class / ideology Dominance of lower classes Aura of poverty Popular taste Less disciplined public behaviour Popular cinema experience Ordinary Community, familiarity, participation
Marginal cinema			
Leopold Catholic cinemas	City centre Suburbs Cheap (fee) Technical inferiority Low-quality facilities	Explicitly adult material (soft-erotic) Explicitly safe family material Low commercial value	Explicit audience (men) Aura of controversy Bad taste Explicit audience (Catholics) Aura of poverty Inferior cinema experience

chapter has explored the importance of ideological segregation and social class from various perspectives. Inspired by other new cinema history projects, we decided to apply a form of triangulation by using different sorts of data, methods, theories and research traditions. This triangulation has made it possible to capture more fully how and where what kind of movies were consumed by what kind of audiences. Applied to the question of the importance of ideology and social class, for instance, an analysis of the structure and the location of cinemas would have been insufficient if not supplemented by programming and audience analysis (Table 5.4). Politicised and ideological (mainly Catholic) film exhibition might have been a substantial part of the film exhibition structure, but its off-centre location, unattractive programming strategies and the audience's pejorative accounts tended to diminish its importance. The Vooruit's public image of a working-class oriented cinema for socialist militants, as another example, became more complex when confronted by programming analysis, which indicated its commercially oriented programme schedules.

Furthermore, the combination of structural analysis with programming data and audience experiences might be more productive than just using the location of cinemas in order to draw conclusions about the class of audiences. As Ben Singer stated on Manhattan nickelodeons, 'one can only infer audience compositions for theaters located in neighbourhoods with a fairly high degree of demographic homogeneity' (Singer, 1997, p. 109). Although more detailed demographic analyses of specific neighbourhoods would add strength to the analysis, we hope to have demonstrated the usefulness of triangulation in order to arrive at a multi-layered concept of cultural and social distinction as a key in understanding the lived experience of cinema.

Notes

1 Richard Maltby, 'How can cinema history matter more?', *Screening the Past*, no. 22 (Dec. 2007). See also Richard Maltby and Melvyn Stokes, 'Introduction', in *Going to the Movies: Hollywood and the Social Experience of Cinema* (eds Richard Maltby, Melvyn Stokes and Robert C. Allen; Exeter: Exeter University Press, 2007), p. 2. As examples, see the contributions to this book by John Sedgwick, Tim Snelson and Mark Jancovich; Karel Dibbets' *Cinema-in-Context* project (www.cinemacontext.nl); and Mark Jancovich, Lucy Faire and Sarah Stubbings, *The Place of the Audience: Cultural Geographies of Film Consumption* (London: BFI, 2003), pp. 3–33.

2 For instance, John Sedgwick and Michael Pokorny, 'The film business in the United States and Britain during the 1930s', *Economic History Review*, 58 (2005), pp. 79–112. See also the contributions by Mike Walsh and Deron Overpeck in this book, and the essays in Kathryn H. Fuller-Seeley (ed.), *Hollywood in the Neighborhood: Historical Case Studies of Local Moviegoing* (Berkeley: University of California Press, 2008).

3 On different forms of triangulation, mainly in the field of social sciences and the humanities, see Norman K. Denzin, *The Research Act* (Englewood Cliffs: Prentice Hall, 1989).

4 Some key works are: Lary May, *Screening out the Past: The Birth of Mass Culture and the Motion Picture Industry* (New York: Oxford University Press, 1980). Peter Stead, *Film and the Working-Class: The Feature Film in British and American Society* (London: Routledge, 1989). Steven J. Ross, *Working-Class Hollywood: Silent Film and the Shaping of Class in America* (Princeton: Princeton University Press, 1998). For an overview of the literature, see: Judith Thissen and André van der Velde, 'Klasse als factor in de Nederlandse geschiedenis', *Tijdschrift voor Mediageschiedenis*, 12 (2009), pp. 50–72. See also: Jeffrey Klenotic, 'Four hours of hootin' and hollerin'', in Richard Maltby, Melvyn Stokes and Robert C. Allen (eds), *Going to the Movies: Hollywood and the Social Experience of Cinema* (Exeter: Exeter University Press, 2007), pp. 130–153. We also refer to the 'Singer/Allen debate' in *Cinema Journal*, on

nickelodeons and their audiences in Manhattan in the first decades of the twentieth century. One of the key questions in the debate was if it is possible to draw a demographic (class and ethnic) profile of audiences based on the geographical situation of the venues in specific areas. See Ben Singer, 'Manhattan nickelodeons: new data on audiences and exhibitors', *Cinema Journal*, 34 (3) (1995), pp. 5–35; Sumiko Higashi, 'Manhattan's nickelodeons. On Ben Singer's "Manhattan nickelodeons: new data on audiences and exhibitors"', *Cinema Journal*, 35 (1996), pp. 72–74; Robert C. Allen, 'Manhattan myopia; or, Oh! Iowa! Robert C. Allen on Ben Singer's "Manhattan nickelodeons: new data on audiences and exhibitors"', *Cinema Journal*, 35 (1996), pp. 75–103. The debate continued in *Cinema Journal*, 36 (4) (Summer, 1997).

5 Flanders is the Dutch-speaking region in the northern part of Belgium. In 2005 it had a surface area of 13 522 km^2, a population of 5.9 million (60% of the Belgian population) and a population density of 434 inhabitants per km^2. Flanders is divided into five provinces and 308 municipalities. Two of them are metropolitan cities (Antwerp and Ghent). Also included in the research project is the bilingual capital Brussels, which is composed of 19 municipalities and over one million inhabitants.

6 The overall research project, 'The "Enlightened" City: Screen Culture between Ideology, Economics and Experience. A Study on the Social Role of Film Exhibition and Film Consumption in Flanders (1895–2004) in Interaction with Modernity and Urbanisation' (Scientific Research Fund Flanders/ FWO-Vlaanderen, 2005–8; promoters: Philippe Meers, Daniel Biltereyst and Marnix Beyen), was based at the universities of Antwerp (UA) and Gent (UGent). The project included students' work, various research seminars, and MA and PhD theses. The authors wish to thank Kathleen Lotze, Gert Willems and the many students involved in the project.

7 Before World War I, Belgium was considered to be the fifth industrial nation in the world with an open, export-driven and expansive economy. Its high-ranked position in international trade was, in part, due to the exploitation of rubber and minerals in its colony, Congo. The country also played a pivotal role in European transport systems, with a widely elaborated, low-tariff railway system and Antwerp as a major world harbour. Its transport system facilitated the distribution of motion picture reels, and Brussels became an important film distribution centre for exports to The Netherlands and northwestern Europe. Gita Deneckere, 'Nieuwe geschiedenis van België', in Els Witte *et al.* (eds), *Nieuwe Geschiedenis van België I: 1830–1905* (Tielt: Lannoo, 2005), pp. 460–461. Ivo Blom, *Jean Desmet and the Early Dutch Film Trade* (Amsterdam: Amsterdam University Press, 2003), p. 147.

8 Conservative Liberals, Communists and Flemish nationalists tried unsuccessfully to create a similar block of organisations in the interwar years.

9 There are some MA theses on film exhibition in Ghent for particular periods. See: Bernadette Dhoore, 'De film te Gent in de periode 1919–1930' (Ghent, 1984). René Van Dessel, 'Preferenties van het Gentse filmpubliek als historische bron voor het mentaliteitsonderzoek, 1930–1934' (Ghent, 1977). Hilde De Martelaer, 'Analyse van de Filmconsumptie te Gent, 1940–1949' (Ghent, 1982).

10 Compared to other European countries with quite similar population sizes and socioeconomic contexts, Belgium had a wide film exhibition sector. By the beginning of the 1930s, Belgium counted 740 theatres, The Netherlands 266 and Switzerland 330. See Ian Jarvie, *Hollywood's Overseas Campaign: The North Atlantic Movie Trade, 1920–1950* (Cambridge: Cambridge University Press, 1992), p. 141. See also George Sadoul, *Histoire Générale du Cinéma (VI): Le Cinéma pendant la Guerre* (Paris: Denoël, 1954), p. IX.

11 These figures are based on a series of microhistorical case studies on the following 46 towns in Flanders: Lier, Oostkamp, Knokke Heist, Sint Kruis, Oostende, Jabbeke, Kortrijk, Harelbeke, Wevelgem, Avelgem, Diksmuide, Nieuwpoort, Veurne, Pittem, Oostrozebeke, Waregem, Roeselare, Lichtervelde, Ieper, Poperinge, Destelbergen/Heusden, Dendermonde, Erpe Mere, Zottegem, Kluisbergen, Oudenaarde, Deinze, Arendonk, Dessel, Liedekerke, Londerzeel, Kontich, Hoboken, Mortsel, Hemiksem, Kessel, Schilde, Hoogstraten, Mol, Borgerhout, Wilrijk, Boechout, Balen, Zwijndrecht, Burcht and Herentals.

12 Sofexim and Cinex became one company in 1969, dominating film exhibition in Ghent. Sofexim managed the Capitole, Eldorado, Savoy and Select, while Cinex managed the Century, Majestic and Rex.

13 In 1952, the Capitole's most expensive ticket cost 30 francs, and the cheapest 10 francs.

14 In Ghent, which is located in the Dutch-language part of Belgium and where the majority of the population spoke Dutch (or Flemish), higher social classes used to speak French in public. With its connotations of French culture and the political and socioeconomic elites, French became an important tool of social distinction.

15 Ghent and its outskirts counted some 164 713 inhabitants and 32 cinemas, or one cinema for 5147 people,

16 Here we will rely upon Ghent 1952 data; the overall database spans from the 1930s until the 1970s. The file for programming strategies in Antwerp comprises data on three years (1952, 1962, 1972). Each record in the database contains information on the cinema, the Belgian and original film title, the programming week, origin of the movie, production year, producer, Catholic morality codes (ranging from 'for all', 'adults' and 'not advised' to 'forbidden') and the official censor's quotation ('children allowed', 'children not allowed' or 16 years limitation).

17 The overall programming data file contains 17 858 entries.

18 It should be noted that the data may somewhat over-represent Catholic cinemas in district and suburb cinemas.

19 In total 389 interviews were conducted, including 155 in Antwerp.

20 On a political economy analysis of audiences, more in particular connected to cinema, see Daniel Biltereyst and Philippe Meers, 'The political economy of audiences', in Janet Wasko, Graham Murdock and Helena Sousa (eds), *The Handbook of Political Economy of Communications* (Oxford: Wiley-Blackwell, 2011).

21 The data file for the programming analysis contains some gaps, including unidentified film titles. It was also not always possible to identify the Catholic morality codes for movies programmed by the socialist Vooruit, because these codes were published in Catholic newspapers, which mainly reported programming schedules from the commercial and Catholic cinemas.

References

Billiet J. (ed.) (1988) *Tussen bescherming en verovering: Sociologen en historici over zuilvorming,* Leuven University Press, Leuven.

Biltereyst, D. (2007) The Roman Catholic church and film exhibition in Belgium, 1926–1940. *Historical Journal of Film, Radio and Television,* 27, 193–214.

Biltereyst, D., Meers, P., Van de Vijver, L. and Willems G. (2007) Bioscopen, moderniteit en filmbeleving. Deel 1: Op zoek naar het erfgoed van bioscopen in landelijke en minder verstedelijkte gebieden in Vlaanderen. *Volkskunde: tijdschrift voor de studie van de cultuur van het dagelijks leven,* 108, 105–124.

Bourdieu, P. (1984) *Distinction: A Social Critique of the Judgement of Taste,* Routledge, London.

Convents, G. (1992) Les catholiques et le cinéma en Belgique (1895–1914), in *An Invention of the Devil?* (eds R. Cosandey, A. Gaudreault and T. Gunning), Presses de l'Université Laval, Sainte Foy, pp. 21–43.

De Martelaer, H. (1982) *Analyse van de Filmconsumptie te Gent*, unpublished thesis, Ghent University.

Dibbets, K. (2006) Het taboe van Nederland: Neutraal in een verzuild land. *Tijdschrift voor Mediageschiedenis*, 9, 46–64.

Jenkins, R. (2002) *Pierre Bourdieu,* Routledge, London.

Kuhn, A. (2002) *An Everyday Magic: Cinema and Cultural Memory,* I.B. Tauris, London.

Lijphart, A. (1977) *Democracies in Plural Societies,* Yale University Press, New Haven.

Maltby, R. (2006) On the prospect of writing cinema history from below. *Tijdschrift voor Mediageschiedenis*, 9, 74–96.

Meers, P., Biltereyst, D. and Van de Vijver, L. (2010) Memory, movies and cinema-going: an oral history project on film culture in Flanders, in *Film Reception* (eds I. Schenk, M. Tröhler and Y. Zimmerman), Schüren, Marburg, pp. 319–337.

Robert, J-L., Prost, A. and Wrigley, C. (eds.) (2004) *The Emergence of European Trade Unionism*, Ashgate Publishing, Surrey.

Ross, S.J. (1998) *Working-Class Hollywood: Silent Film and the Shaping of Class in America*, Princeton University Press, Princeton.

Singer, B. (1997) Manhattan melodrama. A response from Ben Singer. *Cinema Journal*, 36 (4), 107–112.

Stallaerts, R. (2007) De weg naar het paradijs: Socialisme en filmvertoningen in Vlaanderen, in *De Verlichte Stad* (eds D. Biltereyst and P. Meers), LannooCampus, Leuven, pp. 163–169.

Strikwerda, C. (1997) *A House Divided: Catholics, Socialists and Flemish Nationalists in Nineteenth-Century Belgium*, Rowland & Littlefield, Lanham.

Strikwerda, C. (1999) 'Alternative visions' and working-class culture: the political-economy of consumer cooperation in Belgium, 1860–1980, in *Consumers against Capitalism? Consumer Cooperation in Europe, North America, and Japan, 1840–1990* (eds E. Furlough and C. Strikwerda), Rowman & Littlefield, Lanham, pp. 67–92.

6

Distribution and Exhibition in The Netherlands, 1934–1936[1]

Clara Pafort-Overduin

After France came the United States, and by the 1920s US films dominated all cinemas in the Western world for ever after. That is the short version of Hollywood's success. The longer version is a bit more complicated, and leaves room for histories of national film industries trying to cope with a gigantic opponent that seemed to know all the secrets about proper storytelling, efficient production methods, generating money and attracting massive audiences. In his work on German cinema audiences between 1921 and 1971, Joseph Garncarz has shown that too narrow an economic approach to Hollywood's domination leaves out the preferences of film audiences for domestically produced movies (Garncarz, 1994, p. 95). John Sedgwick has also demonstrated that many of the long ignored and despised British 'quota quickies' were far more popular with audiences than has conventionally been described (Sedgwick, 2000, pp. 47–54, 95–96, 250).

This chapter deals with another easily overlooked national history, and begins in 1934 when the first Dutch talkies finally reached Dutch audiences. While *Willem van Oranje* (*William Of Orange*, 1934), the first on the market, did not raise much enthusiasm, *De Jantjes* (*The Sailors*, 1934), released a month later, was accompanied by a national outburst of joy. 'We are able to compete with Hollywood', boasted cinema owner Abraham Tuschinski at its premiere, and his words drew a standing ovation and a resounding rendition of the national anthem, from the audience.[2]

The Sailors seemed to provide a positive answer to the lingering question of whether it was possible for The Netherlands to have a national film industry. Until then, no continuous feature film production had been established. The only Dutch film production company that had produced films on a regular basis was Filmfabriek Hollandia (Film Factory Hollandia), and it had been closed for almost 10 years in 1934. Since then, films had only been made irregularly. Unlike Sweden and Czechoslovakia – two countries that the Dutch film press loved to refer to as models,

Explorations in New Cinema History: Approaches and Case Studies, First Edition.
Edited by Richard Maltby, Daniel Biltereyst and Philippe Meers.

because they were of a comparable size – the Dutch had not been able to build a thriving national film industry (Dittrich, 1986, p. 110). The fact that only one Dutch feature film was produced between 1930 and 1934 illustrates how bad the situation was. With the coming of sound, newspapers and the Dutch trade journal *Nieuw Weekblad voor de Cinematografie* [*New Weekly of Cinematography*] regularly argued that there was a need for Dutch-spoken films, but unlike France, Germany and Italy, where foreign films were commonly dubbed, the arrival of sound had not brought Dutch voices to the cinemas (Dibbets, 1993, pp. 264–273). Dutch audiences did not take to the disembodied voices of dubbed actors, and films were subtitled instead (Dibbets, 1993, p. 101). Apart from the newsreels of the Dutch *Polygoon Journaal* and some experimental short films, no films sounded Dutch. This made cinema owners even more aware of the lack of Dutch features (Dittrich, 1986, p. 108). While the British and French governments had given some protection to their domestic film industries, in The Netherlands there was not even an ailing film industry to protect.[3] After the box-office success of *The Sailors*, however, Dutch fiction film suddenly appeared economically viable, and until World War II it seemed possible to develop a small national film industry. During the war film production was reduced to zero, and in 1945 after the war the Dutch film industry was back where it had started in 1934. This chapter focuses on the first three years of the short flowering of Dutch sound film between 1934 and 1936, when 27 Dutch fiction films were produced.

How did these films enter the Dutch market? What were the prospects of a new, national product succeeding in a well-supplied and internationally oriented market, particularly since the opportunities for Dutch-speaking films were limited to the domestic market?[4] Did Dutch audiences like their domestic movies, and were they willing to spend their money on them? As Karel Dibbets has argued, not much is known about the composition and preferences of Dutch audiences in the 1930s (Dibbets, 1986, p. 244). Statistics were systematically gathered from 1937, making it possible to say something about the general size of the audience from then on, but not about their preferences. Before 1937, only arbitrary and incomplete information is available. It is commonly assumed from a reading of the contemporary national newspapers and the so-called quality magazines that Dutch audiences were unenthusiastic about Dutch film. Kathinka Dittrich cites the journal *Cinema en Theater*'s [*Cinema and Theatre*] claim that Dutch interest in Dutch film evaporated after the release of *Bleeke Bet* (*Pale Betty*, 1934) in September 1934, and there were no hits in the years thereafter (Dittrich, 1986, pp. 141–142). Against this view, my examination of the first three years of Dutch sound fiction film production suggests that Dutch films remained very popular with domestic audiences.

My analysis is built from three complementary sources: a survey of Dutch newspaper and magazine reviews, an examination of distribution strategies in The Netherlands, and an analysis of what was shown in Dutch cinemas. Although the expectations and judgements of Dutch critics were influenced by their differing ideological backgrounds and economic dependencies, they represented at least one aspect of the films' public reception. Reviews provide only one very specific perspective on audience taste, however, and other sources are needed to complement or contrast the views they articulate. One such source is distribution strategy. What did Dutch film distributors expect from this new product on the market? Did they use different distribution strategies for domestic and foreign films? And if so, what does this imply about the audience?

As my third source of information, I will analyse what was actually shown in Dutch cinemas, using the number of screenings of a film as an approximate indication of its popularity. Because cinema owners were engaged in a profit-seeking commercial activity, it is likely that they adjusted their film programmes to maximise the screenings of popular films, and that therefore the frequency of a film's screening provides an indication of its relative popularity. Although the opportunities to return or cancel an unpopular film might have been limited, exhibitors had opportunities to programme extra screenings or to prolong a film's exhibition if there was a demand for it. This method of obtaining information about the relative popularity of films by comparing the number of their screenings is adapted from John Sedgwick's POPSTAT methodology of generating popularity statistics by counting ticket sales (Sedgwick, 2000, pp. 55–73; see also Chapter 7). In the Dutch case, information on ticket sales is not available, and therefore we cannot be certain of any film's box-office earnings, but counting screenings provides an alternative gauge of popularity. Triangulating these three sources of information will result in a better understanding of Dutch audiences, and their role in maintaining the viability of a domestic Dutch film industry.

To compile my sources, I searched a range of national and regional newspapers and magazines, covering the whole country and the breadth of ideological perspectives – Catholic, Protestant, socialist, Communist, liberal, neutral and nationalist – for articles on Dutch films in the period 1934–1936, although because Dutch Protestants rejected movies altogether, Protestant newspapers contained no film reviews or advertisements for films. I also constructed a data set containing programme information from cinemas in 18 cities in The Netherlands, with populations ranging from 9400 to 780 000 inhabitants. Amsterdam, Rotterdam and The Hague were chosen because these three cities together accounted for half of the country's total cinema attendances.[5] The other locations were chosen from various Dutch provinces in order to compare the findings from the three largest urban centres with provincial towns of varying size, spread across The Netherlands. Three towns had populations of between 110 000 and 160 000 inhabitants, seven had between 50 000 and 100 000, and five had between 9000 and 50 000 inhabitants.

Most of the data were gathered by scrutinising cinema advertisements in local newspapers, while the *Cinema Context Collection* provided the programmes from the cinemas in Amsterdam, The Hague, Rotterdam and Groningen.[6] All together, these 18 cities had 145 cinemas, representing 40% of the total number of cinemas in The Netherlands operating between 1934 and 1936. This total of 359 cinemas included venues such as club houses showing films on an irregular basis, and these venues were removed from the data set, along with a small number of cinemas for which little programme information could be found. The final data set contains programme information on 138 cinemas, and includes 23 674 programmes featuring 2402 individual titles shown in The Netherlands between 1934 and 1936. The data set records information on the cinemas, film titles and programmes. Along with its seating capacity, each cinema's geographical location was recorded, so that patterns of distribution and regional differences in audience preferences could be identified. Information on each film's director, stars, production company, and year and country of production was recorded in order to characterise film supply and determine what kind of films were popular. For all films, the number, date and location of all screenings, and details of double bills were entered.

Dutch Film Industry

The Dutch fiction film industry was almost non-existent in 1934. From the beginning, it had been difficult to establish the basis for a national industry. The most successful attempt had been Maurits Binger's Filmfabriek Hollandia [Film Factory Hollandia], but after its collapse in 1923, silent Dutch fiction movies were made only haphazardly. The coming of sound held back production even more: after the failure of *Zeemansvrouwen* (*Sailor's Wives,* 1930) – which had only one spoken line – no Dutch fiction films were produced until 1934.[7] This situation changed dramatically when *The Sailors* triumphantly filled Dutch screens for weeks on end. After this glorious beginning, other entrepreneurs were easily convinced to invest in Dutch film. Between 1934 and 1936, 27 Dutch talkies were made by as many as 21 different production companies. Distributor, exhibitor and producer Loet Barnstijn had so much confidence in the emerging Dutch film industry that he built a fully equipped studio, Filmstad [Film City], which opened in October 1935 boasting state-of-the-art production facilities and equipment, including one of only two electrically driven camera cranes in Europe, according to press reports.[8]

The producers' optimism was not shared by the Dutch press, however, and a divergence of views developed between those journalists who preferred the so-called art or quality film and a minority of commentators who acknowledged that a national film industry needed paying customers, and therefore welcomed every commercially successful Dutch film. After the first wave of positive reviews of *The Sailors*, the more serious newspapers and journals began to take a more critical point of view, and as early as September 1934 they were expressing the hope that Dutch film producers would not continue to invest in low quality movies catering only for the masses. Director Gerard Rutten, who had just received the prize for best cinematography at the Venice Biennale for his film *Dood Water* (*Dead Water*, 1934), predicted that even the masses would eventually be insulted by these films and would turn their backs on Dutch production. Largely shot on location using natural lighting, *Dead Water* strove for documentary realism in its presentation, and Rutten was convinced that his film demonstrated that this realist style of low-budget production, featuring long shots of typical Dutch landscapes and little dialogue, would provide a recipe for successful Dutch films in both the domestic and foreign markets (Cannegieter, 1934). Advocates of art film like Rutten believed that if they were exposed to good examples of more serious genres, the public would eventually come to appreciate them. They could not, however, deny the popularity of the 'wrong' kind of films. When the third Dutch talkie, *Pale Betty*, premiered seven weeks before the Dutch premiere of *Dead Water*, critics of all ideological persuasions and two-thirds of the newspaper reviewers denounced it as another low-class film, but also predicted that the public would love it.[9]

For their part, Dutch producers complained about the negative press they received and defended themselves by arguing that film was first of all a commercial activity. In 1936, the Netherlands Cinema Alliance, which represented distributors and exhibitors, declared in its annual report that 'a certain section of the Dutch press voiced unjustified criticism' of Dutch fiction films.[10] The negative reception of Dutch films was even mentioned in the foreign press. In December 1935, the German trade paper *Der Filmkurier* published an article accusing the leading Dutch newspapers of slaughtering Dutch film, just as they had done previously in attacking Dutch silent film production. The article also suggested that German films had become victims of a Dutch smear campaign, probably referring to a ban on German films proposed by Dutch socialists after Hitler came to power in 1933.[11]

Reviewers' scornful association of high attendances with low quality, especially reviewers in the more serious press, initiated a negative discourse on Dutch film that suggested that the Dutch film industry was only rarely capable of producing a quality film. Historians seeking information about audience preferences can easily be misled by looking at reviews, since a film's critical failure did not by any means result in a failure at the box office. In order to gain an understanding of what audiences went to see without having actual data on the takings of individual cinemas and films, it is necessary to analyse supply as a form of demand. For this purpose, I have taken all films released in the Dutch market between 1934 and 1936 as constituting the supply of product, while the number of screenings of each title is treated as constituting the demand for that film. The relative popularity of each film can be gauged by the frequency of its screenings.

Distribution and Exhibition: The Dutch Film Market 1934–1936

The Netherlands was an open film market, with no quotas or similar restrictions on the number of films that could be imported. Without a national film production industry, limits on importation were in no one's interest, since they would only hurt distributors and exhibitors. In 1934, the Netherlands Cinema Alliance protested fiercely when the government proposed a sharp increase in the import tax on film, and succeeded in convincing the Minister of Finance to maintain the existing 10% tariff.[12] The open Dutch market was dominated by Hollywood, with just over half the films in the data set being produced in the United States (Figure 6.1). Germany was the second largest supplier, with a 26% share, although it had declined rapidly since 1932.[13] The remaining quarter of the Dutch market was very

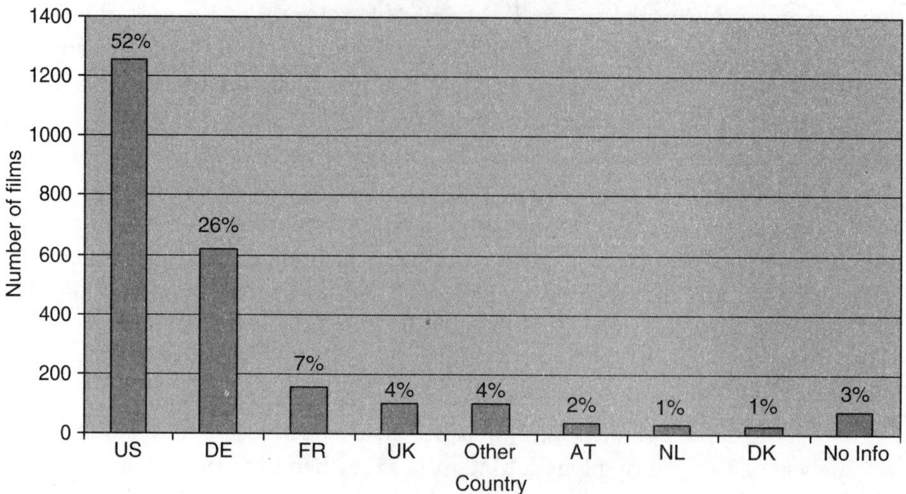

Figure 6.1 Share per country of film titles presented in the Dutch film market, 1934–1936.

fragmented, with the largest other providers being France, with 7%, and Great Britain, with 4%. The Dutch share was an insignificant 1%.[14]

Half the films on the Dutch market were supplied by a few large production companies, while the other half came from many small ones. Only 16 production companies supplied more than 20 films each between 1934 and 1936, but between them these companies, including MGM, Paramount, UFA, Fox Film, Universal and British International Pictures, provided 42% of the total. A further 47% of the market was supplied by 585 other producers, each of which provided fewer than 20 films in the 3-year period. Among these producers were well-known companies such as Pathé-Nathan, Nero Film, Carl Froelich Film, Ariel Film and Majestic Film, but 396 producers supplied only one film in the period. No production information was available for the remaining 10% of the films, but it is most likely that they were also produced by small production companies.

The same pattern is revealed by an analysis of distribution, where there was also a relatively large number of small distributors. According to the list of members of the Netherlands Cinema Alliance, 55 distribution companies supplied the Dutch market, and the data set shows that 28 of these companies distributed fewer than 50 films in the period 1934–1936.[15] Eight companies distributed between 50 and 100 films, four, including Fox Film, between 100 and 150 films. The five largest distributors were UFA (200), the Dutch company Express-Film (192), Paramount (167), the Dutch company City Film (163) and MGM (161); these five companies distributed 37% of all the product in the Dutch market between them, while the half of the market not occupied by Hollywood was fragmented, leaving room for the circulation of many smaller films, including Dutch films.[16]

The number of prints struck of each film indicates the expectations of the distributors and therefore indirectly tells us something about the predicted preferences of the Dutch audience, in that a higher number of prints points to the

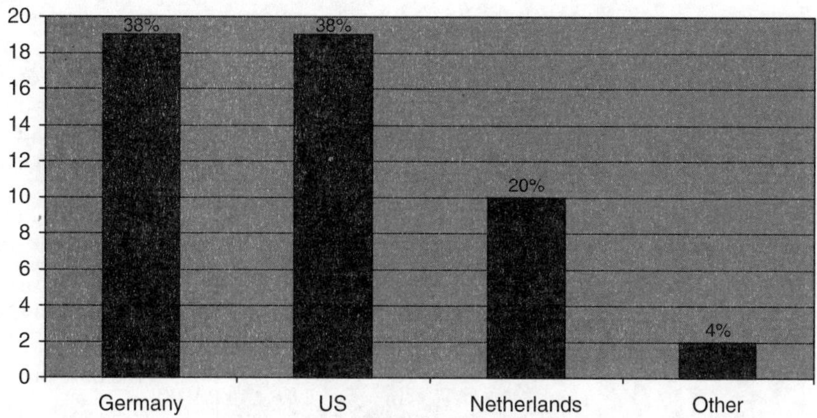

Figure 6.2 Number of films and share per country of the films released with three or more copies.

expectation of a large audience. What did distributors expect from domestic and foreign features? Were Dutch films distributed differently from foreign films, and did their distribution strategy change after the first Dutch films reached the market? In general, the evidence suggests that Dutch distributors did not take much of a risk when distributing a film. For 2090 films (91%) only one copy was initially available, with more copies being made if the film proved successful. This happened in the case of 28% of films. Two copies were initially released for 160 films (7%), and only 31 (1%) had three or more copies.[17] As Figure 6.2 indicates, Dutch films made up a relatively high proportion of this last group.

In analysing distribution strategies for Dutch domestically produced films, I will begin by examining the first three Dutch features released between January and September 1934, and then consider the broader perspective provided by looking at distribution in the whole period to the end of 1936. According to the Dutch press, *William of Orange* was a disappointing production: its cheap sets and poor production values were evident on the large screen, while the acting was theatrical and the tempo of the editing was very slow. Addressing the assembled press and notables at the film's premiere, David Hamburger, chairman of the Netherlands Cinema Alliance, asked the audience to bear in mind the still primitive condition of the Dutch film industry when reviewing the film.[18] As some critics explained in their reviews, this plea for mercy put them in an uncomfortable position: while they did not want to kill the first child of the national film industry, they also did not want to hide their opinions. Most reviewers referred to Hamburger's speech, summarised the film's good parts and ended with a critical note on what could have been done better.[19] Some of them urged their readers to see *William of Orange* as a national duty, because this was a movie about the forefather of the Dutch monarchy.[20] Socialist critics, who opposed the monarchy, ignored the appeal and stressed the film's mistakes and dreadful direction.[21] *William of Orange* premiered simultaneously in four theatres, and this unusually high number of prints points to

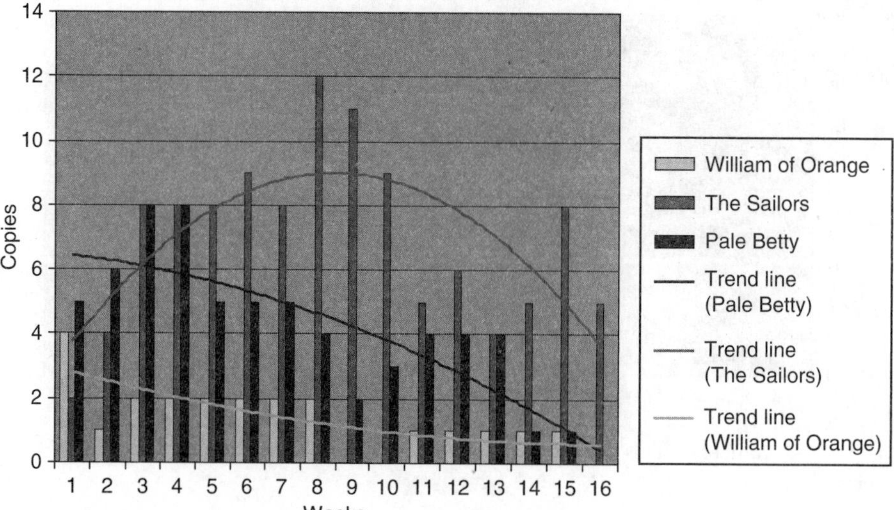

Figure 6.3 Distribution pattern for *William of Orange*, *The Sailors* and *Pale Betty*.

high expectations of box-office success. These expectations, however, belonged only to exhibitor Abraham Tuschinski, who staged simultaneous premieres of the film in three of his nine cinemas.[22] The fourth print was shown in the City Theatre in The Hague, which was owned by one of the film's two distributors.

The Sailors was distributed by Loet Barnstijn's Standaard Film. Barnstijn began with two prints, premiering the film in Amsterdam and The Hague. Within two weeks this had doubled to four prints, and eight weeks after the premiere, 12 prints were being shown at the same time.[23] *The Sailors* also had long runs in cinemas; after 16 weeks four prints were still being shown simultaneously. At the first sign of *The Sailors'* success, Alex Benno, who started to produce *Pale Betty*, the third Dutch feature film, produced and distributed by Monopole Film NV, a film distribution company owned by Max Sprecher, decided to go for multiple prints. Five prints were initially made, with eight prints in circulation in the third week, before dropping off more quickly than had been the case for *The Sailors*. Figure 6.3 shows the number of prints in circulation for the first 16 weeks of release for each of the three films. The trend lines reveal two different distribution patterns: one starting with a high number of copies then falling (*William of Orange* and *Pale Betty*), and the other starting from a low base, rising and then dropping (*The Sailors*).

To see whether distribution strategies changed after the first Dutch talkies had reached the market, Figure 6.4 shows the number of initial prints made of all Dutch feature films that premiered between 1934 and 1936, in chronological order. One film, *De Big van het Regiment* (*The Piglet of the Regiment*, 1935), immediately attracts attention because it was released on 19 April 1935 by Max Sprecher's Monopole Film with the unprecedented number of 13 prints. No explanation was offered in the press for why so many prints – much more than for any film in the

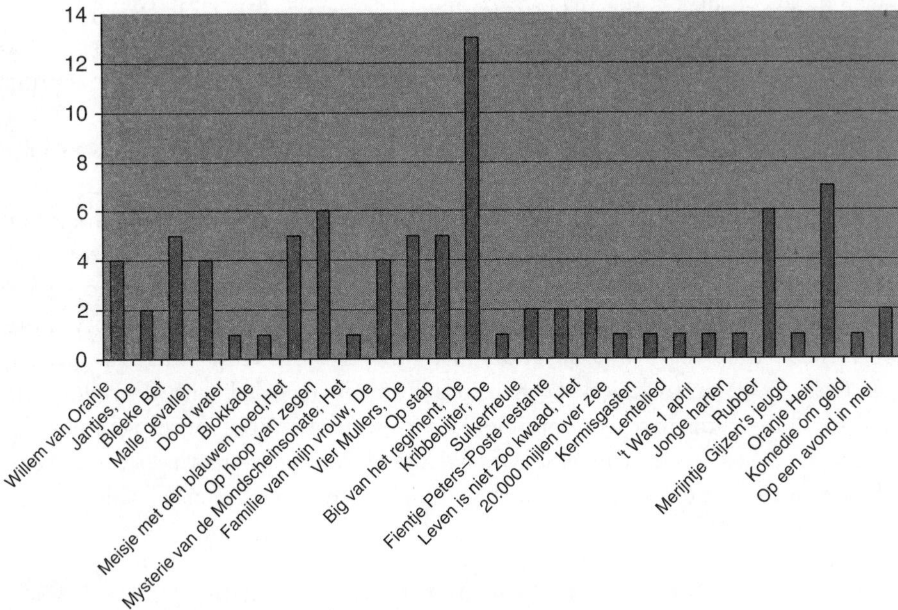

Figure 6.4 Number of premiere copies of Dutch films, 1934–1936.

period – were made, but it was probably the combination of the attractive small boy in the leading role and the fact that Herman Bouber, spiritual father of *The Sailors* and *Pale Betty*, had written the film's dialogue. Certainly circulating this many prints was unusual for Monopole. During this period the company distributed 19 films, of which only three were initially released with more than one print. All three were Dutch: *Pale Betty* (five prints), *The Piglet of the Regiment* (13) and *Oranje Hein* (*Orange Harry*, 1936) (seven), indicating that Monopole's distribution strategy was premised on the attraction of national film products for Dutch audiences and suggesting that Dutch films were expected to do much better at the box office than foreign films.[24]

In 1936, only 3 of the 11 Dutch films premiered were initially released with more than one print, but this was still three times more frequent than the average for the total group, and should not be interpreted as indicating a failing confidence in Dutch features. Rather than a lack of audience interest, it resulted from a change in the type of films being produced. Four of the films with one initial print – *Lentelied* (*Song of Spring*, 1936), *Jonge Harten* (*Young Hearts*, 1936), *Komedie om Geld* (*Comedy on Money*, 1936) and *Merijntje Gijzen's Jeugd* (*The Young Merijntje Gijzen*, 1936) – were 'quality' films, and *The Young Merijntje Gijzen* also featured a main character who was Catholic, which might have been a further occasion for caution.[25] The film *20.000 mijlen over zee* (*20 000 Miles over the Sea*, 1935) was a documentary on the Dutch Navy, and such films were never released in high numbers. Two films raised high expectations: *Rubber* (1936) and *Orange Harry*. *Rubber* was a social drama similar to the 1934 success *Op hoop van zegen* (*In Good Hope*), and like that film was released with six prints. *Orange Harry*, a comedy in the same genre as *The Sailors* and *Pale Betty*, was premiered with the highest number of initial prints (seven) in 1936.

This evidence suggests that distributors expected Dutch comedies to have greater popular appeal than serious or so-called 'quality' films. Quality films were treated in the same way as foreign films, fitting into the normal distribution pattern of an initial release of one or two prints, with more made if demand required. The fall in initial print numbers in 1936 does not indicate that distributors were taking fewer risks, but is instead explained by the fact that more 'quality' films were made that year. In 1934 and 1935, other serious films such as *Blokkade* (*Blockade*, 1934) and *Dead Water* had initially been released with a single print. Almost all the films that were premiered with more than one print were popular comedies. Apart from *William of Orange*, the only exception was *In Good Hope*, which was based on a very popular stage play of the same name.

Measuring Popularity: Programming of Dutch Cinemas, 1934–1936

Information about the supply of films to Dutch cinemas can only tell us what was screened, but not how many screenings of each film there were. The data set provides this other information. More screenings were arranged when a film was expected to do well or when it unexpectedly drew larger audiences, especially in smaller towns. Culemborg, for example, was a small provincial town in the centre of The Netherlands, with 9400 inhabitants and one cinema that only opened for three screenings at weekends. When *The Sailors* played in Culemborg, there were seven shows, and every subsequent Dutch film had additional screenings, although only *Pale Betty* and *Malle gevallen* (*Funny People,* 1934) had as many as seven.

Dutch films took up a much higher proportion of the total number of screenings – 6% – than their percentage of the total number of films shown in The Netherlands during the period. The relationship between the number of screenings and the number of films can be seen as an indicator of demand, and clearly points to the popularity of domestic films. By comparison, American films comprised 52% of films and 53% of screenings, while German films made up 26% of films and 23% of screenings. The total number of screenings of each film in the data set provides a relative scale of popularity. Table 6.1 shows the 20 most frequently screened features in the period. This list suggests that distributors were right to distribute Dutch films with more copies. Seven (35%) of the top 20 were Dutch films, giving the 1% (34) of Dutch films a greater share than American or German films (Figure 6.5).

The popularity of domestic films is even more apparent when the number of films in the top 20 is compared with the total numbers supplied from each country, indicating what percentage of the films from that country were included in the top 20 (Figure 6.6).

Table 6.1 Top 20 most screened films in The Netherlands, 1934–1936.

	Title	Total number of screenings	Year of Production	Country	Director
1	*The Sailors (De Jantjes)*	2514	1934	Netherlands	Jaap Speyer
2	*Modern Times*	1778	1936	US	Charles Chaplin
3	*Bright Eyes*	1751	1934	US	David Butler
4	*Pale Betty (Bleeke Bet)*	1425	1934	Netherlands	Alex Benno and Richard Oswald
5	*Wenn du jung bist, gehört dir die Welt*	1455	1934	Germany	Richard Oswald
6	*The girl with the Blue Hat (Het Meisje met den blauwen hoed)*	1387	1934	Netherlands	Rudolf Meinert
7	*Maternelle, La*	1294	1933	France	Jean Benoît-Lévy and Marie Epstein
8	*In Good Hopes (Op hoop van zegen)*	1117	1934	Netherlands	Alex Benno
9	*Grumpy (De Kribbebijter)*	1111	1935	Netherlands	Henry Koster and Ernst Winar
10	*Devil's Brother*	1105	1933	US	Hal Roach and Charley Rogers
11	*The Little Colonel*	1103	1935	US	David Butler
12	*The Piglet of the Regiment (De big van het regiment)*	1087	1935	Netherlands	Max Nosseck
13	*Funny People*	1075	1934	Netherlands	Jaap Speyer
14	*Ein Stern fällt vom Himmel*	1062	1934	Austria	Max Neufeld
15	*Mazurka*	1035	1935	Germany	Willi Forst
16	*One Night of Love*	989	1934	US	Victor Schertzinger
17	*Mein Herz ruft nach dir*	957	1934	Germany	Carmine Gallone
18	*Vergiss mein nicht*	856	1935	Germany	Augusto Genina
19	*The Lives of a Bengal Lancer*	882	1935	US	Henry Hathaway
20	*Gold*	838	1934	Germany	Karl Hartl

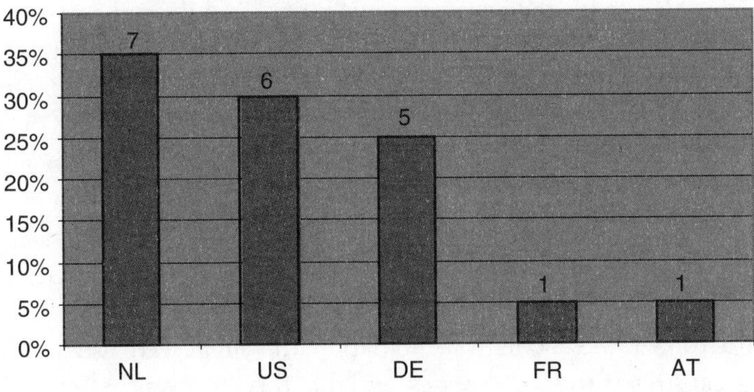

Figure 6.5 Share of countries in top 20 most screened films.

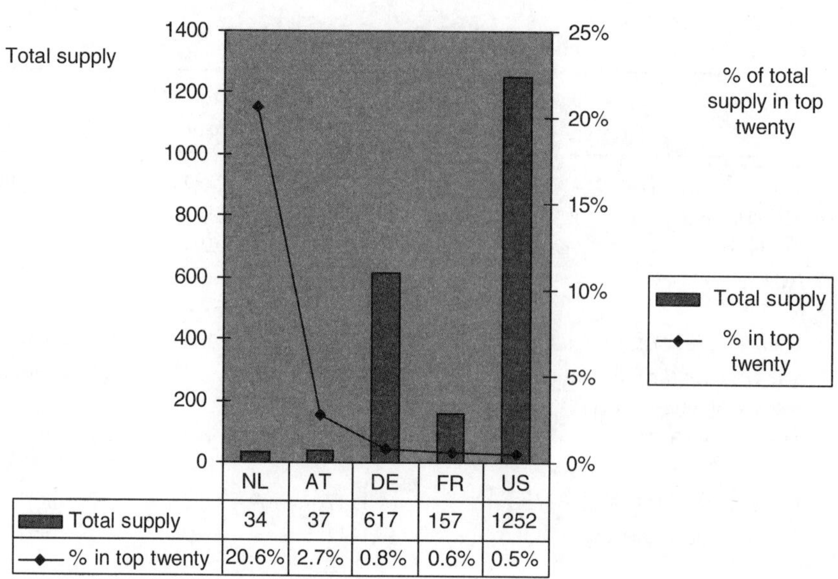

	NL	AT	DE	FR	US
Total supply	34	37	617	157	1252
% in top twenty	20.6%	2.7%	0.8%	0.6%	0.5%

Figure 6.6 Share per country of films in the top 20 most screened films as percentage of the total number of titles offered by a country.

From the total of 34 released Dutch films, seven (slightly over 20%) ended up in the top 20 most screened films, explaining not only why these films were so attractive to Dutch distributors, but also why there was a relative boom in Dutch production after the success of *The Sailors*. Dutch exhibitors and distributors like Alex Benno and Loet Barnstijn were also often involved in the financing of Dutch films. While one might expect significantly lower percentages of American or German films from this method of comparison because of the much greater volume of supply, it is nevertheless safe to conclude that Dutch film was very popular with Dutch audiences.

It is striking that, with the exception of Shirley Temple, none of Hollywood's female stars appear in the list of top 20 films: there are no films starring Marlene Dietrich, Greta Garbo, Mae West or Bette Davis.[26] The only two adult female stars who appear in the list are Hungarian singer and actress Martha Eggerth and Polish actress Pola Negri, who both starred in many German films, suggesting that German stars were more popular in The Netherlands than Hollywood's *femmes fatales*. The same is true for male stars. Apart from comics, only one US star, Gary Cooper, appears in the top 20 list. The other male stars appeared in German films: singer and actor Joseph Schmidt, Hungarian singer and actor Jan Kiepura and Hungarian actor Szöke Szakall. In combination, this suggests that Dutch audiences preferred great singers to star actresses, and that this taste was better catered to by German and Dutch producers than by Hollywood.

Conclusion

In contrast to the impression given by many contemporary reviews and subsequent historical accounts, the evidence from distribution and exhibition patterns suggests very clearly that Dutch movie audiences showed great enthusiasm for Dutch talkies. The most favoured films were optimistic comedies with music, featuring stars of Dutch theatre and revue. These films competed with and often outperformed popular German films in the same genre and lavish Hollywood productions. Although the absence of protective barriers in The Netherlands made it easy for foreign companies to enter the Dutch market, for Dutch distributors this disadvantage was balanced by the fragmentation of the film market. Since there were almost no vertically integrated companies (only UFA owned three theatres), exhibitors were to a large extent free to choose their programmes, and they often chose to screen Dutch films. For Dutch producers, however, fragmentation made it impossible to develop a continuous mode of film production. New finance had to be gathered for every film, and the very small size of the market required that every film be profitable, or else investments were not recovered. This factor made the Dutch film production industry very vulnerable, since the slightest setback could bring disaster. As a result, film production remained an economically very risky business despite the strong demand for domestic films. These conclusions are very much in line with those of other film historians, like John Sedgwick and Joseph Garncarz, who have re-examined the popularity of national films from the perspective of distribution and exhibition. It seems likely that greater attention to the relationship between the supply of films to the market and the demand for each film, as measured by the frequency of its screenings, will provide a significantly more accurate analysis of the relation between Hollywood and domestic films. The results of these enquiries may not change our perception of Hollywood's economic dominance, but it may very well modify our perspective on the extent of Hollywood's cultural dominance of its foreign markets.[27]

Notes

1 This chapter is based on the author's PhD research on the popularity of Dutch film in the thirties. I want to thank Jaap Boter for his great help with the statistics.

2 *De Telegraaf* [*The Telegraph*], 9 February 1934.

3 In Great Britain the Cinematograph Films Act of 1927 obliged exhibitors to show a certain proportion of British films, rising to 10% by 1936. In France the Herriot decree of 1928 stated that for every seven foreign imported films one French film should be made. In Italy all imported films had to be dubbed in Italian. In Germany the Nazi regime restricted Hollywood imports.

4 Little research has been done on the export of Dutch films in this period, but the evidence from the trade press, newspapers, film magazines and the annual reports of the Netherlands Cinema Alliance suggests that Dutch films only rarely penetrated foreign markets. Some producers made attempts to sell their films abroad. *The Sailors*, for example, was shown in Antwerp in Belgium, and Leon Barnstijn also attempted to sell it to England. The film was

also shot in a German version, but this was never finished, apparently because the Dutch actors' German accents were deemed unacceptable.

5 *Jaarverslag van de Nederlandse Bioscoop Bond*, 1939 [*Annual Report of the Netherlands Cinema Alliance*, 1939]. See also Dibbets (1986), p. 244.

6 http://www.cinemacontext.nl. This database contains information about Dutch film programming from 1895 to 1940, and is still expanding.

7 It should, however, be noted that director Gerard Rutten (who was trained in Germany) started shooting *Dead Water* as early as 1932. When the early film footage was destroyed in a fire, he had to start production again.

8 *Nieuw Weekblad voor de Cinematografie* [*New Weekly of Cinematography*], no. 45, 9 August 1935. On *Filmstad* see also Marcel Linneman, 'Loet C. Barnstijn's Filmstad', in *Jaarboek Mediageschiedenis 2* [*Yearbook of Media History*] (Amsterdam: SDU Uitgeverij, 1990), pp. 41–64.

9 In magazines other than journals on popular film and trade papers this negative opinion was even stronger.

10 *Jaarverslag van de Nederlandse Bioscoop Bond*, 1936 [*Annual Report of the Netherlands Cinema Alliance*, 1936], pp. 20–21.

11 Magazines printed by the Arbeiderspers (Labourers' Press) had also called their readers to avoid cinemas where German films were screened. *Jaarverslag van de Nederlandse Bioscoop Bond*, 1933 [*Annual Report of the Netherlands Cinema Alliance*, 1933], pp. 17–18.

12 *Jaarverslag van de Nederlandse Bioscoop Bond*, 1934 [*Annual Report of the Netherlands Cinema Alliance* 1934], pp. 4–6.

13 *Der Filmkurier*, December 1935. *Der Filmkurier* estimated that the German share of the market had fallen from 49% in 1932 to 19% in 1935. This figure is lower than that indicated by the data set, most probably because of a difference in the way films were counted: *Der Filmkurier* provides no information about how it counted films.

14 There is no information (n.i.) available on the country of origin of 3% of the films. The category 'Other' includes countries that supplied only very few films, such as Poland, Czechoslovakia, Sweden and Norway.

15 *Jaarverslag van de Nederlandse Bioscoop Bond*, 1933 [*Annual Report of the Netherlands Cinema Alliance*, 1933].

16 These numbers are extracted from Cinema Context. They include new films and old films, and may require some minor refinement because some films are listed as having two distribution companies.

17 These numbers are based on films that were released between January 1934 and July 1935. This date was chosen so as to be able to follow the distribution pattern after the premiere for a long enough time.

18 *Haagsche Courant*, 5 January 1934.

19 *Haagsche Courant*, 5 January 1934; *Gooi en Eemlander*, 5 January 1934; *De Haagsche Dameskroniek*, 13 January 1934; *Het Centrum*, 6 January 1934.

20 *Arnhemse Courant*, 15 January 1934. The review concluded with the sentences: 'Even as a movie *Prince William of Orange* is worth our full attention, and no one should pass this milestone in our cultural history without pausing a while. Let the people of Arnhem find the Rembrandt theatre!'

21 *Voorwaarts*, 6 January 1934; *Volksblad voor Friesland*, 6 January 1934. The Socialists had called for a revolution right after the Russian Revolution in November 1918. This became known as the failed revolution and was followed by demonstrations of citizens from all over the country expressing their love to the 'endangered' Queen.

22 The three venues were the Grand Theatre in Rotterdam, the Passage in Schiedam and the Tuschinski in Amsterdam.

23 The data set identifies nine copies, but additional research on *The Sailors* has provided the information on the extra three copies.

24 The fourth film was the Austrian film *Heut' ist der schönste Tag in meinem Leben* [*Today Is the Best Day of My Life*], 1936, directed by Richard Oswald.

25 Dibbets argues that in order to be appealing to the largest possible audience, Dutch films had to be neutral on religious matters. *Merijntje Gijzen* is set in a catholic environment. For a full discussion see Karel Dibbets (2006) 'Het taboe van de Nederlandse filmcultuur. Neutraal in een verzuild land' ['The taboo of Dutch film culture. Neutral

in a pillarised society'], *Tijdschrift voor Mediageschiedenis* [*Journal of Media History*], 2, 46–64.

26 Although Marlene Dietrich had started her career in Germany, by 1934 she was promoted as a Hollywood star, as was Garbo, who was born in Sweden.

27 This issue is also discussed, for example, in David W. Ellwood and Rob Kroes *Hollywood in Europe. Experiences of a Cultural Hegemony* (Amsterdam: VU University Press, 1994); Melvin Stokes and Richard Maltby, *Hollywood Abroad. Audiences and Cultural Exchange* (London: BFI, 2004); Geoffrey Nowll-Smith (ed.) *Hollywood and Europe: Economics, Culture, National Identity 1945–1995* (London: British Film Institute, 1998); Thomas Elsaesser (ed.) *European Cinema. Face to Face with Hollywood* (Amsterdam: Amsterdam University Press, 2005).

References

Cannegieter, H.G. (1934) Persoonlijkheden: Gerard Rutten. *Morks-Magazijn*, 36ste jaargang, no. 10, October.

Dibbets, K. (1986) Het bioscoopbedrijf tussen twee wereldoorlogen [Cinema business in the interbellum period], in *Geschiedenis van de Nederlandse Film en Bioscoop tot 1940* [*The History of Dutch Film and Cinema until 1934*] (eds K. Dibbets and F. van der Maden), Het Wereldvenster, Houten, pp. 229–270.

Dibbets, K. (1993) *Sprekende films. De komst van de geluidsfilm in Nederland, 1928–1933* [*Talking Pictures, The Introduction of Sound Film in the Netherlands, 1928–1933*], Cramwinckel, Amsterdam.

Dittrich, K. (1986) De speelfilm in de jaren dertig [The feature film in the 1930s], in *Geschiedenis van de Nederlandse Film en Bioscoop tot 1940* [*The History of Dutch Film and Cinema until 1934*] (eds K. Dibbets and F. van der Maden), Het Wereldvenster, Houten, pp. 107–144.

Garncarz, J. (1994) Hollywood in Germany: the role of American films in Germany, in *Hollywood in Europe. Experiences of a Cultural Hegemony* (eds D.W. Ellwood and R. Kroes), VU University Press, Amsterdam, pp. 94–135.

Sedgwick, J. (2000) *Popular Filmgoing in 1930s Britain. A Choice of Pleasures*, University of Exeter Press, Exeter.

7

Patterns in First-Run and Suburban Filmgoing in Sydney in the mid-1930s

John Sedgwick

Within the materialist framework of a capitalist economy, in which the generation of profits is a key motivation, what Noel Carroll has termed 'mass produced art' blossomed, enabling talent with artistic and technical capabilities to create accessible commodities of an aesthetic and narrative nature that met audiences' demand for novelty (Carroll, 1998). The lineages of film art that developed were never far removed from the economic relations between the various agents of its production and circulation. Exploiting the technologies of mass reproduction and a transport system that made mass distribution possible, the film industry was built upon the mass popular appeal of its products. While the profit imperative has certainly influenced the artistic development of public presentations of non-filmic art, literature, theatre, classical music and classical ballet for at least the past 300 years, the scale of consumption of these 'cultural' commodities was of a different order of magnitude, commonly comprising much smaller and more affluent sections of the population, and the aesthetic lineages that emerged were more strongly influenced by opinion leaders.

The phenomenon of cinema's mass popularity was central to its development, and followed a common pattern, characterised across cultures and territories by a small number of 'hit' movies outperforming averagely popular films by considerable margins. The films that were popular with audiences differed from territory to territory, however, giving us insights into the comparative tastes of audiences in particular localities at particular moments in time. Furthermore, the intensity of filmgoing also differed from territory to territory, drawing attention to non-filmic forces at play. A number of methodological developments have made it possible to study the process by which audiences express preferences for, and between, ever changing flows of recently released films. This chapter discusses the contribution that economic reasoning and statistical methods can make to our understanding of the circulation and consumption of films in different but connected markets, and thus to our understanding of audience tastes and the culture of cinemagoing.

Explorations in New Cinema History: Approaches and Case Studies, First Edition.
Edited by Richard Maltby, Daniel Biltereyst and Philippe Meers.

Data on Filmgoing and Popularity

There are two ways of coming to data about filmgoing. Secondary sources such as government inquiries, entertainment tax returns and trade journals are often rich in data collected for contemporary information and analysis, providing an overview of the film business, whereas primary sources such as newspaper advertisements of cinema programmes draw attention to the practices of exhibitors and audiences in particular localities. In the case of secondary data, Simon Rowson used tax returns to produce his epic account of the British film industry in 1934 (Rowson, 1936). In the English-speaking world, the government inquiries in Australia in 1928, Canada, and New Zealand in 1934, the Marks Inquiry in New South Wales in 1934, the Committee of the Board of Trade in London in 1935, and the US Congressional Hearings in 1936 are all exemplary sources of contemporary evidence and opinion from which important details can be learned about the way the film business operated and the manner in which its various sectional interests competed with one another.[1] Complementing these sources, trade journals such as *Film Daily*, *Motion Picture Herald* and *Variety* in the United States, and *Kinematograph Weekly* in Great Britain, and their associated yearbooks, the *Film Daily Yearbook*, the *International Motion Picture Almanac* and the *Kine Yearbook*, provide lists of agencies, tables of business information and reviews of films on release – generally from an exhibitor viewpoint – that are indispensable for the researcher.[2]

While the use of these secondary sources has been an established practice in cinema history for some time, the more recent growth of interest in audiences and the reception of films has led researchers to draw on local records, such as newspaper advertisements, street and business directories, cinema licensing details, and the Watch Committee reports of local councils. In the United States, Kathryn Fuller and Gregory Waller have produced detailed accounts of cinemagoing in small communities before the outset of World War II; the contributions of Robert Allen, Arthur Knight and Jeffrey Klenotic to this volume also address this issue (Waller, 1995; Fuller, 1996). Outside the United States, research teams based at the Universities of Amsterdam and Utrecht in The Netherlands, Siegen in Germany, Birkbeck College, London University, in the United Kingdom, the Universities of Ghent and Antwerp in Belgium, Flinders University, RMIT, and the University of Wollongong in Australia, and Masaryk University, Brno, in the Czech Republic, have won national research funding to build large databases recording the location of cinemas, and their programmes, across multiple communities at various periods during the twentieth century.[3] From such work it will be possible to provide a very firm empirical framework by which to identify and understand cinemagoing practices within and across communities, and then territories.

My research has been principally concerned with measuring the popularity of films, using quantitative approaches to the analysis of data, particularly when, as is usually the case, exact figures on audience numbers or box-office takings are unavailable. Using cinema advertisements found in local evening newspapers, I have compiled data sets drawing upon the programmes of first-run cinemas in various

English and Scottish cities during the 1930s, and all cinemas in the towns of Bolton, Brighton and the small city of Portsmouth. In a separate project with Mark Glancy and Michael Pokorny, I have constructed a data set based on *Variety*'s weekly reporting of the box-office takings of first-run cinemas in cities across the United States during the 1930s (Sedgwick and Pokorny, 2005a; Glancy and Sedgwick, 2007). These investigations have sought to achieve three aims: to identify statistical patterns of film popularity; to produce tables of films screened in and across localities ranked by their popularity; and to explain, from this evidence, how the system of distribution and exhibition was geared to screening films that audiences wanted to see. If the trade press in Great Britain had carried the box-office records of first-run cinemas in the same way *Variety* did in the United States, recourse to the advertised cinema programmes would have been superfluous. The absence of such box-office records led me to formulate the POPSTAT Index of Film Popularity as a way of dealing with the problem that different cinemas had different seating capacities and charged different prices, meaning that different screenings of a film in different cinemas generated different levels of revenue for the exhibitor. By multiplying a cinema's seating capacity by its mid-range ticket price, POPSTAT estimates the potential box-office revenue of each cinema in a given population of cinemas (e.g. a city or a region), and expresses this as a proportion of the mean box-office potential of the population of cinemas to give a numerical weighting to each cinema's relative commercial status. Using this relative measure of potential revenue, it is possible to approximate more closely the box-office earnings of each film in each population of cinemas.[4]

The research questions I ask and the methods I have developed are closely associated with my training as an economic historian. Colleagues from different disciplinary backgrounds are likely to ask different types of questions, and develop different methods of investigation, producing analyses that differ in scope from my own. The contributions to this book signal that much of the new work on film audiences is unified not by *a priori* high theory, but by a pragmatic evidence-based methodology that facilitates wide-ranging questions and forms of analysis, calling upon a range of disciplines and employing an array of approaches to make the best use of the available evidence.[5]

The most common account of the system of film distribution used until the 1970s explains its operation in terms of the principle of price discrimination. Distributors sought to insert each film into the exhibition hierarchy at the highest available point, in order to secure maximum revenue from those audiences willing to pay more to see it sooner rather than later. Having kept the film in the most profitable venues for as long as it achieved a minimum earning threshold, distributors then cascaded the film down the sequence of exhibition 'runs', maximising its earnings at each tier of the system before dropping to the next. The principle of price discrimination provides a very good explanation of the practice of restricted release to box-office-rich first-run metropolitan cinemas. In researching the film programmes of London West End and provincial city first-run cinemas in Great Britain during the 1930s, however, I became aware that it might not apply so strongly once those films were subsequently distributed to the string of suburban cinemas in the same cities (Sedgwick, 2000). In particular, my studies of filmgoing in Bolton, Brighton and Portsmouth showed that it was highly unusual for a film, when first released, to be held over for a second week, and that beyond the round of second-run cinemas, films were normally screened on double-bill, twice-weekly-change programmes (Sedgwick, 2006). With such a rapid turnover of films, to what extent can any film be said to be more popular than any other film, especially if, as is often supposed, audiences were less discriminating at the lower runs of the distribution/exhibition chain? The research described in this chapter is my first investigation of the diffusion of films across a metropolitan entity.[6] It builds on my earlier work and serves as an example of the kind of incremental advance that evidence-based research can lead to.

Set in Sydney in 1934, the research compares patterns of film distribution and popularity, based upon the exhibition records of all 11 first-run cinemas, four of the eight city-centre second-run cinemas, and 65 of the city's 160 suburban cinemas.[7] At the time, Sydney, with a population of 1 275 000, was the 13th largest city in the world and the second largest in the British Empire, comprising close to 20% of the population of Australia (Commonwealth Bureau of Census and Statistics, 1936, p. 404).

The First-Run Market for Films in Sydney in 1934

Kristin Thompson has shown that during the 1920s the major Hollywood studios set up in-house distribution networks in Australia, with headquarters in Sydney and Melbourne (Thompson, 1985). At this time, two national cinema chains, Hoyts and Union Theatres, emerged, coming to dominate the exhibition sector in the State capitals, and coexisting with a set of much smaller suburban and rural chains and a multitude of independent exhibitors. By 1934 the two chains had merged to form General Theatres Corporation (GTC) in which Fox had a major interest (Shirley and Adams, 1983, p. 107). GTC was dominant in the city centres of the Australian State capitals, while Hoyts' strength was in the metropolitan suburbs.[8] Table 7.1 shows just how dominant GTC was in Sydney's first-run market, holding 72% of the seats.

The trade journal *Everyones* is a particularly important source of information. In addition to the cinema seating capacities, screenings per day and admission prices reported in Table 7.1, the trade journal also recorded the weekly box-office takings of each cinema as a percentage of the cinema's mean weekly takings over the previous 52 weeks, enabling me to reconstruct the pattern of earnings of any single programme over the course of its run. Equipped with information on the size and pricing structure of the cinema, it was then possible to calculate the relative box-office performance of each film being screened there. While I have not had access to the raw data from which these percentages were calculated, it is logical to assume that the actual box-office for any week in 1934 was compared with the mean weekly value for 1933. As a consequence, it is possible to build this measure of relative popularity into the formula by which the POPSTAT Index can be calculated:

Table 7.1 Sydney city centre's first-run cinemas in 1934.

Cinema	*Owner/ operator*	*First licensed*	*Seating capacity*	*Admission prices*[a]	*Screenings per day*	*No. of films screened in 1934*
Capitol	GTC	1928	2752	1/– to 2/7	4	104
State	GTC	1929	2678	1/– to 4/3	4	36
Regent	GTC	1928	2120	1/– to 3/2	4	60
Civic	GTC	1916	1802	1/– to 3/2	4	49
St James	Fuller/MGM	1926	1684	1/– to 4/7	4	25
Plaza	GTC	1930	1589	1/6 to 3/2	4	33
Lyceum	GTC	1909	1402	1/– to 3/2	4	29
Mayfair	Fullers	1909	1370	1/– to 2/6	4	26
Prince Edward	Carroll-Musgrave	1924	1355	1/– to 4/3	4	34
Embassy	GTC	1934	992	1/– to 5/4	4	11
Liberty	Imperial	1934	657	1/– to 4/3	3	16

Sources: *Inquiry into the Film Industry of NSW*, 1934, paras 84, 151, 177; *Daily Telegraph*; *Sydney Morning Herald*; *Everyones*, in the section 'At the box-office'.

[a]Prices are in shillings and pence, where for example 1/– = one shilling and 4/7 = four shillings and seven pence. There were 20 shillings in one pound and 12 pence to each shilling.

$$POPSTAT_{it} = \sum_{j=1}^{n_i} \sum_{k=1}^{k_i} \mathbf{w}_j \star \mathbf{bo}_{ijk} \star \mathbf{bs}_{ij}$$

POPSTAT is designed to develop a series of index numbers by which the relative popularity of individual films can be measured in a given set or population of cinemas over the period under investigation. It is important to recognise that the index numbers in any given POPSTAT series are significant only in relation to each other; their absolute values result from the information available, and are not a direct expression of box-office earnings. The POPSTAT formula will vary, depending on the nature of the information available; in this case, for example, *Everyones* provides more detail on the performance of films in Sydney's first-run cinemas than is available for the suburban-run cinemas, and so the POPSTAT formula for the first-run cinemas has more terms in it. In both versions of the formula, however, the following terms are constant:

n is the number of cinemas in the set under consideration (11 in the case of Sydney's first-run cinemas);
t is the duration of the investigation;
i is an individual film.

So, $POPSTAT_{it}$ is the Film Popularity Index for each film screened during the duration (t) of the investigation.

j is an individual cinema;
w is the 'weight' of a cinema, or the numerical expression of its relative box-office potential compared to the other cinemas in the set.

So, w_j is the weight of an individual cinema.

In the version of POPSTAT used to measure relative popularity in the Sydney first-run market:

k is an individual week in the period under investigation.

So, bo_{ijk} is the box-office performance of each film at each cinema during each week of its exhibition there. Using the data in *Everyones*, this box-office performance is expressed as a percentage of the mean box-office of that cinema, where 100% equals the mean.

bs_{ij} is the billing status of each film at each cinema. Billing status is expressed as: 1.0 for a single billing, 0.8 for the main attraction, 0.2 for a support attraction, and 0.5 for a shared (i.e., equal attraction) billing.

For each film at each cinema, the POPSTAT formula multiplies the weight of the cinema by the film's box-office performance for each week it played at that cinema, and by the film's billing status to derive the film's index score for that theatre for that week. (In the formula, '*' is used instead of '×' to indicate multiplication.) If a film received more than one booking, the index scores of each booking would be summed in order to derive its POPSTAT Index value.

The symbol Σ signifies the instruction to sum the values of the expression that follows it (in this case a product of three terms) over the range of the variable indicated below and above the symbol. The double symbol, Σ Σ, indicates that in this instance the values result from two distinct ranges of variation, corresponding to the two variables j and k.

For instance, *Little Women* (1933) was the third highest scoring film in Sydney's first-run cinemas. It was screened at the State Theatre as a single-bill attraction for five consecutive weeks from late March 1934. The price range and seating capacity shown in Figure 7.1 generate a cinema weight of 1.84368 for the State. The weekly viewing data provided by *Everyones*, expressed as a percentage of the cinema's average for the five weeks, are respectively 200, 200, 170, 135 and 110. As a single-bill feature, the billing weight is 1. Thus the POPSTAT Index value garnered by *Little Women* at the State is calculated as follows: (1.84368*200*1) + (1.84368*200*1) + (1.84368*170*1) + (1.84368*135*1) + (1.84368*110*1) = 1497

Table 7.2 lists the descriptive statistics of the 491 films screened at the 11 Sydney first-run cinemas in 1934, including those films that were premiered in 1933 but received the bulk of their subsequent billings in suburban cinemas during 1934. The statistics are depicted visually in Figure 7.1. Expressed in statistical terms, this is a highly skewed frequency distribution, with a long right tail, in which the median and mean both fall into the first decile group, and the standard deviation is greater than the mean. In plainer terms, this means that only a very small number of films enjoyed the considerable revenues that accrued to the 'hits' of

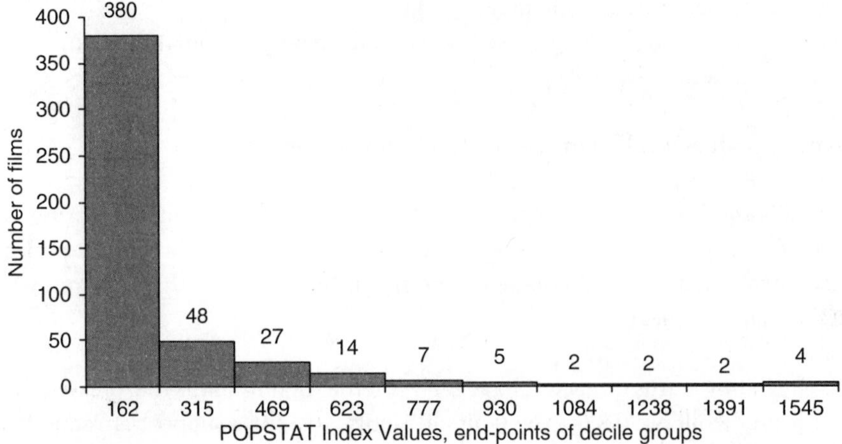

Figure 7.1 Histogram showing the frequency distribution of POPSTAT values for films screened in Sydney's first-run cinemas, organised into decile groups.

Table 7.2 Statistical characteristics of the distribution of POPSTAT values of 491 films released in late 1933 and 1934.

Statistic	*POPSTAT values*
Mean	155
Median	74
Standard deviation	225
Range	1538
Minimum	7
Maximum	1545
Sum	76 253
Count	491

the year. The most successful 30 films (or 0.6% of the total number of films exhibited) generated 35% of the total POPSTAT values for the year, and the top 59 films generated as much as the remaining 432 films put together. This skewed frequency distribution follows a very similar pattern to those derived from datasets of US and British first-run cinemas published in my work with Michael Pokorny, and presented in Figure 7.2. This recurring pattern of highly unequal distributions of box-office revenues, which we have termed an empirical regularity, has shaped the manner in which the film industry has been organised, and provides the underlying economic explanation for the industry's reputation as a high-risk environment (Sedgwick and Pokorny, 2005b, pp. 15–16).

The top-earning 30 films grouped in the upper decile reaches of the frequency distribution depicted in Figure 7.1 are listed in Table 7.3. One of the most revealing

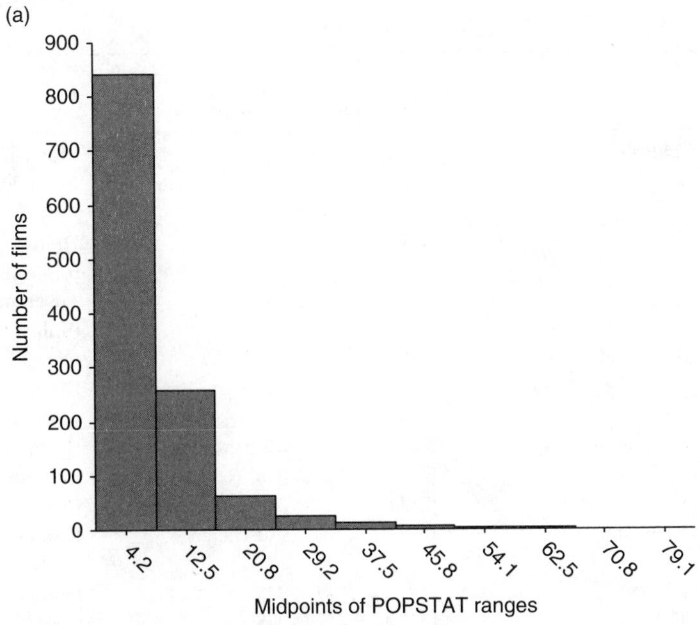

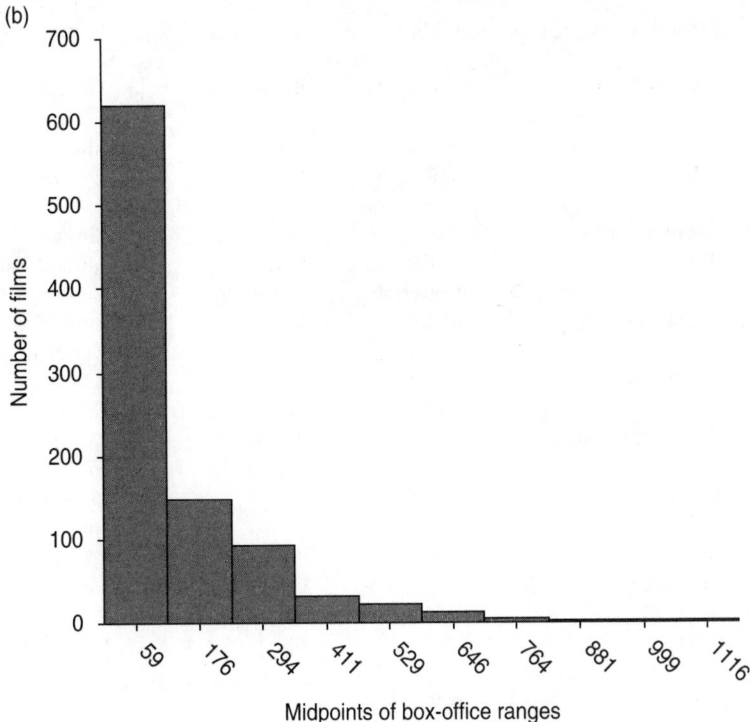

Figure 7.2 Histogram showing the frequency distribution of (a) POPSTAT values for films screened in first-run British cinemas, and (b) US box-office values for films screened in US first-run cinemas in the mid-1930s.

Table 7.3 Top 30 films screened in Sydney's first-run cinemas in 1934.

Rank	*Film*	*Studio*	*Distributor*	*Nationality*	*Genre*
1	*One Night of Love*	Columbia	GAF	US	Musical/romance
2	*Paddy The Next Best Thing*	Fox	Fox	US	Comedy
3	*Little Women*	RKO	RKO	US	Drama/family/romance
4	*The Count of Monte Cristo*	Reliance	UA	US	Adventure/drama/thriller
5	*Squatter's Daughter*	Cinesound	BEF	Australian	Drama
6	*Tell Me Tonight*	F&S [Fellner & Somlo]	GAF	German/British	Comedy/drama/musical
7	*I Was A Spy*	Gaumont British	Fox	British	Drama
8	*Roman Scandals*	Goldwyn	UA	US	Comedy
9	*The Hayseeds*	J.C. Williamson	BEF	Australian	Comedy/musical
10	*The Silence Of Dean Maitland*	Cinesound	BEF	Australian	Drama
11	*The Masquerader*	Goldwyn	UA	US	Drama
12	*Dinner At Eight*	MGM	MGM	US	Comedy/drama/romance
13	*It Happened One Night*	Columbia	GAF	US	Romance/comedy
14	*Private Life Of Henry VIII*	London Films	UA	British	Drama
15	*Gold Diggers of 1933*	WB	WB	US	Musical
16	*The Affairs of Voltaire*	WB	WB	US	Drama
17	*Evergreen*	Gaumont British	Fox	British	Musical
18	*Blossom Time*	BIP	BEF	British	Musical/romance
19	*Ticket In Tatts*	Efftee	Universal	Australian	Comedy
20	*Dancing Lady*	MGM	MGM	US	Musical/comedy/romance
21	*Treasure Island*	MGM	MGM	US	Adventure
22	*Riptide*	MGM	MGM	US	Drama
23	*Good Companions*	Gaumont British	Fox	British	Comedy/musical/romance
24	*Queen Christina*	MGM	MGM	US	Biography/drama/romance
25	*Red Wagon*	BIP	BEF	British	Drama
26	*I'm No Angel*	Paramount	Paramount	US	Comedy/musical/romance
27	*Flying Down To Rio*	RKO	RKO	US	Comedy/musical/romance
28	*The Working Man*	WB	WB	US	Drama/comedy
29	*Only Yesterday*	Universal	Universal	US	Drama/romance
30	*Falling For You*	Gainsborough	Fox	British	Comedy/musical

Star 1	*Star 2*	*Cinema*	*Date*	*Length of run (weeks)*	*POPSTAT Index*
Moore, G	Carminati, T	Liberty	24 Dec 34	39	1545
Gaynor, J	Baxter, W	State	18 Dec 33	6	1528
Hepburn, K	Bennet, J	State	26 Mar 34	5	1497
Donat, R	Landi, E	State	17 Dec 34	6	1442
Worth, C	Lyndsay, G	Civic	2 Oct 33	9	1324
Kiepura, J	Hale, S	Mayfair	12 Jun 33	20	1316
Carroll, M	Marshall, H	Lyceum	22 Jan 34	12	1151
Cantor, E	Etting, R	State	18 Jun 34	5	1131
Kellaway, C	Towers, K	Civic	11 Dec 33	8	1063
Longden, J	Francis, C	State(3)/Civic(4)	28 May 34	7	970
Colman, R	Landi, E	Regent	30 Apr 34	7	872
Dressler, M	Barrymore, J	St James	30 Oct 33	8	841
Gable, C	Colbert, C	Plaza	6 Aug 34	8	822
Laughton, C	Donat, R	Embassy	4 Jun 34	7	788
Warren, W	Blondell, J	State	30 Oct 33	4	786
Arliss, G	Kenyon, D	State	27 Aug 34	4	705
Matthews, J	Hale, S	Embassy	23 Jul 34	9	687
Tauber, R	Baxter, J	Embassy	15 Oct 34	9	675
Wallace, G		Civic	23 Apr 34	6	671
Crawford, J	Gable, C	St James	22 Jan 34	5	669
Beery, W	Cooper, J	St James	17 Dec 34	4	663
Shearer, N	Marshall, H	St James	9 Jul 34	5	645
Matthews, J	Gwenn, E	Prince Edward	18 Sep 33	7	618
Garbo, G	Gilbert, J	St James	26 Mar 34	5	608
Bickford, C	Hanley, J	Civic	26 Mar 34	4	593
West, M	Grant, C	Prince Edward	12 Mar 34	8	591
Del Rio, D	Raymond, G	Plaza	23 Apr 34	4	567
Arliss, G	Davis, B	Prince Edward	7 Aug 33	6	562
Sullavan, M	Boles, J	Liberty	2 Apr 34	12	561
Hulbert, J	Courtneidge, C	Lyceum	13 Nov 33	6	543

aspects of the investigation was the extent to which British- and Australian-made films were screened in Sydney's first-run cinemas. Indeed, of the 11 cinemas, three of the smaller venues – the Embassy, Lyceum and Mayfair cinemas – were given over exclusively to exhibiting British features, while the Civic screened all of the major Australian releases. Five British films were included in the Top 20, and a further three in the Top 30, but even more remarkable was the performance of Australian production companies, taking four of the Top 20 berths. The major Hollywood distributors had somewhat restricted access to the Sydney first-run market, and this became a major issue in the inquiry preceding the Marks Report in 1934. Nevertheless, it is difficult to discount the suggestion that cultural associations played a strong part in first-run audiences revealing a strong liking for home-made and British films.[9]

The Suburban Market for Films in Sydney in 1934

The pattern of film distribution in the Sydney suburbs involved a diffusion outwards from box-office-rich cinemas, often in more prosperous inner city suburbs, such as the 2165-seater Star, Bondi Junction, and the 1553-seater Arcadia, Chatswood, to box-office-poor cinemas in the outer suburbs such as the 988-seater Cinema, Merrylands, and the 1100-seater Mortdale Theatre, Mortdale. The suburban data set consists of 65 suburban cinemas, sourced from a table found daily on page 2 of the *Sydney Morning Herald*, plus four inner-city cinemas that served as second-run cinemas, receiving films in the distribution chain concurrently with the major suburban cinemas.[10] Between them the 69 cinemas in the list provided audiences with a total of 105 933 seats, giving a mean seating density of 1581 seats per cinema.[11] The locations of the suburban cinemas have been identified using *Gregory's Street Directory of 1936*. The cinemas are split 40 to 25 between inner and outer suburbs, with 25 cinemas located in the southern, 18 in the western, 15 in the northern, and 7 in the eastern suburbs. The main chains were Broadway Theatres with six cinemas; GTC-Hoyts with 13; and Western Suburban Cinemas with 10. Of the remainder, most were owned by a single proprietor, although the exhibition records of these cinemas suggest that many of them booked their programmes through one of the chains.

Table 7.4 indicates that the overwhelming majority (93%) of programmes screened at suburban cinemas during 1934 were double bills, changed twice weekly. Of the 13 820 film bookings, only 61 (19 whole-week and 42 half-week bookings) were screened as single-bill attractions. The number of whole-week programmes was more substantial, but this figure is considerably bolstered by the inclusion in the data set of the two city second-run cinemas, each of which ran weekly programmes. In the suburbs, other than the newly opened (September 1934) 600-seat King's cinema, the only cinemas that frequently ran whole-week programmes were the Star, Bondi Junction; the Arcadia, Chatswood; and the Kinema, Mosman.

Table 7.4 Suburban data-set characteristics.

Films screened at least once in 1934	733
Films screened as single-bill attractions for one week	19
Films screened on double-bill programmes for one week	910
One week double-bill programmes	455
Total single-week programmes	**474**
Films screened as single-bill attractions for a half week	42
Films screened on double-bill programmes for a half week	12 840
Half-week double-bill programmes	**6420**
Films screened on a treble-bill programme for a half week	9
Half-week treble-bill programmes	**3**
Total film bookings	13 820
Total programmes	**6897**

With the seating capacities of these cinemas ranging from 540 to 2599, the cinemas in the sample, like those in the first-run sample, would have generated quite different levels of revenue for their owners and the film distributors. As with the first-run sample, my solution has been to give cinemas weights based upon each cinema's revenue potential expressed as an average of the set. Unfortunately, as admission prices and the number of screenings at these cinemas are not known, the weights are, in effect, based upon the cinemas' relative seating capacity, and this requires that I assume that all cinemas in the suburban sample ran a common number of screenings per week, and charged a common range of admission prices. As with the first-run houses, it also assumes that all cinemas experienced the same seat utilisation ratios, irrespective of what film programme was being screened. The biases implicit in these assumptions will underestimate the relative earnings of films being screened in those better accoutred and larger cinemas such as the Star, Bondi Junction, which got their films earlier and probably had higher seat utilisation statistics, than films being shown in smaller and less well furnished cinemas screening films towards the end of their runs, such as the Mortdale Theatre, Mortdale.[12]

The POPSTAT formula on this occasion is somewhat simpler. The crude cinema weight is now multiplied by the length of run in weeks and the billing status of the film. Because of the absence of information in the source data to indicate otherwise, each film on a double-bill programme is assumed to be equally attractive to audiences, and given a billing status value of 0.5. Thus the ith film being screened at the jth cinema with, say, a weight of 1, on a single-bill programme for 1 week, generates the index value of 1 (1*1*1) for that billing, which, when added to the index values generated at each of the $(n - 1)$ other cinemas at which the film was screened constitutes that film's POPSTAT index value:

$$POPSTAT_{it} = \sum_{j=1}^{n_i} w_j \star bs_{ij} \star l_{ij}$$

In this version of the formula, as before:

n is the number of cinemas in the set under consideration (65).

$POPSTAT_{it}$ is the Film Popularity Index for each film (i) screened during the duration (t) of the investigation.

So, w_j is the 'weight' of an individual cinema (j);
bs_{ij} is the billing status of each film at each cinema: 0.5 for a shared billing, 1.0 for a single billing;
l_{ij} is the length of each film's run at each cinema.

For each film at each cinema, the POPSTAT formula multiplies the weight of the cinema by the film's billing status and by the length of the film's run, to derive the film's index score for that theatre for that week. (In the formula, '*' is used instead of '×' to indicate multiplication.) Again, if a film received more than one booking, the index scores of each booking would be summed in order to derive its POPSTAT Index value. The symbol Σ sums this expression in the way explained in the previous example of POPSTAT.

Using the exhibition experience of a single film as an illustration, *Little Women* received 32.5 booking weeks in Sydney's suburban cinemas. It opened in early June 1934 at nine cinemas. One of these was the Star, in the suburb of Bondi, where it played as a single feature for a 1-week booking. The Star was a 2165-seat cinema and based on this has a weight of 1.364047. Thus the POPSTAT index value for this booking was 1.364047, the result of the formula (1.36407*1*1).

Even though films were screened on multiple occasions as they diffused through the suburban cinema circuit, it is immediately noticeable that the range of POPSTAT values in the suburban data set is much smaller than in its first-run counterpart found in Table 7.2. The higher numerical range of the first-run data set can be explained through the inclusion in the POPSTAT formula of the weekly average performance data published by *Everyones* for each film exhibited in a first-run cinema, expressed as a percentage of the cinema's weekly average. However, for comparative purposes, because each POPSTAT series is in effect a series of index numbers, what is important is the relative, not the absolute, values in each series.

Of greater significance, the statistics in Table 7.5 indicate a much less unequal distribution of POPSTAT Index values than that found in Table 7.2, and displayed in Figure 7.1. Here, the standard deviation is less than the mean, and the median and mean values are close, both falling into the third decile of Figure 7.3, and suggesting a bimodal distribution, with a second peak occurring in the fifth decile. This indicates an altogether different pattern of film distribution to that depicted in Figure 7.1.

Table 7.5 Statistical characteristics of the distribution of POPSTAT values of the suburban data set.

Statistic	*POPSTAT values*
Mean	5.10
Median	4.91
Standard deviation	4.41
Range	20.46
Minimum	0.09
Maximum	20.54
Sum	3737
Count	733

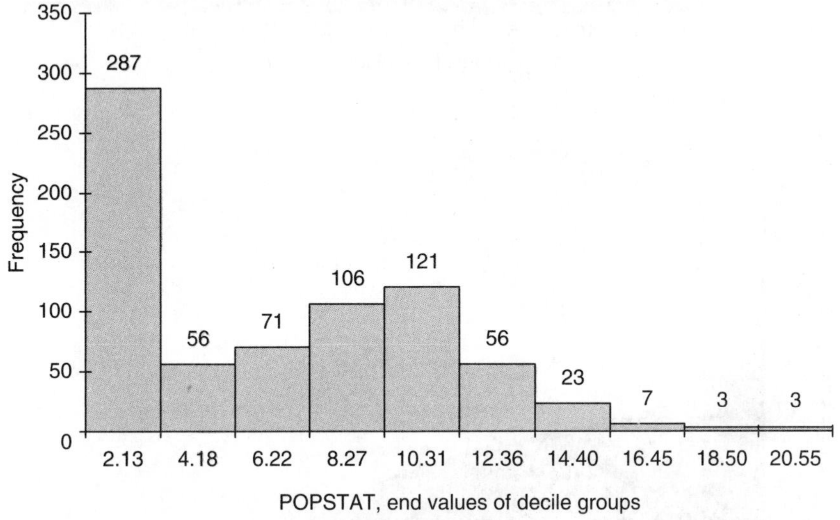

Figure 7.3 Histogram showing the frequency distribution of POPSTAT values for films screened in Sydney's suburban cinemas, organised into decile groups.

Differences Between First-Run and Suburban-Run Markets

In Figure 7.4 films are placed in rank order – from highest to lowest – according to the POPSTAT Index values they generated, illustrating the rate at which POPSTAT values decline with rank. Figure 7.4a is drawn from the first-run market and shows that following an initial precipitous rate of decline, POPSTAT values fell in a pattern of decrements that results in a smooth curve, not unlike that of a rectangular hyperbola in form. The shape of the POPSTAT curve in Figure 7.4b differs markedly from this. Here the POPSTAT curve shows two steep declines separated by a much flatter section associated with the bulge of 177 films contained within the fifth and sixth decile groups of Figure 7.3.

(a)

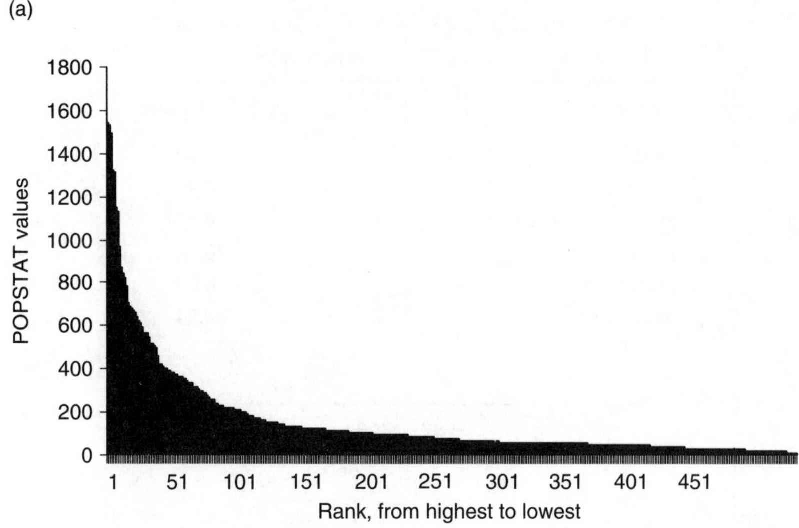

(b)

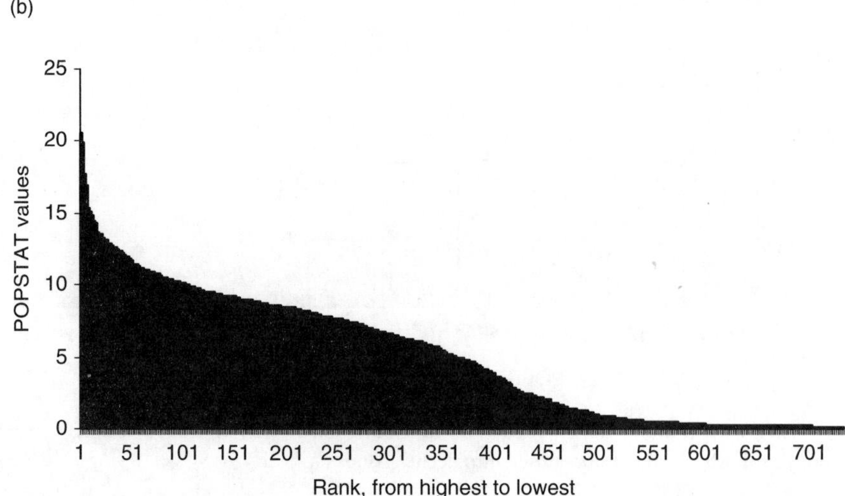

Figure 7.4 The distribution of (a) first-run POPSTAT values and (b) suburban POPSTAT values by ranked order of films.

Although perhaps perplexing at first sight, the plethora of statistics associated with the two sets of diagrams derived from the first-run and suburban cinema data sets provides evidence that the two markets were quite different in form. Whereas the first-run market was organised around the principle of allocating screen time to films according to their popularity, the suburban market was geared to ensuring that the bulk of cinemas operating double-bill programmes changing twice weekly were able to screen 204 films annually. As with first-run cinema managements, suburban exhibitors wanted to screen those films that were most popular with their audiences. The films most likely to prove popular had, however, already received extended exhibition in the first-run market and would have been seen by a large number of patrons working in the city but living in the suburbs. By the time these films reached the suburbs, their novelty value was diminished, and so was their potential audience in a particular locality. As a result, suburban exhibitors required regular changes in film programmes in order to maintain admission levels. To achieve this, distributors needed to organise the planned-for number of prints expeditiously, moving their supply out in steps from box-office-rich inner suburban cinemas screening four programmes a day, to smaller cinemas on the fringes of the suburbs where perhaps only one screening a day took place.[13] By this time, the potential audience for most films had been exhausted.

In order to supply programmes that were attractive to audiences, exhibitors needed to screen not just the small number of films that had proven to be 'hits' with first-run audiences, but also a much larger body of films that had high, but not extraordinary, levels of appeal. They had to maintain the interest of their patrons so that it would not cross their minds to think of alternative uses for their customary moviegoing time slots. The three-day booking policy proved successful because it meant that audiences within particular suburban localities had little opportunity to become sated with films. As a result, middle-ranking films were given much greater exposure in the suburban market than in first-run cinemas. This is what the POPSTAT distributions depicted in Figure 7.4a and 7.4b show us.

To further illustrate this phenomenon, I have compared the POPSTAT scores of the Top 200 films in the suburban market to the Top 200 films in the first-run market, by giving the top-ranking film in each rank order the value 100. The results are shown in Figure 7.5, from which it is clear that, after the most popular eight films in both series, the rate of decline of POPSTAT values in the suburban market is much less than it is in the 'showcase' market of first-run cinemas, for the reasons indicated above.

Conclusion

In her provocative book *Sheep and Australian Cinema*, Deb Verhoeven refers to the 'missing discourse of consumption in the way the Australian cinema is understood' and that an aspect of this would be 'an interest in national audiences' (Verhoeven, 2006, p. 5). While this chapter does not discuss the characteristics of audiences, nor their tastes in any detail, it does give form to the pattern in which films were consumed by first-run and suburban-run audiences. In knowing what films attracted which audiences, and the circumstances of that consumption, film historians have a base for better understanding what Kate Bowles has termed 'the pragmatism of the market place', and through this the social history of the various coexisting cinema cultures (Bowles, 2007, p. 250).

Little Women topped the suburban charts for 1934, followed by *It Happened One Night* (1934), with each securing over 30 weeks of screenings in the cinemas that made up the suburban data set. Both films also did well in the first-run market, but it is clear

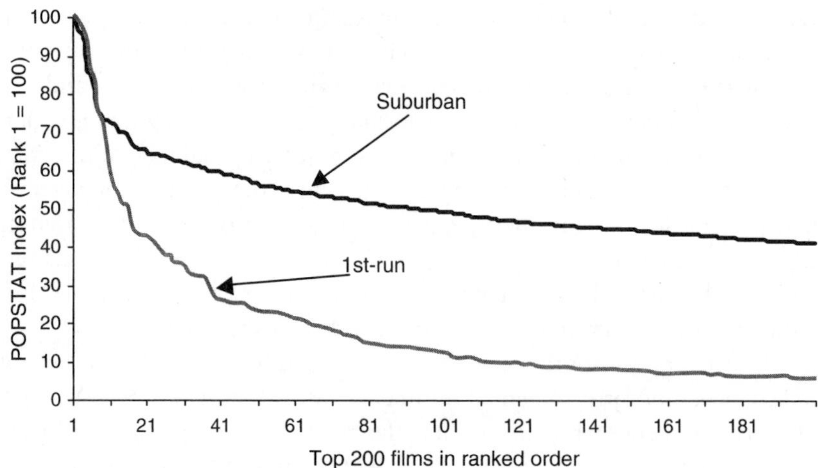

Figure 7.5 Index of the POPSTAT values of the Top 200 films in first-run and suburban data sets.

from the data presented in Figure 7.1, Figure 7.3, Figure 7.4a,b and Figure 7.5 that the two markets differed greatly in form. Whereas in the first-run market the most popular films received single-bill exhibitions over many weeks, normally at a single cinema, suburban exhibition took the form of short duration, multi-cinema screenings over many weeks. The logic behind first-run exhibition was to get as large an audience as possible to pay the highest prices possible to watch a single attraction for as long as a minimum revenue threshold was achieved, and to replace it once this was no longer the case. Typically audiences, and the box-office they generated, declined from above average to below average over the duration of the booking. Films that only generated an average audience on release had short lives in the first-run markets, giving form to the dramatic decline in popularity associated with rank shown in Figure 7.4a and Figure 7.5.

In Sydney's suburban market, on the other hand, revenue maximisation was tempered by a number of interlinked factors. Major film attractions had already been watched by large audiences in city-centre cinemas, as a consequence of which audience demand for them in each suburban area was appreciably lower than it otherwise would have been. This, in turn, meant that suburban cinemas replaced films on a regular schedule rather than holding them over, and this implies that, unlike first-run cinemas, suburban cinema needed large numbers of films in order to continually attract audiences. As a result, distributors were obliged to maintain very tight diffusion schedules in order to service the demands of the suburban subsequent-run market as efficiently and profitably as possible. The outcome was that film popularity in the suburbs manifested itself through multiple cinema billings, over time, throughout the suburban network, and that the velocity with which films circulated was such that considerably more films received a higher exhibition profile in the suburbs than in the first-run market.

This case study demonstrates the distinctly different operation of the first-run and suburban-run markets in Sydney. There is no reason to suppose that there is anything particularly unusual about the arrangement of that location, so it follows that there is a reasonable basis for assuming that other markets operated on the same basis, telling us something very significant about how the two markets interacted, in a manner significantly different from our earlier assumptions of a simple 'cascade' process.

Notes

1 Report of the Royal Commission on the Moving Picture Industry in Australia (Canberra, 1928). Investigation into an alleged combine in the motion picture industry, Ministry of Labour, chairman Mr P. White (Ottawa, 1931). Report on the Proceedings of the Parliamentary Inquiry held by the Industries and Commerce Committee into the Motion Picture Industry in New Zealand, chairman Mr A Harris (Wellington, 1934). Minutes of Evidence taken before the Departmental Committee appointed by the Board of Trade to consider the Position of British Films, chairman Lord Moyne (London, HMSO, 1936). Report of a Committee appointed by the Board of Trade to Consider the Position of British Films, chairman Lord Moyne (London: HMSO, cmd.530, 1936). Hearing before a Subcommittee of the Committee on Interstate and Foreign Commerce, House of Representatives, Seventy Fourth Congress, on Bill to Prohibit and to Prevent the Trade Practices Known as 'Compulsory Block-Booking' and 'Blind Selling' in the Leasing of Motion Picture Films in Interstate and Foreign Commerce (Washington DC, 1936).

2 *Variety* did not produce a yearbook.

3 For details of these projects, see their websites at: http://www.cinemacontext.nl/; http://fk615.221b.de/earlycinema/start/show/; http://londonfilm.bbk.ac.uk/about/project/; http://www.cims.ugent.be/research/past-research-projects/-enlightened-city.

4 This relative weighting of box-office potential, importantly, assumes that every cinema's seating capacity was utilised to an equal extent, irrespective of the film programme being shown or the quality of the cinema. This assumption undoubtedly discriminates against the most popular films and the higher-run cinemas.

5 For example, see Clara Pafort-Overduin's employment of a variation on the POPSTAT methodology in response to a broad but less detailed data set in Chapter 6 of this book. See also the contributions to *Going to the Movies: Hollywood and the Social Experience of Cinema* (eds R. Maltby, M. Stokes and R. Allen), Exeter University Press, Exeter.

6 This research was principally funded by grants from the Menzies Trust and British Academy in 2006. It was also generously supported in 2007 by a visiting fellowship to RMIT in Melbourne, jointly financed by RMIT University and the Australian Film, Television and Radio School.

7 The first-run data set is based on the daily advertisements found in the *Sydney Daily Telegraph* and the *Sydney Morning Herald*, and the listings found in the weekly trade journal *Everyones*. The suburban data set is drawn from the daily listing of suburban cinemas found in the *Sydney Morning Herald*, found apart from the first-run cinema adverts. Knowledge of the total number of suburban cinemas was given to the Marks Inquiry.

8 Hoyts continued to trade after the formation of GTC and, according to Shirley and Adams (1983, p. 123), booked films for its suburban circuit. For a summary of these complicated financial relationships see 'Inquiry into the Film Industry in New South Wales', Legislative Assembly of New South Wales, Chairman: F.W. Marks, (Sydney, 1934), vol. 3, paras 84 to 104.

9 In their contributions to this volume, Clara Pafort-Overduin (Chapter 6) and Peter Krämer (Chapter 9) both examine the audience appeal of domestically produced films.

10 An attempt to uncover the programmes of more suburban cinemas was thwarted by the general absence of suburban newspapers in the archive.

11 This compares to an average seating capacity in the first-run cinema of 1673 seats.

12 Notwithstanding the methodological compromises made above, it would appear that, in this case at least, the aggregate length of run of films across cinemas in the suburban data set is as good a measure of popularity as POPSTAT, since the correlation coefficient describing the closeness of association of the two measures across the 734 films screened at least once in the 69 cinemas in the suburban set is over 0.99.

13 In addition to the suburban runs, these same prints were also required to service country town cinemas.

References

Bowles, K. (2007) 'Three miles of rough dirt road': towards an audience-centred approach to cinema studies in Australia. *Studies in Australian Cinema*, 1 (3), 245–260.

Carroll, N. (1998) *A Philosophy of Mass Art*, Oxford University Press, Oxford.

Commonwealth Bureau of Census and Statistics (1936) *Official Yearbook of the Commonwealth of Australia*.

Fuller, K.H. (1996) *At the Picture Show: Small-Town Audiences and the Creation of Movie Fan Culture*, Smithsonian Institution Press, Washington, DC.

Glancy, H.M. and Sedgwick, J. (2007) Cinema going in the United States in the mid-1930s: a study based on the *Variety* dataset, in *Going to the Movies: Hollywood and the Social Experience of Cinema* (eds R. Maltby, M. Stokes and R. Allen), Exeter University Press, Exeter, pp. 155–195.

Rowson, S. (1936) A statistical survey of the cinema industry in Great Britain in 1934. *Journal of the Royal Statistical Society*, 99, pp. 67–129.

Sedgwick, J. (2000) *Popular Filmgoing in 1930s Britain: a Choice of Pleasures*, Exeter University Press, Exeter.

Sedgwick, J. (2006) Cinemagoing in Portsmouth during the 1930s. *Cinema Journal*, 46, 52–85.

Sedgwick, J. and Pokorny, M. (2005a) The film business in the U.S. and Britain during the 1930s. *Economic History Review*, 58, 79–112.

Sedgwick, J. and Pokorny, M. (2005b) The characteristics of film as a commodity, in *An Economic History of Film* (eds J. Sedgwick and M. Pokorny), Routledge, London, pp. 6–23.

Shirley, G. and Adams, B. (1983) *Australian Cinema: The First Eighty Years*, Currency Press, Sydney.

Thompson, K. (1985) *Exporting Entertainment: America in the World Film Market 1907–1934*, BFI, London.

Verhoeven, D. (2006) *Sheep and the Australian Cinema*, Melbourne University Press, Melbourne.

Waller, G.A. (1995) *Main Street Amusements: Movies and Commercial Entertainment in a Southern City, 1896–1930*, Smithsonian Institution Press, Washington, DC.

8

From Hollywood to the Garden Suburb (and Back to Hollywood)

Exhibition and Distribution in Australia

MIKE WALSH

Most studies of 'national cinema' understand that term as referring almost exclusively to a national production sector. In such a framework, distribution and exhibition are inevitably short-changed. If they figure at all, it is generally either as victims or as *compradors* in the hegemonic dominance of Hollywood. Little has been written on the history of distribution and exhibition in many countries in which Hollywood films have enjoyed a dominant role, even though these activities have framed the way in which most people have interacted with international cinema industries. Using Australia as an example of a country whose screens were (and continue to be) dominated by Hollywood films, I shall look in this chapter at two case studies, in order to sketch the outlines of a more detailed history of the ways distribution and exhibition worked around Hollywood production. In the process, I hope to call into question some longstanding assumptions about the practices that underpinned the circulation of Hollywood movies.

Australia provides a clear example of the prevalence of Hollywood production and the metaphors of weakness and strength, dominance and victimhood through which the relationship between American products and local consumption is usually represented. When Kristin Thompson writes that from the early days of US film export, 'few foreign markets succumbed so thoroughly to US film' as Australia and New Zealand, she reflects a widespread attitude in which Australian film institutions are given little history other than that of victim (Thompson, 1985, p. 42). On the other hand, for those exporting US films, the metaphors were those of robust health. In 1925, First National's international manager rhapsodised in *Film Daily Yearbook* that 'Australia is alive, progressive, and on the upward trend in every way, and it is my belief that the motion picture business is in a healthier condition in Australia than in any country of the world outside of the United States.'[1]

Explorations in New Cinema History: Approaches and Case Studies, First Edition.
Edited by Richard Maltby, Daniel Biltereyst and Philippe Meers.

As an English-speaking country with an international trade economy geared largely to considerations of comparative advantage, Australia has generally proven to be one of the most stable and successful markets for US film distributors. This is also a situation of long standing, since Australia had become the largest single export market for US film footage by 1922. No matter what their public pronouncements, Australian governments chose, until the late 1960s, to import and tax entertainment films rather than subsidise a production industry. In 1918, a correspondent to *Moving Picture World* noted that 'Australia pays more per capita for amusement than any other country in the world, as well as paying proportionately more for her film.'[2] In his annual report on Hollywood's international marketing in the 1929 *Film Daily Yearbook*, C.J. North wrote that 'Australia and New Zealand on a smaller scale are among the best markets in the world and command intensive cultivation'.[3]

For the American companies, this process of cultivation entailed the establishment of local subsidiary companies to distribute their films. We typically assume that the dominance of Hollywood films on the screens of many countries was at least sustained by – and most likely caused by – the industrial dominance of these distribution subsidiaries in their dealings with local exhibitors, through practices such as block-booking, blind bidding and other tactics cited periodically by local politicians, film-makers and some disgruntled exhibitors. A more detailed consideration of the operations of a distribution subsidiary, United Artists Australasia, and an independent suburban cinema, the Colonel Light Gardens cinema in Adelaide, South Australia, will allow us to revise these assumptions and gain a more fine-grained sense of the shifting balance of power that constituted the relations between the distribution and exhibition sectors.

Distribution: The American Subsidiary

On 19 September 1921, the Board of Directors of United Artists (UA) formally authorised an Australian subsidiary, at a meeting that also established subsidiaries in Mexico, South America and the Far East.[4] United Artists (Australasia) Limited was registered in Sydney on 9 February 1922. The company's capital consisted of 5000 £1 shares (£1 being equivalent to US $4.50 at the time). The low level of capitalisation was typical of US subsidiaries in Australia: both Paramount and First National were capitalised at £10 000.[5] Although they were not officially registered, 4993 shares were held on the understanding that they were in the name of the American owners of UA (Mary Pickford, Douglas Fairbanks, Charlie Chaplin and D.W. Griffith). Every care had to be taken to ensure that the Australian subsidiary and the American parent remained legally separate, so that remittances sent to the US parent were classed as business expenses for the Australian company rather than taxable income. In addition to the owners' shares, there were seven non-voting £1 shares, which were held by the subsidiary's officers and their solicitors in order to establish a local ownership component and to satisfy the legal requirement in New South Wales that a public company should have at least seven shareholders.

The company's distribution practices were initially established on the same terms as those accorded UA's British subsidiary, Allied Artists. The local company was to retain 25% of rentals as a distribution fee, with 70% being remitted to the producers and 5% to the UA parent company as its commission. (UA was atypical of the other major US film distributors in that it was not vertically integrated, owning no theatres and limiting itself to distributing films for independent producers.) After a disastrous beginning, during which the company's first manager entered into several disadvantageous contracts, Maurice Silverstone came to Sydney in 1922 to reorganise UA's Australasian distribution operation. Silverstone, who later became head of all UA's operations, anticipated that after renegotiating contracts with the dominant first-run exhibitor, Union Theatres (UT), rentals would increase by 50%. He had come to Australia confident in the market value of UA's films ('we are the only organization worthwhile in the picture business') and positive that he could use this to counter the dominant exhibition position of Union Theatres.[6] Once in Sydney, however, he quickly recognised the power of UT as a possible benefit, and changed policy. Rather than conspiring with other American companies, as politicians often claimed that the distributors did, Silverstone began colluding with UT to gain advantage against other American distributors. He singled out Paramount and Fox as the companies at which exhibitors 'are waiting to take a healthy fling'. When Paramount was locked out of Melbourne suburban exhibition after a dispute with UT in 1922, Paramount's manager approached UA for assistance in taking a stand against UT. Silverstone turned him down flat, declaring 'frankly speaking, I have not a bit of sympathy for Paramount in this situation, for they bought it about themselves by their sledgehammering and bullying methods, and they deserve this punishment'. Silverstone's November 1922 memo to the head of UA's international operations, in which he made this comment, was completely taken up with his activities to undermine the machinations of Paramount in Australia, by driving a wedge between Paramount and Union Theatres.[7]

Australia's smaller state capital cities such as Adelaide became crucial bargaining chips in these manoeuvres, as Silverstone induced Stuart Doyle of UT to break his first-run Sydney contract with Paramount, safe in the knowledge that if Paramount sued, UT could lock it out of first-run exhibition in Adelaide, Perth and Brisbane, where the exhibition chain held a virtual monopoly. Silverstone reported that Adelaide was 'a good instance of how we would be placed if we did not play with Union Theatres for without them our revenue here would be practically nothing'. UT's dominance of the Adelaide market was so complete that UA closed its exchange there, on the grounds that it was wasteful to maintain an office in a city so heavily controlled by a single exhibition company.

At the end of 1922, UA recognised that it could not sustain its international expansion at the initial low distribution rates it had established, and introduced variable rates for different territories. In 1926, the producer's share was lowered to 60% for Australia, but this still proved too high to prevent the local company from continuing to accumulate losses. In September 1927, the Board of Directors again cut the producer's share, reducing it to 50% in a move that contributed to the profitability of the local operation and helped finally to turn it into a stable proposition.[8] The report of the Royal Commission on the Moving Picture Industry in Australia, published in 1928, estimated that the overall percentage of Australian film rentals remitted to the United States ranged between 50% and 65%.[9] The Commission also found, however, that in the 1925–26 financial year £771 000 had been remitted to the United States from a total rentals figure of £1 100 000, while in 1926–27, £740 000 was remitted from the same total rentals. This remittance of over 67% of total rentals suggests that most US distributors must have operated at closer to 75% rather than UA's 50% range.[10] In 1929, First National was remitting a 65% share to its US parent and Paramount was thought to remit 75%. By 1927, UA's distribution fee was among the highest of all the US subsidiaries in Australia, and its overseas remittance rate among the lowest.

One historian of this period in Australian film history, John Tulloch, has characterised the relations of distribution to exhibition in Australia as one in which US distributors held all the cards through the 1920s, with exhibitors being dominated by practices of block-booking (Tulloch, 1982). Against this view, I hope to have indicated in this brief description of UA's entry into Australia that American distributors cannot be seen as a single unified force carrying all before them. Indeed, there were many occasions on which US distributors in general, and UA's managers in particular, felt that the upper hand resided with exhibitors, and as a result they acted in concert with exhibitors and in competition with other American distributors.

Just as generalisations about cultural imperialism have led to a lack of detailed knowledge about the day-to-day activities of American distributors, they have also given us a very poor insight into the business practices of cinema exhibition. In the remainder of this chapter, I want to suggest some of the complexity of exhibition through the analysis of one independent suburban cinema in Adelaide in the 1930s.

Local Exhibition: Colonel Light Gardens Theatre and the Great Depression

Colonel Light Gardens, a suburb 5 km south of Adelaide's central business district, was a bold new experiment in the international garden cities movement that had become prominent after World War I. Popularised in South Australia by Charles Reade, the movement aimed at building planned suburbs that provided a 'low density, self-contained residential environment catering within its boundaries for all residents' needs except employment' (Garnaut, 1999, p. 35). In 1919 the Garden Suburb Bill had passed the South Australian Parliament, authorising housing development for the farmland on the southern fringe of the city that had been used as an army encampment during the war. In 1924, the state government's Thousand Homes Scheme saw the new suburban subdivision development accelerated in order to provide affordable housing for army veterans and families with children. Over 1000 individual dwellings were constructed and purchased in Colonel Light

Gardens between 1921 and 1927. Churches, schools and recreational areas formed part of the planned development, so it is not surprising that a cinema should also be included.

Original plans and specifications for the building were submitted on 2 August 1926 by National Pictures Ltd, a company that already controlled cinemas in the Adelaide suburbs of Prospect, Marryatville, Norwood and North Adelaide, and at Victor Harbour, 'the miniature Naples of Australia', a summer resort 80 km south of the city.[11] The Colonel Light Gardens cinema (CLG) opened on 25 July 1927, with a seating capacity of 1740: 1150 on the ground floor and 590 in the dress circle. When National Pictures went into liquidation in 1928, an independent company, Colonel Light Gardens Theatres, was formed to take over the cinema. This company's Share Register has survived, along with its Minute Books after 1932, and these allow us to reconstruct in minute detail the financial structure of independent suburban cinema exhibition during the Depression.

By 1932, the company had a £1000 overdraft limit with the National Bank of Australia, and as it came closer to that limit in February 1933, some of the shareholders began 'to think it was a dead loss', and contemplate cutting their losses.[12] At the Annual General Meeting for that year, the Chairman spoke of selling or leasing the theatre or putting the company into liquidation, and the meeting decided to defer a decision for 6 months. This issue came back at each board meeting for a number of years.

The figures in Table 8.1 track the fortunes of the cinema through the decade and give us an insight into the financial structure of the suburban exhibition business. These figures show that the overwhelming majority of the theatre's income came at the box office. Amusement Tax was collected by the theatre and simply paid out again to the government. Rents collected from shopkeepers – there was a fruit shop and a confectionery shop in the cinema building – accounted for only £15 to £20 per month with rents at £1 per week. The average price paid per customer was between 11d and 1/1 (without Amusement Tax).[13] When Amusement Tax on tickets over 2/6 was reduced in 1935, manager W.R. Thompson noted that this would have no effect on the suburban cinemas, since they never charged that much. At semi-annual general meetings in 1939, Thompson outlined the ticket prices and the distribution of tickets within this range. (It should be noted that the prices cited here include Amusement Tax, and the lower charges in the second period register the reduction of Amusement Tax on tickets over 1/6d.)

Table 8.2 indicates that the top ticket prices attracted very few patrons, with the bottom adult price of 1/– being overwhelmingly popular. The 6d figures effectively give us the number of admissions for children, as the Motion Picture Distributors Association of Australia insisted on a one shilling minimum for adult admission. The fact that almost 30% of tickets were sold to children is indicative of the marketing efforts made by Thompson. The cinema instituted a Birthday Club for patrons under 15 providing free admission to the Saturday matinee following the child's birthday. Thompson continually stressed his efforts to market the cinema through local schools, by his attending sports days and giving out

Table 8.1 Receipts and expenditures summary, Colonel Light Gardens Theatres (in £).

	1931	*1932*	*1933*	*1934*	*1935*	*1936*	*1937*	*1938*
Total receipts	**£3527**	**£4588**	**£4615**	**£4981**	**£5266**	**£5956**	**£6503**	**£6511**
Box office		£3684	£3709	£4048	£4257	£4886	£5366	£5645
Amusement Tax		£635	£636	£694	£731	£816	£737	£467
Rent/slides		£268	£269	£238	£277	£255	£400	£399
Total expenditures		**£4750**	**£4526**	**£4179**	**£4469**	**£5321**	**£6751**	
Film hire	£1772	£1835	£1664	£1783	£1911	£2154	£2458	£2576
Salaries	£960	£916	£861	£833	£891	£1034	£1116	£1168
Amusement Tax	£607	£635	£640	£693	£732	£811	£746	
Lighting	£157	£183	£181	£122	£131	£156	£181	£176
Advertising	£294	£261	£242	£225	£243		£270	£298
Rates/taxes			£125	£73	£88	£124	£143	£218
Interest/ insurance			£110	£81	£41	£42	£42	£34
Dividends						£327	£832	
Total attendances	**75 155**	**80 126**	**75 605**	**80 457**	**87 480**	**96 218**		

Table 8.2 Distribution of ticket prices, Colonel Light Gardens Cinema, 1938–39.

July 1938 to January 1939		*Percentage of total*	*February to June 1939*		*Percentage of total*
2/4	964	1.8%	2/–	867	1.4%
2/–	5576	10.3%	1/8	6556	10.7%
1/9	9801	18.1%	1/6	11 031	18.0%
1/–	21 646	40.0%	1/–	25 090	40.9%
–/6d	16 117	29.8%	–/6d	17 838	29.1%
Total	54 104			61 382	

prizes. In November 1932 he lamented the number of Sunday School picnics being run on Saturdays by local churches, and announced his hopes that booking *Tarzan, The Ape Man* would get the children back to the Saturday matinees.

At the start of the 1930s, the cinema screened on two nights each week, Saturday and Wednesday, with a matinee on Saturday. With such a relatively small number of screenings, the management saw itself as vulnerable to such events as bad weather, defined as being either too hot, too cold, or wet, as well as to competing leisure attractions. The introduction of harness racing on Saturday nights at nearby Wayville in 1934 caused serious consequences for the rest of the 1930s as 'the trots' regularly attracted crowds of 20 000. When the trots began to offer free admission to children accompanying their parents, the state Exhibitors' Association, of which Thompson was then Chair, tried to agitate against this on moral grounds.

Avoidance turned out to be the best long-term strategy for dealing with this rivalry, however, and by 1936 the cinema had started additional screenings on Monday nights, so that it could pick up the crowds who went to the trots or the motor speedway on Saturdays.

The largest component of the theatre's expenditure was for film hire. In 1932, it accounted for almost exactly 50% of the value of box-office takings, coming down thereafter to between 44% and 46%, and remaining within this range for the rest of the decade. The initial reduction came about as a consequence of the Film War of 1932–33, in which Australia's two dominant first-release exhibitors, Greater Union and Hoyts, formed a joint buying company, General Theatres Corporation, which forced lower rental terms from distributors (Shirley and Adams, 1989, pp. 122–125).

The introduction of sound had brought about an increase in distributor rentals because distributors insisted on contracts that gave them a percentage of the box office rather than a fixed rental sum. The upper hand thus enjoyed by American distributors as a result of the coming of sound fits well with narratives of cultural imperialism, in which all the cards are typically assumed to be in the hands of the Americans. The Film War, however, shows that this was not an uncontested relationship, nor one in which exhibitors were powerless. Throughout 1932, Thompson anticipated that the resolution of this struggle would lead to lower rental prices flowing through to suburban cinemas. When contracts for the next season began to be tabled, they were not the undifferentiated blocks that nationalist legends report as being dumped on exhibitors. Rather than simply being tied to a complete programme through a single distributor, the Colonel Light Gardens cinema had contracts with virtually all the American distributors. Thompson booked well in advance, but he also used spot bookings (contracts for individual films arranged at short notice) as he sought to maintain a supply of films while deferring any decision on contracts he considered too expensive. Contract negotiations with distributors were typically deferred for several board meetings until prices were reduced to within the cinema's price range. After waiting out the initial demand, the exhibitor was generally successful in getting reduced prices. It was an article of faith for exhibitors that wherever possible, films should be booked on a flat fee basis rather than a percentage. Distributors held out for percentages for their bigger films, and Thompson reported that this made it impossible to realise a profit on these films. Instead, the exhibitor's main motive in playing them was to hold patrons and maintain the prestige of the cinema.

The negotiations with Fox for the 1936 season provide an excellent example of the terms under which exhibitor and distributor did business. In December 1935 Fox tendered the following terms:

- four Shirley Temples, at 40% of the box office with a minimum guarantee of £18 10s each;
- three floaters (individually bookable films) at £15 flat fee each, and three floaters at £12 10s each;
- 12 roadshow films at £8 each, 18 at £4 10s each, and 12 at £3 each;

- British Gaumont films: three floaters at £17 10s each, three floaters at £15 each, six programme films at £7 each, eight programme films at £3 each.

The board deferred its decision on this contract for 2 months until Fox came back with a revised offer that reduced prices. The special status of the Shirley Temple films is worth noting. Beginning with *Bright Eyes* in 1935, her movies were sensations at the Colonel Light Gardens, providing the theatre with its first sell-out business. Thompson was even moved to organise a series of Shirley Temple parties at the cinema to strengthen its association with such a potent brand name.

The theatre's negotiations with British Empire Films (BEF) are instructive not only for what they show of distribution and exhibition relations, but also for the light they cast on preferences in national cinema. BEF, a distribution company controlled by the Greater Union Organisation, specialised in distributing British films, a term that also encompassed Australian productions made by Cinesound. In 1937, the CLG cinema reneged on its contract with BEF, refusing to play films with an agreed rental value of almost £67 because 'the films were not suitable for Colonel Light Gardens'. Rather than enforce the contract, BEF accepted the situation and tried to sell the cinema on the proposition that the 1938 films would be greatly improved. They offered three roadshows at £10 each, 12 specials at £4 each, and 10 films at £2 each. It is of considerable note that three Australian films, all directed by Ken G. Hall, were included in the contract under special prices, giving an indication of their estimated value in the market. *Tall Timbers* (1937) and *Lovers and Luggers* (1937) were both quoted at £12 10s, while the rental price for *It Isn't Done* (1937) was £8. While these were not top prices, they were above average, suggesting that Australian films had a significant appeal to suburban audiences.

The CLG cinema also had a distribution contract for 1936 with MGM for 23 films at £5 each, six at £10 each, and seven at £12 10s each; and with First National-Warner Bros for seven films at £15 each and 45 at £4 10s each. An important aspect of this contract was that it gave the CLG theatre access to the first suburban releases of Warner-First National films in Adelaide. A similar arrangement was also part of the contract with Columbia.

This raises the question of clearance windows (the mandated time between different phases in a film's release), and with it the matter of internal divisions within the exhibition sector. The 1932–33 Film War had involved the demands of first-run exhibitors for longer clearance windows after first-release seasons before distributors made films available for suburban theatres. Given that distributors typically imported only six prints of each film into Australia, they were keen to keep the prints working as hard as possible. Four-week windows were made standard, with some special films being given 8-week windows, and in the case of the Academy Award-winning *Cavalcade* (1933), 3 months. Suburban exhibitors were conscious that the Depression sharpened the competition with first run. Thompson prized the CLG's status as suburban first-release, arguing that 'locals will want to see them [here] instead of journeying up to Adelaide'. He clearly saw his theatre as being in competition with the city cinemas, arguing that he could not alter his programming strategy by moving from a double feature to a single feature unless the city cinemas instituted a similar change.

Over the course of 1936, the Colonel Light Gardens Cinema showed 225 films in 211 sessions. The film industry trade paper *Everyones* listed 437 films as having been released in Australia in 1936, and so we can see that, even showing only 3 days a week, a single suburban cinema screened half the total number of films released in the country during the year. Total admissions for the year were 96 218, with an average attendance per session of 456, or just over one-quarter of capacity. If total film hire for the year was £2154, the average price per film was £9.11s. The 225 films were sourced from the following distributors:

Fox (including 12 Gaumont-British)	55
MGM	41
Warner-First National	33
Paramount	29
Columbia	23
Universal	18
United Artists	8
Monogram	7
Associated BEF	6
British Dominions	3
RKO-Radio	2

There was some variation from the initial contracts in what was actually shown. Instead of taking 72 films from Fox, 55 were screened. Instead of 36 MGM films, 41 were screened, and 33 Warner-First National films screened instead of the contracted 52, suggesting a further degree of flexibility in the distributors' operation of block-booking contracts.

Everyones had an evaluation system for film quality, ranking films in six classes. If we plot these descriptors of quality for 1936 against the films shown at Colonel Light Gardens, there is a rough equivalence in their distribution, suggesting that the CLG was an average cinema, in which the proportion of big, expensive films balanced the small, cheap programme pictures. By the mid-1930s, the system appears to have achieved a kind of balance, as exhibitors worked within the bounds of a slowly rising level of attendance, which was nevertheless limited by disposable income and the availability of alternative forms of leisure spending. Within these bounds, exhibitors tried to keep their major expenditure, film hire, within a tightly defined range and constructed their programmes accordingly. Block booking clearly contained a degree of flexibility within it that helped the system maintain itself.

Only one of the 225 feature films screened at the CLG in 1936 was an Australian film: *Thoroughbred*. Twenty-one British films were screened, the majority of them shown only once on the quieter Wednesday night sessions. Roughly 90% of the features shown were American, and this might lead us to ask whether the screen was American, even if local exhibitors had a little more room to manoeuvre than we might have thought. The localism of the programme was clearly something that exhibitors worked to foreground wherever possible. Generally, however, this happened around the margins of the programme. Although sound and the Depression had brought about a decline in live music and stage presentation acts, the CLG cinema persevered with such live acts as a local xylophone player, a tap dance competition winner, and on one occasion a pantomime that replaced its Saturday matinee. Twice during the year, a collection of vaudeville acts played before the films on Saturdays, with acts geared to children at the matinee and to adults at night. These acts often headlined above the films in the advertising, pointing to the value placed on localism.

The major way in which localism seems to have asserted itself in the programme, however, is through featured news films. A news film featuring Adelaide's floral pageant, held to mark the centenary of European settlement, was headlined above the bill. The Easter races at nearby Oakbank were also presented quickly as a special attraction, as was the Melbourne Cup and a film of the first Ashes test cricket match between Australia and England. The promotion and screening of films such as these by the CLG cinema and by two other cinemas operated by Glenelg Pictures indicates that localism of a certain type was encouraged by the association of local independent exhibitors.

Suburban cinemas in Adelaide appear to have recovered much more quickly than first-release city cinemas. The records of the Colonel Light Gardens cinema suggest that 1932 was the low point for suburban exhibition, and that the cinema business slowly revived after that. By August 1933, the CLG was beginning to reduce its overdraft and gain some breathing space under its £1000 limit. It finally eliminated the overdraft in the middle of 1935, buoyed by the influx of new families into the nearby Hollywood subdivision. On the other hand, Wests Olympia, one of Greater Union's main first-release houses in the Adelaide central business district, closed its doors at the start of February 1934, with the company rumoured to be losing £400 a week on its operations in Adelaide. Although Greater Union made an attempt to reopen the cinema during 1934, it quickly closed again. The only city cinema thought to be prospering in 1935 was the Royal, which was controlled by the suburban Ozone circuit.

The two major financial problems for the Colonel Light Gardens cinema had come with the decline in demand as a result of widespread unemployment, and the increase in expenditures caused by the increase in distribution rentals that accompanied sound, and by the installation of sound technology. Although Adelaide suburban cinemas had started to install talkie equipment in late 1929, the CLG did not convert to sound until April 1932, installing a local sound system manufactured by Unbehaum and Johnstone at a cost of over £900. The company took until January 1933 to pay off the instalments and then took a further 2 years to repay the £100 loan it had taken from Mrs Andrews, one of its shareholders, in order to make the initial down payment.

Conclusion

The two case studies I have discussed in this chapter flesh out our sense of how the business of film distribution and exhibition worked during this period. Most writers on the cinema have typically only asked large-scale policy questions about these two facets of the cinema business, and have substituted generalisations about power and influence for more fine-grained analyses of the multiple and shifting sets of relations and balances of power that I have sought to demonstrate here.

During the 1920s, the Australian film industry had become dominated by corporate interests pursuing a policy of specialisation in exhibition. It made sense to specialise in this area because it complemented international inputs into the industry. The major companies involved in the Australian motion picture business saw their role as being to exploit a product that originated further upstream in the marketing process, and so exhibiting films in Australia necessarily involved adapting to changes in supply as well as expecting supply to adapt to what local specificities of exhibition existed. US international distribution took advantage of its capital-intensive production sector, but at least in this period, this did not involve intensive flows of capital from the United States into foreign countries in order to purchase cinemas. Instead, US films created a situation where local capital could be profitably invested downstream in the marketing process, in exhibition. The large exhibition chains, as well as smaller suburban operators, had tied their profitability to the continued supply of a high volume of American films, and a threat to that supply was a threat to their core operations. The partnership of Australian exhibition and foreign distribution undoubtedly involved tensions on a day-to-day basis over the equilibrium of the system but, on a larger level, both participants saw the partnership as a mutually beneficial fit. Clearly there were times when American distributors acted together to support their common interests against local exhibition, but it is important to recognise that these lines of affiliation were easily fractured and that the distribution and exhibition sectors both contained internal lines of opposition and competition. It is only after we have broken the idea that American distributors were an implacable force oppressing Australians that we can start to write a history of Australian cinema that contains positions of agency for Australians, both as operatives within the cinema industries and as audiences. By similarly shifting the focus of their investigations from production to exhibition, historians elsewhere may come to comparable conclusions about other national cinemas.

Notes

1 *Film Daily Yearbook, 1925* (New York: Film Daily, 1925), p. 660.
2 *Moving Picture World*, 19 October 1918, p. 428.
3 *Film Daily Yearbook, 1929* (New York: Film Daily, 1929), p. 1009.
4 Minutes of the United Artists Board of Directors, 19 September 1921. United Artists' Collection, O'Brien Legal Files, Series 2A, Wisconsin Centre for Film and Theater Research, Madison, Wisconsin (hereafter 'O'Brien').

5 Of the 10 000 shares in the Paramount subsidiary, 9708 were held by the US parent company. *Everyones*, 4 July 1928, p. 7; Ruth Megaw, 'The American image: influence on Australian cinema management, 1896–1923', *Journal of the Royal Australian Historical Society*, 54 (2) (June, 1968), p. 199.

6 Maurice Silverstone to Hiram Abrams, 11 September 1922, O'Brien 60/2.

7 Silverstone to W. Hodkinson, 13 November 1922, O'Brien 55/9.

8 Minutes of United Artists Board of Directors, 14 September 1927.

9 Report of the Royal Commission on the Moving Picture Industry in Australia, Commonwealth of Australia, *Parliamentary Papers*, 1926–28, no. 227, p. 9.

10 Report of the Royal Commission, p. 22.

11 Letter from National Pictures Limited, dated 2 August 1926. State Records of South Australia, GRG67/33/106/1926; Charles R. Hodge, *Guide-book to Victor Harbour (the Miniature Naples of Australia) and the South Coast* (Adelaide: The Advertiser, 1930).

12 All quotations directly concerning the reports of the Colonel Light Gardens Cinema come from the Minute Books, Colonel Light Gardens Cinemas (Greater Union Collection, BRG234, State Library of South Australia Archival Collections).

13 Prices are in shillings and pence, where, for example, 1/1 equals one shilling and one penny. There were 12 pence (d) in a shilling (s), and 20 shillings in a pound (£).

References

Garnaut, C. (1999) *Colonel Light Gardens: Model Garden Suburb*, Crossing Press, Darlinghurst.

Shirley, G. and Adams, B. (1989) *Australian Cinema: The First Eighty Years* (revised edn), Currency Press, Sydney.

Thompson, K. (1985) *Exporting Entertainment: America in the World Film Market, 1907–1934*, BFI, London.

Tulloch, J. (1982) *Australian Cinema: Industry, Narrative and Meaning*, Allen and Unwin, Sydney.

9

Hollywood and its Global Audiences

A Comparative Study of the Biggest Box Office Hits in the United States and Outside the United States Since the 1970s

PETER KRÄMER

For almost a century, film industry representatives, politicians, scholars and cultural commentators have been debating the relationship between Hollywood and the world beyond the borders of the United States.[1] Non-American film audiences play a two-fold role in these debates. On the one hand, there is a widespread assumption that Hollywood exports have long been very successful in cinemas (and later also on television, video and DVD) around the world and that, therefore, Hollywood has played an important part in the life of non-American film audiences, exerting various kinds of cultural and ideological influence on them, which are usually subsumed under the heading 'Americanisation'.[2] On the other hand, precisely because Hollywood's successful exports have generated a considerable share of the industry's overall income, the film preferences and objections of non-American audiences (the latter often mediated through censorship boards and other official organisations in particular countries) can in turn be assumed to have played an important part in the operations of Hollywood and influencing its output.[3]

As Joseph Garncarz has pointed out, the discussion of Hollywood's success around the world has traditionally relied on figures relating to supply – that is, to Hollywood's share of all films released in a particular country – rather than to demand, expressed as Hollywood's share of total ticket sales in that country (Garncarz, 1994, p. 96). His analysis of the German market across much of the twentieth century strongly suggests that Hollywood's often dominant share of film

Explorations in New Cinema History: Approaches and Case Studies, First Edition.
Edited by Richard Maltby, Daniel Biltereyst and Philippe Meers.

supply in countries around the world has rarely translated into an equivalent share of ticket sales; indeed, before the 1980s, in countries such as West Germany, France and Japan, Hollywood's share of box-office revenues tended to be less than 50%, with the majority of revenues going to domestic productions and imports from neighbouring countries.[4] Investigations of Hollywood's influence around the world have to take these limits of its success into account, and may also usefully concentrate on those Hollywood imports that are most successful in each country (Krämer, 2005a). At the same time, if the number of widely successful Hollywood exports is not as large as is often assumed, it is important to identify those outstanding films that do in fact succeed in a range of countries because they are in the most likely position to exert some kind of global influence.

Reversing the perspective, the influence that audiences around the world can exert on Hollywood's output usually depends on the share of Hollywood's overall income generated in their countries. This in turn depends on the relative size of that market, the share of ticket sales (as well as television, video and DVD sales) going to Hollywood films, and the exchange rate between the local currency and the dollar. Hence it is worth determining precisely in which countries Hollywood earns most of its export revenues. Additionally, one might ask which films earn the lion's share of this export income (presumably by being successful with audiences in all or most of the major export markets), because Hollywood will be more inclined to invest in the types of film that repeatedly perform extremely well abroad than in those that are consistently less successful. This raises the further question of whether Hollywood's biggest export hits are the same films, or at least the same types of films, as its greatest domestic successes (in which case the film preferences of foreign audiences would not make much difference to Hollywood's operations), or whether the two sets of hits form different patterns (in which case the distinctive pattern of export hits might influence Hollywood's output).

This chapter offers a comparative study of Hollywood's domestic and foreign theatrical markets since the 1970s, leaving non-theatrical film markets and developments up to the 1970s aside for future research.[5] The first section identifies which foreign markets generate most of Hollywood's export revenues for theatrical releases, relating them to the total world cinema market and the total world population, and demonstrating that Hollywood earns most of its foreign theatrical revenues in a small number of highly developed mid-sized countries. The second section compares Hollywood's biggest theatrical hits in its domestic market since 1977 with its biggest theatrical hits in foreign markets, outlining both overlap and differences along generic and thematic lines between the two lists. The third section then offers a case study of one of Hollywood's biggest foreign markets, comparing German box-office charts with their American counterparts and showing that some of the differences between the two are in line with the differences explored in the previous section, while others are specific to Germany.

Major Export Markets

Hollywood has long been dependent on income from the theatrical release of its films outside the United States. Since World War II, the share of Hollywood's total theatrical revenues coming from abroad has been in the region of 30–50%.[6] The majority of Hollywood's revenues from foreign theatrical distribution come from a small number of countries. *Screen Finance* calculated in 1989 that 70% of the rental income of the major Hollywood studios from outside the United States came from Japan, Canada, France, West Germany, the UK, Italy, Spain and Australia (listed here in order of market share).[7] In 1999, the share of total non-US theatrical revenues for both the major studios and American independents coming from these eight markets was about 80%.[8] These eight countries contain less than 10% of the world's population outside the United States, and only about a fifth of the world's cinema screens outside the United States.[9] What is more, average annual cinema admissions per head in these eight countries were much lower than they were, for example, in India, Singapore and Hong Kong, and not much higher than they were in many other countries in the world: in 1997, for example, the annual average was 1.12 cinema admissions per head in Japan, compared to 0.93 in much more populous Indonesia (Acland, 2003, pp. 250–255).

The eight markets making up the vast majority of the American film industry's international theatrical revenues account for only a small fraction of worldwide paid cinema admissions. Indeed, ticket sales in India alone have far exceeded ticket sales in Hollywood's eight main foreign markets, and in the 1980s the same was true for ticket sales in China (Acland, 2003, pp. 253–255). The huge number of admissions in foreign markets outside these eight countries do not translate into substantial box-office income for Hollywood for several reasons. Most obviously, the market share of US exports in those countries may be comparatively small. In the two largest markets in terms of cinema admissions since the 1970s, India and China, Hollywood has accounted for only a small share of paid admissions (Lent, 2008, p. 280; Govil, 2008, p. 286). More generally, ticket prices in developing countries are much lower, and unfavourable exchange rates may prevent box-office income from translating into substantial amounts of dollars.

This brief overview suggests two cautions concerning claims about Hollywood's influence on global audiences, and the influence of global audiences on Hollywood. Firstly, with regard to India, China and other of the world's most populous countries, the exposure of cinemagoers to Hollywood movies on the big screen is probably extremely limited.[10] Secondly, despite the tremendous growth potential for Hollywood exports in the world's most populous countries, the majority of Hollywood's export revenues since the 1970s have consistently come from a few mid-sized countries, and only the cinemagoers in these countries are likely to have exerted any influence on Hollywood's output. But are their film preferences different from those of American audiences?

Domestic Versus Export Hits

For several years, Hollywood has made box-office returns from foreign markets publicly available through its trade press and various websites. The most accessible source for these data is the Internet Movie Database's 'All-Time Non-USA Box Office' chart (http://www.imdb.com/boxoffice/alltimegross?region-non-us). As with most available box-office data, the IMDb includes Canadian revenues with those for the domestic US market, so that 'non-USA' in fact means: outside the United States and Canada.[11] The chart lists all films with a box office gross of $100 million or more outside the United States and Canada. Because of ticket price inflation around the world and fluctuating exchange rates, the revenue figures given for films in this chart are not comparable across decades, but the scale of these variations can be significantly reduced by breaking the chart down into 5-year periods. The IMDb chart does not include a single film made before the 1970s, and only three films made before 1977: *The Godfather* (1972), *The Exorcist* (1973) and *Jaws* (1975). From 1977 onwards, however, several films from each year appear on it. For this and other reasons to do with changing hit patterns in the United States and Canada before and after 1977, I have chosen 1977 as my starting point (Krämer, 2005b). For each 5-year period, I have listed the 10 top grossing films outside the United States and Canada in Table 9.1, as well as the 10 top domestic hits.[12]

There is considerable overlap between the two lists and, on average, six titles appear in both top tens in each 5-year period. Examining the films that do not make it into both top ten lists provides some indication of which broad types of Hollywood product fare better in which market. Only four of the animated films in the domestic top tens are also in the foreign top tens: *Beauty and the Beast* (1991), *Aladdin* (1992), *The Lion King* (1994) and *Finding Nemo* (2003). The domestic animated hits that do not make it into the foreign top tens are: *Toy Story* (1995), *Toy Story 2* (1999), *Shrek* (2001), *Monsters Inc.* (2001) and *Shrek 2* (2004). While one might expect animation to transfer with particular ease from one country to the rest of the world, the received wisdom that humour on the big screen is difficult to export may find some confirmation here; after all, these animated films are comedies. In addition, there are a range of other comedies that appear in the domestic but not in the foreign top ten lists: *Smokey and the Bandit* (1977), *Animal House* (1978), *Tootsie* (1982), *Ghostbusters* (1984), *Beverly Hills Cop* (1984), *Three Men and A Baby* (1987), *Mrs Doubtfire* (1993) and *How the Grinch Stole Christmas* (2000).

It is worth noting that these are not primarily romantic comedies (although several of these films, especially *Smokey and the Bandit* and *Tootsie*, feature romantic relationships). By comparison, films placing a strong emphasis on romantic comedy frequently appear in both top tens, most notably *Pretty Woman* (1990), but also *Grease*, *Aladdin* and *Beauty and the Beast*, as well as the more action-oriented *Crocodile Dundee* (1986). Romantic dramas also tend to appear in both charts, especially when they are infused with a sense of tragedy or loss, most notably in the case of

Table 9.1 Top grossing films in the United States and Canada, and outside the United States and Canada. Box-office figures are not adjusted for inflation or for changing exchange rates. They include revenues from re-releases. Films that do *not* appear in both the domestic and the foreign top ten are in bold italics.

	Top grossing films in the United States and Canada	*Top grossing films outside the United States and Canada*
1977–1981		
1	*Star Wars* (1977, $461 m)	*Star Wars* (1977, $337 m)
2	*The Empire Strikes Back* (1980, $290 m)	*The Empire Strikes Back* (1980, $244 m)
3	*Raiders of the Lost Ark* (1981, $242 m)	*Grease* (1978, $199 m)
4	*Grease* (1978, $181 m)	*Close Encounters of the Third Kind* (1977, $172 m)
5	***Animal House*** (1978, $142 m)	*Superman* (1978, $155 m)
6	*Superman* (1978, $134 m)	***Saturday Night Fever*** (1977, $143 m)
7	*Close Encounters of the Third Kind* (1977, $128 m)	*Raiders of the Lost Ark* (1981, $142 m)
8	***Smokey and the Bandit*** (1977, $127 m)	***Moonraker*** (1979, $140 m)
9	***On Golden Pond*** (1981, $119 m)	***The Spy Who Loved Me*** (1977, $139 m)
10	***Superman II*** (1980, $108 m)	***For Your Eyes Only*** (1981, $133 m)
1982–86		
1	*E.T.* (1982, $444 m)	*E.T.* (1982, $322 m)
2	*Return of the Jedi* (1983, $309 m)	*Return of the Jedi* (1983, $264 m)
3	***Ghostbusters*** (1984, $239 m)	***Rocky IV*** (1985, $173 m)
4	***Beverly Hills Cop*** (1984, $244 m)	*Top Gun* (1986, $168 m)
5	*Back to the Future* (1985, $211 m)	*Crocodile Dundee* (1986, $154 m)
6	*Indiana Jones and the Temple of Doom* (1984, $180 m)	*Indiana Jones and the Temple of Doom* (1984, $153 m)
7	***Tootsie*** (1982, $177 m)	***Out of Africa*** (1985, $152 m)
8	*Top Gun* (1986, $177 m)	*Rambo: First Blood Part II* (1985, $150 m)
9	*Crocodile Dundee* (1986, $175 m)	*Back to the Future* (1985, $140 m)
10	*Rambo: First Blood Part II* (1985, $150 m)	***Octopussy*** (1983, $116 m)
1987–91		
1	*Home Alone* (1990, $286 m)	*Terminator 2* (1991, $312 m)
2	***Batman*** (1989, $251 m)	*Ghost* (1990, $300 m)
3	*Ghost* (1990, $218 m)	*Indiana Jones and the Last Crusade* (1989, $298 m)
4	*Terminator 2* (1991, $205 m)	*Pretty Woman* (1990, $285 m)
5	*Indiana Jones and the Last Crusade* (1989, $197 m)	*Home Alone* (1990, $248 m)
6	*Dances With Wolves* (1990, $184 m)	*Rain Man* (1988, $240 m)
7	*Pretty Woman* (1990, $178 m)	*Dances With Wolves* (1990, $240 m)
8	*Rain Man* (1988, $173 m)	***Robin Hood*** (1991, $225 m)
9	*Beauty and the Beast* (1991, $171 m)	***Back to the Future II*** (1989, $214 m)
10	***Three Men and a Baby*** (1987, $168 m)	*Beauty and the Beast* (1991, $207 m)
1992–96		
1	*Jurassic Park* (1993, $357 m)	*Jurassic Park* (1993, $563 m)
2	*Forrest Gump* (1994, $330 m)	*Independence Day* (1996, $505 m)
3	*The Lion King* (1994, $328 m)	*The Lion King* (1994, $455 m)
4	*Independence Day* (1996, $306 m)	*Forrest Gump* (1994, $350 m)
5	*Twister* (1996, $242 m)	***The Bodyguard*** (1992, $289 m)
6	***Mrs Doubtfire*** (1993, $219 m)	*Aladdin* (1992, $285 m)

(continued)

Table 9.1 (Cont'd).

	Top grossing films in the United States and Canada	*Top grossing films outside the United States and Canada*
7	*Aladdin* (1992, $217 m)	***Mission: Impossible*** (1996, $272 m)
8	***Toy Story*** (1995, $192 m)	***Die Hard with a Vengeance*** (1995, $265 m)
9	***Batman Forever*** (1995, $184 m)	*Twister* (1996, $253 m)
10	***The Fugitive*** (1993, $184 m)	***Se7en*** (1995, $250 m)
1997–2001		
1	*Titanic* (1997, $601 m)	*Titanic* (1997, $1,235 m)
2	*Star Wars: Episode I – The Phantom Menace* (1999, $431 m)	*Harry Potter and the Philosopher's Stone* (2001, $651 m)
3	*Harry Potter and the Sorcerer's Stone* (2001, $318 m)	*The Lord of the Rings: The Fellowship of the Ring* (2001, $547 m)
4	*The Lord of the Rings: The Fellowship of the Ring* (2001, $314 m)	*Star Wars: Episode I – The Phantom Menace* (1999, $491 m)
5	*The Sixth Sense* (1999, $294 m)	***The Lost World: Jurassic Park*** (1997, $385 m)
6	***Shrek*** (2001, $268 m)	*The Sixth Sense* (1999, $368 m)
7	***How the Grinch Stole Christmas*** (2000, $260 m)	***Armageddon*** (1998, $353 m)
8	***Monsters, Inc.*** (2001, $256 m)	*Men in Black* (1997, $337 m)
9	*Men in Black* (1997, $250 m)	***Mission: Impossible II*** (2000, $330 m)
10	***Toy Story 2*** (1999, $246 m)	***The Matrix*** (1999, $285 m)
2002–06		
1	***Shrek 2*** (2004, $436 m)	*The Lord of the Rings: The Return of the King* (2003, $752 m)
2	*Pirates of the Caribbean: Dead Man's Chest* (2006, $423 m)	*Pirates of the Caribbean: Dead Man's Chest* (2006, $637 m)
3	***Spider-Man*** (2002, $408 m)	***Harry Potter and the Chamber of Secrets*** (2002, $604 m)
4	*Star Wars: Episode III: Revenge of the Sith* (2005, $380 m)	***Harry Potter and the Goblet of Fire*** (2005, $602 m)
5	*The Lord of the Rings: The Return of the King* (2003, $377 m)	*The Lord of the Rings: The Two Towers* (2002, $581 m)
6	***Spider-Man 2*** (2004, $373 m)	***Harry Potter and the Prisoner of Azkaban*** (2004, $540 m)
7	***The Passion of the Christ*** (2004, $370 m)	***The Da Vinci Code*** (2006, $540 m)
8	*The Lord of the Rings: The Two Towers* (2002, $340 m)	*Finding Nemo* (2003, $525 m)
9	*Finding Nemo* (2003, $340 m)	*Star Wars: Episode III – Revenge of the Sith* (2005, $468 m)
10	***Star Wars: Episode II – Attack of the Clones*** (2002, $311 m)	***The Matrix Reloaded*** (2003, $454 m)

Source: Internet Movie Database, http://www.imdb.com/boxoffice/alltimegross, http://www.imdb.com/boxoffice/alltimegross?region-non-us, accessed 12 August 2007.

Ghost (1990) and *Titanic* (1997); one might also include *Forrest Gump* (1994) here. Two similarly inflected romantic dramas, *Out of Africa* (1985) and *The Bodyguard* (1992), are in the foreign top ten lists but not in the domestic ones, supporting the overall impression created by these lists that romantic dramas do better outside the United States and Canada.

Films based on classic American comic strips are significantly less successful in foreign markets. Only *Superman* (1978) appears in both lists, while *Superman II* (1980), *Batman* (1989), *Batman Forever* (1995), *Spider-Man* (2002) and *Spider-Man 2* (2004) only appear in the domestic top tens.[13] Similarly, the adaptation of the classic American children's book *How the Grinch Stole Christmas* only makes it into the domestic top ten list. At the same time, many films based on well-known non-American source material (usually British novels) in the foreign top tens fail to make it into the domestic top tens, including four James Bond films, *Out of Africa* (based on a Danish novel) and three Harry Potter adaptations (only the first is in both lists); one could also add *Robin Hood: Prince of Thieves* (1991) as it is based on a legendary figure in English history. Among the adaptations of foreign source material that do appear in the domestic top ten, two have changed the originals' foreign settings into American settings: *Three Men and a Baby*, which is a remake of a French movie (*Trois Hommes et un Couffin*, 1985), and *Mrs Doubtfire*, which is an adaptation of a British children's novel (*Alias Madame Doubtfire*, 1988).

Perhaps not surprisingly, films with foreign settings, often featuring foreign actors, are much more prominent in the foreign top tens than in the domestic ones: *Rocky IV* (1985, partly set in Russia), *Mission: Impossible* (1996, Europe), *The Lost World: Jurassic Park* (1997, exotic island), *Mission: Impossible II* (2000, Australia), *The Da Vinci Code* (2006, Europe).[14] Of course, many of the fantasy, futuristic and animated films appearing in both sets of top tens have non-American settings featuring some non-American actors, but the tendency for hit movies to do so is much more pronounced in the foreign top tens. By contrast, almost all of the (largely non-romantic) non-animated comedies that failed to translate their domestic success into a place on the foreign top tens have American settings and stars.

Finally, there are hints at other possible patterns. For example, the presence of *Se7en* (1995) in the foreign top ten and its absence from the domestic list might indicate that extremely violent films do better in foreign markets than in the United States and Canada. Similarly, the fact that *The Passion of the Christ* (2004) has been more successful domestically than abroad could indicate the greater resonance of emphatically Christian films in the United States and Canada. There is also an indication that the status of star vehicles for African Americans may have changed. The biggest such domestic hit before 1997, the Eddie Murphy vehicle *Beverly Hills Cop* (1984), does not make it into the foreign top ten, but the Will Smith vehicle *Men in Black* (1997) is in both lists.

It is also important to compare the actual domestic and foreign earnings of films, rather than just their respective rankings. To begin with, some general observations can be made. During the decade 1977–86, films appearing in both top ten lists tend to have higher earnings in the domestic market than abroad. After 1986, this relationship is reversed.[15] Indeed, for several films appearing in both top tens, such as *Terminator 2* (1991), *Pretty Woman* (1990) and *Independence Day* (1996), foreign earnings are about 50% higher than the domestic earnings. In extreme cases, foreign earnings are twice as high as the domestic figure: *Titanic* (1997), *Harry Potter and the Philosopher's Stone* (2001) and *The Lord of the Rings: The Return of the King* (2003). Set against this general trend, it is possible to identify some exceptional films. For example, *Close Encounters of the Third Kind* (1977) made more money abroad than domestically during a period when most top ten films did better domestically. Conversely, *Home Alone* (1990) did better domestically when most other top ten films during this period earned more abroad, while *Forrest Gump* (1994) and *Twister* (1996) were among the few top ten films after 1986 to earn almost as much domestically as in the foreign market.

These exceptional films broadly support the patterns identified earlier, emphasising the success in foreign markets of romantic comedies and dramas and films based on foreign source material, while non-romantic comedies (both animated and live action) often fail to translate their domestic success into the same level of profitabilty in foreign markets. Perhaps the comparatively low foreign earnings of *Forrest Gump* (when compared to the film's domestic earnings) relate to the earlier observation that films that are rooted too specifically in particular aspects of American popular culture often fail to replicate their domestic success abroad. On the other hand, the comparatively high foreign earnings of *Close Encounters of the Third Kind*, *Terminator 2* and *Independence Day* suggest that films dealing with transformative events for humanity as a whole (encounters with extraterrestrials of a redemptive or destructive nature, the imminent destruction of most of mankind by computers) can have a particularly strong appeal in foreign markets (Krämer, 2009).

The potential importance of such divergent hit patterns for Hollywood's operations is indicated by the substantial share of the industry's total theatrical revenues that is generated by a small number of big hits. In 2000, for example, the major studios had foreign theatrical revenues of $6.6 billion. *Mission: Impossible II*, one of the top ten export hits of 1997–2001, but not on the equivalent domestic list, earned 5% of these $6.6 billion, while *How the Grinch Stole Christmas*, a film on the domestic list but not the foreign one, earned 3.5% of the $7.5 billion total US theatrical revenues (Hayes, 2001). If the differences between domestic and foreign hit patterns observed for the limited number of films discussed here also applied to a wider range of films (e.g. the annual top ten, which between them usually account for about a quarter of Hollywood's theatrical revenues), then it is conceivable that export markets could exert a distinctive influence on Hollywood's output by, for example, encouraging the production of romantic comedies and dramas, and of films with non-American settings and those based on foreign source material.

Case Study: Germany

Since the 1970s, Germany has been one of Hollywood's main sources of export revenues, making up around 10% of Hollywood's foreign box office (Krämer, 2008, p. 242). Until the early 1970s, West German box-office charts were dominated by domestic productions, in conjunction with imports from Austria in the 1950s and from other European countries in the 1960s.[16] Hollywood imports only rose to a very prominent position during the 1970s and only came to dominate the annual top ten list in the 1980s. Comparing the annual top ten hits in West Germany (until 1990) and the reunified Germany (after 1990) with those in the United States and Canada reveals considerable overlap.[17] There are, however, some striking differences, including the continuing presence of one or two German productions or European imports in each year's German charts. Continuing trends established in the late 1960s and early 1970s, certain kinds of American imports achieved much higher levels of success in Germany than in their domestic market. This applies especially to Disney films and to erotic films: *Mandingo* was the seventh highest grossing film in West Germany in 1975; *Caligula* fourth in 1980, and *The Blue Lagoon* tenth in 1981; none of these were in the domestic top ten.

In sharp contrast to the virtual absence of traditional Disney productions from the domestic top ten until 1989, it is remarkable that the company placed on average one animated feature or live action children's film per year in the West German top ten between 1975 and 1988, taking one of the two top positions on six occasions.[18] West German audiences' enthusiasm for animation, in evidence since the late 1960s, also supported Disney's rivals, notably ex-Disney animator Don Bluth, whose films *The Secret of NIMH* (sixth in 1982) and *The Land Before Time* (seventh in 1989) were much more successful in West Germany than in the United States and Canada. After 1990, Hollywood animation was about as prominent in the German top tens as it was in the American/Canadian top tens, although the animated films making it into the respective top tens were not necessarily the same. The German preference for animation before 1989 indicates that Hollywood animation can travel well across national borders, while the variations found after 1990 confirm my earlier observation that huge success for Hollywood's animated features in the domestic market does not always translate into the same level of success abroad.

Like animated films, James Bond films were also much more successful in West Germany in the 1970s and 1980s than they were in the United States and Canada, where they disappeared from the domestic top ten list for over a decade after *Octopussy* (1983), In West Germany, however, *Never Say Never Again* was fifth in 1984, *A View to a Kill* seventh in 1985, *The Living Daylights* fourth in 1987, and *License to Kill* fifth in 1989. A noticeable difference between the German and American charts concerns films relating to the Nazi era and war. In the wake of the top ten success of the German documentary *Hitler – Eine Karriere* (*Hitler, a Career*), Ingmar Bergman's Nazi drama *Das Schlangenei* (*The Serpent's Egg*, a German-American co-production), and the epic United Artists release *A Bridge Too Far* in 1977, a range of films about World War II and also about other wars appeared in the West German top ten list, including several Hollywood productions that did not make it into the domestic top ten. As part of this general trend at the West German box office, a series of Vietnam movies became major hits: *Apocalypse Now* (sixth in 1979); *First Blood* (seventh in 1983), *Rambo: First Blood Part II* (fourth in 1985), *Platoon* (sixth in 1987) and *Full Metal Jacket* (ninth in 1983). While *Apocalypse Now*, *Rambo II* and *Platoon* also entered the domestic top ten, the West German market quite surprisingly generated a larger number of top ten hits about the Vietnam war.

A striking feature of the German top ten is the outstanding success of romantic comedies and romantic dramas, which took one of the two top positions in the annual charts from the mid-1980s to the mid-1990s much more frequently than such films did in the United States and Canada. The high point of the reign of romances came in the mid-1980s, when three West German productions, the comedy *Männer* (*Men*, 1986) and two romantic farces featuring TV comedian Otto, *Otto – Der Film* (*Otto – The Movie*, 1985) and *Otto – Der neue Film* (*Otto – The New Movie*, 1987), occupied first place. American imports profiting from this trend included *Out of Africa* (second in 1986), *The Bodyguard* (second in 1993) and *While You Were Sleeping* (second in 1994), whereas the success of *Basic Instinct* (first in 1992) echoes the appearance of sexually explicit films in the German top ten of earlier decades. While most of these Hollywood imports also featured in the domestic top tens, they were ranked much lower. These observations about the German market are in line with my earlier discussion of Hollywood's foreign markets in general.

In addition to conducting such comparisons between the annual top tens, we can also compare the top grossing films across a longer period.[19] The lists of the 30 highest grossing films from 1990 to 2004 in the United States and Germany both include the romantic epics *Titanic* (by far the most popular film in both markets) and *Forrest Gump*, as well as a number of animated, science fiction, fantasy and action films with strong romantic storylines. The German list also includes the straightforwardly romantic imports *Pretty Woman* (1990), *The Bodyguard* (1992) and *What Women Want* (2000) as well as the sex comedies *American Pie* (1999) and *American Pie 2* (2001), again indicating that sexually explicit material and romantic films do better in Germany than in the United States and Canada. By contrast, films featuring classic American comic strip characters or based on classic American children's books do much better in their domestic market than in Germany: neither of the two *Spider-Man* movies nor *How the Grinch Stole Christmas* replicated their domestic success. The German list also includes much more English material: it features the British slapstick comedy *Bean* (1997) and includes all of the first three Harry Potter films – whereas only one of them makes the American list. The *Lord of the Rings* trilogy also ranks much higher, providing a further example of the differences between Hollywood's domestic and foreign markets discussed in the first section of this chapter.

The most obvious difference between the lists of the most popular films in Germany and the United States and Canada is, not surprisingly, the former's German bias. The top 30 for 1990–2004 include the German-themed Hollywood import *Schindler's List* (1993) as well as the German comedies *Der bewegte Mann* (1995), *Der Schuh des Manitou* (*Manitou's Shoe*, 2001), *Good Bye, Lenin!* (2003), *(T) Raumschiff Surprise – Periode 1* (*Dreamship Surprise, Period 1*, 2004) and *7 Zwerge – Männer allein im Wald* (*Seven Dwarfs*, 2004). Even in the new millennium, individual German productions, especially those featuring TV comedians, have competed with Hollywood imports in the German market as successfully as the Otto films and *Männer* did in the 1980s. The German example would, therefore, lead us to expect that even in those countries with a preponderance of Hollywood imports in their annual charts, the top grossing films of recent years are likely to include a small number of domestic productions, and that the Hollywood hits in those countries will form some distinctive patterns. Even though audiences in different countries may share a strong inclination towards Hollywood, they still make distinctive film choices.

Conclusion

As an audience study, the preceding discussion is obviously very limited. Audiences feature only as abstract aggregates; actual people or sociologically profiled social groups are absent from it. As a comparative study of domestic and foreign hit patterns, it also has severe limitations. It focuses only on the top ten movies for each 5-year period, is merely observational and looks only at broad generic and thematic trends. A much wider range of films could be selected, statistical analysis could be employed, and a broader range of factors (ranging from budgets to the presence of stars) could be examined.[20] Alternatively, a more qualitative approach could be taken, exploring the textual meanings and attractions offered by individual films in more detail, examining the marketing materials that frame their reception, analysing the responses of critics and cultural commentators, and conducting surveys, focus group discussions or interviews about these films with actual audience members (see, e.g., Barker and Mathijs, 2008). Furthermore, the focus of this study has been only on theatrical exhibition when in fact most Hollywood films since the 1970s have been viewed on the small screen (through television broadcasts, video and DVD), and since the mid-1980s Hollywood has generated most of its income through video and later DVD. Finally, the study has largely been concerned with patterns discernible fairly consistently across a 30-year period, rather than with changes taking place within those 30 years, or with longer-term processes of historical change.[21]

Having said all this, my preliminary investigation has illuminated two points that may prompt future research. Firstly, much greater attention needs to be paid to those countries in which most of the world's population lives (notably China, India, Indonesia, Brazil, Pakistan, Bangladesh and Russia, which between them contain half of the world's population), and in which most film viewing takes place. These markets have only generated a tiny portion of Hollywood's overall income, and Hollywood films in turn have probably had only a small, even negligible presence in most of them.[22] Secondly, a film's success at the American box office does not always translate straightforwardly into success abroad; both the export market as a whole (perceived in terms of financial returns rather than in terms of ticket sales) and individual countries are characterised by distinctive hit patterns. It continues to be worth asking why this is so, and what these similarities and differences might tell us about the cultural exchanges between the populations of different countries after a century of 'Americanisation'.

Notes

1 See, for example, Kristin Thompson, *Exporting Entertainment: America in the World Film Market 1907–1934* (London: BFI, 1985); and Deniz Göktürk, *Künstler, Cowboys, Ingenieure: Kultur- und mediengeschichtliche Studien zu deutschen Amerika-Texten 1912–1920* (München: Wilhelm Fink Verlag, 1998).

2 For a recent critical summary of debates about 'Americanisation' see Richard Maltby, 'Introduction: "The Americanisation of the World"', in Melvyn Stokes and Richard Maltby (eds), *Hollywood Abroad: Audiences and Cultural Exchange* (London: BFI, 2004), pp. 1–20.

3 See, for example, Stephen Prince's comments on the importance of foreign markets for the careers of action stars Sylvester Stallone and Arnold Schwarzenegger, in *A New Pot of Gold: Hollywood Under the Electronic Rainbow, 1980–1989* (Berkeley: University of California Press, 2000), pp. 175, 183; Ruth Vasey, *The World According to Hollywood, 1918–1939* (Exeter: University of Exeter Press, 1997).

4 David Waterman, *Hollywood's Road to Riches* (Cambridge, MA: Harvard University Press, 2005), pp. 4, 158, 182. Waterman concludes (on p. 273): 'other things equal, movie patrons prefer domestically produced movie content.'

5 For a discussion of one European market, The Netherlands, in the 1930s, see Clara Pafort-Overduin (Chapter 6) in this volume.

6 David A. Cook, *Lost Illusions: American Cinema in the Shadow of Watergate and Vietnam* (New York: Scribner's, 2000), p. 21. Kerry Segrave, *American Films Abroad: Hollwood's Domination of the World's Movie Screens from the 1890s to the Present* (Jefferson: McFarland, 1997), pp. 287–288. Figures can vary considerably from source to source, depending on whether only the major studios or all American production companies are counted, and on whether Canada is included as part of the domestic rather than the foreign market.

7 Soaring Overseas Demand Creates Studio Upheaval. *Screen Finance*, 17 May 1989, p. 10.

8 Int'l Shrinks for Studios, Boosts Indies. *Screen International*, 28 July 2000, p. 6.

9 *The Economist, Pocket World in Figures 2007. A Concise Edition* (London: Profile Books, 2007).

10 This is not to deny that these films may be more widely viewed on television, video and DVD, or that the films dominating the cinema screens may be influenced by Hollywood productions.

11 Canadian revenues make up around 5% of US revenues. Soaring Overseas Demand Creates Studio Upheaval, *Screen Finance*, 17 May 1989, pp. 8–10; and Acland (2003), p. 6.

12 It should be noted that box-office figures include revenues from much later re-releases, which means that initially films such as the *Star Wars* trilogy and *E.T.* were not quite as far ahead of the competition as they are here; nevertheless, their top rankings are not dependent on the inclusion of re-release revenues.

13 *Men in Black* (1997), which appears in both lists, was based on an obscure comic strip first published in 1990.

14 Considering their post-apocalyptic settings, *The Matrix* (1999) and *The Matrix Reloaded* (2003) could also be included here.

15 This is not simply a consequence of the general increase in revenues from foreign theatrical markets. Throughout the 1980s, the share of the American film industry's box-office revenues coming from outside the United States remained fairly stable, with only a slight rise at the very

end of the decade. See 'Soaring Overseas Demand Creates Studio Upheaval', *Screen Finance*, 17 May 1989, pp. 8–9. A somewhat more volatile picture (with a decline of export revenues share at the beginning of the decade and an increase at the end) emerges from statistics provided in Segrave, K. (1997) *American Films Abroad: Hollywood's Domination of the World's Movie Screens from the 1890s to the Present*. McFarland, Jefferson, NC, p. 288.

16 Both the charts and a thorough analysis of the major trends within them, in particular the changing role of Hollywood imports, can be found in Garncarz (1994), pp. 94–135.

17 For the German market, I have used the charts up to 1990 reprinted in Garncarz's essay and, for the period after 1990, I have used the annual charts printed in one of the January issues of the German trade paper *Filmecho/Filmwoche*. For the American charts I have used data from a range of sources, which all rely on the American trade paper *Variety*. Unfortunately, the (West) German charts do not account for a film's total ticket sales, but only for sales within a given calendar year, whereas the American/Canadian charts I have compiled are based on a film's total ticket sales. Hence, films released late in the year are likely to do much better in the American/Canadian chart. Although the figures in the two charts are not, therefore, exactly comparable, their differences do not invalidate the broad conclusions I draw from them.

18 *Robin Hood*, second in 1975; *The Rescuers*, second in 1978; *The Jungle Book*, first in 1980 and second in 1988; *The Aristocats*, second in 1981; and *The Fox and the Hound*, first in 1982.

19 The list for the United States and Canada is derived from Box Office Mojo, 'Domestic Grosses Adjusted for Ticket Price Inflation' (http://www.boxofficemojo.com/alltime/adjusted.htm), accessed 13 August 2007; the German list is derived from figures published in German trade papers since 1990.

20 See, for example, the analysis of generic patterns in annual hit lists in David Waterman, *Hollywood's Road to Riches* (Cambridge, MA: Harvard University Press, 2005), pp. 226–227, 320–324.

21 For a study of changes in hit patterns from the 1940s to the 1980s in the US, see Krämer (2005b).

22 It is worth keeping in mind what Jeremy Tunstall has recently concluded about American media influences: 'Even in small population countries the majority of audience time goes to national media. In larger population countries the national, regional, local, and across-the-border media typically achieve audiences between 6 and 12 times those of global or American media.' Jeremy Tunstall, *The Media Were American: U.S. Mass Media in Decline* (New York: Oxford University Press, 2008), p. 10.

References

Acland, C.R. (2003) *Screen Traffic: Movies, Multiplexes, and Global Culture,* Duke University Press, Durham NC.

Barker, M. and Mathijs, E. (eds) (2008) *Watching The Lord of the Rings: Tolkien's World Audiences,* Peter Lang, New York.

Garncarz, J. (1994) Hollywood in Germany: the role of American films in Germany, 1925–1990, in *Hollywood in Europe: Experiences of a Cultural Hegemony* (eds D.W. Ellwood and R. Kroes), VU University Press, Amsterdam, pp. 94–138.

Govil, N. (2008) India: Hollywood's domination, extinction, and re-animation (with thanks to *Jurassic Park*), in *The Contemporary Hollywood Film Industry* (eds P. McDonald and J. Wasko), Wiley-Blackwell, Oxford, pp. 285–294.

Hayes, D. (2001) Late Rally Lifts Wilted Wickets. *Variety*, 8 January, pp. 9–10.

Krämer, P. (2005a) Big pictures: studying contemporary Hollywood cinema through its greatest hits, in *Screen Methods: Comparative Readings in Film Studies* (eds J. Furby and K. Randell), Wallflower Press, London, pp. 124–132.

Krämer P. (2005b) *The New Hollywood: From Bonnie and Clyde to Star Wars,* Wallflower Press, London, pp. 89–103.

Krämer, P. (2008) Germany: Hollywood and Germany – a very special relationship, in *The Contemporary*

Hollywood Film Industry (eds P. McDonald and J. Wasko), Wiley-Blackwell, Oxford, pp. 240–250.

Kramer, P. (2009) Welterfolg und Apokalypse: Überlegungen zur Transnationalität des zeitgenössischen Hollywood, in *Film transnational und transkulturell. Europäische und amerikanische Perspektiven* (eds R. Strobel and A. Jahn-Sudmann), Wilhelm Fink Verlag, Paderborn, pp. 171–184.

Lent, J.A. (2008) East Asia: for better or worse, in *The Contemporary Hollywood Film Industry* (eds P. McDonald and J. Wasko), Wiley-Blackwell, Oxford, pp. 277–285.

10

Blindsiding

Theatre Owners, Political Action and Industrial Change in Hollywood, 1975–1985

Deron Overpeck

During the 1970s, the growth of pay cable television stations threatened to reduce the supply of both films and audiences to American movie theatres. The studios, which saw pay cable as a growth opportunity, were already producing fewer films than many exhibitors believed was healthy for the future of the industry. Compounding the problem, the studios were also transferring much of the financial risk of production onto theatre owners through the distribution practice of blind bidding, which required exhibitors to guarantee rental payments long in advance of a movie's release. Exhibitor groups disagreed on how best to address these issues, and the resulting uncertainties hampered theatre owners' plans for expansion. Although many exhibitors wanted to build new theatres or convert their current single screen theatres into multiplexes, others, along with some studio executives, were unsure if economic conditions warranted such growth.

Rather than wait passively for economic conditions to improve, exhibitors took matters into their own hands. Working primarily through their trade organisation, the National Association of Theatre Owners (NATO), exhibitors confronted these and other issues threatening their business. Although NATO was unable to forestall the spread of pay television, it lobbied the studios, the Federal Communications Commission and various local regulatory agencies to ensure that theatrical exhibition remained the first venue for most films. In order to increase their cash flow and thus make expansion more affordable, the exhibitors also fought a state-by-state campaign to end blind bidding, the distribution practice that exposed them to so much risk. This chapter examines how NATO prevailed in the confrontation over blind bidding. It uses NATO memoranda, trade press reports and interviews with key individuals to shed new light on the relationship between exhibition and production–distribution in the American film industry.

Explorations in New Cinema History: Approaches and Case Studies, First Edition.
Edited by Richard Maltby, Daniel Biltereyst and Philippe Meers.

In his seminal study of the exhibition industry, *Shared Pleasures*, Douglas Gomery has detailed how national theatre chains established themselves as the dominant forces in the industry, and has also indicated the importance of individual exhibition executives such as Sam Katz and Garth Drabinsky (Gomery, 1992). Scholars such as Gregory Waller, Kathryn Fuller-Seeley and Taso Lagos have detailed the exhibition practices in specific cities of various sizes, while William Paul has focused on the architectural specifics of various venues (Paul, 1994; Waller, 1995; Lagos, 2003; Fuller-Seeley, 2008). Barbara Wilinsky (2000) and Eric Schaefer (1999) have provided important histories of alternative exhibition sites including the art house and exploitation markets. Although these scholars have all contributed to our field's understanding of the importance of exhibition to the health of the film industry, they have in most cases done so in a way that effectively separates exhibition from production–distribution, or otherwise reinforces the perception that it is the junior partner in the industry. Histories of the conversion to sound in the late 1920s, for example, tend to emphasise the actions of studios and minimise the resistance provided by independent exhibitors who could not afford to convert their theatres (Crafton, 1997; Gomery, 2005). Similarly, the Paramount case and the resulting divorcement decrees are usually presented as crises for the film studios, while much less attention is paid either to the role of independent exhibitors in spurring the federal government to action during the 1930s, or to the suffering of exhibitors of all classes in the aftermath of the decrees (Conant, 1960; Izod, 1988; White, 1988).

Other scholars have begun to examine the role of exhibitors in the central controversies in the film industry. Gary Edgerton (1983) has analysed how national chain and independent exhibitors negotiated an industrial structure that allowed production–distribution to dominate exhibition. Ben Singer (2004) has explored how smaller exhibitors, who had previously permitted patrons to come and go as they pleased throughout the day, changed their programmes and policies to accommodate the longer feature films in the 1910s. Susan Ohmer (2007) has examined how, from the late 1930s, exhibitors used audience research to ascertain what would bring audiences back into theatres. In his study of how the experience of exhibition has shifted in the past two decades, Charles Acland (2003) addresses the response from exhibitors and studio executives to the potential for vertical reintegration in the mid 1980s. It is in this latter tradition that the present study falls.

Because of its direct impact on their cash flow, blind bidding was the most critical issue that exhibitors faced in the mid-1970s. It was a problem that affected all exhibitors, national chain and independent alike, regardless of size or location. Blind bidding required exhibitors to pay for the licence to offer a film in their theatres without being able to see it beforehand. Before production began on a film, the distributing studio would send to theatre owners a brief report on it, including a plot synopsis and the names of attached actors and other talent. Based on this information, each exhibitor would submit a sealed bid that detailed how much money he would advance to the studio for the licence to the film, how long beyond the studio-mandated minimum period the film would appear on the theatre's screens, and the minimum amount of the box office gross the exhibitor would guarantee to pay the studio. The film studios claimed that blind bidding was an essential element in funding the blockbuster hits that everyone craved. Without that guaranteed money, producers would be forced to take out more high-interest loans to finance their projects. The Motion Picture Association of America (MPAA) President Jack Valenti warned that the industry would face a shortage of theatrical films during peak moviegoing periods.[1] Furthermore, the studios maintained, blind transactions were an unavoidable part of doing business in the film industry, arguing that they '"blind [bought]" everything from the original script to media advertising ... [and] exhibitors should not be exempt from taking the business risks that accompany the blind bidding on a new film' (Linck, 1981).

In response, NATO charged that the practice was 'unethical' because it required exhibitors to invest money in films that that they knew next to nothing about and would quite possibly have rejected had they been able to see them beforehand.[2] Box office disappointments made blind bidding an even more bitter pill to swallow. A. Alan Friedberg, a Boston-based exhibitor and president of NATO from 1978 to1980, pointed to *A Bridge Too Far* (1977) as an example of how inaccurate could be the information from which exhibitors were expected to make their blind bids. 'It was advanced to us as an epic film starring Robert Redford', he said, adding that based on United Artists' solicitations he put up a $100 000 advance payment in order to secure the film for his theatres. 'As it turned out', he continued, 'the film was three hours long and Redford was in it for maybe seven minutes. The film was a huge bomb.'[3]

Other films cited by exhibitors as flops that they would have avoided had they been able to trade screen them included John Boorman's infamous *Exorcist II: The Heretic* (1977), *The Other Side of Midnight* (1977), *The Wiz* (1978) and Sylvester Stallone's labour drama *F.I.S.T.* (1978). All had been expected to be great box office draws: the sequel to one of the decade's most successful horror films, an adaptation of a popular novel, an adaptation of a Broadway musical that was itself an adaptation of a classic movie, and Stallone's first film after the Oscar-winning *Rocky* (1976). But all were critical and commercial disasters. Even successful films that had been blind bid could cause problems for exhibitors, as the 1977 hockey comedy *Slap Shot*, starring Paul Newman, demonstrated. Theatre owners expected the film to be in the mode of *Butch Cassidy and the Sundance Kid* (1969). Instead, they received a profane, raunchy comedy and found themselves having to explain to offended patrons that, thanks to blind bidding, they had had no idea what they were getting when they scheduled the film for their theatres.[4]

The blind bidding system also assumed that a film would be completed and released on schedule. Film releases continue to be delayed for any number of reasons, and these delays can cause problems for exhibitors. In 1978, for example, Paramount, United Artists and Warner Bros all delayed films that had been solicited and bid on as summer releases, including *Superman*, which many exhibitors had expected to be the cornerstone of their summer schedules. Exhibitors were forced to tie up a lot of their cash flow in order to secure the licence for a film, and if the film was delayed they were left scrambling to find an affordable replacement.[5] Little wonder, then, that theatre owners considered blind bidding such a threat. In January 1978, NATO conducted a mail-in survey of its members, asking them to comment on the state of the exhibition business. It sent out 8000 survey forms, and received 4800 replies. Ninety percent of the respondents agreed that blind bidding was a major problem confronting them.[6]

On the other hand, blind bidding was in part a beast of exhibition's making. Prior to the Paramount case, which ended the vertical integration of the studio system era, blind bidding was virtually non-existent. The vertical integration of the film industry guaranteed studios the most important screens on which to show their films. The block booking system, by which distributors sold theatre owners a slate of between 5 and 50 films at a time, ensured that theatres not owned or affiliated with the studios also screened the studios' films. Independent exhibitors' persistent complaints against block booking during the 1930s led the Department of Justice (DOJ) to pursue its antitrust case against the major studios. In 1940, the studios signed a consent decree that temporarily halted the antitrust suit; among its conditions was one requiring them to trade screen films to exhibitors before distributing them. Because the industry remained vertically integrated, trade screenings were largely a formality and were in fact poorly attended. This consent decree ended in 1943, although trade screenings continued until 1948 (Aarons, 1966, p.7).

The postwar antitrust trials inadvertently made blind bidding a prominent part of the distribution of films in the United States. In 1946, in an attempt to address the imbalance of commercial power between affiliated and independent exhibitors, the trial court created a system of competitive bidding in which each film was offered on an individual basis to exhibitors, with no requirement that an exhibitor take any one film in order to receive another. Blind bidding was not prohibited in this system, and the studios were not required to trade screen any film. The court recognised that this process was 'capable of some abuse' and thus included a provision that allowed exhibitors 'to reject a certain percentage of their blind-licensed films within a reasonable time after they shall have become available for inspection' (Aarons, 1966, pp. 7–8). The studios, exhibitors and government all denounced the court's system when the case was heard before the Supreme Court in 1948. When the Court handed down its verdict against the studios, the District Court's competitive bidding system was rejected as well (Schatz, 1997; Lewis, 2000).

Blind bidding became an increasingly important part of the studios' business plans throughout the 1950s. As Valenti would later claim in the 1970s, the practice did secure production funds that would otherwise have come from bank loans. It also allowed the studios to continue to dominate exhibition in the post-studio system era. By tying up exhibitor dollars in as-yet unmade films, the studios were able to ensure that the films they produced or distributed reached the nation's theatres, that independent and foreign films were relegated to art-house theatres, and thus that the lion's share of the nation's box office found its way into their coffers. The goal of the Paramount case had been to free theatrical exhibition from studio dominance; the effect of the Paramount decision was to give the studios the mechanism by which to maintain that dominance.

Exhibitors spent the next two decades complaining that blind bidding placed them in dire jeopardy and hoping that some further federal court action would prohibit it. In 1966, Judge Edmund Palmieri, who oversaw the implementation of the consent decrees, considered a modification of the Paramount consent decrees that stipulated under what circumstances blind bidding would be permitted. Trade screenings would be required for all films other than those the studios intended to roadshow, a distribution format reserved for prestigious pictures, such as *2001: A Space Odyssey* (1967), in which prints of a film would 'tour' the country in much the same way as a Broadway play or musical. The modification was offered to the court by the studios themselves and supported by the DOJ. It was opposed by NATO, which pointed out that it allowed the studios to blind bid the most financially risky films.[7] Judge Palmieri approved the modification in 1968, but, according to NATO executive Jerome Gordon, the studios continued to blind bid all films. When the modification expired in 1973, the studios had no theoretical limits on their ability to blind bid films.[8]

Dissatisfied by the court's action on blind bidding, NATO began to explore other options. Its first step was to approach the federal government and again ask for its intervention. In 1974 and again in 1975, NATO's counsel, Peter Fishbein, asked the DOJ to pursue antitrust action against the film studios over blind bidding, in the hope that federal lawyers would respond with the same sympathy that their counterparts had in the 1930s and 1940s. By the early 1970s, however, the arguments of the Chicago School of economists and legal theorists that industrial concentration benefitted consumers had become ascendant in the federal government, and the regulatory mood had begun to shift away from intervention in the affairs of industry (Stigler, 1966; Posner, 1970; Bork, 1978; Geisst, 2000). When the DOJ responded to NATO, it announced that the federal government now supported blind bidding, with only one caveat. So long as all exhibitors were subject to blind bidding, the practice was permissible. If any exhibitor were permitted to see a film before the bidding process began, then the studios would have to trade screen the film for all exhibitors everywhere.[8]

For the exhibitors, then, the goal was to create a situation in which the studios would be required to trade screen a film for at least some exhibitors; if NATO could achieve that, the studios could be compelled to trade screen the film for all exhibitors. The federal government had already signalled that it was not interested in creating such a situation; not only had the DOJ refused to pursue any antitrust action against the studios, but both the Senate and the House of Representatives had also declined to hold any hearings on blind bidding. So, in a plan designed to take advantage of the prominence of the nation's theatre chains, NATO turned to individual state legislatures. In 1978, American theatrical exhibition was, as now, dominated by chains operating theatres in more than one state.

Exhibitors working for a theatre chain in a state where blind bidding was forbidden would be able to see a film at trade screenings and communicate their opinions of the film to other exhibitors in the same chain operating in states that allowed blind bidding, giving those exhibitors a competitive advantage over independent exhibitors. NATO's campaign aimed to bring this evidently unfair trade situation in being, and thus force the studios to abandon blind bidding or the Federal government to prohibit it.

According to Jerome Gordon, who was then the Special Assistant to NATO President Marvin Goldman, no one person suggested the campaign, nor did NATO conduct any prior research to determine that it was likely to succeed. NATO's national office contacted its state chapters to ascertain which of them already had strong relationships with their local lawmakers, and decided that 'the South would be a good place to start', because 'Southern exhibitors were closer to their legislatures'.[8] The first state to pass anti-blind bidding legislation was Alabama in March 1978. The Alabama Motion Picture Fair Competition Act forbade any bidding or negotiation for the licence to exhibit a picture 'before the motion picture has been trade screened, or before such motion picture, at the option of the distributor, otherwise has been made available for viewing by all exhibitors'.[9] Once a film had been trade screened and bids submitted, the bids were to be publicly opened and made available to exhibitors for their inspection. If the distributors found the bids unsatisfactory, they could reject them all, but the bill required that bids for the film then be resolicited to ensure that licences were to be awarded only through an open-bidding process. The bill also provided for civil actions and criminal injunctions against distributors who were found to be violating the law.

Other Southern states, including South Carolina, Georgia and Louisiana, soon followed Alabama's lead. Within 18 months, a total of 16 states throughout the nation had enacted anti-blind bidding legislation.[10] Ohio and Pennsylvania passed the two most stringent laws. Both states prohibited not only blind bidding but also minimum guarantees of box office: any contract that required exhibitors to submit a bid for a film before it had been trade screened, to pay any amount of money in advance of receiving the film, or to promise a minimum percentage of the box office to distributors was null and void in those states, even if the exhibitor had willingly entered into it.

Gordon coordinated the national organisation's participation in the state-by-state strategy, but the anti-blind bidding campaign was not really a national effort. Federal law prevented the national organisation from acting on behalf of its members, and the state NATO chapters had to pursue anti-blind bid legislation themselves, although national NATO provided legal assistance, financial support and a model bill that local exhibitors could offer to friendly legislators. Gordon himself made personal appearances before some state legislatures, but for the most part, national NATO's role was to keep its members abreast of which states had passed blind bidding laws and how those victories had been accomplished, through a series of 'Blind Bidding Hotlines'.[11]

The studios took NATO's anti-blind bidding campaign seriously and fought the passage of anti-blind bidding legislation in many of the states in which it was introduced. Their strategy included lobbying efforts before state legislatures and film commissions, and making threats about product delays and lawsuits. As early as 1977, Jack Valenti began to warn that producers would eschew doing any location shooting in states that passed anti-blind bidding laws because they would not feel welcome there.[12] Star power was also employed to make this threat. Jerry Reed, a country singer then appearing in the *Smokey and the Bandit* films, hosted a luncheon in Tennessee in 1981 at which he urged state legislators to repeal their anti-blind bidding law. His remarks betrayed a somewhat contemptuous attitude towards exhibitors. 'Are we going to say we don't care about losing this money', he wondered aloud, 'because it's more important to please those damn exhibitors? Let's make the exhibitor work a little bit. He ain't going to get hurt that bad.'[13] The lawmakers ignored Reed's pleas, but the allegation of lost location shoots was serious all the same. Production companies spent a great deal of money during location shoots, and states were loath to lose this income, as Arkansas governor Bill Clinton indicated when he vetoed an anti-blind bidding bill passed by the state legislature.[14] NATO worked diligently to counteract the MPAA's assertions. Jerome Gordon met with several state film commissions to argue that the MPAA could not prevent independent production companies from filming on location wherever they chose. NATO also brought Valenti's claim to the attention of the DOJ, arguing that such a deliberate boycott of filming locations would constitute illegal collusion on the part of the studios. The DOJ agreed, and announced its intention to investigate the matter in 1981. Valenti quickly denied ever having claimed that the studios would deliberately avoid any state; he had, he insisted, merely meant to assert the studios' rights to film wherever they felt most welcomed.[15]

The MPAA also warned that states that forbade blind bidding would receive films at a later date than those that permitted blind bidding, because the studios could not trade screen films until they were completed. In some isolated cases, studios did appear to delay distributing their films in anti-blind bidding states. During the Christmas season of 1978, for example, *Superman* was held out of Louisiana for several weeks after it debuted in other states, and when moviegoers travelled into Texas to see the film, some exhibitors in the Pelican State petitioned legislators to repeal the anti-blind bidding law. As A. Alan Friedberg pointed out, however, the states in which films were held back were relatively less populated; the studios were not willing to risk losing profits in the more populous states and as such never followed through on its threat with any vigor.[16]

Warnings of production embargoes and late movies were not the only weapons the studios had in the blind bidding fight. In 1980, the studios filed federal lawsuits to overturn the laws in Ohio and Pennsylvania. Although neither state is as large as California or New York, each is home to large urban centres served by the national exhibition chains. As such, to lose either state would be a serious threat to the future of blind bidding. The lawsuits alleged that the laws violated the commerce clause of the Constitution, which reserves to the federal government the right to regulate interstate commerce, by denying the studios their rights of equal protection and due process, pre-empting applicable federal laws, including the Copyright and Sherman Antitrust acts, and denying the studios their First Amendment rights to free speech by forcing them to open films in some theatres months later than when they would have preferred to. Although the Pennsylvania suit was initially decided in favour of the studios, that decision was overturned on appeal, while the Ohio lawsuit was decided for the defendants.[17] Unsuccessful in the federal court, the studios also filed lawsuits in Utah and Georgia, hoping that those courts would find the anti-blind bidding laws to be violations of state constitutions, but those attempts also ended in defeat for the studios.[18]

The MPAA's last attempt to preserve blind bidding involved negotiating a compromise with NATO. This was entirely unsuccessful, for a variety of reasons. To begin with, it was of dubious legality, since federal law prohibited the MPAA and NATO from acting as bargaining agents for their members, because neither represented all studios or all exhibitors. One meeting between the two parties, scheduled for early 1979, was blocked by the DOJ.[19] For the next five years, the two parties continued to find some way around the law in order to discuss a mutually satisfactory end to the fight, although NATO had little reason to concede while it continued to add to the roster of states prohibiting blind bidding. Indeed, NATO leaders' giddiness at their success in the blind bidding battle hamstrung early efforts at conciliation. During his terms as NATO president, A. Alan Friedberg took pleasure in nettling Valenti. He openly disputed the financial figures used by the MPAA in its arguments about the impact of blind bidding on theatre owners, and castigated the studios for telling state legislatures that anti-blind bidding laws were unconstitutional when the matter was still being adjudicated in federal court. Friedberg likened Valenti to convicted Watergate 'dirty trickster' Donald Segretti, and implied that the studios behaved like Nazis during negotiations with exhibitors.[20] These statements outraged Valenti, and contributed to the cancellation of one attempted exhibitor–distributor summit. Tensions between the MPAA and NATO were so great that Friedberg refused to invite Valenti to his traditional speaking engagement before the 1979 NATO convention. Insulted, Valenti vowed not to associate with NATO outside the courtroom. Despite the fact that the convention was held in Anaheim, 50 miles from Hollywood, the major studios also boycotted it in protest of Friedberg's treatment of Valenti.[21]

The blind bidding battle was won entirely by the exhibitors. In 1984, when the MPAA effectively conceded defeat after the last appeals of the studios' various lawsuits were rejected, 24 states, a county in Maryland and the Commonwealth of Puerto Rico had enacted anti-blind bidding legislation. NATO never managed to win the three biggest states: California, New York and Texas all rejected anti-blind bidding legislation. In fact, Texas – Jack Valenti's home state – not only voted down anti-blind bidding legislation, but instead passed a resolution and held a party in his honour. This must have refreshed Valenti, who had promised to resign if Texas went with NATO.[22] But as the rest of the country went with NATO, the MPAA recognised that it would be defeated. Valenti decried the amount of time and money spent on legal challenges, to which NATO responded that the financial drain could easily be stopped by the MPAA dropping its legal challenges. In 1984, Valenti announced he was 'sick' of the blind bidding battle and ready for new challenges.[23] The MPAA dropped its plans to appeal its various lawsuits to the Supreme Court and quietly conceded that the exhibitors had won the day.

According to Friedberg, the reason the exhibitors won the blind bidding battle was simply that their cause was just. In February 1979, he described NATO's mission in patriotic tones: 'To vote against legislation eliminating blind bidding is getting to be as unpopular … as voting against God, motherhood, country or apple pie.'[24] More than 30 years later, he also suggested that the state-by-state strategy mitigated the MPAA's lobbying advantage.[25] Although the MPAA maintained a lobbying presence before local and state governments, NATO's members had personal connections with their legislators and offered a personal element to exhibitors' stories of financial peril.

The blind bidding battle stands as an instance in which exhibitors, usually seen as the junior partner in the production-distribution-exhibition triad, successfully fought back against studio domination and managed to make their voice heard in the industry. Whereas independent exhibitors in the 1930s and 1940s had persuaded federal lawyers to defend their interests, the fight over blind bidding involved exhibitors representing themselves and winning in an arena – lobbying – traditionally regarded as an MPAA stronghold. Theatre owners shuffled off the burden of production risk and exchanged it for the risk of real estate speculation. Their success had rapid and lasting ramifications on both theatrical exhibition and on film form. It facilitated the growth that exhibitors had been planning since the beginning of the decade. With an improved cash flow, exhibitors were able to build new theatres and refurbish existing buildings into multiplexes. The number of indoor screens in the United States increased by 8000 during the 1980s.[26]

The end of blind bidding also contributed to the development of the kinds of glitzy, action-oriented high concept movies associated with the multiplex. In October 1979, Valenti warned that without the financial security provided by blind bidding, the studios would be forced to become more conservative with their projects. 'There won't be any *Close Encounters of the Third Kind* or *Apocalypse Now* pictures [if blind bidding is illegal]', he argued. 'The major studios, like any businessmen, won't be willing to take any risks. If they have to prepare budgets without any guarantees, they'll produce fewer big budget blockbusters, fewer imaginative films, and more and more sequels and remakes.'[27] Although, as Justin Wyatt has pointed out, the studios' fondness for high concept fare had begun in the early 1970s, movies based on other movies or television series, comic books, video games or theme park rides are now the dominant forces at American movie theatres. It is true to say that the film studios have always prioritised quick and easy profit over artistry: the countercultural cinema of the late 1960s and early 1970s was more an attempt to find ways to attract a youthful audience than it was a commitment to artistic progress. But one would be hard-pressed to name many films made during the 1980s or 1990s that were as artistically ambitious or intellectually engaging as *Apocalypse Now* (1979) or *Raging Bull* (1981). The end of blind bidding took away the financial safety net that encouraged studios to support more challenging film-making. If not the primary cause of the growth of high concept film-making, it was certainly a contributing factor.

I make this point not to blame NATO for any perceived degradation of film-making quality, but rather to suggest that the struggle outlined here demonstrates more than a localised rupture in the typical relationship between studios and exhibitors. It also demonstrates that actions taken by exhibitors have significantly influenced the American film industry's transition out of its post-studio system malaise into the current converged entertainment industry. No matter how well they are remembered now, *A Clockwork Orange* (1971), *Chinatown* (1974) and *The Conversation* (1974) were qualified box office successes. Hollywood's resurgence – and the rise in the number of movie theatres – in the 1980s came as a result of movies such as *Raiders of the Lost Ark* (1982), *Flashdance* (1983) and *Top Gun* (1986). Far from ruing the shift to adaptations and other popcorn fare, exhibitors were most likely to welcome it.

Although the relationship between the MPAA and NATO is now cordial, important disagreements remain, particularly in relation to the continually shrinking window between theatrical exhibition and home video release. Whether or not the exhibitors will have the same success in protecting their interests now as they did three decades ago remains to be seen. The blind bidding fight illustrated the extent to which exhibitors have been active forces in the film industry throughout its history, with the organisational strength to shift the terms of industrial debate in their favour, at least on occasion. Further scholarly attention on their activities, both historical and current, will enrich our understanding not only of the development of American theatrical exhibition, but of the American entertainment industry in general.

Notes

1 'Distribs Will Combat State-by-State Parity', *Variety,* 18 May 1977, p. 7. See also 'On Making Flop Films', *Variety,* 13 October 1976, p. 7; and 'Boone to NATO: Risks Justify Bid System; TV as Lethal Interloper', *Variety,* 25 October 1978, p. 6.

2 'NATO's Roth Urges Unity for Solving Problems', *Boxoffice,* 24 March 1975, p. 4; 'Film Rental Demands for Exhibitors Financial Homicide', *Boxoffice,* 25 October 1975, p. 5. Harlan Jacobson, 'NATO: Bids Could Hit 2d, 3d Runs, Too', *Variety,* 16 May 1979, p. 7.

3 Telephone interview with A. Alan Friedberg, 1 December 2006.

4 'Victims of locust attacks!!!', *NATO Flash Bulletin* 1 July 1977, p. 2. 'Just-a-short-note-why-what-NATO-is-doing-is-important Dept', *NATO Flash Bulletin,* 5 May 1978. Position paper by the National Association of Theater Owners [sic], and a rebuttal to the booklet 'Motion Picture Licensing' published by the Motion Picture Association of America on the subject of 'Blind Bidding of Motion Pictures'. Contained in Anti-Blind Bidding Bill Legislative Packet, revised 10 October 1979, p. 63. From the personal files of Jerome Gordon.

5 'NATO president blasts film companies', *NATO Flash Bulletin,* 13 January 1978, p. 1. 'Model bill progress', *NATO Flash Bulletin,* 27 January 1978, p. 1.

6 'The following are the overall results....', *NATO Flash Bulletin,* 7 April 1978, pp. 3–5.

7 Undated memorandum filed on behalf of National Association of Theatre Owners, in the United States District Court for the Southern District of New York, United States of America vs. Paramount Pictures, Inc., *et al.* MSS 1446, National Association of Theatre Owners Manuscript Collection. L. Tom Perry Special Collections, Harold B. Lee Library, Brigham Young University, LTPSC, Box 1, Folder 5.

8 Telephone interview with Jerome Gordon, 30 November 2006.

9 Text of the Alabama bill (H. 152) contained in the Anti-Blind Bidding Bill Legislative Packet, pp. 1–3. Personal files of Jerome Gordon.

10 The full roster of states that had prohibited blind bidding as of October 1979 (in order in which the legislation was passed): Alabama, South Carolina, Louisiana, Virginia, Ohio, Georgia, Tennessee, West Virginia, Idaho, Utah, North Carolina, New Mexico, Washington, Maine, Oregon and Massachusetts.

11 30 November 2006 and 4 December 2006 telephone interviews with Jerome Gordon. Mr Gordon also provided a copy of one of his Blind Bidding Hot Lines from his personal files.

12 'NATO of Illinois fights blind bidding', *NATO News*, 20 May 1977, p. 3.

13 '"Concrete Cowboy" attempts to corral Tenn. Lawmakers', *NATO News,* 26 June 1981, p. 2.

14 'Cite one motive in bid bill veto: Ark. feared film location hurt', *Variety*, 25 April 1979, p. 5.

15 'NATO's Orear blasts bid-linked boycotts', *Variety,* 3 June 1981. '"Disinclined", yes', *Variety,* 3 June 1981.

16 'Valenti Hails Bid Drive Curbs; Says Public Indifferent, Not Aroused; 11th Anti Law Due', *Variety,* 25 April 1979, p. 5. '"Late access" called MPAA mythology', *Variety*, 25 April 1979, p. 5. Telephone interview with A. Alan Friedberg, 1 December 2006.

17 Tony Rutherford, 'CARA director testifies in trial on Ohio bid law', *Boxoffice*, 30 July 1979, pp. 1, 3. 'Exhibition the winner in Ohio blind bidding ruling', *Boxoffice*, 14 July 1980, p. 1. 'MPAA tries litigious shortcut to oust Pa. blind bidding nix', *Variety*, 18 June 1980, p. 6. Jim Robbins, 'Tough Pennsy anti-blind law reaffirmed by Appeals Court', *Variety*, 28 July 1982, p. 3.

18 'Utah's fair-bidding act is upheld in federal court', *NATO News and Views,* 8 January 1982, p. 1. 'Georgia court issues summary judgment against Paramount's anti-blind bidding suit', *NATO News,* 19 February 1982, p. 2.

19 'Blind bidding talks terminated', *NATO News*, 16 March 1979, p. 4.

20 'Says MPAA apes Donald Segretti', *Variety*, 31 January 1979, p. 7. Gregory Tobin, 'Friedberg takes offensive', *Boxoffice*, 5 February 1979, p. 1.

21 'MPAA bows out of NATO convention; key panel canceled', *Boxoffice*, October 1979, p. 1. 'NATO party: nobody came but Disney', *Variety*, 7 November 1979, p. 7.

22 'Texas loves Valenti: no bid law as proof', *Variety*, 15 July 1981, p. 3. Telephone interview with Jerome Gordon, 30 November 2006.

23 '"Sick & weary" blind bid impasse persists', *Variety*, 18 November 1981, p. 5.

24 'Friedberg takes offensive', *Boxoffice*, 5 February 1979, p. 1.

25 Telephone interview with A. Alan Friedberg, 1 December 2006.

26 The number of outdoor screens decreased by 2400 during the same period, so the net gain of screens was approximately 5600. Stephen Prince, *A New Pot of Gold: Hollywood under the Electronic Rainbow, 1980–1989* (Berkeley: University of California Press, 2000), p. 79.

27 'Friedberg's discount excludes blind bid films', *Boxoffice,* 29 October 1979, p. 1.

References

Aarons, S.H. (1966) The legal case against blind bidding: a special report. *NATO Newsletter,* May.

Acland, C. (2003) *Screen Traffic: Movies, Multiplexes and Global Culture,* Duke University Press, Durham, NC.

Bork, R. (1978) *The Antitrust Paradox: A Policy at War with Itself,* Basic Books, New York.

Conant, M. (1960) *Antitrust in the Motion Picture Industry,* University of California Press, Berkeley.

Crafton, D. (1997) *The Talkies: American Cinema's Transition to Sound, 1926–1931,* Charles Scribners' Sons, New York.

Edgerton, G.R. (1983) *American Film Exhibition and an Analysis of the Motion Picture Industry's Market Structure, 1963–1980,* Garland, New York.

Fuller-Seeley, K. (2008) 'What the picture did for me': small-town exhibitors' strategies for surviving the Great Depression, in *Hollywood in the Neighborhood: Historical Case Studies of Local Moviegoing* (ed. K. Fuller-Seeley), University of California Press, Berkeley, pp. 186–207.

Geisst, C. (2000) *Monopolies in America: Empire Builders and Their Enemies from Jay Gould to Bill Gates,* Oxford University Press, Oxford.

Gomery, D. (1992) *Shared Pleasures: A History of Movie Presentation in the United States,* University of Wisconsin Press, Madison.

Gomery, D. (2005) *The Coming of Sound,* Routledge, London.

Izod, J. (1988) *Hollywood and the Box Office, 1895–1986,* Columbia University Press, New York.

Lagos, T. (2003) Film exhibition in Seattle, 1897–1912: leisure activity in a scraggly, smelly frontier town. *Historical Journal of Film, Radio and Television,* 24 (2) (June), 101–115.

Lewis, J. (2000) *Hollywood v. Hard Core: How the Struggle over Censorship Saved the Modern Film Industry,* New York University Press, New York, pp. 57–65.

Linck, D. (1981) Studios using purse strings to strangle blind bidding laws. *Boxoffice,* June, p. 16.

Ohmer, S. (2007) Speaking for the audience: double features, public opinion and the struggle for control in 1930s Hollywood. *Quarterly Review of Film and Video,* 24 (2) (March), 143–169.

Paul, W. (1994) The K-Mart audience at the mall movies. *Film History,* 6 (4) (Winter), 487–501.

Posner, R. (1970) A statistical study of antitrust enforcement. *Journal of Law and Economics,* 13 (October), 365–419.

Schaefer, E. (1999) *Bold! Daring! Shocking! True! A History of the Exploitation Film, 1919–1959,* Duke University Press, Durham, NC.

Schatz, T. (1997) *Boom and Bust: American Cinema in the 1940s,* University of California Press, Berkeley, pp. 160–164.

Singer, B. (2004) Feature films, variety programs and the crisis of the small exhibitor, in *American Cinema's Transitional Era* (eds C. Keil and S. Stamp), University of California Press, Berkeley, pp. 76–100.

Stigler, G. (1966) The economic effects of antitrust laws. *Journal of Law and Economics,* 9 (October), 225–258.

Waller, G. (1995) *Main Street Amusements: Movies and Commercial Entertainment in a Southern City, 1896–1930,* Smithsonian Institution Press, Washington, DC.

White, T. (1988) Life after divorce: the corporate strategy of Paramount Pictures Corporation in the 1950s. *Film History,* 2 (2), 99–119.

Wilinsky, B. (2000) *Sure Seaters: The Emergence of Art House Cinema,* University of Minnesota Press, Minneapolis.

Part 3

Venues and their Publics

11

'No Hits, No Runs, Just Terrors'

Exhibition, Cultural Distinctions and Cult Audiences at the Rialto Cinema in the 1930s and 1940s

Tim Snelson and Mark Jancovich

Introduction

In his history of film exhibition, *Shared Pleasures*, Douglas Gomery argues that the Balaban and Katz chain became the most successful and imitated exhibitors of the 1920s, despite their theatres having little initial access to Hollywood's top films (Gomery, 1992, p. 43). Instead, the success of the chain, which was bought by Paramount and rebranded as the Publix Theatre chain in 1926, derived from other aspects of the cinematic experience. Its theatres were distinguished by five key features: locations; theatre buildings; service; stage shows; and air conditioning. The chain offered its patrons an experience in which the opulence of the theatre and the attentive staff addressed their aspirational fantasies, while the areas in which they were located not only ensured easy access from most areas of the city but also associated the cinema with prosperous middle-class neighbourhoods.

Although the exhibition practices of the Rialto Cinema in Times Square, New York, were in stark opposition to those of the Balaban and Katz chain, its success in the late 1930s and 1940s, when it was known as the city's 'cinematic chamber of horrors', also depended very little on the movies it screened (Strauss, 1941). Once a centre of upmarket cultural consumption, Times Square had gone into serious decline by the 1930s, after Prohibition had ruined the lobster palaces and cabarets that had been central to its prosperity and ambience (see, e.g., Taylor, 1991; Bianco, 2004; Traub, 2004). The Depression exacerbated the area's financial decline, and the Square acquired a seedy and even disreputable image as 'growing numbers of young men – many of them migrants from the economically devastated cities of Pennsylvania, Massachusetts, New York and the industrial South' were attracted to

Explorations in New Cinema History: Approaches and Case Studies, First Edition.
Edited by Richard Maltby, Daniel Biltereyst and Philippe Meers.

its already established homosexual underground (Chauncy, 1991). As one veteran Broadway critic protested, 42nd Street had become 'cheapened and nightmarish' by 1934: 'a screeching amusement park bedlam that presented guess-your-weight stands, gypsy tea rooms, chop suey, and there at the curb was the man with the giant telescope, ready to show you the craters of the moon for a dime'.[1]

Arthur Mayer took control of the Rialto at the height of the Depression, and drastically changed its character, converting it from a plush movie palace into a grind house cinema. Rather than playing to aspirational cinemagoers, Mayer cultivated an overtly disreputable image for his cinema, aiming to appeal to people 'slumming' it. He publicly rejected notions of 'cultural uplift' precisely when the Hollywood studios, their exhibition chains and the administrators of the Production Code were labouring to counter accusations of impropriety (Maltby, 1993, pp. 53–64). The Rialto was, however, no 'fleapit'. Rebuilt in 1935 as an ultramodern Art Moderne theatre, its décor was suited to the most educated of modern bourgeois tastes. What is so significant about the Rialto is the way in which it distinguished itself from other movie palaces in Times Square by constructing an image that did not necessarily reflect the reality of either its physical characteristics or its patronage.

The Rialto is a particularly striking example of a cinema imbued with a character that not only exceeded its function as a place to show films, but even transformed the meanings of the films shown within them (Jancovich and Faire, 2003, p. 12). As a venue specialising in 'the M product – mystery, mayhem and murder' or, as the *New York Times* put it, a cinema that made a 'goose pimple its trademark', the Rialto did not so much attract audiences because of its films as give its brand to the films themselves (Strauss, 1941; Mayer, 1953, p. 169). Throughout the 1940s, both 'Hollywood conferences' and the New York papers often referred to horror films as 'Rialto-type pictures', and judged them on the basis of their appropriateness to the venue at which they were shown (Mayer, 1953, p. 180). For example, the *New York Times* doubted that the audience at Mayer's 'shriek-and-shiver emporium' would take to *The House of the Seven Gables* (1940), which it dismissed as a 'watered-down treatment of a nineteenth century shocker'.[2] Its review of *The Hunchback of Notre Dame* (1939) made the point even more clearly, suggesting that the film was simply at the wrong venue: 'at the Rialto, yes; at the Music Hall – and on a holiday showing – no!' (Nugent, 1940).

The Rialto was a critical venue for the emergence of the cult movie scene, a phenomenon that is usually associated with the 1950s, 1960s or 1970s (Taylor, 1999). From the mid-1930s, the cinema positioned itself as a place of cult connoisseurship and camp appropriation, and the strategies of cult interpretation that it encouraged became quite commonplace in some mainstream reviews in the late 1930s, particularly in relation to 'Rialto-type pictures'.[3] This chapter examines the ways in which, in his promotion of the cinema, Arthur Mayer defined the Rialto against mainstream Hollywood by presenting it as an oppositional space through an othering of femininity and an identification with subcultural tastes. At the same time, the Rialto's sensational and disreputable image was often ironised by humour both by the mainstream press and by Mayer himself, and the knowingness of this humour is the topic of the third section.

The chapter focuses on the discursive construction of the Rialto's audience, rather than the audience's experience of the cinema. The ways in which the cinema's audience were portrayed in Mayer's promotional strategies or in the observations of other commentators did not necessarily accurately represent its demographic composition. Mayer's writing in his journalism and autobiography are prone to frequent embellishment and self-promotion, whilst the *New York Times'* complex positioning with regard to the Rialto has to be understood in the context of the paper's wider attitude to the 'trashy' genres that the cinema specialised in (see Jancovich, 2008). While these sources provide us with some information about the actual experiences and make-up of the Rialto's audiences, this chapter's main concern is to explore the Rialto and its audience as discursive formations. The discursive Rialto of these writings was a self-conscious construction: attempting to manufacture a distinction from its competitors, it appealed to the very bourgeois dispositions and tastes that it appeared to exclude (Bourdieu, 1984). For example, Mayer's overt othering of the feminine was not designed to exclude women, and the cinema actually became very popular with female audiences during the late 1930s and early to mid-1940s. Rather, Mayer aimed to differentiate the Rialto from a conception of mass culture as feminised, in the belief that this stance would appeal to a segment of the bourgeois audience. While it was often presented as a place of lowbrow tastes, the Rialto proved a considerable draw for specific sections of the New York intelligentsia, championed by critics such as Manny Farber and James Agee.

Even more middlebrow publications, such as the *New York Times*, displayed a fascination with and affection for the cinema and its film culture. Mayer and his cinema were the focus of numerous *Times* articles, and he was occasionally given the opportunity to promote the cinema through articles under his own byline. Both the newspaper's interest in Mayer and his cinema and Mayer's own use of the *Times* as a means of promoting his cinema demonstrate that the Rialto and its policy of 'no hits, no runs, just terrors' were consciously marketed to middle-class audiences searching for an alternative to middlebrow culture (Mayer, 1953, p. 170). While the Rialto management and New York press's construction of a 'Rialto faithful' provides only glimpses of the 'real' Rialto audience, the complex discursive processes they do reveal highlight how institutions such as these 'create', in Pierre Bourdieu's terms, 'groups with words' (Bourdieu, 1990, p. 139).

Reversing the Deluxe Policy: Location, Service, the Building and Programming

When the Rialto opened in 1916, it was described as 'a new palace of polite pleasure for thousands', located on 'one of the finest theatrical sites in the world', where Oscar Hammerstein's Victoria Theatre had previously stood.[4] Built on the site of the old Market Livery Stables in 1898, the Victoria had established the corner of 42nd and Broadway as 'the most famous amusement corner in the world', and introduced 'a new form of family entertainment' that was considered the forerunner of vaudeville. With the increasing gentrification of the area in the 1910s, the theatre was bought by local impresario 'Roxy' Rothafel, who opened the Rialto as New York's first stageless motion picture house, a sumptuous 'Temple of Motion Pictures, Shrine of Music and the Allied Arts'. Famous Players-Lasky bought a controlling interest in the theatre in 1919, and for much of the 1920s it was one of Paramount's most prestigious venues, known as the 'House of Hits'. By the early 1930s, however, the golden age of 42nd Street entertainment had ended, the character of Times Square changed dramatically and Paramount's deluxe policy had become increasingly unfeasible in the austere climate of the Depression. By 1933, the Rialto was reportedly operating at a $2000 a week deficit, and Paramount relinquished control of the theatre to manager Mayer.[5] Mayer claimed that the day he first opened the doors, 'the banks closed ... undaunted, I ordered anyone lacking cash should be admitted to the theatre in return for an IOU, and a six-foot notice was posted outside to that effect' (Mayer, 1953, pp. 166–167).[6]

Mayer had learned his trade from Sam Katz, who had built the Balaban and Katz empire and then joined Paramount when it purchased the theatres, converting them into the Publix Theatre Chain. Believing 'that anyone who couldn't successfully operate a theatre at the world's busiest crossroads was a dope', Mayer took over the Rialto by offering to share all profits with Paramount and cover any losses out of his own pocket (Strauss, 1941). In his autobiography, he claimed to have taken the Rialto 'out of the red immediately' by simply cutting 'a five-thousand weekly advertising budget to less than five hundred dollars', cancelling the 'free list' of 'politicians, bankers and friends of the former management', and reducing 'the service staff'. More than simply cost cutting, these measures were crucial to his overall strategy. Mayer knew that Times Square was not what it had once been, and he tailored the cinema experience to fit the new environment, which required something quite different from the aspirational movie palaces and 'deluxe policy' of his mentors. Although he reversed many of his mentors' strategies, he did so because he had learned that a cinema's success could not simply depend on the films. In the absence of an advertising budget, or the money to compete for the top films, his cinema needed to have 'a distinctive personality' that would prove an attraction in itself and provide a guarantee to customers that they would 'know what [they] can expect' when they frequented it (Mayer, 1935, p. X3).

Balaban and Katz had employed a large number of 'male college students' to provide service to their customers, evoking 'an image that most patrons associated with a fine hotel, country club, or bank' (Gomery, 1992, pp. 49–50). Claiming that 'the place was bristling with overpaid West Point-trained ushers instructing customers kindly to expectorate only in the urns', Mayer 'heaved most of [the staff] overboard', replacing them with 'genial, slouchy, underpaid boys, the most underpaid being my son, Michael' (Mayer, 1953, p. 167). While the Balaban and Katz ushers were dressed in 'in red uniforms with white gloves and yellow epaulets', Mayer announced that his ushers would have 'no resemblance to Arrow-collar ads [and] will let you take whatever seats are available' (Mayer, 1935, p. X3; Gomery,

1992, p. 49). He actively pursued a disreputable image in which his ushers did not encourage a sense of decorum but rather a sense of moral laxity and even abandon, even claiming that they are 'in the cinema so much of the time, hearing such esoteric language and seeing so many sights of violence' that they 'have acquired the less desirable characteristics of the personalities they see on the screen'.[7]

Mayer's mentors had made their cinema buildings attractions in themselves, surpassing 'the splendor of the vaudeville and legitimate theatres' and spelling 'opulence to the average Chicago moviegoer' (Gomery, 1992, p. 47). Once he had freed himself of his initial partnership with Paramount, Mayer's first decision was to remodel the cinema so that the 'accoutrements of the theatre' would be 'tailored' to his new clientele: 'There will be an absence of geegaws, rococo plaster, plush carpets, and paintings of cows in lush meadows.' Rather than signifying 'opulence', the new décor was minimal and signified a place of relaxation where patrons 'will be able to smoke where and when [they] want' (Mayer, 1935, p. X3).

The reconstructed Rialto was far from the 'fleapit' that some of Mayer's comments would suggest, but rather reflected the modern tastes of its new clientele. The old Rialto building was demolished in May 1935 and replaced by a modern four-story Art Deco block containing offices, shops, restaurants and a new 700-seat movie theatre: the new Rialto, which was considerably smaller than the previous theatre's 2000-seat capacity. Following the opening in December 1935, the *New York Times* explained that 'Times Square's newest theatre' was the first to be accessible from the subway level; the city's first truly 'underground' movie theatre. The article also featured photographs of the theatre's new ultramodern interior, highlighting its aluminium-trimmed lighting coves and acoustic plaster ceiling.[8] Mayer's new Art Moderne theatre was distinguished from other movie palaces not by its shabbiness, but by its minimalism, utilitarianism and restraint. Its décor and architecture were still aimed at bourgeois tastes, but modern bourgeois tastes defined through a rejection of excessive embellishment and showy splendour.

The programme also diverged from the Balaban and Katz model. While theatre bookers had conventionally assumed that 'desirable movie entertainment required a well-balanced bill – comedy with romance, or adventure with music' in order to address a broad audience, Mayer recognised that he 'could not compete … with left-over second-rate musicals, routine love stories and polite, innocuous comedies' and began to book the 'only other type of B pictures consistently available to an independent operator … the M product … and shortly to specialize in them' (Mayer, 1953, p. 169). Using this situation to distinguish his theatre Mayer 'jammed the Rialto for several weeks with two old horror films' and so 'made Broadway history by double-featuring *Dracula* and *Frankenstein*' (Mayer, 1953, pp. 178–179).

Under Mayer, the Rialto's programming was positioned in direct opposition to the post-1934 Hays Office, which sought to promote 'better pictures' aimed at 'a new movie-going public recruited from the higher earning income earning classes' (Maltby, 1993, p. 62). As part of its attempt to acquire a more respectable image, the Hays Office promoted prestige 'adaptations of literary classics and historical biographies', and stressed the cultural and pedagogical functions of these 'better pictures' (Maltby, 1993, pp. 62–63). Mayer showed no interest in this audience of middle-class readers of *Parents Magazine* and *Ladies Home Journal*. In a *New York Times* article of March 1934, entitled 'Who Killed the Movies?' Mayer attacked the 'better pictures' designed to make audiences 'historically, if not hysterically, screen conscious', complaining that after the box-office success of *The Private Life of Henry the Eighth* (1933) 'the leading picture executives are spending their spare hours studying biography and history'. These films were not, he claimed, greeted warmly by exhibitors, who were 'as bitterly opposed to cycles and conventional, stereotyped products as much as the most radical experimenter in Hollywood.' Cinema managers, he asserted, welcomed 'sex in the luscious form of Mae West' and abhorred quality pictures, but they had not been given 'anything to say about this cycle' by the Hays Office (Mayer, 1934).

Three years later, Mayer was still condemning 'the precocious starlets – Bartholomew, Breen and Temple – along with their grownup counterparts – curly haired crooners, wan lovers and sophisticated sinners', and positioning the Rialto's unrefined policy, in which 'G-men and free men will reign supreme', in opposition to the Hays Office, its 'better pictures', and the more general 'feminization' of cultural life. He planned to 'eliminate ultra-refined non-moving movies' from his programme, and to 'surfeit Rialto regulars' with 'horror, mystery and menace'.[9] In 1939, he blamed the 'Production Code requirement that evil doers be punished on this earth not the next', for Hollywood's 'sappy endings', and urged patrons to leave five minutes before the end of such movies (Nugent, 1939).

'As Offensively Unfeminine as a Sailor's Pipe': Gender, Taste and Subcultural Capital

Although Mayer claimed that his rejection of the 'deluxe policy' and the 'better pictures' was a product of 'hunger, not acumen', it was also consistent with his overall strategy. The Rialto did not market itself at aspirational moviegoers or the industry's image of the general or family audience. Recognising that five times as many men passed the theatre as women, Mayer regarded his 'only chance of survival' as being to appeal 'to a segment of the population sick of saccharine romance, cute kiddies and fondly addicted to murder, mayhem and mystery' (Mok, 1937). He rhetorically presented the theatre as a space that would be 'as uncompromisingly masculine as a turbine and as offensively unfeminine as a sailor's pipe'.

Mayer contrasted his theatre not only with the picture palace it had replaced but also with the long established notion of the middle-class suburbs as a feminine space, in which men were dominated by their families:

> Women and children first is not only the law of the sea. It is also the basic assumption on which Manhattan's economic and social life is predicated. Papa commutes from the suburbs so the kiddies can frolic in the sunshine and learn the facts of life from the birds and flowers. He slaves at the office while Mamma plays contract and

> throws cocktail parties. His hard-earned cash vanishes for shoes for baby, the cutest Parisian models for sister and a purple runabout more refulgent than Mrs. Jones's. (Mayer, 1935, p. X3)

In 1935, he presented the Rialto as 'the last refuge of the oppressed sex', in direct opposition to a middlebrow leisure culture that was feminised through metaphors of consumption and domesticity. Declaring that 'it is high time to head a male revolt', and dedicating the new Rialto to that role, Mayer insisted that there would be 'more spittoons than mirrors in the lobby … no perfume machines and no candies on sale', and that 'Shirley Temple will be barred; and what she stands for' (Sennwald, 1935). He looked back nostalgically to the 'early movie theatre, dirty, ill-ventilated, uncomfortable', as 'a male paradise', and described himself as a man with strong 'misogynist principles'.[10] His 'gloating house manager' even boasted that his clientele included 'practically every notorious gangster in New York' (Mayer, 1953, p. 179). His choice of films was designed to emphasise this anti-feminine character; he claimed that his programming ministered to 'the masculine escapist urge: adventure, horror, blood' (Sennwald, 1935). In 1936, discussing his attempts to find a slogan for the venue, he asserted that he had rejected the idea of calling it 'The Home of Horror Pictures' on the grounds that 'my horror patrons are ill-disposed to home, and home folks hate horror'.[11]

Despite what he called his 'haunting dread that in spite of all our efforts the women will adore' the new Rialto, Mayer's anti-feminine rhetoric was not so much directed at women as at middle-class respectability, for which the feminine and the domestic have operated as an image (Mayer, 1935, p. X3). In defining the gendered appeal of cult cinema, Joanne Hollows has argued that 'the rejection of the feminine functions not only to secure the masculinity of cult but to assure its (allegedly) oppositional politics' (Hollows, 2003, p. 40). Mayer's revolt against the suburban family resembled the 'male revolt' that Barbara Ehrenreich has identified with *Playboy* magazine in the 1950s, and shared many of the same criticisms of the 'housewife role' voiced by later feminists (Ehrenreich, 1983; see also Hollows, 2000). Mayer declared that his cinema was 'not prejudiced against women and will effect no unfair barriers against them'; he expected his cinema to attract women who were, as Sara Thornton puts it, 'culturally one of the boys' (Thornton, 1995). In 1936, he claimed that since the opening of *Dracula's Daughter* (1936) it had become impossible 'to keep women out of the theatre … They are keen on seeing a member of their sex destroy vaunted male prestige in cold-blooded villainy'.[12] Subsequently Mayer conceded that he was 'grateful for the recent surge of female attendance, and hope[d] to continue in the ladies' good graces'.[13]

By the 1940s, horror was no longer seen as a predominantly male genre. After the success of *Rebecca* (1940), many women's films were clearly marked as horror films, while many horror films featured female leads and were predominantly directed at a female audience (Snelson, 2009). Part of the pleasure of the Rialto for women seems to have been its potential for them to transgress traditional gender roles, and thus distance themselves from certain negative associations of femininity. Commenting on the changes in female spectatorship, brought about by wartime shifts in employment and leisure practices, Mayer later observed: 'For several years my clientele remained largely and defiantly male ... In time, however, to our consternation, feminine attendance started to zoom. Whether this proved that women are not as tender as advertised and as Hollywood still believes, or whether they finally could no longer stand the idea that men were having a good time without them, I do not know (Mayer, 1953, p. 179). During the wartime prize fights staged at the theatre, he reported, 'there could be heard more feminine than masculine voices in the darkness yelling "hit him with the right," "kill the bum" and other such expressions of maidenly advice' (Mayer, 1953, p. 180).

Making Fun: Sensational, Humorous and Disreputable

From the outset, Mayer was concerned to position his cinema as an offensive space that was opposed to the 'safe' and 'censored', and he explicitly stated his objection to the Hays Office. Not only did he object to a type of picture which he described as 'a Hays version of one of the classics, recognizable, but strangely altered, like some old classmate encountered after many years of separation', but he also presented his films as challenging the PCA's notions of good taste (Mayer, 1935, p. X3):

> I would like to tell you how the villain learns the secret of creating zombies and how he makes the sweetheart who jilted him perform his every wish. I'd like to. But there's trouble enough running a horror theatre without getting into trouble with Mr. Hays.[14]

On at least one occasion in 1936, the Hays office threatened him with an injunction over his advertising of Paramount's *Lady, Be Careful* under the title of the 'objectionable' stage play on which it was based, *Sailor Beware*.[15] By the 1940s, Mayer frequently presented himself as chafing at the restrictions that censorship imposed on him. In an interview commemorating the 25th anniversary of the cinema, Mayer was described as a purveyor of horror 'as far as he is allowed':

> For through the Legion of Decency and sundry other factors the Grade B movies, among which are found most of the horror and action films, have lost much of their one-time vigor and forthrightness. There was a time, Mr. Mayer remembers, when he posted a nurse in the house to revive victims of 'Frankenstein's Daughter', and once a United States Marine passed out cold when a clammy hand reached for the heroine's throat. But that was almost two years ago. Today Frankenstein is only a shadow of his former self. (Strauss, 1941)[16]

Because Mayer sought to present himself as operating at the very limits of what was permissible, a lowbrow image was central to the Rialto's discursive claim to disrepute, and Mayer occasionally transformed the connotations of the films being shown so that they matched the cinema's 'lurid' reputation, renaming them to make them sound more sensational:

> Handicapped by weak casts, the titles of pictures we played assumed even more importance than ordinarily. *A Son Comes Home* was by itself too innocuous to attract patrons, so on the marquee we added *From Gangland*. We strengthened *Fit for a King* by inserting the word *Murder* ahead of it. We were playing *Hollywood Boulevard* when a well-known movie actress achieved notoriety through the publication of her diary – an impressive tally of her daily indiscretions. We converted the title to the more timely *Hollywood Diary*. (Mayer, 1953, p. 175)

Mayer's cultivation of a disreputable image was marked by a knowing humour that relied on puns and plays on words to display his own sophistication and wit, although his accounts serve more as a projection of the disreputable image that he wished to promote for his theatre and himself than as a completely reliable description of his actual exhibition practices.

In this active pursuit of 'disrepute', Mayer also courted bad reviews and baited film critics, presenting his cinema as an inversion of their values and demonstrating that, as Sara Thornton has argued, the mechanisms and spaces provided by the media and the perceived conformist masses they service are 'instrumental in the congregation of [fans] and the formation of subcultures' (Thornton, 1995). On one occasion, Mayer jokily dismissed 'the theory that there is no good critic except a dead one', by suggesting that this misconception was 'based on the superficial resemblance of critics to Indians, their strange outcries on the war path, the scalps which they display on their teepees, their love of white man's fire water'.[17] In a 1937 *New York Times* article, Mayer thanked a reviewer for the bad review of the picture then on offer, declaring 'Give me a vitriolic abusive review and I won't give you an empty seat in the house'.[18]

Tastelessness and hyperbole were part of Mayer's promotion of the Rialto to his audience. In 1936, responding to a survey indicating that audiences favoured single features programmes over double bills, he claimed to be considering adopting the slogan 'Not such a Good Picture, but Only One'.[19] In 1942 he complained to the *New York Times* that its policy of confining its list of the year's ten worst pictures to million-dollar pictures automatically excluded the Rialto, which 'week in week … has maintained its undisputed supremacy in the field of bad pictures' (Mayer, 1942).

The Rialto also became famous for its carnival atmosphere and outlandish promotions. Its lurid and grotesque attractions – onscreen, in the foyer and on the storefront displays – were a calculated attempt to embrace Times Square's return to the carnivalesque spirit of the turn of the century, when Hammerstein grazed cattle on the Victoria's roof and salacious acts were promoted through rowdy 'ballyhoo' outside on the street. In the mid-1930s, Mayer's Rialto claimed to share its location 'with a raucous bazaar hawking cashew nuts, cheroots, knockwurst, gin and hair-cuts', while 'a casual passerby is apt to have his wits dislodged by sudden unearthly sounds from a marquee loudspeaker, or a quick faintness may pass over him when looking up from the baseball scores he sees a desiccated face staring down from the lobby display' (Strauss, 1941). Having slashed the advertising budget, Mayer used 'the theatre front and the lobby for my major shilling' (Mayer, 1953, p. 174), and his displays became notorious. On one occasion, he

> re-created a tropical jungle kingdom in the lobby ... full of mangy lions, moth-eaten tigers, gaudy, beady-eyed birds, and live monkeys swinging from papier-mâché coconut trees. An added effect of a lion roaring – so loud it could be heard two blocks away over heavy Broadway traffic – was, I thought, an imaginative touch in a blood-curdling way, but the Police department felt differently about it and I had to throttle my king of the jungle down to the anaemic purr of a superannuated lion. ... the Police Department's tender ears, in fact, remained a constant menace to our sound attractions.

These displays also earned the disdain of the critics. To promote *The Mummy* (1932), Mayer had his staff build 'a colossal and terrifying character combining the most repulsive features of Frankenstein's monster and Dracula', with 'an electrical device which vibrated waves of crimson and orange from his belly to his brain ... and a sound effect of grunts ... from his aboriginal jaws'. One critic 'commented in print that the show staged outside the Rialto was far more entertaining than the one inside ... In appreciation of his appreciation, we sent him [the creation] as a gift' (Mayer, 1953, p. 175).

'Homicide Connoisseurs': Cult Audiences, Cultural Capital and Class Tastes

These conflicts with the press were also part of the process by which Mayer constructed his disreputable image. When one critic 'in a moment of exasperation so far forgot himself as to refer to my Harvard background', he not only saw this as 'the final insult' but immediately responded by booking *Abdul the Damned*, 'a picture replete with oriental intrigue, perfidy and sadism, not to mention occasional vistas of life in a harem and in the torture chamber'.[20] The *New York Times* was fond of contributing to his notoriety by referring to his privileged background or his 'charmingly fitting, almost feminine, headquarters above the Rialto Marquee', jokingly calling him 'the eminent educator of Times Square' and his cinema as having 'the atmosphere of refinement and good taste reminiscent of the elm-shaded confines of old Harvard'.[21] Rather than puncturing the Rialto's image, these references only contributed to it, revealing the doubleness of the cinema's appeal. Mayer and his cinema were the objects of intense fascination for the *New York Times*, which published numerous stories about them and frequently revealed considerable enthusiasm for the cinema in its film reviews. Mayer was also a regular contributor to the newspaper, and the *Times* presented him as a figure of authority and prestige when it came to the history of the Rialto and of the Square more generally.[22]

The Rialto's clientele has often been described as lower class; Anthony Bianco, for example, suggests that the 'typical' Rialto 'patron probably was a bus driver or

Midtown secretary' (Bianco, 2004, p. 101). The articles in the *New York Times*, however, clearly addressed a fairly prosperous and privileged middle-class readership. Mayer's first article about the Rialto, indeed, presented it as a place that existed primarily for the middle-class male who 'commutes from the suburbs' to work, where he 'slaves at the office' (Mayer, 1935, p. X3). Expecting the Rialto to conform to the disreputable image that Mayer had manufactured, the *Olean Times Herald* was 'startled' at the 'high degree of apparent respectability amongst the pew-holders' when it made a special trip to the all-night *Frankenstein* and *Dracula* double bill in 1937 (Ross, 1938).

While the Rialto was presented as a 'lurid place', its audience – the 'Rialto habitués', the 'Rialto faithful', or the 'Rialto's monster-of-the-week-club' – was not simply seen as a dedicated group of horror fans, but also as knowledgeable and sophisticated connoisseurs of homicide who 'can spot a killer before the scenario author himself knows who committed the crime' (Crowther, 1944; Critics Theatre Review Staff, 1944/1945). Mayer claimed that, 'like Macbeth, our patrons supped so deep on murder that now any picture with less than a score of killings is dismissed as sissy'.[23] This was typical of the discourse about refined tastes in low culture that circulated widely in discussions of Mayer and his cinema, referring to him as a 'macabre maestro' with an 'exquisite taste in murder and mayhem'.[24]

The Rialto audience earned the respect of highbrow critics such as Manny Farber and James Agee. In his review of *Curse of the Cat People* (1944), Agee referred to it as 'a specialized audience ... poor, metropolitan, and deeply experienced', and far superior to the 'art-theatre' audiences at venues such as the Museum of Modern Art. 'As long as such an audience exists', Agee maintained, 'no one in Hollywood has a right to use the stupidity of the public for an alibi' (Agee, 1944).

These references to knowledge, sophistication and refinement described an audience high in subcultural capital (see Thornton, 1995; Jancovich, 2002). Although the Rialto was presented as appealing to low-class audiences and tastes, its overt cultivation of a disreputable image was at least in part designed to appeal to educated and cultured audiences who were looking to 'slum it'. The *New York Post* even joked about its clientele as being made up of 'intellectuals who come into the Rialto to gain respite from their heavy thinking chores' (Winsten, 1944).

Conclusion

In a brief reference to the Rialto in *Shared Pleasures*, Douglas Gomery notes that despite the cinema's success 'there were few imitators, but in the 1930s and 1940s there were few cities like New York' (Gomery, 1992, p. 138). The Rialto's exhibition practices would, however, become central to the emergence of cult film, particularly in the ways in which it constructed a culture of alternative film consumption through discourses of transgression, urbanity, masculinity and active spectatorship. Mayer consciously positioned his 'cinematic chamber of horrors' in opposition to the consumption, domesticity and conformity of a discursively feminised middlebrow culture. Subverting his mentor Sam Katz's slogan that 'You don't need to know what's playing at a Publix house. It's bound to be the best show in town', Mayer promised a uniquely 'lurid' cinematic experience irrespective of the particular movie playing onscreen. Although it positioned itself as hostile to the comforts of the domestic sphere, the Rialto's discomforting sights and uncomfortable seats provided a reassuring refuge for a community of middle-class male and female patrons wishing to escape the real terrors of Depression and war.

Notes

1 Ward Morehouse, quoted in Taylor (1991), p. xxiv.
2 B.C., The House of the Seven Gables, *New York Times* 15 April, 1940, p. 23.
3 For more on the *New York Times*'s complex relationship to lowbrow horror fandom in the period, see Mark Jancovich (2010) 'Two ways of looking': affection and aversion in the critical reception of the 1940s horror, *Cinema Journal*, 49 (3) (Spring), 45–66.
4 'Rialto Theatre Opens its Doors', *New York Times*, 22 April 1916.
5 'Rialto Theatre Closes its Door', *New York Times* 2 February 1933, p. 21.
6 According to the *New York Times*, the Rialto actually reopened on 10 March 1933. 'Rialto to Be Re-opened', *New York Times*, 8 March 1933, p. 15. Derived from the phrase 'I owe you', an IOU is a promissory note acknowledging debt that does not specify the time of repayment.
7 'The "Merchant of Menace"', *New York Times*, 20 December 1936, p. X6.
8 'Times Square's Newest Theatre', *New York Times*, 12 January 1936.
9 'A Film Man's Resolution', *New York Post*, 26 December 1936.
10 'Where Menace is Menace', *New York Times*, 28 June 1936, p. X4; 'Cup Bearer to the Bloodthirsty', *New York Times*, 17 May 1936, p. X3.
11 'The "Merchant of Menace"', p. X6.
12 'Cup Bearer to the Bloodthirsty', p. X3.
13 'A Film Man's Resolution'.
14 'Cup Bearer to the Bloodthirsty', p. X3.
15 'Hays Objects to Title', *New York Times*, 10 October 1936, p. 21.
16 The anecdote highlights Mayer's capacity for embellishment and misremembering, since *Frankenstein's Daughter* was not produced until 1958. Mayer was probably referring to *Dracula's Daughter* (1936), which he had promoted by encouraging women to attend and thereby transgress gendered and generic expectations.
17 'Mayer the Masochist', *New York Times*, 25 July 1937, p. 133.
18 'Mayer the Masochist', p. 133.
19 'The "Merchant of Menace"', p. X6.
20 'Cup Bearer to the Bloodthirsty', p. X3.
21 'Cup Bearer to the Bloodthirsty', p. X3; 'Mayer the Masochist', p. 133; 'The "Merchant of Menace"', p. X6.
22 See, e.g., Strauss (1941) and 'The "Merchant of Menace"'.
23 'Cup Bearer to the Bloodthirsty', p. X3.
24 'The "Merchant of Menace"', p. X6; Strauss (1941).

References

Agee, J. (1944) Films. *The Nation*, 1 April, p. 402.

Bianco, A. (2004) *Ghosts of 42nd Street: A History of America's Most Infamous Block*, William Morrow, New York.

Bourdieu, P. (1984) *Distinction: A Social Critique of the Judgement of Taste*, Harvard University Press, Cambridge MA.

Bourdieu, P. (1990) *In Other Words: Essays Towards a Reflexive Sociology*, Polity, London.

Chauncey G. Jr (1991) The policed: gay men's strategies of everyday resistance, in *Inventing Times Square: Commerce and Culture at the Crossroads of the World* (ed. W.R. Taylor), Johns Hopkins University Press, Baltimore.

Critics Theatre Review Staff (eds) (1944/45) *New York Motion Picture Critics' Review,* Critics' Theatre Reviews, New York.

Crowther, B. (1944) A Child's Mind. *New York Times,* 4 March.

Ehrenreich, B. (1983) *The Hearts of Men: American Dreams and the Flight from Commitment,* Pluto, London.

Gomery, D. (1992) *Shared Pleasures: A History of Movie Exhibition in the United States,* British Film Institute, London.

Hollows, J. (2000) *Feminism, Femininity and Popular Culture,* Manchester University Press, Manchester.

Hollows, J. (2003) The masculinity of cult, in *Defining Cult Movies: The Cultural Politics of Oppositional Taste* (eds M. Jancovich, A. Lazaro Reboll, J. Stringer and A. Willis), Manchester University Press, Manchester.

Jancovich, M. (2002) Cult fictions: cult movies, subcultural capital and the production of cultural distinctions. *Cultural Studies,* 16 (2), 306–322.

Jancovich, M. (2008) Pale shadows: narrative hierarchies in the historiography of 1940s horror, in *The Shifting Definitions of Genre: Essays on Labelling Film, Television Shows and Media* (eds L. Geraghty and M. Jancovich), McFarland, Jefferson, NC, pp. 15–32.

Jancovich, M. and Faire, L., with Stubbings, S. (2003) *The Place of the Audience: Cultural Geographies of Film Consumption,* British Film Institute, London.

Maltby, R. (1993) The Production Code and the Hays Office, in *Grand Design: Hollywood as a Modern Business Enterprise: 1930–1939* (ed. T. Balio), University of California Press, Berkeley, pp. 37–72.

Mayer, A. (1934) Who Killed the Movies? In Which an Exhibitor, Replying to Critics, Says He Didn't. *New York Times,* 11 March.

Mayer, A. (1935) A New Deal for the Forgotten Man. *New York Times,* 26 May.

Mayer, A. (1942) Noted For the Record. *New York Times,* 4 January.

Mayer, A. (1953) *Merely Colossal,* Simon and Schuster, New York.

Mok, M. (1937) Hurrah for Horror! Down with Sex! *New York Post,* 18 February.

Nugent, F.S. (1939) Cure For the Sappy Ending. *New York Times,* 8 October.

Nugent, F.S. (1940) The Hunchback of Notre Dame. *New York Times,* 1 January, p. 29.

Ross, G. (1938) Broadway's Stay-Ups and Stay-Outs Flock to All-Night Moving Theatre. *Olean Times Herald (New York),* 24 October, p. 11.

Sennwald, A. (1935) Frank Buck's 'Fang and Claw', at the New Rialto. *New York Times,* 28 December, p. 10.

Snelson, T. (2009) Horror on the Home Front: the female monster cycle, World War Two and historical reception studies. PhD thesis, University of East Anglia.

Strauss, T. (1941) Roll Out the Barrel: The Convivial Ghosts of the Old Rialto Are Summoned for an Anniversary. *New York Times,* 20 April, p. X5.

Taylor, G. (1999) *Artists in the Audience: Cults, Camp, and American Film Criticism,* Princeton University Press, Princeton, NJ.

Taylor, W.R. (ed.) (1991) *Inventing Times Square: Commerce and Culture at the Crossroads of the World,* Johns Hopkins University Press, Baltimore.

Thornton, S. (1995) *Club Cultures: Media, Music and Subcultural Capital,* Blackwell, Oxford.

Traub, J. (2004) *The Devil's Playground: A Century of Pleasure and Profit in Times Square,* Random House, New York.

Winsten, A. (1944) 'Weird Woman' Brings Anthropology to Students at Rialto Theatre. *New York Post,* 1 April.

12

Going Underground with Manny Farber and Jonas Mekas

New York's Subterranean Film Culture in the 1950s and 1960s

PETER STANFIELD

In New York's film culture, the meaning of the term 'underground film' shifted during the late 1950s and early 1960s. This chapter aims to track the move from the underground cinema defined by the critic and painter Manny Farber to that defined by film critic, publisher, archivist and film-maker Jonas Mekas. For Farber, underground film was loosely characterised by a set of styles, forms, attitudes and intensive moments displayed in male-oriented action movies and best experienced in the rundown flea-bitten cinemas located off Times Square. While Farber mined a rich seam of critically ignored, economically marginal Hollywood products, Mekas championed a group of film-makers who were geographically removed from Hollywood and economically independent of the major studios.[1] Both versions of underground film, however, shared sites of exhibition, and sometimes audiences.

In the 1950s, west of Broadway, where the first-run houses the Roxy, Loew's State and the Paramount were located, there was a strip of theatres each of which specialised in a certain type of movie:

> The Times Square presented westerns. The Hudson offered violence and action-genre films. The Victory offered war movies, the Empire domestic, non-military violence (e.g. Fritz Lang's *The Big Heat,* 1953), the Lyric showed non-advertised first runs. The Selwyn ran second-run box-office flops, and the Liberty less successful, third-run mainstream misses. The Apollo specialized in foreign films, and the Rialto 'art,' mostly horror and soft-core sex. (Eliot, 2001, pp. 96–97)[2]

These theatres were at the heart of Farber's underground.

Explorations in New Cinema History: Approaches and Case Studies, First Edition.
Edited by Richard Maltby, Daniel Biltereyst and Philippe Meers.

In the 1930s the New York theatre district concentrated in and around Times Square entered into a period of economic decline that would not be halted until the 1990s. The 1939 WPA (Works Progress Administration) guide to New York noted that on 'Forty-second Street west of Broadway, once the show place of the district, famous theaters have been converted into movie "grind" houses devoted to continuous double feature programs of burlesque shows.'[3] Theatre historian Brooks McNamara wrote: 'As huge, elaborate movie palaces like the Paramount and the Roxy arose on Broadway and Seventh Avenue, the old Forty-Second Street houses could no longer compete and were forced to lengthen their hours and lower both their prices and artistic sights' (McNamara, 1991, p. 186). All the 42nd Street theatres had midnight screenings and many stayed open to 3.30 am.

At the intersection of 42nd Street and Broadway stood the Rialto, which had been run as a cinema specialising in horror and action since 1933. Arthur Mayer, a former Paramount employee and public relations operative for Mae West and Marlene Dietrich, managed the theatre. At the Rialto he 'instituted the profitable policy of playing nothing but bad pictures', he recalled:

> The type of picture we featured was rated strictly masculine fare. ... It was a source of gratification, morally and financially, to see so many male patrons assert themselves by patronizing the Rialto and not meekly following their women into the Valentino traps operated by my competitors. (Mayer, 1953, pp. 178–179)

The Rialto could be entered at street level and via the subway, making it Manhattan's only truly 'underground' cinema.[4]

Mayer's sentiments were echoed in Manny Farber's 1957 essay 'Underground Films: A Bit of Male Truth', in which he rebuffed the lure of Hollywood's more pretentious productions, featuring a 'list of ingredients that anyone's unsophisticated aunt in Oakland can spot as comprising a distinguished film' (Farber, 1998, p. 14). In its stead he found more honest work in roughneck films culled from vulgar, low-pulp material that lay hidden beneath the critical horizon of all but the most astute observers.

Against all the 'polishing', 'bragging', and 'fake educating' that went on in Hollywood, there was a group of film-makers who had 'tunneled' inside the action movies at which they excelled, directors who accepted the role of 'hack so that they can involve themselves with expedience and tough-guy insight in all types of action: barnstorming, driving, bulldogging. The important thing is not so much the banal-seeming journeys to nowhere that make up the stories, but the tunneling that goes on inside the classic Western-gangster incidents and stock hoodlum-dogface-cowboy types ... private runways to the truth.' Farber labelled Howard Hawks, William Wellman, Raoul Walsh, Anthony Mann, Phil Karlson and Robert Aldrich 'underground directors', who made 'faceless movies, taken from a half-polished trash writing'. In these movies, the 'small buried attempt to pierce the banal pulp of underground stories with fanciful grace notes is one of the important feats of the underground director' (Farber, 1998, pp. 16, 17, 19). In 'Underground Magic, Eccentric Vitality and Artful Direction Salvage Banal Stories' Farber wrote:

> the *real* fascination of a movie isn't the sum total of aesthetic effects, but the underground channels created by each artist pursuing his path. When considered only as whole works somewhere between dud and masterpiece … films not only shrink in interest but are too easily pigeon-holed. (Farber, 1959)

The critical act was not to search for a masterpiece or to dismiss the dud, but to recognise that 'each movie has an iceberg's hidden resources – the continuity of interest represented by each technician's following or veering from a battle-scarred path that has been "long abuilding" and seems more crucial than the generalization of any single picture' (Farber, 1959).

The context of the viewing experience helped fashion Farber's habit of viewing movies with a truant eye, feeding back into the films he connected with as if there was a symbiotic loop linking critic, film and audience.[5] In his 1946 review of *The Killers* (1946), Farber wrote: 'Besides its brutality, it has noise, the jagged, tormenting movement of keyed-up, tough, flashy humanity that you get from a walk through Times Square' (Farber, 1946). The demimonde of Times Square was also the perfect audience with whom to watch underground movies:

> The hard-bitten action film finds its natural home in caves: the murky, congested theatres, looking like glorified tattoo parlors on the outside and located near bus terminals in big cities. These theatres roll action films in what, at first, seems like a nightmarish atmosphere of shabby transience, prints that seem overgrown with jungle moss, sound tracks infected with hiccups. The spectator watches two or three action films go by and leaves feeling as though he were a pirate discharged from a giant sponge. (Farber, 1998, p. 15)

Farber's authentication of his filmgoing experiences, and his acts of discrimination between Hollywood's commercial products, was a form of slumming, a crossing of the proverbial tracks. Like the white patrons of the 1920s and 30s who went uptown to Harlem to the black-and-tan clubs to consume a more delirious, spontaneous, invigorating, physical spectacle than could be found in the feminised sphere of cultural sophistication below 110th Street, Farber got his movie fix in cinema's urban terminus.

The trance-like pull of 'punk movies', as critic and novelist Meyer Levin called run-of-the-mill films in the 1930s, was best experienced, he believed, in second-run theatres such as the Sheridan Square in Greenwich Village where an 'expectant mood raised by the advance promotion is no longer in effect', and where, on almost 'any evening, you can run into some of the nation's highest thinkers, standing in line at the box-office, to get their weekly or bi-weekly dosage' (Levin, 1971). As Tim Snelson and Mark Jancovich discuss in Chapter 11 of this book, underground or punk movies in a suitably non-bourgeois setting had a clear appeal to certain segments of the intelligentsia.

While on a 'reviewer's holiday', and covering similar ground to Farber and Meyer, James Agee chanced upon a screening of Val Lewton's *The Curse of the Cat People* (1944), which he watched with a 'regular Times Square Horror audience'. This is a 'specialized audience, unobstreperous [sic – he surely meant they are 'obstreperous'], poor, metropolitan, and deeply experienced. The West Times Square audience is probably, for that matter, the finest movie audience in the country (certainly, over and over, it has proved its infinite superiority to the run of the "art theater" devotees – not to mention, on paper which must brave the mails, the quality and conduct of Museum of Modern Art film audiences)' (Agee, 2005, p. 105). The validation of a proletarian audience's taste over and above the acts of distinction performed by an educated elite may not have been quite the act of obscenity that Agee suggested would get the Postmaster General hot under the collar, but it may have provoked a reaction from his readers who would not generally be inclined to attend a cinema specialising in horror movies.

In a 1953 review for *The Nation,* Farber took time out to defend the audiences west of Times Square from other critics' condescending descriptions of 'the largely male audience for action and horror pictures as being "made up of a desperate crew – perverts, adolescent hoodlums, chronic unemployeds, and far-gone neurotics."' He tallied with the proletariat because they were 'movie critics who simply couldn't be fooled by the expensive or pretentious' (Farber, 1953). In seeking 'to encourage moviegoers to look at the screen instead of trying to find a freak show in the audience', Farber was following the lines laid down by Otis Ferguson, whom he listed among the 'toughest, most authentic native voices' history had buried (Farber, 1953; Kael, 1963, p. 12). The following is a fine example of the rough poetry Farber found in Ferguson's criticism:

> The Globe is one of those Broadway fleatraps which hawk at modest prices the pick of the refuse left in the distributor's bin after every theatre exhibitor with any kind of decent pitch has had first, second, and third choice on everything from fair to awful. It has naturally built up its own kind of audience, a trampling, hoarse, and hoodlum pack off the garish sidewalks of what ranks today among the first gutters of the world, Broadway and Seventh, from Fortieth to Fifty-Second … You … find the picture starting half an hour later than schedule, part of which waiting time is taken up with a throwaway advertising short, and most of the rest of the time is devoted to sweat and suffocation and being walked over. If you can imagine a Turkish bath in a tight seat with all your clothes on, the steam coming from roiling vats of old underwear, you will know what fusty anachronism is ahead of you. (Wilson, 1971, pp. 331–332)

When, in 1963, Pauline Kael called Andrew Sarris and the British *Movie* critics to account for their boyhood devotion to 'virile' film-makers, she produced a critique that could more readily be laid against Agee, Ferguson and Farber.

Compare the following from Kael with Farber's description of the underground moviegoing experience:

> These critics work embarrassingly hard trying to give some semblance of intellectual respectability to a preoccupation with mindless, repetitious commercial products – the kind of action movies that the restless, rootless men who wander on 42nd Street and in the Tenderloin of all big cities have always preferred just because they could respond to them without thought. These movies soak up your time. (Kael, 1963)

In the male critic's fascination with the low-brow he aligns himself with the illegitimate, positioning himself as a cultural outsider – a hipster even. The figure of the hipster hanging around the 42nd Street film dives was fixed as early as 1952 in Chandler Brossard's novel *Who Walk in Darkness*, where, in between the bebop jam sessions, drinking, sexual promiscuity, drug taking, indolence and watching the fights, Greenwich Village's latest boho set take themselves to the pictures: *Casablanca* (1942) at the Museum of Modern Art, a double bill of *The Treasure of the Sierra Madre* (1948) and *Manhandled* (1949) at the Waverly. But it is the character Max Glazer, the novel's 'underground man', 'spiritual desperado', a 'smart guy' and 'very hip', who looks like a 'street-corner hoodlum' and is the 'finest lyric poet in America' who digs the movies the most:

> Max said he was going to a movie, a double-feature on Forty-Second Street. There was nothing else to do. Porter said that must be the fourth movie he had gone to in the last week. Max said so what. He liked the movies. (Brossard, no date, p. 79)

In the cold war years, the new subculture of the Beats and hipsters made their playground at the intersection of Broadway and 42nd Street, beneath the advertising light show, in the pinball arcades, cafes, bars, shooting galleries, automats and chop suey houses, the bookstores peddling smut and sensation, and the fleatrap theatres grinding out horror, westerns and crime pictures.[6] Here the new bohemians mixed with the drunks, pimps, prostitutes and junkies. Cruising homosexuals and their rough trade mingled with transvestites, panhandlers, pickpockets, pornographers, and grifters and drifters. Here among New York's underworld stirred a new underground, that would eventually spin out to include Mekas and his underground cinema, including such luminaries as Jack Smith, Kenneth Anger, John Cassavetes, Stan Brakhage and Andy Warhol.

'The underground man, both as literary figure and social type, first entered European awareness in the nineteenth century', claimed the critic Irving Howe; 'In the twentieth century the underground man comes into his own and, like a rise of pus, breaks through the skin of tradition. … Author, central character, and chorus, he is running the whole show … As rebel against the previously secure Enlightenment, he rejects the claims of science, the ordered world-view of the rationalists, the optimism of the radicals. He speaks in the accents of Romanticism, but a Romanticism gone sour and turned in upon itself' (Howe, 1970). In twentieth century arts in the United States the figure is inescapable, dominating the imagination of successive generations from the hot jazz aficionados of the 1930s, the bebop musicians of the 1940s, the abstract expressionists and beatniks of the 1950s, the rock musicians of the 1960s, and the New York punk avatars of the 1970s, to name only the most obvious. The term 'underground' for these revolts into style had its roots in the industrial revolutions that transformed the mythical vertical cosmos of sky, earth and underworld, with its sacred journeys into the netherworld, into a secular space where the lower depths have been penetrated by technology and invaded by mankind (Williams, 1990, pp. 16–17).

Artists have made profound use of real and imaginary subterranean worlds that promised places of mystery and a search for truth and power. This quest was mirrored in the excavations carried out by geologists, palaeontologists, anthropologists and archaeologists who sought, through their tunnelling, mining and drilling to unravel the 'Mystery of lost time' (Williams, 1990, pp. 23–24). The excavations uncovered a truth about the world's development; its strata and fossils exposed to the light a time before man, as archaeological digs exposed a hitherto unknown history of man.

The literal excavation of the underground produced a parallel set of ontological investigations. As Rosalind Williams observes, 'both Marx and Freud depend so much upon subterranean imagery that it is now virtually impossible to read a text about the underworld without filtering it through a Marxist or Freudian interpretation – without reading the buried world as the subconscious, or the working class' (Williams, 1990, p. 48). Going underground therefore formed the substructure of modern life, a place as fascinating as it is fearful: 'The social degradation of underground labor, as much as unconscious psychological terrors, explains why the underworld was dreaded as the region of sorrow and death' (Williams, 1990, p. 55). The underworld of literary social realism took the middle-class reader on journeys down among the lower ranks of society, with writers like Dickens and Hugo offering a moral education. 'What the writer unearths, however, is less fruitfully read as a description of lower-class reality than as a reflection of middle-class anxieties that the writer shares' (Williams, 1990, p. 21).

The social realist's underground journey eventually gave way to the transvaluation of middle-class ideals expressed by Bohemian deities such as Rimbaud and Céline, whom Howe described to such good effect as underground men: 'A creature of the city, he has no fixed place among the social classes; he lives in holes and crevices, burrowing beneath the visible structure of society … Even while tormenting himself with reflections upon his own insignificance, the underground man hates still more – hates more than his own hateful self – the world above ground' (Williams, 1990, pp. 121–122). The 'holes and crevices' are not the geological formations inhabited by primitive man, but the bolt-holes and watering holes in the architecture of the modern city. As Williams pointed out, the imagery of 'hyperurbanity resembles that of the underground', particularly the extreme verticality of Manhattan with its neo-cave dwellers (Williams, 1990, p. 6).

Farber's journeys into the underground were akin to those of the anthropologist visiting a lost tribe of primitive cave dwellers, or an archaeologist interpreting cave paintings, or the acts of a slumming aesthete. With its implied climb down the social and cultural ladder, his underground film experience was soon eclipsed, though not entirely wiped out, when 'underground' was reassigned as a noun for films made outside of Hollywood.[7]

In 1961, experimental film-maker Stan Vanderbeek published his picture essay 'The Cinema Delimina: Films from the Underground' in *Film Quarterly*. His underground was not the same as Farber's:

> Meanwhile, what of the artists, poets, experimenters in America, who must work as if they were secret members of the underground? (Vanderbeek, 1961)

The avant-garde film historian David E. James dates the formation of a New York underground cinema to the period between 1961 and 1963, when Jonas Mekas set up screenings first at the Charles Theater on Avenue B and East 12th Street and then at the Bleecker Street Cinema and the Gramercy Arts:

> The underground was coming into full flower and an unprecedented social visibility, not to say notoriety, with works in which the tradition of social realism associated with New York was rapidly giving way to bizarre sexual extravaganzas: the films of Ron Rice, Ken Jacobs, and especially Jack Smith, soon followed by Andy Warhol's early films. (James, 1992, p. 10)

In his introduction to Parker Tyler's *Underground Film*, Jim Hoberman wrote:

> A rubric rich with romantic connotation, Underground Film suggests movies that erupt out of individual libidos and channel beneath the surface of public consciousness, clandestine spectacles produced to be shown in subways or bomb shelters, experiences shared by a deviant (if not oppositional) sub-culture, films that might be subject to police harassment, a cinema that is anti-bourgeois, anti-patriotic, and anti-religious, as well as anti-Hollywood. (Tyler, 1994, p. v)

In the mid-1960s, Mekas was discussing the 'underground' in singular possessive terms as '*we* – *the* underground' [my emphasis], which he used as a catch-all for his various cinematic endeavours (Mekas, 1967). Discussing Mekas's co-option of the term 'underground', film historian Juan A. Suárez noted that it had 'great critical fortune, due to its descriptive power and its cultural history, which pointed to both the modernist and the avant-gardist components of the movement' (Suárez, 1996, p. 81). It signified, in other words, both a burrowing into and a withdrawal from mass culture. By the late 1960s, underground film was felt to be a term that best described American avant-garde film practice and exhibition.[8] In its anti-art stance, its cultural illegitimacy, its evocation of the primitive, its willingness to investigate the lurid and the taboo, this form of underground film would appear to find a rich complement in the pulp films admired by Farber. The films produced by underground artists such as Jack Smith, Andy Warhol and Kenneth Anger drew liberally from the common currency of Hollywood archetype and myth. Arch-reflexivity and exaggeration were endemic to this form of underground film, symptoms of a camp sensibility. But this new underground also readily inverted the gender certainties of underground film as established by Farber. As the 1960s progressed, the common ground of cultural illegitimacy shared by the two undergrounds induced production overlaps, mutually supportive exhibition practices, and corresponding critical and scholarly pathways. Not the least of these is the suggestion, made by David James, that the Farber-esque action film contested Hollywood from within while the avant-garde did it from without (James, 2005, p. 95).

In his 1968 article 'Experimental Films', Farber himself implicitly recognised and endorsed the shifting meaning of the term 'underground'; he wrote:

> The theatres of the Underground – often five or six docile customers in an improbable place that looks like a bombed-out air shelter or the downstairs ladies room at the old Paramount – offer a weirdly satisfying experience. For two dollars, the spectator gets five bedraggled two-reelers, and, after a sojourn with incompetence, chaos, nouveau-culture taste, he leaves this land's-end theatre feeling unaccountably spry. (Farber, 1998, p. 246)

The sites and descriptions of the underground/experimental film screenings bore a strong comparison with the cinema experience found on 42nd Street and other terminal zones that Farber had encountered in the 1950s:

> In the cliquish, subdued atmosphere of the New Cinema Playhouse or Tambellini's Gate, there is more than an attempt to dump the whole history of films. One glance at the pock-marked terrain and the placid spectator suggests a new concept of honesty and paradise. The Gate, on Second Avenue, starts as an entrance to an old apartment house, moves through a 1920's marble hallway, and engulfs the customer in a black chamber. God help him. The big sensation here is the ancient unreliable floor, which, like the ceiling in this blitzed miniature cathedral, is indescribable. Sometimes, the shredded carpeting, with its patches of masking tape, feels as spongy and sandy as the beaches at Waikiki. (Farber, 1998, p. 246)

Whether watching action movies or a Kuchar brothers' two-reeler, the experience still involved a tunnelling action, and the happening remained 'spongy'.

The key forum for encouraging correspondence between the two undergrounds was Mekas. In his *Village Voice* column he wrote a number of pieces on Times Square cinemas:

> Go to 42nd Street, where you can always find a Western. The Times Square Theatre, which shows Westerns exclusively, is always full, day or night. A sad, lonely crowd, made up usually of older people. It's like an old people's home, a hundred per cent male. The American Western keeps them company. They sit there, in the midst of all that poetry sweeping grandly across the screen, dreaming away. (Mekas, 1971, p. 12)

Like Farber, he cast this audience and its environs as an underground, a secret world of shadows and the forbidden:

> I hear some people want to clear up 42nd Street. What would we do without our movie joints, our hamburgers, our secret places? Clean places! We need more shadows, that's what I say. There we can cultivate forbidden virtues and forbidden beauties. Man needs unnecessary, unclean corners. (Mekas, 1971, p. 75)

Mekas's anarchic tastes, and open and eclectic approach to editing his journal *Film Culture*, produced some marvelous juxtapositions; the Winter 1962/63 issue included Sarris's 'Notes on the Auteur Theory', Kael's review of Truffaut's *Tirez sur le Pianiste* (*Shoot the Piano Player*, 1960), Jack Smith's homage to Maria Montez, and Farber's development of his theory of underground movies in 'White Elephant Art vs Termite Art'. In the Spring 1964 issue, which was largely devoted to Kenneth Anger's work, a letter to Sarris from Samuel Fuller was reproduced alongside a production still from *The Naked Kiss* (1964) and a series of frame enlargements from the film's opening scene. The images of a bald Constance Towers attacking the camera are not out of place alongside the journal's more usual avant-garde fare, and in retrospect at least, the idea of Fuller touting his sexploitation film to long-hairs like Sarris and Mekas suggests an ideal marriage of the two undergrounds.

In a 1990 interview with Sarris about his work with Mekas, film historian Tom Gunning asked about the shared use of provocation in Sarris's auteur theory and Mekas' New American Cinema. Sarris replied by more clearly drawing links between the two 'undergrounds':

> There was an aspect that was common to both things – the underground aspect, the covert aspect, the revolutionary aspect. In the one case you had people who are genuinely underground. Very many of them had subversive ideas of one type or another, either political, or social, or sexual, or behavioral, or formal, or artistic ideas. Then there was the second underground thing. It was the perception that a great many things that were considered disreputable, grubby, cheap, vulgar, were really much more interesting than that. And that there was something underneath all of this. The process of getting underneath is basically an intellectual process. It's a high-art process. It's not random, it's not undisciplined enthusiasm. It's overturning something. (Gunning, 1992, p. 74)

In her attack on auteur theory, Kael proffered a particularly astute reading of Mekas' and Sarris's critical symbiosis: 'And doesn't the auteur theory fit nicely into the pages of an "independent filmakers" [sic] journal when you consider the work of those film-makers might compare very unfavorably with good films, but can look fairly interesting when compared with commercial products. It can even look original to those who don't know much film history.' Kael argued that Mekas and Sarris had a shared view: both addressed themselves to a selective and exclusive group of films and film-makers; both resorted to the 'the language of the hipster';

both put a 'peculiar emphasis on virility'. She was also 'prepared to believe that for Jonas Mekas, culture is a "Big Lie". And Sarris, looking for another culture under those seats coated with chewing gum, coming up now and then to announce a "discovery" like Joanne Dru, has he found his spiritual home down there?' – *down there*, in the dark, sticky, spongy underground where the avant-garde and pulp mixed it up (Kael, 1963).

The disparate elements of the underground found a shared site of exhibition in New York's The Charles Theatre circa 1962. In *Midnight Movies*, Hoberman described the cinema as 'a moldering seven-hundred-seat movie house on Avenue B, a few blocks north of Tompkins Square Park. Like the handful of other Manhattan revival theatres (the Thalia, the New Yorker, the Bleecker Street Cinema) that catered to the rising interest in offbeat movies, the Charles offered an eclectic program' (Hoberman and Rosenbaum, 1991, p. 41; see also Hoberman, 1982). Mekas organised the weekend midnight screenings. The *New York Film Bulletin* called attention to the Charles' 'really audacious film selection' and hoped it would 'serve as an off-beat (truly off-beat) revival house … the New Yorker's beatnik brother'.[9]

In March 1961, the *Bulletin* announced the programme for a season of films called 'Young American Directors' at the Bleecker Street Theater. The chosen films were *Stakeout on Dope Street* (1958), *T-Bird Gang* (1959), *The Young Stranger* (1957), *The Cry Baby Killer* (1958), *The Strange One* (1957), *High School Big Shot* (1959), *Crime and Punishment, U.S.A.* (1959) and *A Time Out of War* (1954) – generic low-budget, drive-in fare. The season had been organised by Sheldon Rochlin, cameraman on Mekas' film *Guns of the Trees* (1961):

> 'Obviously, my method of selection was not based on any standards of accepted critical recognition. These films represent what I consider to be the outstanding examples of what is being done by young American film directors,' Mr Rochlin explained. 'The stories, mostly imposed on the directors, are admittedly poor: unmistakably a case of the form-over-content school. But yet they contain some of the best cutting, editing, and camera work we have seen in the post-war American films. The deficient story material provides an opportunity for the director to infuse a personal element into the *mise-en-scène*. Recently, neophyte directors in this country have been forced to work on stock studio properties and teen-age exploitation movies in order to gain a foothold; it can only be hoped that they may be given a chance in the near future to exercise their more obvious talents on more substantial material.'[10]

The cineaste's interest in low-budget movie-making looped back to the position outlined by Farber in his 'Underground Films' essay. The cinephiles and cineastes celebrated the honesty of the hack work, the authenticity of its world view, talent's tunnelling inside commercial material, and for those with sharp, well-attuned eyes, the recognition of 'grace notes' that 'pierce' through the bland outward shell of the formulaic fiction.

Though no doubt of only marginal critical concern, the idea that the low-budget film and creativity had something in common was a felt presence in 1950s' film criticism. In his *Village Voice* column in the late 1950s and early 1960s, Mekas wrote often 'In Defense of Action Films':

> You fools who look down on Westerns, who go only to 'art' films, preferably European – you don't know what you are missing. You are missing half of the cinema, you are missing the purest poetry of action, poetry of motion, poetry of the Technicolor landscapes. (Mekas, 1971, p. 75)

On another occasion he wrote:

> *Navarone* insults your intelligence? There you go, always searching for ideas. The best intelligence today is no intelligence at all, if you know what I mean. No intelligence is better than false intelligence. So enjoy the mountain dangers. Enjoy the man in action. Explosions. Ocean storms. Close escapes. Gregory Peck. Simple things like that.
>
> As for cinema, let's not fool ourselves. *Village of the Damned*, *Underworld U.S.A.*, or *Mad Dog Coll* has as much of it (in any case not less) as any 'art' movie you see today … Yes there are films which enrich our understanding of man and ourselves in a more realistic or, one could say, scientific manner. *L'Avventura*, for instance, or *Ashes and Diamonds*, or *la Dolce Vita*. But that doesn't give you the right to deny the other cinema, other kinds of knowledge, the knowledge gained through slapstick or a murder story, to name but two. (Mekas, 1971, p. 31)

This viewpoint came to a kind of apotheosis with Pauline Kael's 1969 essay 'Trash Art and the Movies', wherein she argued that 'The lowest action trash is preferable to wholesome family entertainment. When you clean them up, when you make movies respectable, you kill them. The well-spring of their *art*, their greatness, is not being respectable … If we have grown up with the movies we know that good work is continuous not with the academic, respectable tradition but with glimpses of something good in trash, but we want the subversive gesture carried to the domain of discovery. Trash has given us an appetite for art' (Kael, 1970).

In America's largest cities, the overlapping of the sites of consumption of genre and avant-garde films was paralleled in exhibition and promotion by the linking of exploitation and European art films. In the 1950s and 60s, European art and American sexploitation cinemas were, as Mark Betz notes, 'thoroughly interdependent and mutually informing', sharing sites of exhibition, marketing strategies and audiences (Betz, 2003, p. 217). The historian of exploitation film, Eric Schaefer, suggests that 'Because foreign films spilled over categories, because they were narratives, because they contained the spectacle of exploitation films, because they employed symbolism and made use of modernist techniques, because they could play in the few existing art theatres as well as Main Street houses that specialized in exploitation films, they were not contained within traditional boundaries and thus were obscene' (Schaefer, 1999, p. 334). The entrepreneur of exploitation films, David F. Friedman, noted that there were two distinct markets for such films: 'one for the select, sophisticated white-wine-and-canapés crowd, the other, and much larger one, for the less discriminating, cold-beer-and-grease-burger gang. As diverse as the two audiences were, both were intent, oddly enough, on viewing pictures in which human female epidermis was exposed' (Schaefer, 1999, p. 335). Arthur Mayer not only booked action and horror movies into his theatres; he was also responsible for importing and playing European films such as *Roma, Città Aperta* (*Rome, Open City,* 1945), *Paisà* (*Paisan*, 1946), *Ladri di biciclette* (*The Bicycle Thief,* 1948) and *Seven Days to Noon* (1950) (Schaefer, 1999, p. 235).[11]

In his valedictory essay on Stanley Kubrick, Michael Herr spins back to the 1940s to discuss the 'Art House Transmission', which so deeply informed the films of Kubrick, the young cineaste, and rolls forward to the 1960s when he, too, received an education in New York's film theatres:

> I spent my nights and a lot of afternoons rocketing between the Bleecker Street Cinema, the Thalia, the New Yorker, and the Museum of Modern Art, running after the hundreds of films that had been unavailable to me living upstate, in the provinces. Films by Bergman, Resnais, Kurosawa, Ophuls, Satyajit Ray, Antonioni, Visconti, Buñuel, Bresson, Godard, Melville, Fellini, to say nothing of Sirk, Lang, Hitchcock, Nicholas Ray, Sam Fuller, and not forgetting the final films of Ford and Hawks and Renoir, blew in and out of New York with great velocity and frequency. It's amazing how much luster those names had, and for how many people. They kept the arbitrary rectangle brimming with drama and spectacle, nuance and magic. (Herr, 2000, pp. 93–94)

It is not too much of a stretch of the imagination to say that postwar American film culture was invented in that 'rocketing' between the 42nd Street theatres, Greenwich Village picture houses, Lower East Side cinemas and MOMA.

Notes

1 For an essential discussion of Farber's film criticism, see Greg Taylor, *Artists in the Audience: Cults, Camp and American Film Criticism* (New Jersey: Princeton, 1999).

2 Another popular history of the locale is Anthony Bianco, *Ghosts of 42nd Street: A History of America's Most Infamous Block* (New York: William Morrow, 2004).

3 *The WPA Guide to New York City: The Federal Writers' Project Guide to 1930s New York* (New York: Pantheon Books, 1982), pp. 29–30, 175. The guide has a short description of motion picture theatres in and around Times Square, noting those with stage shows, those that specialise in newsreels and those that show foreign-language pictures, Yiddish, Russian, Chinese, and so on. There is a map of the theatre district showing the location of the movie houses on pages 168–169.

4 WPA (1982), p. 172.

5 The image of the 'truant eye' comes from Roger Cardinal (1986) 'Pausing over Peripheral Detail', *Framework* #30/31, 112–130.

6 For anecdotal histories of Times Square, Greenwich Village and the Beats see James Traub, *The Devil's Playground: A Century of Pleasure and Profit in Times Square* (New York: Random House, 2004), pp. 113–18, and Ronald Sukenick, *Down and In: Life in the Underground* (New York: Beach Tree Books, 1987).

7 Sheldon Renan offers a very impressionistic genealogy of 'underground film' as it extends from Farber in 1957 through its use by Lewis Jacobs in *Film*

Culture in 1959 through its use by experimental filmmaker Stan VanDerBeek; see *The Underground Film: An Introduction to its Development in America* (London: Studio Vista, 1968), p. 22.

8 'Underground Film as an exclusively American phenomenon (Jack Smith, Harry Smith, Anger, Brakhage, Warhol, et al.) with European/surreal antecedents.' Tony Rayns, 'The Underground Film'. *Cinema* 1 (December 1968).

9 *New York Film Bulletin* (17 July 1961) Series 2, No. 11 (37), pp. 1–2. The *Bulletin* ran an infrequent column by Chas. F. Kane called 'Notes from the Underground – a column of praise and protest' from 1960 to 1961. For a review of the programming at the New Yorker see Raymond J. Haberski Jr, *Freedom to Offend: How New York Remade Movie Culture* (Lexington: University Press of Kentucky, 2007), pp. 112–116.

10 *New York Film Bulletin* (13 March 1961), Series 2, No.4 (30), p. 1.

11 Towards the end of his autobiography, Mayer (1953) surveys the state of film fare and concludes that things have become moribund, the future, he believes, is with organisations such as New York's Cinema 16, which shows its 'strange avant-garde documentaries in a high school auditorium to an audience composed of people under twenty-five years of age'.

References

Agee, J. (2005) *Agee On Film: Reviews and Comments,* Library of America, New York.

Betz, M. (2003) Art, exploitation, underground, in *Defining Cult Movies: The Cultural Politics of Oppositional Taste* (eds M. Jancovich, A. Lazaro-Reboll, J. Stringer and A. Willis), Manchester University Press, Manchester, pp. 202–222.

Brossard, C. *Who Walk in Darkness,* Lancer Books, New York, p. 79 [no date].

Eliot, M. (2001) *Down 42nd Street: Sex, Money, Culture, and Politics at the Crossroads of the World,* Warner Books, New York.

Farber, M. (1946) Caper of the Week, *New Republic,* 30 September, pp. 415–416. Quoted in Taylor, G. (1999) *Artists in the Audience: Cults, Camp and American Film Criticism,* Princeton University Press, New Jersey, p. 45.

Farber, M. (1953) Times Square Moviegoers, *The Nation,* 4 July. Reprinted in Bromley C. (ed.) (2000) *Cinema Nation: The Best Writing on Film from The Nation, 1913–2000,* Thunder Mouth Press, New York, p. 405.

Farber, M. (1959) Underground magic, eccentric vitality and artful direction salvage banal stories. *New Leader,* 42 (16) (20 April), 27–28.

Farber, M. (1998) *Negative Space: Manny Farber on the Movies,* DaCapo, New York.

Gunning, T. (1992) Loved him, hated it, in *To Free the Cinema: Jonas Mekas & The New York Underground* (ed. D.E. James), Princeton University Press, New Jersey, pp. 62–84.

Herr, M. (2000) *Kubrick,* Picador, London, pp. 93–94.

Hoberman, J. (1982) The short happy life of the Charles, *American Film,* 7 (5) (March), 22, 34.

Hoberman, J. and Rosenbaum, J. (1991) *Midnight Movies,* Da Capo, New York.

Howe, I. (1970) Celine: the sod beneath the skin, in *Decline of the New* Harcourt, Brace & World, pp. 54–57.

James, D.E. (1992) *To Free the Cinema: Jonas Mekas & the New York Underground,* Princeton University Press, New Jersey.

James, D.E. (2005) *The Most Typical Avant-garde: History and Geography of Minor Cinemas in Los Angeles,* University of California Press, Berkeley.

Kael, P. (1963) Circles and squares. *Film Quarterly,* 16 (3) (Spring), 12–26.

Kael, P. (1970) *Going Steady,* Temple Smith, London, pp. 115–129.

Levin, M. (1971) The Charge of the Light Brigade, originally published in *Esquire,* reprinted in Cooke A. (ed.) (1971) *Garbo and the Night Watchmen,* Secker & Warburg, London, p. 109.

Mayer, A. (1953) *Merely Colossal: The Story of the Movies from the Long Chase to the Chaise Longue,* Simon & Schuster, New York.

McNamara, B. (1991) The Entertainment District at the end of the 1930s, in *Inventing Times Square: Commerce and Culture at the Crossroads of the World* (ed. W.R. Taylor), Russell Sage Foundation, New York, pp. 178–190.

Mekas, J. (1967) Where are we – the underground?, in *The New American Cinema: A Critical Anthology* (ed. G. Battcock), E.P. Dutton, New York, pp. 17–22.

Mekas, J. (1971) *Movie Journal: The Rise of a New American Cinema, 1959–71,* Macmillan, New York.

Schaefer, E. (1999) *"Bold! Daring! Shocking! True!" – A History of Exploitation Films, 1919–1959*, Duke University Press, Durham, NC.

Suárez, J.A. (1996) *Bike Boys, Drag Queens, and Superstars: Avant-garde, Mass Culture, & Gay Identities in the 1960s Underground Cinema*, Indiana University Press, Bloomington.

Tyler, P. (1994) *Underground Film*, Da Capo Press, New York.

Vanderbeek S. (1961) The cinema delimina: films from the underground. *Film Quarterly*, 14 (4) (Summer), 5–15.

Williams, R. (1990) *Notes on the Underground: An Essay on Technology, Society, and the Imagination*, MIT Press, Cambridge, MA.

Wilson R. (ed.) (1971) *The Film Criticism of Otis Ferguson*, Temple University Press, Philadelphia.

13

Searching for the Apollo

Black Moviegoing and its Contexts in the Small-Town US South[1]

Arthur Knight

When I moved to Williamsburg, Virginia, in 1993, after more than a decade spent in Chicago, Illinois, researching African American movies and moviegoing, I assumed that my new home town would not provide much of interest for my studies. Williamsburg was a small, Southern town. At the turn of the twentieth century it and the adjacent James City County had 5732 inhabitants; at mid-century they had 13 502; and at the millennium 60 100. At those intervals, 53%, 30% and 14% of the population was black. Beside its small population, Williamsburg was in a state that, until the 1960s, enforced strict racial segregation laws, which it was willing to take to extremes like its 'massive resistance' to school integration in the late 1950s, when it shut down public schools rather than integrate them racially. Given this history and demography, Williamsburg's socio-cultural landscape seemed unlikely to be a rich terrain of black moviegoing.

My perspective may have reflected prejudices created by my time researching Chicago's large and vibrant 'Black Metropolis', but it also had scholarly support. Thomas Cripps, a pioneering scholar on the topic of African Americans and American film, had argued in his 1970 essay, 'The Myth of the Southern Box Office', that despite Hollywood's claims that the South 'could carry a movie "out of the red" ', the region was a very small part of the US movie market, implying that the black South was an even smaller part (Cripps, 1970). In 1988, Cripps made this claim explicit: 'A considerable segment of black society rarely went to movies.' By Cripps' estimate, in the period between the World Wars as few as 10% of African Americans (just over 1% of the US population) were moviegoers. 'If this seems like an improbably low figure', he wrote:

> it must be remembered that if a black person wished to attend a movie the desired experience was nothing like its white equivalent. Far from a 'picture palace' with glittering constellations painted on the ceiling, gilt plaster imps lining the lobby, and

Explorations in New Cinema History: Approaches and Case Studies, First Edition.
Edited by Richard Maltby, Daniel Biltereyst and Philippe Meers.

> soldierly ushers at the doors, a black movie house was sure to be a reminder of the shabby world just outside the curtains of a black bourgeois parlor. In the South, the movie house would have been segregated by law; in the North, by custom. Moreover, even if a black family decided to go, they knew the regulars in the audience would catcall at the screen. (Cripps, 1988)

Just before my journey from Chicago to Williamsburg, Gregory Waller outlined the struggles of the very few theatre operators attempting to serve the black population of Lexington, Kentucky (population 35 000 in 1920; 30% African American), early in the twentieth century. Those struggles made kindred efforts in a much smaller town seem improbable (Waller, 1992).[2] At the same time, Douglas Gomery, in his history of US moviegoing, seconded Cripps by detailing both the humiliations of segregation and chronic 'underseating' for African Americans in the South. Drawing on a 1932 study of African Americans as a potential consumer market, Gomery argued that 'blacks in the South tended to rely on radio [for entertainment], because they were sometimes unable to secure access to theatres and radio provided a solution to the embarrassment associated with going out to the movies' (Gomery, 1992, p. 159; Edwards, 1932). When I arrived in Williamsburg a sampling of theatre advertisements in local press sources supported this scholarship: no movies for African Americans in town, at least for the first six decades of the century.

Then a few years ago I discovered the 1936 *Film Daily Yearbook*'s annual state-by-state/town-by-town listing of theatres in the United States. I checked the Williamsburg listing. There were the two theatre names I expected from my press survey, but there was also a mysterious 'New'. The New Theatre was in the *Yearbook* again in 1937, but in 1938 it disappeared, to be replaced by an equally mysterious 'Apollo'. I had never seen evidence of either of these theatres or heard any long-time Williamsburgers speak of them. The Apollo was listed again in 1939, and in 1940 the *Yearbook* also published a state-by-state/town-by-town list of 'Negro Theaters', and the Apollo appeared on that list, too. Perhaps my inference about black moviegoing was wrong. In 1941, the Apollo vanished from the list. Perhaps my inference was not too wrong.

Long a champion of examining 'the spatial and social conditions of the cinematic experience', Robert Allen has recently surveyed the last decade's effusion of scholarship on moviegoing. Allen finds much of importance in this work, but he also notes that – like me upon leaving Chicago – most of it is 'fixat[ed] on the metropolitan [and Northern] experience of cinema'. For Allen this fixation has 'obscured' the importance of the hyper-racialised, 'hyperterritorialized' experience of 'Southern urban modernity… [vs] Northern or Midwestern metropolitan modernity' in the history of US moviegoing. Having made this argument, Allen begins work on clearing the obscurity, but he also laments, 'There is so much we do not know about the cultural and social complexities of black moviegoing, particularly in the South, and the historiographic challenge represented by its reconstruction is especially daunting'. Specifically considering the effects of racial segregation on Southern moviegoing, Allen suggests, like Cripps, 'it is quite possible … that moviegoing was much more occasional than regular or habitual for most African Americans for the first 65 years of American film history, and that, as a consequence, what we might call movie culture was not a prominent feature of the lived experience for most African Americans for most of the twentieth century' (Allen, 2006, pp. 48, 69, 71, 77–78).

Spurred by what seem to have been Williamsburg's inhospitable conditions historically for black moviegoing as well as by the tantalising flash of the Apollo in the American film industry's historic record, this chapter attempts both to discover more about black moviegoing in the non-metropolitan US South and to demonstrate the 'historiographic challenge' that Allen discusses. A novelty of this study is that I will not confine myself to the era of pre-sound cinema, as most of the existing studies of black moviegoing and exhibition have.[3] Rather, I will pursue my case through the era of desegregation (roughly 1955–1965) to the start of the multiplex era (1969 in Williamsburg), where experiences of race and the space of the cinema continued to shape one another in complex ways. The case of Williamsburg certainly will not disprove Allen's carefully framed proposition about Southern black moviegoing. But it will suggest that long before we might have suspected, there was at least a desire amongst African Americans for moviegoing to be a part of black life in the small-town South.

The Surround: Town and Country, White and Black

A case study of black moviegoing in Williamsburg – and the means to judge its representativeness, generalisability or importance – can only make sense with some broader understanding of the town's history, as well as with some attempt to understand the national market for African American moviegoing. Founded in 1699, Williamsburg thrived for 75 years as the Virginia colony's capital and as a marketing and cultural centre for the large plantations that made up much of seaboard Virginia. At the eve of the American Revolution, the City had a population of almost 2000, about half black and half white. In 1780, Virginia's first non-colonial governor, Thomas Jefferson, feeling that Williamsburg was too vulnerable to British troops, moved the capital to Richmond, and Williamsburg was transformed from an urban centre into a quiet backwater for about the next 120 years.

Williamsburg entered the era of cinema as a small town housing a small College, a state-supported asylum, and a growing number of industries serving the local agrarian communities: a lumber mill, a knitting mill and a cannery. Just as the town seemed poised at the threshold of the industrial era, a preservation-minded group of clergymen, scholars and progressives noticed that one of the effects of the abrupt removal of the capital and Williamsburg's subsequent quiescence was that many colonial era buildings remained comparatively undisturbed. They began a campaign to 'restore' the town to their vision of its grandeur at the eve of the revolution. In the mid-1920s, this group convinced John D. Rockefeller Jr, philanthropist scion of the Rockefeller oil fortune, to support the project. In 1926–27,

Rockefeller's agents bought the majority of the property at the centre of Williamsburg, and over the next decade what had been central Williamsburg was recreated as 'Colonial Williamsburg' (or 'CW'), a town-sized antiquities and living history museum dedicated to retelling the story of the United States' founding moments. Not surprisingly, CW has never represented the colonial era city as 50% African American, and it has long struggled with how to represent slavery.[4]

The founding of CW had three prominent effects in relation to race and social space in Williamsburg. Firstly, it caused massive displacements of the population of the town, as people were bought out of their homes and moved to the developing periphery. In this process, the town, which had been integrated in its lower middle class and working class neighbourhoods and its business zones, became much more strictly segregated. Secondly, the town's economy reoriented toward tourism as other attractions developed to capture the attention of visitors to CW. This switch in economic focus for the area racialised employment patterns, creating a comparatively affluent black community of service workers. Thirdly, even as it amplified segregation in the town, tourism brought area blacks and whites into regular contact with outsiders who did not uniformly share white Virginia's investment in segregation. After World War II, the tourism and service economy of Williamsburg drew many new residents, creating a second order of large demographic changes and perhaps further complicating the locale's commitment to strict segregation. According to many long-time locals, these aspects of the Williamsburg community and economy at once eased and blunted (or softly repressed) the transformations of the Civil Rights era in Williamsburg.[5] On the one hand, many people were emphatically aware of the injustices of segregation, especially since those injustices had been materially emphasised in the CW restoration. On the other hand, activities that would disrupt tourism, including protests and racial violence, were undesirable for many people, white and black, whose livelihoods depended on it.

Considered in terms of population and geography, Williamsburg could fairly be viewed as representative of many small Southern, mid-Atlantic towns. At the same time, after the founding of CW the town clearly acquired some unique aspects that likely made it less representative. In the second section of this chapter, I will address in some detail how this shift in Williamsburg's make-up manifested itself in the townspeoples' – and especially local African Americans' – moviegoing opportunities. Before doing that, some attention to the history of the national scene for African American moviegoing will help provide useful context.

Concrete data on African American filmgoing – or, more accurately, on exhibition for African Americans – are scant and fragmentary. However, they do exist, and are suggestive, as shown in Table 13.1.

The numbers given in Table 13.1 need to be qualified in a host of ways. Aside from a few instances, it is not clear who collected these data, and because of that, it is often not entirely clear what is being counted and what is not. For example, for the 1942 number of 430 reported in the *Motion Picture Herald*, we know the data were collected by the US Department of Commerce (DOC) and 'checked by' Sack

Table 13.1 Numbers of African American cinemas in the United States.

Year	*No. of theatres*	*IL*	*NY*	*VA*	*NC*	*TX*	*FL*	*LA*	*AL*	*MS*
1909	112*									
1921	308*									
1923	<600*									
1925	425*									
1931	455 (30)	23	16	4	42	56	35	11	23	3
1932	445									
1933	300									
1937	[232 MPH] (28)									
1939	264 [388 MPH]									
1940	399/332 (28)	21	39	22	19	29	40	17	17	18
1941	393									
1942	413 [430 MPH]									
1943	410									
1944	421									
1945	452/442 (28)	21	39	33	21	39	44	21	19	21
1946	481									
1947	584									
1948	622									
1949	983									
1950	953/952 (34)	34	54	61	62	88	95	60	38	54
1951	956									
1952	1039									
1953	1049									
1954	1048									
1955	1045/1064 (37) 'estimated'	27	49	63	68	111	114	65	45	56

* Sources for the numbers marked with an asterisk are detailed in note 37.
'MPH' indicates numbers published in the *Motion Picture Herald*.
All other data come from the *Film Daily Yearbooks* (*FDYB*). The numbers for the years 1931–33 come from sections listing 'Colored Houses' state-by-state and town-by-town. All others come from the 'Industry Statistics' section. The second number in 1940, 1945, 1950 and 1955 was derived by counting the individual theatres listed in the state-by-state and town-by-town 'Negro Theaters' listings that the *FDYB* ran from 1940 to 1955. The number in parentheses in 1931, 1937, 1940, 1945, 1950, 1955 indicates the number of states (including the District of Columbia and, in 1955, the Bahamas and US Virgin Islands) listed as having 'Negro Theaters'. The columns provide the number of theatres in a sample of nine states as found in the *FDYB*'s state-by-state and town-by-town 'Negro Theaters' listings.

Amusement Enterprises of Dallas, 'one of the largest distributing firms of Negro films in the country'. In gathering these data they did not count 'theatres throughout the South which maintain balconies for Negro audiences or operate on a "midnight' show policy"' or theatres that split their weeks between days for white and days for black audiences.[6] Consequently, this number certainly underestimates black access to the movies across the United States, perhaps especially in the South, though it is not possible to know by how much.

In reporting its numbers, the *Film Daily Yearbook* (*FDYB*) never specifies what constitutes a theatre 'catering to Negro patronage', but it seems to mean: (i) in states where segregation was a legal requirement, theatres that served African Americans but not theatres with segregated facilities; and (ii) in states where segregation was illegal, theatres for which the majority of the audience was African American.[7] This puts *Film Daily Yearbook* practices in accord with the DOC, but over time the *FDYB* also started to add to its count drive-ins (which were segregated rather than black-only), some non- or semi-commercial venues, and 'portable' theatres or tent shows. The *FDYB*, then, was more liberal in its method than the DOC. Nevertheless, by not counting segregated accommodations in 'white' theatres (as opposed to drive-ins) in the South or any trends in integrating moviegoing in the North, it still likely yielded a conservative estimate of black access to the movies. That the DOC's conservative collection method yielded higher numbers than the *FDYB*'s unspecified method for the only two years in which both sources collected information – 1939 and 1942 – perhaps further emphasises the likelihood that all these numbers are underestimates. Moreover, since the numbers for those two years (especially 1942) are in rough accord, it seems probable that the dramatic increase reported in 'Negro Theaters' from 1931 to 1955, and especially after World War II, is both broadly accurate and indicative of an important trend in film exhibition's recognition of an underserved market – a market that the sample state-by-state numbers suggest saw most of its expansion in the South.

Aside from these figures, some fugitive bits of evidence suggest that, especially after the Great Depression, African Americans had more access to the movies in the South than we previously thought. Several cinema chains operating 'Negro Theatres' either in whole or in part began in the 1920s and 1930s and expanded and thrived into the early 1960s. The most notable of these was Lichtman (later District) Theatres, which began in Washington, DC in the late 1920s and expanded in the late 1930s and early 1940s to run more than 25 theatres for African Americans down the mid-Atlantic coast into North Carolina. Other chains following a similar pattern were the Bijou chain across the middle South, the large Wilby-Kincey chain affiliated with Paramount, and the six-theatre Booker-T chain in North Carolina, which went out of business with desegregation in 1963.[8]

Social scientists studying black Chicago in the 1930s and 1940s had found that 75% of African American youths (compared to 66% of whites) went to the movies at least once a week (12% went three times compared to 3% of whites), but others also found the movies were important outside the black metropolises of the North (Witty *et al.*, 1941). Observing black audiences in Washington, Atlanta, New Orleans and Birmingham, Rayford Logan argued in 1940 that 'The interest of Negro youth in almost any type of picture in which Negroes play a role is … incontrovertible' (Logan, 1940, p. 433). In his 'research memorandum' on 'Recreation and Amusement Among American Negroes', prepared for Gunnar Myrdal's *American Dilemma*, sociologist E. Franklin Frazier found that for blacks in the rural South 'one of the major attractions in town is the movie', and that 'the movies undoubtedly provide the means by which modern popular dances are communicated to youngsters in these small towns'. He also cited a 1929 survey in Richmond, Virginia, that found that going to the movies (preferred by 25% of 1587 respondents) trailed only going to church (33%) as a favoured form of leisure. Frazier detailed the often very objectionable conditions under which black Southerners could see movies, but he also noted that considerable sections of the audience – particularly youth and the 'lower classes' – were willing to endure these conditions to attend (Frazier, 1940). Writing after World War II, Phil Carter, a publicist for MGM (by his accounting, one of only two 'behind the camera' black employees in Hollywood), made a case for why:

> Negroes and others at the bottom of the economic heap attend movies proportionally more than whites to whom various forms of diversion and entertainment are open. Denied access to beaches, golf courses, swimming pools, skating rinks, and bowling facilities, and having few country places to dash off to for the weekend, *there is no other place for Negroes to go but the movies*. (Carter, 1946) [emphasis in original]

There is no question that conditions for black moviegoing in the South were very different from conditions for moviegoing in general, and even those for black moviegoing in the urban North and Midwest, and certainly those conditions kept some African Americans away from the movies. But there is also compelling, if not quite conclusive evidence that African Americans in many places in the South, and especially after World War II, did have regular and increasing access to the movies and that at least a substantial number made use of this access. In the broadest terms, in 1937 the *Motion Picture Herald* noted estimates that African Americans comprised 6% of the US movie audience; by 1967, *Variety* reported that the industry believed its audience might be as much as 30% African American.[9] While African Americans saw movies under radically different circumstances from whites, and while habits of African American moviegoing may have developed (or been allowed to flourish) later than those of whites, the *Motion Picture Herald*'s claim in 1942 that 'Negro America is movie-conscious' seems to have some merit. The case of Williamsburg will provide some means for testing this judgment.

Searching for the Apollo: The Many, Elusive Places for Black Moviegoing in Williamsburg

Williamsburg's first cinema – the nickelodeon-like Palace Theatre – opened in 1910 in the centre of town, conveniently positioned to draw custom from all parts of town.[10] In 1915, however, the local African American chapter of the Odd Fellows fraternal organisation began showing movies for black audiences twice a week at their lodge. This suggests that black Williamsburgers did not have access to the Palace and also that they wanted access to this emphatically modern amenity and entertainment.[11]

This expression of desire is very much in keeping with Jacqueline Stewart's finding that Chicago's African American audiences were engaged, in several senses, with the movies as a modernising force (Stewart, 2005, pp. xiii, 1–19). In Williamsburg, however, this engagement with modernity did not necessitate urban migration.

We do not know when the Odd Fellows stopped showing movies, but by the 1920s movies were being shown for African Americans in a location near their Hall, in what was probably an old and fairly unprepossessing building that one local woman, Mrs Bessie Gerst, called the 'tin theatre'.[12] Movies were also shown – perhaps after the tin theatre shut down – on Saturdays at the James City County Training School for African Americans, which opened in the same area of town in 1924.[13] The existence of these venues suggests that the Imperial, the main movie theatre in town in that era, did not have segregated facilities and thus did not admit African Americans.[14]

As the Colonial Williamsburg project acquired land to make way for the restoration and the commercial district that would serve it, all of Williamsburg's movie theatres, white and black, were bought up. The Odd Fellows Hall and the tin theatre fell to the wrecking ball as, in the late 1930s, did the Training School. Because the Imperial Theatre occupied what was envisioned as the commercial heart of town, CW purchased it, razed it, and in 1933 built a new RKO affiliated theatre, the Williamsburg Theatre, which has operated there ever since.

The Williamsburg Theatre definitely made no accommodations for and did not admit blacks, but, not surprisingly, it did employ African American labour to build it, and it also employed some black staff.[15] However, the New Imperial Theatre, which opened in 1932, before the Williamsburg and about a block away on the border of what was developing into a new African American neighbourhood, did include a balcony and separate accommodations for blacks. The Williamsburg Theatre's chain affiliation ensured that the New Imperial only got access to downmarket films. Moreover, female students at the College of William & Mary were, at least until 1934, forbidden to attend the New Imperial, perhaps because of its multiracial, though segregated, clientele.[16] Whatever the causes, the New Imperial lasted only through 1936 before leaving the field to the Williamsburg Theatre alone and, perhaps, leaving black Williamsburgers with no local movie theatre.

In 1936 the Apollo, its name most likely a gesture to the famous Apollo Theatre in New York City's Harlem, made its elusive appearance in the *Film Daily Yearbook*. The Harlem Apollo hosted many celebrated black performers, whose appearances there were noted by black newspapers around the country. In addition, it was home to a popular radio broadcast amateur hour responsible for launching many professional careers, and it was also a movie theatre.[17] To borrow this name for a black theatre was, potentially, to make an aspirational, community statement.

The historiographical problem posed by the Apollo Theatre is that in present-day Williamsburg there is no documentary or oral historical evidence of the existence of such a place, at least under that name. What did exist – and what may have been the Apollo – was a venue that its customers called Crutchfield's, or Mr Crutchfield's, Theatre. Crutchfield's was located at the edge of town, near a predominantly black neighbourhood, and it was a nondescript structure, probably less cinema-like in its appearance than even the early Palace Theatre. It apparently ran only on weekends.[18] This put it in line with the Palace's practice in the early teens, but by the 1920s, Williamsburg's white theatres had professionalised, showing every night with matinees on Saturday. Weekend-only showings put Crutchfield's squarely in a continuing and not very Apollonian line with Williamsburg's previous intermittent, non-professional venues for blacks.

Jack Morpurgo, an Englishman who had attended William & Mary in the late 1930s and penned a memoir about living and travelling in the United States, used the differing standards of movie availability he found in Williamsburg to illustrate and criticise racial inequality in the United States. In this context he referred to what must have been Crutchfield's as a 'negro shack' (Morpurgo, 1949, p. 14). Morpurgo's notice of Crutchfield's hints at several interesting issues: Firstly it was apparently a somewhat rough-and-tumble place. The memories of Mrs Doris Rainey, who was in her early teens in the late 1930s, support this inference. She knew of the theatre but was never allowed to attend because it was too boisterous. Her older brothers could go and so could her older sister, if she was accompanied by her brothers. Secondly, Crutchfield's was, by all accounts, a mixed race – or inverted race – space. Several rows of seats were reserved in the back of the theatre for whites – apparently mostly boys who liked to come to the B-westerns that were the theatre's standard fare.[19] Morpurgo does not claim to have attended Crutchfield's, but it is possible that he spoke from direct participation. Did the inverted segregation at Crutchfield's have anything to do with the boisterous atmosphere or Mrs Rainey's mother's sense of the place's dangerousness or inappropriateness? It seems likely.

One way of looking at this version of segregation is as a mode of white surveillance of African Americans – maybe even an extreme version with the white owner/manager's gaze at and over 'his' black clients being amplified by the gazes of the white boys in the back, who could be amused by both the film and the black audience and who were ideally situated to amuse themselves by baiting the African Americans in front of them. The letter from a local historian that first brought Crutchfield's to my attention suggests that this is probably an important way to think about the segregated social space at Crutchfield's: 'Doug [Johnson] said that the *white owner* of the theater kept the back two rows open for white clientele.'[20] Doug Johnson's uncle, Frank Gore, was the 'white owner'. According to Mr Johnson, Thomas Crutchfield had built the building and initially ran the theatre before Gore. And Thomas Crutchfield was black. Crutchfield developed the theatre's admissions practices and, at least for the theatre's black clientele, even when Gore ran the theatre, it bore Crutchfield's name.[21] A 1938 survey of the 'occupational and social needs of Negroes in the Williamsburg area' suggests the theatre was a vital local institution (and backs up Phil Carter's assertion that 'there is no other place for Negroes to go but the movies'): 'No recreational facilities are provided in any community in the area except a motion picture house for Negroes in Williamsburg, and a temporary bathing beach on the James River' (Carter, 1946).[22] Perhaps this complex status in the racialised landscape hints that Crutchfield's was the elusive Apollo after all.

The Apollo disappeared from the *Film Daily Yearbook* in 1940, though some locals recall it running as late as 1945. However, when the Bruton Heights School (BHS), a new facility for blacks, opened in 1941, it also included an auditorium equipped to show movies. Initially the BHS only had 16 mm equipment, but after a 2-month trial showed sufficient interest to support 'semi-commercial' movie exhibition at the school, it upgraded to professional 35 mm equipment.[23] During World War II, when BHS also served as a black United Services Organization (USO), the school eventually showed movies five or more nights a week. The Williamsburg Theatre's manager and programmer (and thus a CW employee), Tom McCaskey, consulted closely on this project and for more than the first year collaborated on its programming, drawing on his connections to negotiate favourable rates and attempting, apparently at the behest of the black audience, to track down black-directed and cast films. Remaining records are not entirely clear, but it seems McCasky had little luck getting black cast features at a rate the BHS could afford, and instead programmed a number of old black-cast shorts. It is also not clear in exactly what capacity or why McCaskey took on this work. He may have been formally tasked to do so, since he made frequent reports of his activities to the President of CW, or he may have been aware that this project interested the Rockefellers, who helped fund the BHS, and thought it wise to interest himself. Alternatively, he may have been genuinely interested and community-minded; he seems to have thrown himself into the work, and his memoranda on the project make clear that he saw the African American staff and students of the school as the 'owners' of the show. Certainly the white school board and the black staff of the BHS thought of him as working in a voluntary capacity and wrote him several notes expressing their thanks. There was, however, never any apparent consideration of making accommodations for blacks in the Williamsburg Theatre that McCasky managed.[24] Exactly when the BHS movie stopped is uncertain, but it appeared in the *Film Daily Yearbook*, in both the general and the Negro Theatres listings, for the last time in 1955.[25]

Almost simultaneously with the opening of the BHS movie, Williamsburg's first drive-in opened: the Stockade Auto-Torium. In his initial exploratory report about the possible BHS movie, McCaskey noted this pending development and opined, 'It will make a heavy play for colored business and will probably depend on it'. He also noted that 'A great number of our colored citizens drive to Hampton and Newport News for movies'.[26] McCaskey's prediction was correct. The Stockade did appeal directly to African Americans. Its advertisements in the local paper pointed out that it accommodated whites and blacks and, unlike any of the other theatres described in this chapter, it advertised regularly in regional African American newspapers. The entrances to the Stockade were segregated, as were the bathroom facilities, but the segregated parking lots were directly adjoined – next to one another, rather than with blacks placed behind whites – and split about equally, with an adjustable rear area that could accommodate overflow of either race. Additionally, the same snack bar served both blacks and whites, albeit from opposite ends of the counter. In the racialised landscape of 1941 this clearly counted as a progressive gesture, and Williamsburg's African Americans recognised this with regular custom and fond memories. Mrs Rainey recalled that 'we had one drive in movie … that was segregated: whites on this side, black on this side – BUT … we all went to the same concession stand. And we could hear them, they could hear us.'[27]

In the postwar era, which has been a fairly steady economic 'boom' period for Williamsburg, the movie scene seemed to stabilise: the Williamsburg Theatre for whites, the Stockade (9 months a year) for blacks and whites, and the Bruton Heights School or other occasional venues (e.g. the basement of the First Baptist Church in the late 1950s) for African Americans. This stability, though, soon had to contend with the developing Civil Rights movement. There are competing accounts of how and when the Williamsburg Theatre was desegregated. Bobby Braxton, a local African American man with a light complexion, tells stories of periodically buying two tickets at the Williamsburg Theatre in the early 1950s and then bringing in a much darker skinned friend and not encountering any trouble.[28] Other informants tell of a section in a rear corner of the theatre cordoned off for black patrons. When that section came into being is not clear – perhaps the mid or late fifties – but it is clear that although some African American moviegoers used it, others did not like it, possibly with spectacular results. Mrs Rainey again, though she emphasised this was 'hearsay':

> They had a movie … on Duke of Gloucester street – it's there now – and they had a rope that divided the blacks from the white. And John Tabb, who's dead and gone, he decided this was not going to be. … He went to the movie, cut the rope, they had him arrested, and he beat up about seven cops. And after that there was no more segregation, BUT the blacks did not go. We – and when I say 'we' I say that literally, a lot of us don't feel the same way that I do – we did not go to places that did not want us first and today if I know that this place had done me wrong when I was a child, I don't go.

Another local man, Mr Dennis Gardner, tells a different story: a local black clergyman, Reverend Collins, negotiated the quiet desegregation of the Williamsburg Theatre, probably in the late 1950s, initially with the roped section, which was eliminated by no later than 1963 when several locals recall seeing *To Kill a Mockingbird* (1962) as part of an integrated audience.[29] In fact, this quiet, gradualist account of how desegregation of public facilities and, to a lesser and later degree, schools happened in Williamsburg accords with other stories, including others of Mrs Rainey.

In 1969 Williamsburg got its first multiplex – and its first cinema that had never been a site of segregation. The Blane Twin Cinemas was in a new shopping centre at the outskirts of town, meant to serve locals better, who found it increasingly inconvenient to make their way into the tourist-clotted town centre. Paul Blane, the white owner/manager of this cinema, had begun a many-faceted career in show business management working for an uncle who ran cinemas serving African American audiences.[30] Perhaps because of his awareness of this historically underserved audience, as well as an apparent interest in spectacular youth cultures, Blane regularly included 'blaxploitation in his very mixed programme that included standard Hollywood fare, family movies, some art films, and exploitation film.[31] The Chamber of Commerce quickly began to worry that the area around Blane's cinemas was showing, in the words of one memo, signs of 'Honky Tonk blight'.[32] It is hard to imagine that anxieties around race and the still fresh desegregation of public amusements were not part of this assessment, but they were soon supplanted, or supplemented by anxieties over sex, when in 1972 and 1973 Blane showed *Deep Throat* (1972) several times before being pressured by the State's Attorney General to cease. Not long after, Blane sold out to a chain, which pointedly sought to avoid controversy of any sort.[33] Consequently, even as Williamsburg was about to 'urban renew' some its black neighbourhoods out of existence and replace them with municipal buildings and a public library, the town lost what may have been its only post-segregationist institution that acknowledged and invited Williamsburg's multiple publics through its programming.

Conclusion

Mrs Rainey's image of John Tabb with his desegregating scissors is powerfully appealing, although so far her 'hearsay' remains uncorroborated.[34] Whether true in all its particulars or not, the fact that the story of John Tabb's active and activist moviegoing circulated among some African Americans in Williamsburg distils four important things that this case study suggests. Firstly, it emphasises that there was a black moviegoing culture in the South, including the small-town South, well before the Civil Rights movement desegregated theatres. Secondly, it suggests that black moviegoers recognised that the material conditions of their moviegoing culture were different from those of mainstream movie culture, and that they sought to maintain some of the features of that difference – a proud community identity forged, in part, in resistance to terrible adversity – while erasing others – most notably the strong, material markers of unequal access. Thirdly, even as I am convinced that African American moviegoing was more robust in the South than scholars (and I) had thought previously, John Tabb's story demonstrates that the historiographical challenges of both gathering further evidence of that moviegoing and, then, working out what it may have meant in African American cultures remain daunting. Much of such evidence and much of the interpretation will have to come from individual and community memory and may resist being stitched into larger, representative patterns.

Finally, the story of John Tabb raises the question: What movie did he miss when (if) the cops took him away? Does it matter, and if so, how? Important studies of the memory of movies and moviegoing suggest that memory of the sociocultural space of the cinema endures much more vibrantly than memories of the movies shown in them.[35] But is this true for moviegoers who were marginalised in the theatre and on screen? At a national level, African American activism around the movies often went forward in two parallel tracks: attention to cinema access and critical attention to representation (or, lack thereof) of blacks. We know these tracks met in Durham, NC, in 1960, when segregated screenings of *Porgy and Bess* (1959) became a locus for Civil Rights activism that helped speed cinema desegregation.[36] There are hints that *To Kill a Mockingbird* may have played a symbolic role in marking the end of theatre segregation in Williamsburg, but what of other confluences – for example, black cast shorts at Bruton High School or blaxploitation at the Blane Twin? In her work on women spectators for silent cinema, Miriam Hansen has argued that we may have to be satisfied with establishing the 'conditions of possibility' for non-dominant spectators and their 'counter-publics' (Hansen, 1991, p. 125). But Hansen could be confident that the women she considered had, if they sought it, access to (say) Valentino movies. One of the great frustrations of searching for the Apollo is that, even once we have proven its existence (and have we?), we do not – and it appears we cannot – know what it played. So we can, it seems, only establish conditions of possibility once removed (if you will, conditions of possibility for the conditions of possibility) for small-town, Southern, African American moviegoing. But perhaps what we can know is this: Those conditions are marked by a double desire – the desire of the scholar to know more and, much more crucially, the desire of at least a half century's worth of black Southern audiences to enter fully the complex spaces that the movies represented in the United States. The first desire will likely never be fulfilled. Has the second been?

Notes

1 Thanks to my colleague Terry Meyers for guiding me to a number of sources for this essay. Thanks also to William & Mary undergraduate Andrew Jungclaus for research assistance in the Williamsburg/James City County Archives; to W&M undergraduate Brian Mahoney for sharing his work on local desegregation; to Cary Carson for his help negotiating the Colonial Williamsburg Corporate Archives; and, most especially, to the many people who have consented to oral history interviews with my students and me. Those whose knowledge and memories have been directly relevant to this research are cited by name below and in the References, but all the people we have talked to, too many to name here, have contributed. This project grows out of the Williamsburg Theatre Project (http://moviegoing.wm.edu/wtp; see also http://homerproject.wmblogs.net/); Rob Nelson, technical director emeritus of the WTP, always deserves thanks.

2 Waller expands on this research in *Main Street Amusements: Movies and Commercial Entertainment in a Southern City, 1896–1930* (Washington: Smithsonian Institution Press, 1995).

3 Besides Waller and Gomery, cited above, see Mary Carbine, '"The finest outside the loop": motion picture exhibition in Chicago's black metropolis, 1905–1928', *Camera Obscura* 23 (May 1990), pp. 9–42; Alison Griffiths and James Latham, 'Films and ethnic identity in Harlem, 1896–1915', in Melvin Stokes and Richard Maltby (eds), *American Movie Audiences: From the Turn of the Century to the Early Sound Era* (London: BFI, 1999), pp. 46–63; Charlene Regester, 'From the buzzard's roost: black moviegoing in Durham and other North Carolina cities during the early period of American cinema', *Film History* 17 (1) (2005), pp. 113–124; Matthew H. Bernstein and Dana F. White, '*Imitation of Life* in a segregated Atlanta: Its promotion, distribution, and reception', *Film History* 19 (2) (2007), pp. 152–178;

Christopher J. McKenna, 'Tri-racial theaters in Robeson County, North Carolina, 1896–1940', in Maltby *et al.* (2007), pp. 45–59; Dan Streible, 'The Harlem Theater: black film exhibition in Austin, Texas: 1920–1973', in Manthia Diawara (ed.), *Black American Cinema* (New York: Routledge, 1993), pp. 221–236; Douglas Gomery, 'The two public spaces of a moviegoing capital: race and the history of film exhibition in Washington, D.C.', *Spectator* 18 (2) (1998), pp. 8–17; Elizabeth Abel, 'Double take: photography, cinema, and the segregated theatre', *Critical Inquiry* 34 (supplement, Winter 2008): s2–s20; and Stewart (2005).

4 Colonial Williamsburg's story has been visited and revisited many times over the years in scholarly and popular works. Three useful sources are Anders Greenspan, *Creating Colonial Williamsburg* (Washington, DC: Smithsonian Institution Press, 2002); Richard Handler and Eric Gable, *The New History in an Old Museum: Creating the Past at Colonial Williamsburg* (Durham, NC: Duke UP, 1997); and Kim Andrea Foster, '"They're turning the town all upside down": the community identity of Williamsburg, Virginia before and after the reconstruction', PhD dissertation, George Washington University, 1993.

5 For more detail on the quietness of Williamsburg in the Civil Rights era, see Rex M. Ellis, 'The African-American community in Williamsburg (1947–1998)', in Robert P. Maccubbin (ed.) *Williamsburg, Virginia: A City Before the State, 1699–1999* (Williamsburg, VA: City of Williamsburg, 2000), pp. 231–245.

6 'Negroes Movie-Conscious; Support 430 Film Houses', *Motion Picture Herald* 24 January 1942, p. 33.

7 *Film Daily Yearbook, 1940.*

8 According to the *Motion Picture Herald*, the Bijou and Wilby-Kincey chains ran mixes of cinemas that were all-Negro, that had segregated accommodations, and that were all-white; 'Negroes Movie-Conscious', p. 34. Additional information from the 'Theatre Chains' section of *FDYB* 1930–66. For more on the Lichtman chain see Robert K. Headley, *Motion Picture Exhibition in Washington, D.C.: An Illustrated History of Parlors, Palaces and Multiplexes in the Metropolitan Area, 1894–1997* (Jefferson, NC: McFarland, 1999), pp. 118, 131, 170; Gomery (1998), p. 13; and Katherine Fuller-Seeley, *Celebrate Richmond Theater* (Richmond, VA: Dietz Press, 2002), pp. 84–88.

9 '232 Negro Theatres' (this article argued that, in light of the apparent number of Negro theatres, this 6% estimate was high); Lee Beaupre, 'One-Third Film Public: Negro; Columbia and UA Pitch for Biz', *Variety* 29 November 1967, p. 3 (thanks to Peter Krämer for this reference).

10 It is not absolutely certain that this first theatre was what became the Palace in 1911, but it is probable. See Julia Woodbridge Oxreider, 'Williamsburg claims the amenities of life, 1880–1920', in Maccubbin (2000), p. 165. Movies did occasionally show in Williamsburg before 1910, most notably at the Eastern State Asylum auditorium, but we have been able to uncover no detailed information about these shows.

11 Oxreider has found that Theodore Harris, a member of a well-to-do black merchant family, 'in 1916 paid $25 total for two moving picture licenses', but it is not clear whether these were for a venue in Williamsburg – even possibly the movie show at the Odd Fellows Hall – or for elsewhere in the area; see Oxreider, J.W., *Rich, Black, and Southern: The Harris Family of Williamsburg (and Boston)* (New Church, VA: Miona Publications, 1998), p. 23.

12 Oral History Interview with Mrs Bessie Gerst, 6 April 2006; interviewer Arthur Knight (with Margaret Freeman). See also 'Pre-Restoration Williamsburg as recalled by Lydia R. Gardner, From 1912 to…', map printed on the inside dust jacket of Maccubbin (2000).

We should note here that virtually all available conventional documentary sources for the history of twentieth century Williamsburg are 'white'. The newspapers that served (and continue to serve) the town have been published, edited, and staffed by whites and the government apparatuses of Williamsburg and James City County were, at least until about 1960, staffed by whites. Consequently, practices of segregation typically went unmarked, because they were not news. Perhaps because of reluctance or shame, the same appears to have been true, by and large, of both formal and informal changes in those practices. There were two prominent African American newspapers published in cities in the region – the *Norfolk Journal and Guide* and the *Richmond Planet* – but they were sufficiently distant from Williamsburg and its small population that they did not carry regular reports about the town or its surrounding rural areas. Because of this, we have relied a great deal on oral histories with Williamsburg residents. These are accessible to researchers via the Williamsburg Documentary Project at http://wdp.blogs.wm.edu/.

13 Mrs Gerst mentions movies at the JCC Training School, as does Oral History Interview with Mrs Doris Crump Rainey, 22 November 2007; interviewer Heather Huyck (with Arthur Knight). See also Oxreider (1998), p. 165.

14 Newspaper advertisements show that the Palace and the Imperial coexisted briefly in the mid-1920s but by 1926 the Imperial had apparently supplanted the Palace.

15 This story of black labour building a white facility was commonplace in the South, but, interestingly, could not be taken for granted in the North. In the late 1920s, when Balaban and Katz built the Regal Theatre on Chicago's African American South Side, the *Chicago Defender* protested that no black labour was being used in the construction. See 'Draw Color Line on Theater Building', *Chicago Defender* 19 March 1927, sec. I, p. 2.

16 The College of William & Mary Yearbook, *The Colonial Echo*, for 1934 contains this note: 'the co-eds voted for rights to visit the Imperial Theatre on occasion and won the appeal ... on occasion' (n.p.; ellipsis in original).

17 For more on Harlem's Apollo see Ralph Cooper with Steve Dougherty, *Amateur Night at the Apollo: Ralph Cooper Presents Five Decades of Great Entertainment* (New York: Harper Collins, 1990).

18 Phone interview with Mr Doug Johnson, 27 July 2007; interviewer Arthur Knight.

19 Mr Johnson Interview; Oral History Interview with Mr Dennis Gardner, 27 August 2007; interviewer Ryan Clark (with Arthur Knight). Headley claims that Washington, DC's famous Howard Theatre (a flagship theatre in the Lichtman chain) had a similar policy in the 1950s; see Headley (1999), p. 273.

20 Personal correspondence, Will Molineux to Arthur Knight, 10 April 2006; emphasis added.

21 What form the transition from Crutchfield to Gore took or when exactly it happened is not clear; neither man shows up in county records as having owned the land. In the 1930 census, Crutchfield (the only male with that surname in the area) was listed as an insurance agent; in 1942 draft records, he was listed as self-employed. In the same records, Gore was a mechanic in 1930 and an employee of the Yorktown Naval Weapons Stations in 1942.

22 'Proposed Educational Program for the Occupational and Social Needs of Negroes in the Williamsburg Area' [typewritten manuscript hand-dated 13 May 1938, held in Colonial Williamsburg Foundation Archives], p. 11. This survey was conducted by a committee made up of the Williamsburg schools superintendent, faculty members at the historically black Hampton Institute, and the state supervisor of Negro education.

23 Who paid for this upgrade is not clear. It may have been Colonial Williamsburg or the Rockefellers, since the local school board seemed ambivalent about this use of the auditorium. Much of my information on the Bruton Heights School comes from Linda H. Rowe, 'A history of black education and Bruton Heights School, Williamsburg, Virginia: research report submitted to the Colonial Williamsburg Foundation, May 1996' [manuscript held in Colonial Williamsburg Archives].

24 The Corporate Archive of the Colonial Williamsburg Foundation holds a series of memos and reports from McCasky to Kenneth Chorley (President of CW) and miscellaneous correspondence with distributors and other interested parties that runs from 17 April 1941 to 1 April 1943, when McCasky ceased his consulting role because he expected war service to take him out of the area soon.

25 The *FDYB* continued its general state-by-state/town-by-town listings until 1966, and the fact that the BHS does not appear in those listings is not proof certain that it ceased operating. These listings could be inconsistent (e.g. there are years when the BHS appears in the 'Negro Theaters' listing but not in the general listing or vice versa), although they also did capture information from far-flung locales, like the 'Auditorium' theatre for

blacks in the very small and isolated town of Gloucester, Virginia; for corroborating evidence, see Judith Haynes, 'Gloucester Family Prized Many Forms of Learning', *Hampton Roads Daily Press* 22 February 1998, A11.

26 Tom McCasky, 'Report and Recommendations on the Bruton Heights Movie', 16 April 1941, p. 2.

27 Mrs Rainey Oral History.

28 Oral History Interview with Robert Braxton, 3 April 2008; interviewer Brian Mahoney.

29 Mr Gardner Oral History (on Reverend Collins); Oral History Interview with Mr John Austin and Mrs Scottie Austin, 4 April 2008; interviewer Brian Mahoney (with Austin Wright) (on *To Kill a Mockingbird*).

30 Phone interview with Paul Blane, 8 August 2007; interviewer Arthur Knight.

31 See the Williamsburg Theatre Project database for examples of the Blane's programming in the early 1970s: http://moviegoing.wm.edu/wtp/.

32 James S. Kelly, President Williamsburg Chamber of Commerce, letter to members, 8 June 1969.

33 'Blane Cinemas Changes Hands', *Virginia Gazette* 5 April 1974, p. 5.

34 Another local man, Phillip Cooke, told a similar story, set sometime between 1957 and 1964, in which he simply took down a rope segregating a section of a local summer stock amphitheatre. Mr Cooke: '[The white usher] said, "But these are orders I got." He said, "The orders came down from the governor." So I sat there and I burned up, I burned up 'til finally I was sitting at the end of that rope and I took it loose and dropped it. The usher had already told me that he want' going to see it. He didn't pay no attention to it. We dropped the rope and immediately it became integrated.' Oral History Interview with Mr Phillip Cooke, no date; interviewer unknown [transcript held in Williamsburg Historic Records Association Collection, Swem Library Special Collections, William & Mary].

35 The fullest such study is Annette Kuhn, *Dreaming of Fred and Ginger: Cinema and Cultural Memory* (New York: NYU Press, 2002). Our oral histories have generally backed up Kuhn's findings: very few of the people we have interviewed, whether they identify as regular moviegoers or film fans or not, recall specific movies; the Austin's memory of *To Kill a Mockingbird* is exceptional in this regard.

36 See Thomas Doherty, 'Race houses, Jim Crow roosts, and Lily White palaces: desegregating the motion picture theater', in Maltby *et al.* (2007), pp. 196–214; Allen (2006), pp. 74–75; and Janna Jones, *The Southern Movie Palace: Rise, Fall, and Resurrection* (Gainesville, FL: University Press of Florida, 2003), especially pp. 49–57.

37 1909: *Indianapolis Freeman,* 7 May 1910, p. 6, quoted in Waller, *Main Street Amusements*, p. 162; 1921: J.A. Jackson, '308 Colored Theatres Found by Jackson', *Baltimore Afro-American,* 30 December 1921, p. 10, quoted in Regester, p. 123; 1923: 'The T.O.B.A.', *Billboard,* 15 December 1923, p. 102, quoted in Regester, p. 118; 1925: *Negro Yearbook* 1931–32 (no publication data supplied), p. 379, quoted in Streible; 1937 MPH: '232 Negro Theatres: 1½% of All Houses', *Motion Picture Herald* 24 April 1937, p. 78 (this number was gathered by surveying distribution exchange centres, not all of which responded); 1939 and 1942 MPH: 'Negroes Movie-Conscious; Support 430 Film Houses', *Motion Picture Herald* 24 January 1942, pp. 33–34.

References

Allen, R.C. (2006) Relocating American film history. *Cultural Studies,* 20 (1), 48–88.

Carter, P. (1946) It's only make believe. *Crisis,* 53 (2) (February), p. 45 [emphasis in original].

Cripps, T. (1970) The myth of the Southern box office: a factor in racial stereotyping in American movies, 1920–1940, in *The Black Experience in America: Selected Essays* (eds J.C. Curtis and L.L. Gould), University of Texas Press, Austin, pp. 116–144 (especially pp. 121–128).

Cripps, T. (1988) Thomas Cripps Responds to Jane Gaines. *Cinema Journal,* 27 (2), 57–58.

Edwards, P. (1932) *The Southern Urban Negro as Consumer*, Prentice-Hall, New York.

Frazier, E.F. (1940) Recreation and amusement among American negroes: a research memorandum, 15

July, pp. 21–31, 57–58 [manuscript held in Special Collections, Regenstein Library, University of Chicago].

Gomery, D. (1992) *Shared Pleasures: A History of Movie Presentation in the United States,* University of Wisconsin Press, Madison.

Gomery, D. (1998) The two public spaces of a moviegoing capital: race and the history of film exhibition in Washington, D.C. *Spectator,* 18 (2), pp. 8–17.

Hansen, M. (1991) *Babel and Babylon: Spectatorship in American Silent Film,* Harvard University Press, Cambridge, MA.

Headley, R.K. (1999) *Motion Picture Exhibition in Washington, D.C.: An Illustrated History of Parlors, Palaces and Multiplexes in the Metropolitan Area, 1894–1997,* McFarland, Jefferson, NC.

Logan, R.W. (1940) Negro youth and the influence of the press, radio, and cinema. *Journal of Negro Education,* 9 (3), 425–434.

Maccubbin, R.P. (ed.) (2000) *Williamsburg, Virginia: A City Before the State, 1699–1999,* City of Williamsburg, Williamsburg, VA.

Maltby, R., Stokes M. and Allen R.C. (eds) (2007) *Going to the Movies: Hollywood and the Social Experience of Cinema,* Exeter University Press, Exeter.

Morpurgo, J. (1949) *American Excursion,* Cressett Press, London.

Oxreider, J.W. (1998) *Rich, Black, and Southern: The Harris Family of Williamsburg (and Boston),* Miona Publications, New Church, VA.

Stewart, J.N. (2005) *Migrating to the Movies: Cinema and Black Urban Modernity,* University of California Press, Berkeley.

Waller, G.A. (1992) Another audience: black moviegoing, 1907–16. *Cinema Journal,* 31 (2), 3–25.

Witty, P., Garfield, S. and Brink, W. (1941) Interests of high-school students in motion pictures and the radio. *Journal of Educational Psychology,* 32 (3), 179–182.

14

Film Distribution in the Diaspora

Temporality, Community and National Cinema

Deb Verhoeven

Every conception of history is invariably accompanied by a certain experience of time which is implicit in it, conditions it, and thereby has to be elucidated. Similarly every culture is first and foremost a particular experience of time, and no new culture is possible without an alteration in this experience.

Giorgio Agamben (1993, p. 91)

Time, much like language, is a carrier of significance, a form through which we define the content of relations between the Self and the Other.

Johannes Fabian (2002, p. xxxix)

Introduction

Films are manufactured in order to be distributed through space and time to audiences. Many recent research initiatives have begun to explore in detail the spatial dimensions of film distribution.[1] But the diffusion of films also occurs through time. In an era tantalised by the thought of 'day and date' releasing it is important to remember that the careful orchestration of film distribution across defined time periods ('windows') has been a long-standing feature of film industry business practice.[2] By granting exclusivity to different exhibition and distribution companies at every stage of a film's release, 'windows' allow film producers to coordinate multiple restricted dealings for the commercial exploitation of a title. This system of distribution relies on a continuous supply of new titles and the ready obsolescence of films at the conclusion of their sequence.

Although digital distribution technologies have raised the prospect (if not yet the full reality) of 'simultaneous' global film releasing, geographies and economies of scale have until recently precluded the idea of instantaneous, non-exclusive release.[3] The expense involved in striking prints for all cinemas and the further cost of

Explorations in New Cinema History: Approaches and Case Studies, First Edition.
Edited by Richard Maltby, Daniel Biltereyst and Philippe Meers.

physically delivering films over vast distances to the theatre door have been given as prime factors for the staggered dispersal of cinema. The division of the world into spatially defined release territories has also had the effect of segmenting them temporally, naturalising a relation between the space and time of film distribution. In these depictions time, understood as a temporal disjuncture or interval in the diffusion of films, is the direct correlate of the spatial distance between global markets. The greater the distance from a film's domestic market, the longer the delay in its arrival. This line of reasoning also seems to apply to the distribution of films within markets.

At different times in the history of cinema, different release stages *within* distribution territories have also applied. For most of the last century, Hollywood movie distribution-exhibition was organised into a progression of 'runs'. Whereas most major film titles today are released on as many screens as possible ('general release') for maximum exposure and a prompt return on investment, prior to the mid-1970s this was not usually the case. In the early years of the twentieth century a 'zone-run-clearance' system was implemented, in which markets (usually cities but sometimes entire states) were classified as zones and the venues within them identified as either first-, second- or third-run theatres (although in some larger markets there may have been as many as five or six runs). The attribution of 'run' status was based on several factors including a theatre's location, size and perceived quality. First-run theatres were usually found within a confined downtown radius and were granted exclusive rights to screen a new title. After this the film would be temporarily removed from circulation for a short period of 'clearance' before reopening on second-run theatres in the inner suburbs. This strategy of sequential 'runs' would continue as the film moved further and further away from the centre of town. In the postwar period, which particularly concerns this chapter, alternative distribution strategies such as 'showcase' and 'roadshow' releasing were also practised.[4] Despite these innovations, the vast majority of Hollywood film titles were distributed according to the zone-run-clearance system into the 1970s.

It is easy to see how the spatial contours of this form of film distribution are arranged as a concentric expansion around the centrifugal locus of the downtown theatre district within spatially defined territories that also fan out from the point of a film's domestic origin. Describing the postwar distribution of films in the city of Melbourne, for example, film exhibitor Brian Miller noted:

> Distributing films across the city and its suburbs was like turning on a garden sprinkler. First turn of the tap covered the city theatres, another turn covered the inner suburbs and each subsequent turn reached further out until suburban Melbourne was saturated. (Miller, 2006, p. 24)

For Miller, the spatial expansion of cinema across the suburbs is also implicitly temporal, operating as a clearly defined sequence of 'turns'.[5] Windows, clearances and defined runs act as interruptions or stops in a linear temporal sequence. Each twist of the faucet identifies which specific market is entitled to view a film at which time, identifying whose 'turn' it is (and who should wait for, or even perhaps miss, a turn). The timing of film diffusion is not simply a transparent consequence of the spatial distribution of markets but is also a ranking of markets.

In accounts such as Miller's, film distribution rests on a conception of time that is thoroughly spatialised, in which temporal differences are also distances. The temporal character of this spatial movement is, however, fitful and contingent, subject to both uneven variation and interruption, fundamentally challenging the idea that global media flows are smooth in their transnationality or unimpeded in their localisation. The business of film distribution is founded on the establishment of temporal hierarchies, and its specific practices at once *promote* and *demote* markets through temporal relegation. The relative velocity of film distribution is not simply a matter of industrial, technological or economic organisation. It matters culturally and politically.

This chapter is particularly concerned to understand better the 'politics' of temporality entailed in the detailed analysis of film distribution as a practice of temporal ranking. Exploring the time experience of cinema spectatorship as it occurs in Australia for Greek diasporic audiences who are themselves the subjects of a spatial and temporal dislocation, it emphasises that neither the quantitative nor qualitative aspects of time have been sufficiently theorised in relation to the historical practice of film distribution and exhibition.

Thinking Time: Theorising the Temporality of Film Distribution and Exhibition

> Ithaca is an idea: to get there one day. Stathis Raftopoulos, Greek and foreign language film distributor and exhibitor[6]

In the course of a film's theatrical distribution in a zone-run-clearance system, films 'descend' through social hierarchies, eventually arriving at those least privileged audiences who receive the last access to a once-new release. As they proceed through their chain of runs, films lose value, and both rental and ticket prices are reduced as a film's prints age and deteriorate through use. The uneasy splices, the perceptible hiss or mismatched dialogue of a damaged soundtrack, the palimpsest of green, yellow and white lines that run amok over the drama, reveal the layers of a film's meaning for those in the cinema. They are a film's defining marks, serving to both position and address its audiences, alerting them to their status at the end of the line.

Examining circuits of film consumption in Bolivia, media anthropologist Jeffrey Himpele has described how the movement of films around the city of La Paz 'marks, separates, connects, and ranks human differences' (Himpele, 1996, 48). Himpele's study is centrally concerned with the ways in which the circulation of film itself distributes difference by dispersing audiences. For Himpele:

> Distribution is not a passive conduit merely linking the sites of production and consumption of film. It separates and connects differences among viewers in the social field. (Himpele, 1996, 59)

Similarly, Sean Cubitt observes the constitutive role that media distribution has in relation to consumers, noting how 'restrictions of media flows to specific audiences at specific times indicate a key task of distribution: participation in the construction of audiences' (Cubitt, 2005, p. 205). For Cubitt and Himpele film distribution wields time as an instrument for differentiating the spaces of consumption and the consumers who frequent those spaces by delaying or accelerating delivery. Charles Acland's work on the rise of the multiplex cinema in the late twentieth century also acknowledges the key role that the global circulation of cinema plays in the creation of lines of spatial and temporal difference in public life (Acland, 2003, p. 245). For Acland the industrial orchestration of commodities and markets unevenly circulates forms and establishes zones of consumption, distinguished by the velocity with which cultural forms arrive and depart from their audiences' attention (Acland, 2003, p. 244). Nowhere is this more apparent than in the organisation of the cinema. Acland is one of several film theorists to argue that recent innovations in communication, information and transportation technologies have created a sense of global synchronicity, which he alternatively calls 'popular cosmopolitanism' or 'felt internationalism'.[7] For Acland, popular cosmopolitanism is a 'structure of feeling about senses of allegiance and affiliation – about being in step – with imagined distant and synchronized populations' (Acland, 2003, p. 237). Acland charts an emerging international simultaneity in contemporary cinema, and a resultant revaluation of the space and time of new film events.[8]

In suggesting that this cultural simultaneity has produced new transnational communities that reside in people's imaginations but also bear material consequences for the organisation of social life, Acland extends to a global scale Benedict Anderson's conceptualisation of nations as communities imagined in the same time. For Anderson, national identity is embedded in temporality:

> An American will never meet, or even know the names of more than a handful of his 240,000,000-odd fellow-Americans. He has no idea of what they are up to at any one time. But he has complete confidence in their steady, anonymous, simultaneous activity. (Anderson, 1991, p. 26)

Anderson suggests that imagined communities or nations emerge from this calendrical coincidence, which is practised through the simultaneous consumption of media, such as the reading of daily newspapers. For Acland, the rise of coordinated opening weekends across the globe gives the impression of connecting people 'to geographically distant and temporally synchronised communities' (Acland, 2003, p. 239). But following Anderson, Acland goes further, stressing that it is not just the coincidence of a film's consumption but the wider expectation of a globally shared experience of cinemagoing, in terms of tempo, timing, duration, sequence and rhythm, that overrides geographical distinctiveness or the 'temporal particularity' of different time zones and which fashions the cosmopolitan audience (Acland, 2003, p. 240).

Both Anderson and Acland share an operative assumption that communities are by definition co-temporal, but Acland's admission of temporal particularities suggests that it is possible to imagine the global diffusion of cinema in such a way that temporal differences (no matter how particular or abbreviated) are acknowledged rather than disregarded. This in turn would suggest there are possibilities for developing and sustaining a sense of community in circumstances that may incorporate multiple permutations and combinations of the temporally discontinuous, geographically distant, temporally coincident and / or geographically near. Instead of the 'before and after' of temporal sequence (with its attention on cultural lag, queuing, waiting) perhaps we might imagine a role for temporal differentiation in experiences of coexistence or community.

One key task for the study of film distribution would be to imagine how the various practices that constitute the cinema might operate *at* the same time but not necessarily *in* the same time. Another is to conceptualise these different temporalities without bringing them into a hierarchical or sequential ordering. The history of Greek cinema in Australia provides an empirical example of how alternative temporal orientations in different social systems and settings can coexist and produce synergies. For the diasporic communities in this study, cinemagoing was in fact an activity constituted by and through diverse temporalities and locations, particularly in terms of the qualitatively different times of cinema consumption in various locations in Greece and Australia. The analysis of these diasporic film circuits reveals a wide range of temporal differences in the various cultural settings of cinema attendance: distinctions that were negotiated, exploited and affirmed by the specialised distributor / exhibitors working the circuit. Diasporic film distributors and exhibitors were adept at practices of de- and re-temporalisation, continually accommodating, altering, adjusting and applying different film itineraries and cinema schedules. Rather than proposing that cultural alacrity and coincidence are the key criteria through which transnational or cosmopolitan identity is measured, the study of diasporic film circuits suggests that there is a place for examining the role of global media circulation in enabling the coexistence of people and communities living in overlapping, intersecting, disparate, parallel, hybrid and contradictory temporalities.

Much theorisation of diaspora has focused on spatial flexion in transnational experience, in which 'diasporic space' is understood as both general and particular, global and local, individual and collective, and is understood as being based on contiguous or 'encountered' relationships as well as imagined and remembered ones.[9] This chapter adds to the reconceptualisation of the complex spaces of the diaspora a similar rethinking of its temporality through the vantage of cinemagoing; a discussion that bears on the commercial organisation of film viewing, on the articulation of specific audience preferences, on remembered cinema experiences, and extends to an acknowledgement of the oral history methodology that partially informs the research itself.[10] Through this analysis of the temporality of cinemagoing, the Australian Greek diaspora appears in fact to be less marginal, less homogenising and less historically discrete than we might imagine (or choose to remember).

Territories and Circuits of Time: The Specifics of Film Distribution in Australia in the 1950s and 1960s

> Distance is as characteristic of Australia as mountains are of Switzerland … The distance of one part of the Australian coast from another, or the distance of the dry interior from the coast was a problem as obstinate as Australia's isolation from Europe. (Geoffrey Blainey, 2001, p. ix)

The movement of films to and within Australia in the postwar period has not yet been the subject of detailed scholarly analysis. Speaking generally, films deriving from the United States took approximately two months – never less – to arrive on screens in Australia.[11] Within Australia the circulation of films varied widely according to studio, distributor, exhibition chain and specific title. There was never a nationwide simultaneous release strategy and it was not uncommon for capital markets outside Sydney to wait for months for a particular film.

Conventionally films arrived in Australia as a fine-grain master positive print. This print was held in a bond store (usually located in Sydney) and was released only after censorship classification and customs duties (levied on a per foot basis) were finalised. The film exchange then arranged for a negative to be struck and from this negative a number of prints (in this period, usually around 12) were printed for the Australasian market.[12] A maximum of three or four prints would arrive in each state for release. Films opening in Melbourne often had a simultaneous regional release, so that Ballarat, Mildura and Albury might screen the film before it reached the Melbourne suburbs. There was usually a one-week clearance period between first and second runs, but no further clearances as the film made its way to the outer suburbs. After a release had run its course, each state branch of the distribution company retained two prints for the possibility of extra screenings (e.g. doing the rounds of the migrant Italian or Greek circuits). Although revivals in suburban cinemas became more common during the 1950s as the studios trimmed their production slates, they were never the mainstay of cinema programming, and Hoyts cinemas, Melbourne's dominant theatre chain, seldom screened reissues. In the 1950s some suburban cinemas moved to simultaneous first-release screenings with the city (splash' release), making the scheduling of print movements much more difficult. Because of the limited number of prints available in each city, exhibitors resorted to 'switching' films, the practice of sharing prints between theatres on the same night by moving them between cinemas on a reel-by-reel basis.[13] As many as five theatres might share the same print on a given night, with reels being choreographed between cinemas by motorcycle, public transport or foot. The practice was so prevalent that Hoyts issued a 36-page handbook to theatre managers describing how switching should be organised and programmed.[14]

It is possible to see how delays in the arrival of films on Australian screens serve to define the Australian market as culturally dependent, with 'production' occurring in one place (there) and 'consumption' occurring in another (here), linked only by the transparent but tardy dealings of distributors. This representation, however, rests on a questionable understanding of the role and agency of distributors and exhibitors in defining the social fields of their audiences. For example, Melbourne's Greek cinemas almost invariably received US films as a last rental.[15] But Greek exhibitors in turn relegated these titles to a supporting role in a double-bill programme in which the feature presentation was nearly always a prominent Greek movie.[16] According to distributor/exhibitor Panayiotis (Peter) Yiannoudes, being the last 'run' for Hollywood films presented a commercial opportunity rather than a problem, because of the low flat-rate rental charges incurred:

> We don't mind because we have our own [films]. But many times our support gave us more money than the feature. If you have a good American film with Greek subtitles, then we never put a good film with that. We put only any rubbish. But usually we have [Greek] blockbusters and we have [US] supporting films. (Peter Yiannoudes)[17]

The position of US and Greek films on the programme was very rarely altered, but the quality mix of the programme could be adjusted. The programming of specific titles was also subject to a multitude of institutional, cultural and social schedules to accommodate the temporal demands of dual national citizenship and the observance of both Greek and Australian holidays in quite distinct ways:

> We never put a good film on a name day or Greek Easter. The best week of the year was the week after Christmas, then the March Labour Day, and Easter, the Australian Easter. At Greek Easter we always closed most of the cinemas. The Queen's Birthday was a good week, and so was the week of Melbourne Cup. Always then that we have good films, special films. (Peter Yiannoudes)[18]

In the mid-1960s, Greek exhibitors were active in the successful push for Sunday cinema trading in Victoria and New South Wales, bringing about a change of state government policy that significantly altered the tempo of cinema consumption.[19] Within the evening's entertainments other adjustments were made:

> Our intervals were quite long, because the audience wanted to see and talk to each other. I used to say to my dad, 'I wish we had an area where we could make a nice coffee place here, they'd stay after the theatre'. (Loula Anagnostou)[20]

Exhibitor-distributor Loula Anagnostou's romantic memory of a lingering audience is, however, challenged by cinemagoer Arthur Gioulekas, who found the late finishes a particular difficulty, as well as a contrast to his experience of watching films in Greece:

> We used to go to Richmond. We used to go about nine o'clock and we used to finish twelve o'clock. But we had a shop ... We went down there, saw the film, come back. In the morning I had to open the shop, you know? (Arthur Gioulekas)[21]

Anna Vlattas, a Sydney exhibitor-distributor, linked the success of the Greek cinemas to the delays in other forms of communication, suggesting the cinema was a prescient form of cultural contact, anticipating correspondences-to-come:

> There's no doubt the Greek cinema has kept Greeks happy here. They were very, very homesick those years, because communication was virtually nil. It was a matter of waiting for a letter, which sometimes took up to a month to communicate with their mothers, fathers or sisters or whoever. Wives. So the Greek cinema did give a lot of entertainment to the Greeks.

For Vlattas, the cinema screenings were a way of passing time, bridging a temporal and spatial breach, diminishing subjective time.[22] For audience member George Siskamanis, however, attendance at screenings only served to highlight his temporal and spatial dislocation:

> The cinema during the period was 'let's take a trip to Greece.' ... when we entered for a few hours, we forgot our commitments, our problems and we lived our need, meaning Greece, with her way of life, all those things. The problem was we would come out of the cinema, strangled by nostalgia, because we hadn't managed to get used to this life and we felt foreign in a foreign place. (George Siskamanis)[23]

For both Siskamanis and Vlattas the temporal experience of the cinema was always counterposed with another temporality, constituting the cinema as place of reckoning – of weighing up – and of comparison. Accounts such as these enable us to look at the way diasporic cinemagoing participates in breaking the assumption that cultural consciousness is inextricably linked to specific categories of space or geographic locations (which are usually understood as *either* where you are from *or* where you are at). Diasporic cinema attendance entails remembering locations of belonging as an outcome of both imaginary and physical processes. It suggests that there are multiple temporal and spatial rifts between locations of residence and observations of identity that are constituted through the acknowledgement of both presence and absence in cinema experiences. In the diaspora 'location' is always already explicitly temporal, relational and interconnected. As such it offers insights into how we might also think about the migrations of cinema as it traverses the globe, in this case from various locations (but principally Greece) to Melbourne.

Marking Time: Greek Film Distribution in the Diaspora

> The cinema would bring our country to us. (Anastasha and Paul Tamvakis)[24]

The rise of the Greek film industry during the 1950s and 1960s was enjoyed not just in Greece but internationally throughout the Greek diaspora. This was especially apparent in Australia, where waves of postwar migration provided a ready audience for imported Greek cinema (alongside sometimes subtitled films from other popular national cinemas, i.e. America, India, Turkey, USSR and Hong Kong). Between 1952 and 1974, some 220 000 Greeks came to Australia, with a very high proportion of them settling in Melbourne. In 1947 there were a mere 2500 Greeks in Melbourne. By 1971, the city boasted more than 98 000, and Melbourne remains the ethnolinguistic centre of Hellenism in Australia, and is sometimes described as the third largest Greek city in the world.[25] Between 1949 and 1970 there were more than 16 000 documented film screenings at Greek language venues in Australia, the majority of these featuring Greek films.[26] Greek diasporic entrepreneurs had entered the Australian cinema business in the 1920s and 1930s as theatre owners and/or managers. But it was not until the 1950s that a distinctive film circuit was established for Greek audiences (Cork, 1998). A thriving Greek cinema circuit made up of some 30 different inner city and suburban venues operated in metropolitan Melbourne alone. Screenings also occurred in the state capitals of Sydney (which also featured a successful theatre circuit), Adelaide, Brisbane, Hobart and Perth as well as in many regional centres such as Geelong, Ballarat, Mildura, Albury, Wollongong and Newcastle.[27]

Greek films were initially distributed and exhibited around the country on an itinerant basis, but by the early 1960s, a series of complex national circuits based on a modified zone-run-clearance system had developed. Taking Melbourne as a case study, it is possible to identify patterns in the timing of runs and the location of theatres that would suggest that within the Greek diaspora a spatial distribution of social hierarchies was also observed. The dominant Greek theatre chain in Melbourne was operated by Cosmopolitan Motion Pictures. By the early 1970s Cosmopolitan owned and leased 10 venues that screened regularly, as well as leasing some additional venues on occasion (Figure 14.1). Usually these cinemas were restricted to screening on weekends and only three venues regularly programmed matinees. Tickets could be reserved only at the National, Westgarth, Kinema and Paramount cinemas, which indicates that seats at these venues were in high demand. According to Peter Yiannoudes, a typical system of runs operated across the cinemas (see Table 14.1). Films would then be sent to Sydney (and vice versa for the Sydney circuits), followed by other capitals and regional centres or locations overseas, such as Wellington. A clearance period would then apply before the films were revived; some films reappeared as many as five or six times.

The circuit relied on importation of single film prints, and therefore relied on 'switching' prints between cinemas in weeks one and two. Since the cinemas involved in switching were not located in adjacent suburbs, and there was no evident efficiency to be gained from sharing prints, the practice suggests that Cosmopolitan made a conceptual connection between the cinema audiences frequenting these early-run venues. More generally, the circulation of films did not conform to a concentric expansion from a point of origin but rather criss-crossed the city. Although the circuit of runs does broadly correspond to Cosmopolitan's chronological acquisition of the cinemas themselves, there are several notable exceptions to this observation. Yiannoudes himself suggests that the movement of films in the circuit was principally focused on keeping competitors at bay. Films

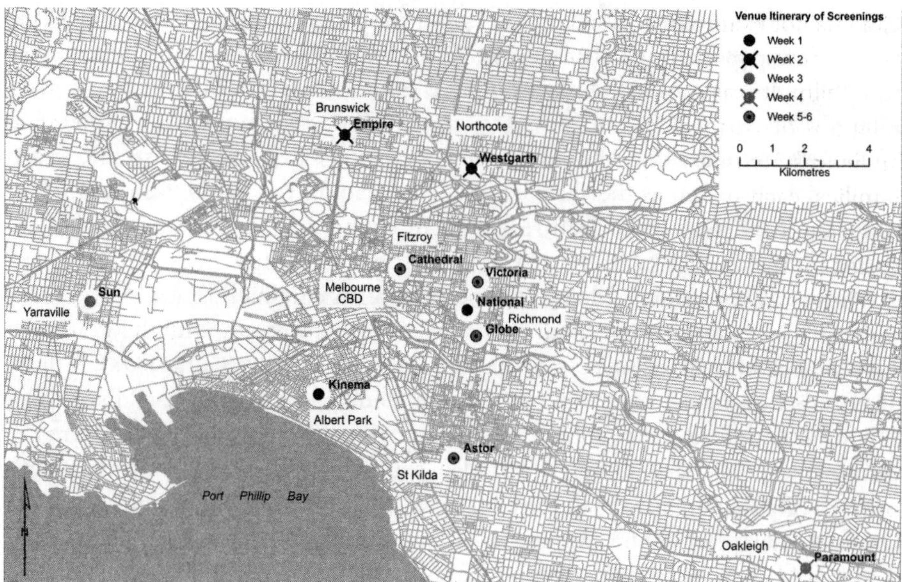

Figure 14.1 The Cosmopolitan Greek cinema circuit in Melbourne in the late 1960s.

Table 14.1 Cosmopolitan Motion Pictures: itinerary of screenings, late 1960s.

Week	*Venue*	*Location*	*Programme schedule*
1	National	Richmond	Mon–Sun (with a Saturday matinee)
	Kinema	Albert Park	Fri–Sun (with a Saturday matinee)
2	Westgarth	Northcote	Sat–Sun
	Empire	Brunswick	Sat–Sun
3	Sun	Yarraville	Sat–Sun
4	Paramount	Oakleigh	Sat–Sun
5–6	Astor	St Kilda	Sat–Sun (with a Saturday matinee)
	Cathedral	Fitzroy	Saturday only
	Globe	Richmond	Sat–Sun
	Victoria	Richmond	Sat–Sun

started in Richmond because of the presence of rival Greek cinemas there, moving to Yarraville for the same reason. This explanation only goes so far, however.

Cosmopolitan's circuit operated by distinguishing venues on the basis of the timing or 'window' between the first and subsequent screenings of a film, as well as the specific scheduling of films throughout the week according to various key attributes: whether the film was Greek or American, whether it was subtitled, and the film's genre and leading actors. All of these distinctions served to distil and distribute social and cultural differences within the diasporic audience. The National

Cinema, for example, operated as the circuit's flagship and was promoted with the largest newspaper advertisements, which often incorporated images from the featured film. It was open for trade even when other cinemas in the circuit closed for religious or national holidays. According to Yiannoudes, the National attracted audiences across the social spectrum: small business owners, shift workers and families, each of whom frequented the cinema on different nights, according to the routine of their work commitments. The programming of films would be varied for these different audiences.

The organisation of the circuit's other cinemas was notable for the relegation of migrants in the poorly serviced western suburbs and the outer eastern suburbs (the Sun in Yarraville in week 3, the Paramount in Oakleigh in week 4) (Figure 14.1). The Cathedral (week 6), which was frequented by the Macedonian community, is a particularly acute example of how the circuit delineated social and cultural distinctions. This became especially apparent when many Macedonians 'crossed over' to other cinemas in the circuit in order to attend screenings of *Alexander the Great* (Rossen, 1956), a film of particularly high interest for them.[28] As Loula Anagnostou recalls, this made for a particularly tense atmosphere:

> Then, for instance, we had *Mega Alexandro* (*Alexander the Great*), I would be the ticket seller, and we'd get a lot of the Macedonian Greeks who were not – the more Bulgarian side of it – they wanted to come of course. Well, I ran out of tickets: 'I'm sorry, there's no more.' Well, did I cop it. 'You put the Greeks in, but you don't want to let us in.' I said, 'No, it's not like that at all, go and have a look, there's no seats.' So I was the in-between person and look, there were funny nights, very funny nights, but there were some very sad ones too. They called me for everything that night, I remember that. Another thing was that when a lot of them were in the theatre and Philip of Macedonia comes out with Alexander as a baby and says, 'This is Philip of Macedonia, Philip of Greece', half of them walked out, they didn't like it you see. And we had a lot of that.
>
> Q: Did you get that cross-over often?
> A: Not always, no. It was only with *Mega Alexandro*. We translated it of course, word for word. They enjoyed it, but they didn't like that little bit, because they wanted him for themselves, and I could understand that too. I mean look at it, it's still going on. It's still going on. (Loula Anagnostou)[29]

After its acquisition by Cosmopolitan in the late 1960s, the Victoria was also singled out for screenings of culturally distinct films such as Yugoslavian and Italian titles (week 6). After the introduction of the R certificate in 1971, Cosmopolitan established a further nuance to audience segregation: some fathers deposited their families at one cinema and went on to themselves attend another without them.[30]

With the exception of Loula Anagnostou's admissions above, not one of the industry professionals identified the major Greek ethnic communities in Australia – Ithacans, Kytherans, Kastellorizians, Macedonians – as being of any significance in terms of the spatial or temporal segregation of audiences.[31] Nor did they consider political divisions in the Greek community relevant to audience behaviour, despite some evidence to the contrary. As far as the distributors were concerned, they serviced one big, coherent, happy audience. They were, however, prepared to acknowledge one key distinction: between prewar and postwar migrants. Most prewar Greek migrants living in Melbourne were Ithacan, while in Perth and Adelaide non-Kastellorizian postwar migrants were sometimes referred to as 'new Australians'. In this way a temporal distinction served to express a cultural one that could not otherwise be admitted.

Perhaps the most striking division to emerge from this research was the one drawn by film distributors between themselves and their audiences. In various interviews, Greek diaspora distributors speak of cinema audiences as if a distinct Other:

> When I used to go and see the films and to buy the films, I never put my feelings, I never buy anything for myself. I used to buy the film for the others.[32]

The audience, for the most part, was characterised as being less developed, locked in the past and oriented to tradition. Loula Anagnostou described her conception of the audience as a prime consideration in selecting programmes for the Victoria:

> I chose the films that I thought that the Greeks would like here, because Greek producers also made films that were not for this public ... You see we were getting the migrant here. The migrant was coming from all over Greece. A lot of them had primary education, and only some of them had tertiary education. So you had to look at their mentality, what they would like. What they could understand better, you know? What they would enjoy.

Paris Vlattas concurred:

> They like heavy drama because a lot of these people who came out here were single and they wanted drama that related back to their home. 'Oh mother I miss you', and this sort of thing that reminded them of what they've left behind.

In centring their narrative on the ways in which the audience experienced films as a form of nostalgia, these accounts of the various diasporic cinema audiences obscure the contemporaneity of Greek popular culture for Australian Greeks and the temporal specificity of the Greek circuit in the context of other cinema temporalities in Melbourne. Greek cinemas, for example, often screened foreign language film titles well before those same films were scheduled by specialised art cinemas. In characterising the audience as being both preoccupied with a past time, and as indicative of that past, these descriptions reveal that distributors were deliberately perpetrating the production of anachronism in the Greek film circuit. This is further emphasised by their management of the flow of films from Greece, and their regular use of revival screenings.

Because of its near monopoly on film exhibition in Melbourne, Cosmopolitan could afford to take their time bringing films over from Greece. Once the release season in Greece had ended and they could determine the relative success or failure of particular titles, the distributors would make their selections. Cosmopolitan only paid a deposit in advance to the one or two producers who could guarantee high-quality supply, so that in most cases they had no compelling financial motive to release the films promptly to recover their investment. The earliest a film could expect to arrive in Australia was within a month, but there was a further delay as the film wound its way through customs for 3 or 4 weeks, and censorship for a further week or so. Even if a film completed this process within a 2-month time-frame it was unlikely to be screened, since it might be reserved for special calendar dates, or held back in order to subdue a potential rival or more generally to heighten market expectation. Imported films were also not always drawn from the most current or recent releases. Between 1959 and 1965, Cosmopolitan contracted to take one film from the back catalogue of Finos films for every two new films they screened.

The majority of films arrived for their premiere screening in Melbourne or Sydney within 12–24 months of their Greek film release (Table 14.2), but the impact of rerelease or revival screenings on the overall temporal character of the circuit is evident in further analysis of the data. So, for example, from 1956, when the circuit developed critical mass and was distributing more than 20 films a year, the mode, or most commonly occurring time-lapse between the release date in Greece and the release date in Australia, varies wildly from year to year (e.g. in 1967 it is 1–2 years but in 1968 it is 11 years or more). However, the median time (the interval centrally positioned between the shortest and longest wait) ranges only between 3–4 and 5–6 years over the entire observed period (1949–1970) and the average or typical time lapse also sticks within a limited range – from the fastest turnaround of 3.6 years in 1960 to the longest delay of 5.5 years in 1968. These figures suggest that distributors were programming the mix of new release and revival films in order to 'balance' for an overall sense of temporal consistency. For Anna Vlattas the inclusion of revivals was a way of ensuring that successive waves of migrants arriving in the country would have access to cherished films:

> And of course we had the titles that were famous. Greeks would see them over and over again. But they might have seen them when they were little and they would have loved to see them again when they're adults. Films like *To Koritsi me ta mavra* [*The Girl in Black*, Kakogiannis, 1956]. (Anna Vlattas, Paris Vlattas and Costas Margaritis)[33]

Loula Anagnostou remembers actively seeking direct feedback from the audience in order to determine repeat programming decisions:

> Many times they would ask for screenings again. We guided ourselves by the public, how they liked it, and sometimes if it was a very interesting film I would get on the microphone and say, 'Would you like to see that again?' Just to see how the reactions, you know? (Loula Anagnostou)[34]

Table 14.2 Gap between release year in Greece and screening in Australia (Greek films only).

	Years since first release in Greece												
Year	*0–1*	*1–2*	*2–3*	*3–4*	*4–5*	*5–6*	*6–7*	*7–8*	*8–9*	*9–10*	*10–11*	*11 or more*	*Total*
1949							1						1
1950		2						1					3
1954		1											1
1955	2		2	1									5
1956	4	1		5	4	1	4					2	21
1957	1	5		4	5	2	1	3	1				22
1958		1	1			1			1				4
1959	5	4	5	3	1	4	1	2	2	1	1	1	30
1960	4	5	6	5	6	3	3	1	1	1	1	1	37
1961	7	10	10	4	5	3	5	8	2	2	1	7	64
1962	6	8	16	15	7	7	3	6	6	3	3	8	88
1963	3	10	5	8	8		3	5	3	5	1	6	57
1964	4	11	18	9	11	10	4	3	2	5	5	7	89
1965	9	8	11	12	6	14	11	3	2	4	3	2	85
1966	5	11	12	11	11	8	7	7	2	1	1	3	79
1967	4	6	5	3	4	6	5	6	3	2	3	3	50
1968	3	25	20	23	19	15	15	14	18	11	5	30	198
1969	4	7	14	12	22	16	7	7	12	9	6	8	124
1970		29	8	11	12	11	7	5	10	3	4	13	113
Total	61	144	133	126	121	101	77	71	65	47	34	91	1071
Percentage	5.7	13.4	12.4	11.8	11.3	9.4	7.2	6.6	6	4.4	3.2	8.5	

The popularity of return viewings goes some way to explaining the success of the Greek video distribution outlets that succeeded the film circuits in the early 1980s. What is notable about the specific temporal horizons of the Greek cinema circuit is the way it demonstrates that it is not the diffusion of films through space that somehow causes film industries to 'temporalise' but that there are underlying conceptualisations of space and time at the core of any globalising cinema that constitute and enable a variety of meanings to the specific distribution of films.

Conclusion

This chapter considers some of the ways that migrant film distributor/exhibitors used cinema circuits to produce new temporalities (and spaces) in Australia. It also examines how enterprising film distributors brandished time to define social relationships and hierarchies within the Greek-Australian community. This example of diasporic entrepreneurism in the global film industry reveals how the commercialisation of time (delineating temporal differences between audiences with window releasing and other distribution practices) supported the existence of internal differences within, and overlap between, apparently enclosed communities.

However, this essay seeks to go beyond simply recognising the difference that time makes to the social world. Certainly, understanding *when* film events occur contributes a great deal to understanding *how* and *why* they occur. But this essay also proposes that time is itself transformed by a multiplicity of practices and is not fixed or regular, that the imagined social relations between various 'selves' and 'others' also define our perceptions and uses of time, and that in a way these constitute time itself. Time as portrayed in this chapter then is not an objective phenomenon existing independently of its contents but can be seen to affect the events within it *and* is also affected by them. Through understanding cinemas as temporal intersections – as multiple and heterogeneous forms of affiliation that move across and between different temporalities and social groups – it may be possible to imagine new ways of writing about and researching the cinema.

Similarly, in analysing how the arrangements made for ethnic media consumption imagine, transform and mobilise new communities of belonging, this chapter does not suggest that the distribution of Greek cinema is a transparent carrier of globalisation. Rather, diasporic film audiences are constituted through ethnic media events and are constitutive of them. More generally, it shows that culturally defined communities can affiliate themselves translocally, through their imaginative comparisons of other places and other times. The formation of these communities need not be premised on perceptions or myths of spatial and/or temporal commonality. So although Australia's Greek cinema circuits may be understood as part of a specific process of 'Hellenisation', they also prompt us to redefine our understanding of 'national cinemas' as politically, linguistically or geographically bounded entities. We also need to reconsider some of our assumptions about the transportability of non-Hollywood popular cinema: the activities of Cosmopolitan Motion Pictures clearly point to what is typically left out of the summary description of the Greek film industry such as in the *Encyclopedia of European Cinema*:

> The output of commercial Greek cinema consisted mainly of quickly made low-budget films aimed exclusively at the domestic market. A few films attempted to meet 'European' or Hollywood standards but met with little success abroad. Only Greek sex films had some impact on foreign markets. (Vincendeau, 1995, p. 190)

Finally then, in suggesting that cinema studies needs to undertake more culturally and temporally nuanced work, this essay acknowledges that the film historian is not outside the production of time either. There are inherent complexities in re-presenting oral histories for example, particularly when the interview subject does not distinguish past and present as sequentially distinct tenses in the same standardised way as the film historian is expected to write. Insofar as there is emerging an 'historical turn' in cinema studies there might also be an opportunity to rethink time in the practice of film history itself; to encourage histories that are accepting of alternative temporal conceptions, and that above all are accepting of the familiar dictum, that all time is relative.

Acknowledgements

I would like to acknowledge the assistance of Michelle Mantsio, Olympia Szilagyi, Alwyn Davidson and Dean Brandum in the preparation of this chapter, and to thank Jill Julius Matthews and Colin Arrowsmith for their helpful feedback on earlier drafts.

Notes

1 See a discussion of some of these in Deb Verhoeven, Kate Bowles and Colin Arrowsmith, 'Mapping the movies: reflections on the use of geospatial technologies for historical cinema audience research', in *Digital Tools in Film Studies*, eds Michael Ross, Manfred Grauer, Bernd Freisleben (Bielefeld: Transcript Verlag, 2009), pp. 1–13. Other significant projects investigating and mapping the spatial dimensions of film distribution and exhibition include: in the United States the longstanding efforts of Jeffrey Klenotic and more recently Robert C. Allen; in Australia, Alwyn Davidson; in Germany, Jens Wagner, Roger Sennert and Michael Ross; and in Canada, Sebastien Caquard.

2 'Windows' may also refer to different stages in a film's format, which are also conventionally spread over a period of time – such as a release in cinemas (theatrical and non-theatrical), as packaged media (video or DVD rental and sell-through), for broadcast (television, video-on-demand, cable) and as digital files.

3 Day-and-date releasing may be calendrically coincident but is never strictly simultaneous, with territories east of GMT opening films before those to the west.

4 Showcasing entailed bypassing the zone-run-clearance system and opening a film simultaneously in a number of second-run venues (perhaps 20 in a smaller market and up to 100 in a major city). This form of distribution was generally reserved for low-budget genre titles. Roadshow releasing was characterised by opening films in a limited number of theatres in big cities for a specific period of time before moving them onto a general release. With its reserved seats, premium ticket prices, souvenir programmes and intermissions, roadshow releasing was Hollywood's attempt to differentiate product by offering a prestige form of presentation for audiences. For a detailed history of these practices, see Sheldon Hall and Steve Neale, *Epics, Spectacles and Blockbusters: A Hollywood History* (Detroit: Wayne State University Press, 2010).

5 Miller explains that this expansion of the distribution network across the suburbs was based on the growth of suburbs themselves and the subsequent construction of theatres. Older and more central cinemas generally got the films before newer ones further from the centre of the city.

6 Stathis Raftopoulos in 2000, interviewers unidentified, posted by 'Rainscratch' online at http://www.youtube.com/watch?v=pORfzQtuZPQ on 13 October 2007. Accessed 5 November 2007.

7 Acland's observations, for example, bring forward Anne Freidberg's earlier description of an intensification of the temporality of cinema spectatorship produced by new forms of engagement with cable television, the multiplex and the VCR. Anne Friedberg, *Window Shopping: Cinema and the Postmodern* (Berkeley: University of California Press, 1993), p. 126.

8 See in particular, Charles Acland, '"Opening everywhere": multiplexes, E-cinema and the speed of cinema culture', in *Hollywood and the Social Experience of Movie-going*, eds Richard Maltby, Melvyn Stokes

and Robert Allen (Exeter: University of Exeter Press, 2007), pp. 364–382.

9 See in particular Avtar Brah, *Cartographies of Diaspora; Contesting Identities* (London: Routledge, 1996).

10 To date, 26 interviews with members of the Australian Greek community have been recorded. A record of films and screenings was compiled and added to the Cinema and Audiences in Australia Project (CAARP) database (caarp.flinders.edu.au). This database holds records of Greek and non-Greek films screening in community-specific venues in Australia, and particularly in Melbourne. The database holds records for 1260 films that screened between 1949 and 1967 at 7598 screening events intended specifically for Greek audiences at various Australian venues. An additional 8786 screening events were held between 1967 and 1970 and are to be added to the CAARP database. By 2011 records for 1970–1980 will be added resulting in a total data set of more than 36 000 records.

11 There were very occasional world premieres, such as *On the Beach* (Kramer, 1959), a Hollywood location film shot in Melbourne and which premiered 'simultaneously' in 18 cities including Moscow. See Philip R. Davey, *When Hollywood Came to Melbourne: The Story of the Making of Stanley Kramer's On the Beach* (Melbourne: Philip R. Davey, 2005).

12 An exception occurred for Technicolor films. Because of the lack of local Technicolor laboratory facilities all 12 or so prints were imported.

13 This practice, which used to be done illegally by exhibitors in the 1910s and 1920s, was then known as 'bicycling'.

14 Referred to by Brian Miller (2006).

15 One exception was *El Cid* (Anthony Mann, 1961), which they received immediately but was not particularly successful.

16 One of the few US films that was screened as a main feature was *Atlantis: The Lost Continent* (George Pal, 1961), which flopped on first release, and was given to Cosmopolitan after only 3 weeks.

17 Peter Yiannoudes, interview by Michelle Mantsio and Deb Verhoeven, 13 April 2006. Greek subtitles were added to many Hollywood films by Greek exhibitors in this period. For a detailed description of this practice see Bowles, K., Maltby, R., Verhoeven, D. and Walsh, M. (2007) More than Ballyhoo?: The Importance of Understanding Film Consumption in Australia, *Metro Magazine*, 152, March: Special feature section on 'The Changing of Cinema Experience', pp. 96–101.

18 Peter Yiannoudes, interview by Michelle Mantsio and Deb Verhoeven, 13 April 2006.

19 Anna Vlattas, Paris Vlattas and Costas Margaritis, interview by Michelle Mantsio and Deb Verhoeven, 29 November 2006.

20 Loula Anagnostou, interview by Michelle Mantsio, 22 July 2006.

21 Arthur Gioulekas, interview by Michelle Mantsio, 12 December 2007.

22 It is not surprising that many venues made available traditional Greek snacks such as roasted pumpkin seeds, called *pasatempo* ('passing the time').

23 George Siskamanis, interview by Michelle Mantsio, 3 December 2007.

24 Anastasha and Paul Tamvakis, interview by Michelle Mantsio, 15 May 2007.

25 The most rapid period of Greek migration to Australia began in the wake of the 1952 bilateral agreement on immigration between the two countries. In 2005, the Greek and Greek-Cypriot population of Melbourne was approximately 215 000, compared to approximately 160 000 in New South Wales. These figures probably underestimate the number of Greeks in Australia, since temporary Greek migrants would have been missed in the periods between censuses, and census documents fail accurately to distinguish ethnic identity from nationality thereby missing ethnic Greeks born in places such as Turkey, Egypt or even the Australian-born children of Greek parents. On this basis, Melbourne is sometimes described as the third largest Greek city (after Athens and Thessaloniki), although variations in the definition of the term 'city' suggest considerable caution is required in making this claim. See Anastasios Myrodis Tamis, *The Greeks in Australia* (Melbourne: Cambridge University Press, 2005), p. 63.

26 Preliminary analysis of the film titles that have an identifiable country of origin suggests that between 1949 and 1970 films from Greece comprised approximately 66% of all screenings, films

from the United States 23%, and films from other countries of origin 11%.

27 For a detailed history of the foundation and early years of Melbourne's Greek distribution-exhibition circuit see Deb Verhoeven (2007) 'Twice born: Dionysos Films and the establishment of an Antipodean Greek film circuit', *Studies in Australasian Cinema,* 1 (3), 96–152.

28 For the attitudes of Macedonian audiences to the Greek film circuit see Pat and Stan Delov, interview by Michelle Mantsio, 28 November 2007.

29 Loula Anagnostou, interview by Michelle Mantsio, 22 July 2006.

30 Adult films were not permitted to be screened in the same cinema as family programmes, so in 1971 an additional cinema was added to the circuit specifically for these R-rated screenings, The Galaxy (which had previously specialised in screening Arabic and Italian films), and which was aptly renamed The Liberty.

31 These are the largest and most influential of Greek migrant groupings which followed chain migration patterns, drawing together settlers from the same region and in many cases the same entire village to the one place in Australia; from the islands of Ithaca (who settled principally in Melbourne), Kythera (in Sydney) and Kastellorizo (Perth and Adelaide). Macedonians dominated settlements in Shepparton and Werribee (both in Victoria). See Tamis (2005), p. 43 ff, for a description of the fierce parochialism which dominated Greek Australian life in the prewar and postwar period.

32 Peter Yiannoudes, interview by Michelle Mantsio and Deb Verhoeven, 13 April 2006.

33 Anna Vlattas, Paris Vlattas and Costas Margaritis, interview by Michelle Mantsio and Deb Verhoeven, 29 November 2006.

34 Loula Anagnostou, interview by Michelle Mantsio, 22 July 2006.

References

Acland, C. (2003) *Screen Traffic: Movies, Multiplexes and Global Culture,* Duke University Press, Durham, NC.

Agamben, G. (1993) *Infancy and History: The Destruction of Experience* (trans. Liz Heron), Verso, London.

Anderson, B. (1991) *Imagined Communities*, Verso, London.

Blainey, G. (2001) *The Tyranny of Distance*, Pan Macmillan, Sydney.

Cork, K. (1998) Parthenons Down Under: Greek motion picture exhibitors in NSW, 1915 to 1963. Unpublished PhD thesis, University of Western Sydney; posted by George Poulos in 2004; available online at http: // www.kythera-family.net (accessed 22 October 2007).

Cubitt, S. (2005) Distribution and media flows. *Cultural Politics*, 1 (2), 193–214.

Fabian, J. (2002) *Time and the Other*, Columbia University Press, New York.

Himpele, J.D. (1996) Film distribution as media: mapping difference in the Bolivian cinemascape. *Visual Anthropology Review*, 12 (1) (Spring), 47–66.

Miller, B. (2006) Reels across the city. *Cinema Record*, 514.

Tamis, A.M. (2005) *The Greeks in Australia,* Melbourne, Cambridge University Press.

Vincendeau, G. (ed.) (1995) *Encyclopedia of European Cinema*, Cassell, London.

Part 4

Cinema, Modernity and the Local

15

The Social Biograph

Newspapers as Archives of the Regional Mass Market for Movies

PAUL S. MOORE

The home paper is the mirror in which those at a distance see us.

Local News column, *Paris (ON) Star-Transcript*, 1 May 1907

In 1904 the *Fort William Times-Journal* introduced a new column called the 'Social Biograph', compiling local curiosities and gossip from all over northern Ontario.[1] The feature had begun with the title 'Social Chat', but its new name seemed to elevate its purpose beyond gossip into a more significant record and review of the intricate details of ordinary life. The 'Social Biograph' lasted into 1909, in its later years often sitting next to advertising for the town's new nickel shows. This edited collection of curiosities provided a biography of the social, graphing the lifeworld for its public of readers. Like the aphorism printed in the *Paris Star-Transcript* in 1907, the small town newspaper's social biograph was a mirror that allowed those at a distance to see its community. The visual dynamic of this metaphor inverts the mass media roles of cinema, since moving pictures conversely allow us here to see them at a distance.

Early twentieth-century newspapers are an archive of cinema's reorganisation of social life. Every small town and village newspaper had a local gossip column, under a heading such as 'Town Topics', offering a nonchalant compilation of the indiscriminate social and commercial happenings of the past week. These columns often recorded the first appearances of five-cent picture shows in not-quite-rural places across North America. More than advertising, more than news stories, these passing comments amidst the village gossip fascinate me most in studying early cinema. Altogether they paint a surprisingly detailed picture of the regional diffusion and institutionalisation of the novelty in the years before it was a mass practice. My book-length study of early moviegoing in Toronto emphasised urban routines and municipal governance as the foundation for making a mass culture out of big-city moviegoing (Moore, 2008). In keeping with some recent

Explorations in New Cinema History: Approaches and Case Studies, First Edition.
Edited by Richard Maltby, Daniel Biltereyst and Philippe Meers.

film exhibition histories, my own archival research has shifted its attention from downtown to acknowledge the point succinctly made by Kathryn Fuller-Seeley, that 'motion pictures seem to have been well tolerated wherever they were shown in villages and towns across the [U.S.] nation. Many itinerant showmen were successful, and nickelodeons cropped up as quickly in smaller towns and cities as they did in Manhattan' (Fuller-Seeley and Potamianos, 2008, p. 7). Even more vociferously, Robert C. Allen has continued to fight against the 'Manhattan myopia' of '*New Yorker* map' film history, most recently arguing that 'our [US] national map of the history of the social experience of moviegoing is schematic, conceptually primitive, geographically distorted, not drawn to historical scale, and hence, of limited epistemological utility' (Allen, 2007; see also Allen, 2006). While agreeing with the general emphasis of these arguments, my prior urban research, in combination with my recent research into early exhibition in Ontario's small towns and villages, leads me to retain the significance of the metropolis, but now as a focal point of a region.

The emergence of mainstream cinema was metropolitan – not simply urban – insofar as it almost simultaneously included the hinterland in creating first a mass market for cinema, and subsequently a mass practice of cinemagoing. The modernity of cinema was not simply the electric apparatus, nor just the commercial form of its pastime, nor the edited sensations of its depictions. It was also, and perhaps primarily, a mass practice that connected all places in a region, not to each other so much as to the mass market. Whatever was on screen, cinema provided a way to practise modernity as it constructed a modern mass public. Of course, newspapers did this first.

About half of Canada's population lived in Southern Ontario, spanning the northern shores of the Great Lakes.[2] This was the most densely populated part of Canada, and the only part of the country with an industrial economy rooted in transportation and metropolitan networks comparable with, and indeed integrated with, those in the bordering United States.[3] After government regulation became standardised and theatre inspection centralised, the bureaucracies of these processes created a rich archive of architectural and administrative records. These archives, however, do not cover the beginnings of everyday moviegoing from 1906, before regular advertising and government inspection became the norm, and the history of the emergence of cinema must be constructed from other sources, particularly from the trade press and local newspapers. As I pursued the emergence of nickelodeons (a strictly American term, it turns out, as these places were known in Ontario as 'theatoriums' or simply 'picture shows'), it seemed at first as if every city, town and village was entirely unique and required an entirely distinct way of searching through its newspapers. The following analysis, however, formulates a more systematic methodology, gradually developed in the process of researching dozens of towns across all of Ontario. It provides not only a typology of cinemas and relations to their localities, but also a typology of newspapers' relations to their localities, in which the local appearance of cinema is embedded and archived.

Newspapers and Modernity

Despite our collective scholarship on the nickelodeon years in North America, it remains surprisingly difficult to recover histories of specific early picture shows. Especially in the biggest cities, nickel shows opened almost anonymously, without advertising, reporting or building permits: the entertainment equivalent of corner stores. The mass market for movies in North America was successfully entrenched through the independent planning of thousands of entrepreneurial showmen, largely because film exhibition began with precisely the radical decentralisation that mass production of celluloid entertainment allowed. Recovering the history of this process consequently needs to be equally decentralised, and locally attuned.[4] There is no single archive of the spread of the nickel shows. Instead, there are thousands, resting in almost every local newspaper and municipal record of the period. Tracking how these variously local appearances of cinema existed in a concerted network requires as many methods as there were routes into showmanship. Exhibition was the avenue through which cinema became culturally meaningful to the population of North America, who gained access to cinema practically simultaneously but initially as somewhat isolated regional publics. A composite local history of nickel shows describes the origins of cinema as a transition from metropolitan curiosity to mass culture during the 'transitional' period from 1907 to 1913 (Keil, 2001; Keil and Stamp, 2004). The regional mass market was an important transitional scale, mediating the initial perception of picture shows as local enterprises, which were then transformed into an institution providing entry into a continental popular culture.[5] Along with the other contributors to the project of New Cinema History, I would argue that the research effort required to verify this process through grounded social history is as valuable to film history as time spent investigating the more centralised processes of production and distribution.[6]

Mapping the nickel show's appearance on a regional scale collects local cases into a mass market without abstracting the process to global or national generalisations. Such a project requires grounded research to bring into view the networks of localities sharing a common subcultural experience of mass culture.[7] To define cinema as mass culture implies the existence of showmen and audiences themselves oriented to moviegoing as a modest way of participating in the mass market of modern metropolitanism. Little remains of their perceptions, of course, but promotional journalism and advertising can stand in as an archive of showmanship and of the ways that it enticed audiences into going to the movies. Newspapers are an important empirical record of transitional cinemagoing because they provided a route for the normalisation of cinema, and were themselves a similarly modernising means of connecting readers in one location to the modern mass market everywhere.[8] This nexus of communication, consumption and public participation (whether through newspapers, cinema, railroads, the telegraph or postcards) defines the very foundation of modernity, but for this assumption to be securely grounded historically, it needs to be supported by contemporary observations of cinema that provide evidence of its arrival being discussed as a sign that localities were becoming modern through their connection to the mass market.[9]

Given my advocacy of empirical grounding, a few examples are in order. Most overtly, showmen often showcased metropolitan business connections, such as the boast of one making 'arrangements to secure, with the leading moving picture theatre of Toronto, the latest films', or another's claim that 'these films are brand new and have never been shown outside the larger cities'.[10] Moving pictures were evidence of communities becoming modern and more like larger cities. Consider the rhetoric of an advertisement for a tent show set up on a town square for the summer, defending the townsfolk against the dismissive attitude of a nearby city: 'Berlin says Galt never wakes up till it's too late. Hundreds have wakened to the good things at the Tentorium'.[11] In the town topics of Newmarket, well north of Toronto but connected by electric railway, the opening of the Scenic put the town 'in the swim' with other places, a cogent, if colloquial, way of denoting modernisation as a network, as connection and circulation rather than hierarchy and progress.[12] Metropolitan downtowns might have taken the plunge earlier, but once 'in the swim' anywhere could be part of modernity. Interpreting newspaper discourse as linking peripheral sites to the metropolitan market even revives the clichés of showmen's advertising copy: new and up-to-date, first-class and refined, the latest and the best. These became vital signs of cultural currency, and could even be transferred from the films to the town or audience itself: 'Scott's Colloseum Coming to the City – Peterborough Up-to-Date', and simply the command, 'Be Up-to-Date. Visit Wonderland'.[13]

From 1995 to 1997, *Cinema Journal* staged a debate over methodologies for studying early cinema, centred around Ben Singer's attempt to defend the working-class and immigrant associations of early cinema against Robert Allen's foundational tracing of 'Manhattan Nickelodeons' corresponding with areas of middle-class consumption much earlier than the mythology of working-class cinema implies (Allen, 1979).[14] Part of the discussion was the need for a more contextualised methodology for studying immigrant moviegoing, marginal theatres and research outside of Manhattan. Subsequent research on Jewish and Italian picture shows in Manhattan has indeed demonstrated an affinity between these marginal audiences and early cinema, regardless of the coexistence of mainstream moviegoing elsewhere. The evidential basis for this casework of the margins has largely been provided by the subcultural newspapers of their communities.[15]

For example, Jacqueline Stewart's history of migrant black moviegoing in Chicago successfully describes cinema as a key route for becoming modern in this viciously marginalised population (Stewart, 2005). One of Stewart's primary sources is the *Chicago Defender*, which contains a surprising wealth of early information on south State Street picture shows (far more than we know of Loop nickelodeons), and richly detailed information on black entrepreneurial film-makers (much more than the *Chicago Tribune* ever published about Essanay or Selig).[16] Early cinema and the community newspaper are perfectly aligned to promote their common audience's integration into the modern public sphere, not just politically but also through consumption and leisure. The appearance of cinema in the *Defender*, however, is less the result of its racialised or class-based marginality than the consequence of the newspaper's role in forming an identifiable community as a public of readers within the larger metropolis. Cinema's place in the *Defender* was, therefore, similar to its early and detailed appearance in the *Englewood Economist*, serving the affluent, white suburb nearby the University of Chicago. The role of the newspaper in promoting readerships to become modern publics was similar in both subcultural communities, and cinema was a valuable tool for integrating each community into a mass-marketed modernity while nevertheless remaining distanced from the Loop. In both cases, the community paper and local cinema became ways to cope with the problems of the wider public sphere, whether those problems were racism or regressive corruption.

Methodologically, such community studies require the researcher to understand the ways in which a history of early cinema is embedded in the promotional discourses of newspapers that envisioned their own roles as serving their readerships as a public. The difference between mainstream and ethnic moviegoing was not simply a matter of who the empirical audience was, but of how those publics were differently included in documents recording the public life of a locality. Most strikingly, major metropolitan dailies, which constituted their readership as a public encompassing the entire city, did not treat cinema with the same promotional zeal shown by the weekly papers of ethnic ghettos, affluent suburbs or small communities, until years later when the movies had unquestionably become a mass culture.

Consider the methodological implications of the following four 'first appearances' of moving picture shows in distinct types of towns.

In the metropolis of Toronto, the earliest trace of five-cent shows occurred at the end of April 1906, when one burnt down. Small news articles about the fire reported the destruction of showman John Griffin's Trocadero near City Hall, explaining why Griffin filed a building permit to rebuild the theatre the next day. The next report of the nickel shows also recorded a fire in November 1906 in Griffin's Lyceum a few blocks away.[17]

The earliest advertising for a moving picture show was not in Toronto, but in the much smaller city of Brantford, about halfway between Toronto and Niagara Falls. The Allen Brothers opened their Theatorium, perhaps the first nickel show opened in Canada outside of Montreal and Toronto, with modest fanfare in November 1906 by purchasing a two-column advertisement in both of the small city's daily newspapers.[18]

In 1907, picture shows began to open throughout Ontario. In small towns, neither news nor advertising was the norm, but a careful search through the 'town topics' column reveals such needles-in-haystacks as 'The Theatorium is again running', in May 1907 in Paris; 'The Majestic Theatre, giving moving pictures and illustrated songs, opened up in the Samson Block last week – Performances every night', in September 1907 in Petrolia; or again 'Dreamland will be open each day 4 p.m.' in October 1907 in St Mary's.[19]

In the Great Lakes port city of Owen Sound in March 1907, there was the smallest of notices for the opening of its first picture show, worded exactly the same in the town gossip column of all three weekly papers: 'Watch for the Opening of the Theatorium, corner Poulett and Union', although one paper repeated this sentence three times and added the smallest further detail that the showman was Mr T. Joy of Brantford. When more shows opened two months later, the Wonderland secured a full article about its owners' plans, while the showman of the Star instead purchased a single advertisement to announce his opening, in just one of the three papers.[20]

These various 'first notices' of cinemas in newspapers constitute a set of distinct relationships between a theatre and its locality, all of which need to be included simultaneously in a methodology accounting for a regional review of early cinema. In metropolitan centres, nickel shows tended to be first noticed only when something 'newsworthy' happened: something out of the ordinary routines of operation, usually negative in effect. In smaller cities, however, the local daily newspaper apparently allowed a very different relation between the theatre and the public, and picture shows were 'adworthy' from the start. In villages, where newspapers had only weekly editions, the first remarks about moving picture shows were more variable, but were dominated by merely 'noteworthy' passing comments about the appearance of cinema in town life. With these three prototypical examples as a starting point, some towns with several weekly newspapers such as Owen Sound presented a combination of these forms. Nonetheless, the typology of the newsworthy, the adworthy and the noteworthy by and large corresponds with the relatively distinct methods that I now use, with a considerable degree of reliability, to find cinema in metropolitan daily papers, small city dailies, and small town weekly newspapers respectively. I have also found that the typology holds for the earlier decade of the cinema of attractions: although booked and promoted by the same advance agent, the 1896–97 travels of the Cinématographe and other cinema shows around Ontario receive news stories but minimal advertising in metropolitan cities, relatively large display advertisements in smaller cities, and often only after-the-fact notes in the 'town topics' in small towns.[21] In later decades, I have noticed that small town papers do indeed profile such phenomena as industrial and educational films much more prominently than big city papers, while the relative standardisation of mainstream advertising and promotion after 1913 confirms the cultural homogenisation of classical cinema.

My typology is, importantly, less a representation of variation in the relation of a theatorium to its local audience than a codification of newspapers' relations to their local readerships. What I am really outlining here is not simply an empirical map of the emergence of regional cinemagoing, but an analysis of how the rapid spread of the movies was embedded within the various relations a community could have with its newspaper. Cinema did not immediately change how local publics congregated, how local businesses promoted themselves, or how local news was communicated; instead, it fitted into the existing norms and routines of what was expected to be mentioned, advertised, noted as merely curious, or reported about in detail. Before cinema was institutionalised – before it was bureaucratically regulated, before film distribution was consolidated, before film showmanship became a big business – hundreds of independent showmen may have worked independently of each other, but they did not, taken altogether, work independently of local norms. They left regular traces that can be used to recover and scrape together a grounded history of movie exhibition.

Verifying the Typology's Reliability

With just a few exceptions, my typology of the ways cinema appears in newspapers can be classified in terms of town populations at the time:

- metropolitan centres of more than 50 000 people with several hefty daily papers;
- small cities of 8000 to 20 000 people with one or two brief daily papers;
- towns of 4000 to 7500 people with multiple weekly papers; and
- villages of fewer than 4000 people with a weekly paper.

There was a fifth type of place, which had a population of less than 2000, but these are marginal to my typology because while they sometimes had a weekly paper, only very rarely did these places have a picture show.[22]

In 1907 in Ontario, there were four cities with a population exceeding 50 000, all with multiple daily newspapers, cosmopolitan in content with distinctly more elaborate illustrations, lengthier editions and significant amounts of international news on the front page.[23] What appeared in a metropolitan daily paper needed to appeal to a mass readership that was by definition polyglot, heterogeneous and fractious. Metropolitan advertising implied that the entire city was welcome and that a wide swathe of the public was likely to attend, something that was only rarely true of the early nickel shows, even those located downtown. Metropolitan daily news needed to appeal to readers' common concerns in politics, their common human interest, or their common ground of consumption downtown. Only extraordinary news and extra-special events tended to be reported, not routine business. Neighbourhood, ethnic or class-based subcultures were by definition marginalised except when they were turned into curiosities or framed as affecting the common good of a democratic society. What made cinema newsworthy was remarkably invariant from one big city to another: fire safety cut to the core of real estate value as the very basis of urban form; children's moral education, immigrants' integration and women's leisure consumption were each crucial concerns affecting the viability of democratic ideals in an increasingly secular, commercial society.[24]

All but two of the remaining daily papers in Ontario were published in small cities of between 8000 and 20 000 population, and all but two such small cities had a daily paper.[25] Downtown was usually the only shopping area, rather than the primary one among peripheral neighbourhoods. Ethnic and class diversities rarely amassed themselves into identifiable subcultures, and were usually connected to specific industries or services, such as Jewish merchants, Italian manual labourers, Greek restaurateurs and Chinese laundrymen. Rather than pare and edit out the routine chaos of everyday life, the daily newspaper in a small city more typically filled its columns with the trivia of routine business notes. Every business was geographically within easy reach of every citizen; and the daily frequency of the paper encouraged a planned, public relation between reading and consumption. Advertising predominated, costing less than in big city daily papers and being more effective than handbills or word of mouth in a smaller village. Picture shows were relatively prominent among amusements; the filigree and cost of a storefront nickel show was more like a small town opera house than a big city vaudeville palace or syndicate playhouse. The daily deadline for advertising easily allowed small city showmen to promote film and song titles for every night right from their grand opening, and these small city papers have provided the most comprehensive archive of film programmes for the transitional period.

The towns of between 4000 and 7500 population are most difficult to codify. These towns tended to have several competing weekly instead of daily papers. The format and content of a town weekly paper was, however, more variable: some emphasised town news, sometimes using headlines, while others printed dense notes from surrounding villages, and yet others featured boilerplate national or international news. There might be many or very few advertisements, much or very little local gossip. In turn, the appearance of picture shows varied without pattern between adworthy and noteworthy from one show to another, even within a single newspaper. Just as a town could seem neither entirely urban nor strictly provincial, these papers needed to be regionally sensitive, covering commercial news in town but also attending to the happenings of the many small villages just outside town. Both advertisements and articles had to be useful to a public not necessarily sharing a daily site of consumption in town. The specific problem for picture showmen in such towns was that the weekly dateline of the newspaper required planning several days ahead for advertising. Advance promotion of film titles was, as a result, extremely rare in weekly newspapers until much later in the 1920s.

Village weekly newspapers typically included political news and opinion, syndicated columns of curiosities from afar, and fiction for leisurely reading. Their original, local content could be characterised simply as local gossip, most often headed with the phrase 'Town Topics'. Summarising the past week's events with scattered previews of the coming week, the village weekly provided a baseline of common knowledge about the commercial doings of local businesses, the travels and transitions of local people, even the weather. Was this really needed in such a small place? The irony is that a village picture show opening would truly have been an event compared to one in a town or city, but the newspaper was not necessary to spread the word in advance. Its opening was instead noted as a matter of fact the following week. Village weekly newspapers, even in places with a population below 4000, still served a catchment of nearby, even smaller places. There seems to be a cut-off point of about 2000 people: in villages with smaller populations than this there might be a weekly paper, but it was unlikely to serve smaller communities nearby. Not coincidently, there was also only rarely a picture show in the village.

An important aspect of this typology of newspapers is a hierarchy of attentiveness: each attends to events in the municipal level just below, so that metropolitan newspapers included news from nearby cities, city newspapers included events from nearby towns, towns from neighbouring villages, and villages from surrounding farming areas. The inverse was much rarer, because publishing deadlines usually prevented weekly village papers from being the first to report newsworthy events, even those that occurred locally. Thus, the network of newspaper attentiveness marked out mutually exclusive markets of social life. While the metropolitan city-dweller might read competing morning and evening editions and be inundated with choice, the farm dweller might conceivably subscribe to a village weekly, a city daily and a condensed, weekly mail-order edition of a metropolitan paper in order to have all levels of events covered. This sometimes explicitly extended to picture show promotions, especially in weekly papers serving farming areas: 'When in Goderich, Don't Miss Seeing the Moving Pictures at Wonderland'.[26]

The picture show spread throughout Ontario as a region just as it did in the markets of the Midwest and Northeast United States. Through advertisements, articles or notes, I have identified 251 'first appearances' of picture shows in 88 different towns in Ontario from the first in Toronto in April 1906 to the end of 1909. These include 220 different theatres and 31 seasonal shows in pre-existing theatres (but not travelling one-nighters) or changes in theatres' names. Almost two-thirds of the notices recorded the exact opening date of the theatre (something either an advertisement or an article might do). Twenty-eight theatres were identified from municipal documents or directories such as *Billboard*, although they were not noted in newspapers before 1910. Thirteen theatres were open in Ontario in 1906, 85 new shows opened in the boom year of 1907, 78 in 1908 and 75 in 1909. Although Toronto was the largest single location, with 28 different shows, it did not predominate. It was quite distinct from American cities of the same size, with relatively few theatoriums before a spree in 1909 and 1910. In February 1908, there were still only eight shows in Toronto, a shockingly small number for a city of 350 000. By comparison, Cleveland had over 50 shows, Pittsburgh about 40, Montreal 26, and Buffalo, Detroit, Cincinnati and Milwaukee about 20 each.[27] The full domestication of the Canadian film market into the American was less a result of how cinema worked in Toronto downtown than of how the whole region worked as a mass market bordering the United States.

The most common form of 'first notice' was an advertisement: a boxed display laid out in the newspaper to attract attention. Sixty percent of the theatres were first announced with a newspaper advertisement, more than twice as many as were first announced with an article (with a headline) and more again than with a note (within a list of other nondescript town topics). Advertisements were, however, often combined with articles or notes that had been paid for, and it is impossible to distinguish which articles were bought as a form of advertising, and which

Table 15.1 Methods of searching newspapers by population of place (columns are independent of each other, compare proportions in each column against total sample).

	Adworthy – promotional advertising	*Noteworthy – nondescript notice*	*Newsworthy – promotional or news article*	*Total sample*
Metropolis (50 000 or more) Multiple daily papers	23%	0 (far lower than expected)	21%	24%
City (8000 to 20 000) Daily paper	49% (higher than expected)	37%	36%	36%
Town (4000 to 7500) Multiple weekly papers	16%	18%	21%	17%
Village (less than 4000) Weekly paper	13% (lower than expected)	46% (far higher than expected)	22%	23%
Total (sub)sample sizes	100% $n = 146$	100% $n = 68$	100% $n = 76$	100% $n = 251$
Significance (χ^2 test)	$p = 0.00$ Significantly different from total sample	$p = 0.00$ Significantly different from total sample	$p = 0.71$ As expected, similar to total sample	

were simply a matter of editors looking for any local events to fill up their newspaper's space. Most promotional articles accompanied advertisements, although the more anonymous notes only rarely appeared when advertising was placed elsewhere in the paper. Only 1 in every 20 theatre openings was first noted in news items, and these were predominantly in metropolitan cities. For the purposes of the statistical summary in Table 15.1, I have grouped both promotional articles and news event articles together. Although qualitatively distinct, they are methodologically equivalent, relying on the researcher reading headlines to filter out the mass of inapplicable material on any page. Notes without headlines, on the other hand, require a distinct method of scanning newspaper content by reading the content of every item in the 'town topics' column, rather than attending carefully to every page in the paper.

As outlined above, I distinguished between four sizes of towns: the four metropolitan centres, 24 cities, 22 towns and 38 villages. The town–city distinction provided an almost perfect correlation with the break between daily and weekly papers. Almost everywhere with a population of more than 2000 had a picture show open by 1910; nowhere with a population of 3000 failed to have one. By far the most common name for early picture shows was 'Wonderland', especially if it was the first show in town. Over one-third of all localities had a theatre with this name, with 'Theatorium' and 'Lyric' distant runners-up. Although 'nickelodeon' is now the generic term for these places, only four Ontario theatres used any variant of the word 'nickel' in their name.

Table 15.1 indicates that scanning metropolitan daily newspapers for topical notes about early cinema is unrewarding, while simply looking for advertising in village newspapers might mislead you into thinking that cinema was almost absent from these locations. Although newsworthy events are important for all places and all types of newspapers, checking for newsworthiness is generally unproductive unless the event and time are already known. Keeping a systematic eye out for advertising is easier because it is visually distinct. Advertising is especially useful in cities, but much less so in the biggest metropolitan centres. Picture show advertisements were the most common way for cinema to appear everywhere except in the smallest villages, where noteworthy curiosities predominated. These nondescript notes also appeared in cities and towns, but never in the biggest metropolitan centres. They were sometimes richly detailed with names, costs, programmes, business connections and locations, providing vital information for the earliest shows, which often had only brief lifespans.

The methods of reading newspapers that I first developed for Toronto and the largest cities turned out to be inapplicable elsewhere, and I had to return to smaller city and small town newspapers many times, always discovering something new, expanding my method to incorporate different ways of searching. For the biggest cities, newspapers are in fact an altogether unreliable source for studying early cinema, and instead I turned to the trade press (*Moving Picture World*, *Billboard* and *Variety*) and especially to bureaucratic archives like police records, tax assessments and building permits. Municipal records were, on the other hand, not at all useful in smaller places, where they were less likely to be archived or even recorded in the first place. In smaller cities and especially in the smallest villages, newspapers proved a much more important archive of local cinema, both more exact and more thorough in capturing the appearance of early cinema. Advertisements alone are a relatively reliable method for documenting cinema history in small cities, while the village gossip columns are as reliable for documenting the appearance of picture shows in the smallest villages. Towns show the least consistent patterns and include all types of announcements, but in every type of smaller municipality advertisements, news and notes all need to be kept in mind.

Another statistical test can address the accuracy of newspapers as archives of early cinema, at least in the minimal sense of whether the exact opening date is mentioned in the 'first notice'.

Table 15.2 clearly illustrates that using newspapers to trace the history of early cinema is far more accurate than relying on the trade press or more general histories, and up to 87 times more accurate if a theatre first appears with both an advertisement and an article or note. The table also demonstrates that the least useful way of reading the newspaper for cinema's appearance is for news: town gossip and advertising are much more likely to offer detailed information, especially when any two sources are combined. News, even including promotional articles, does not catch cinema in its routines but in exceptional, anecdotal, random events when it breaks its everyday character. Such news might be illuminating, but it cannot be gathered methodically, and it will not represent the important aspect of cinema's being, essentially an everyday habit. These results are not greatly affected by the

Table 15.2 Logistic regression on whether the first announcement indicates the exact opening of the picture show (interpret results as the odds, or likelihood, of recovering exact opening date).

	E(b) 'odds'	*Sig.*	*Interpretation*
Type of first announcement (compared to none in newspaper but something elsewhere, e.g. Billboard, MPW, city directory)			
News article only	12.9	**	13 times more likely, significant result
Advertising only	18.3	***	18 times more likely, highly significant result
Note only	21.8	***	22 times more likely, highly significant result
Advertisement and article both	68.3	***	68 times as likely, highly significant result
Advertisement and note both	86.9	***	87 times as likely, highly significant result
Type of locality (compared to metropolis)			
City	3.32	**	Three times more likely, significant result
Town	0.96		No significant difference
Village	2.00		Twice as likely, but not significant
Year opened (compared to 1906)			
1907	3.26	*	Three times as likely, some chance not significant
1908	1.40		More likely, but no significant difference with 1906
1909	0.71		Less likely, but no significant difference with 1906
If first show in town	0.67		Less likely, but not significant
Cox & Snell R^2 (test of predictive power)	0.29		29% of the sample's variation is explained

* $p < 0.10$; ** $p < 0.05$; *** $p < 0.01$.

type of locality, and are consistent from year to year. The suggestion that local newspapers are more accurate and detailed than continental sources such as *Moving Picture World* is hardly original, nor is it surprising that more information will also be more accurate, but the results provide a way to verify the intuitive assumptions behind our methods. It is worth dwelling for a moment on the observation that the accuracy of our research depends almost entirely upon the character of the archive, rather than the locality or year or whether the show was first in town. This means that the detail and richness of our moviegoing history depends more heavily on local journalism than it does on film trade journalism or processes internal to the development of the film industry.

Newspapers are especially useful and accurate for smaller cities compared with either metropolitan centres or small towns and villages. The main instrument for subsequently promoting and announcing Hollywood or institutional cinema – routinised advertising for the coming days' shows and show times – appeared in prototypical form in smaller cities right from the opening of their first picture shows in 1907, before it was applied in a centralised and standardised way in the metropolitan centres and throughout the continent from 1913. The institutionalised promotion of cinema *originated* outside the metropolis, and it is especially important to note how production centres in New York and Chicago were among the last places to use newspaper advertising as a way of announcing cinema. This point is vital: promotion made cinema a mass practice, because it explained and made meaningful the idea that there was a common audience dispersed across the continent. Newspaper announcements of cinema collected and collectivised the mass audience, connecting these people here to everyone, everywhere. This happened first at the regional scale, from the periphery inwards, as each town saw cinema as a small way to make a modern connection to the metropolis.

Distribution companies' branch film exchanges eventually took responsibility for newspaper advertising and promotion. As part of the codification of the run-zone system, newspaper advertising became the primary mode of promoting 'Hollywood' cinema, irrespective of locality, theatre, date, ticket price or audience. But advertising has its own transitional history, shifting as it did from smaller cities to metropolitan centres between 1907 and 1913, as important a part of 'transitional cinema' as the development of classical production techniques or institutional vertical integration. As a neglected part of the cinema of transition, newspaper promotion can also be seen as a neglected component of debates over the 'modernity thesis'. The nickelodeon period began with the promotion of cinema locally controlled by showmen and attuned to regional audiences, and ended with standardised advertising provided by production-distribution companies and focused on movie stars and film titles. Key moments in this transition were the *What Happened to Mary?* fiction supplements in the *Ladies Home Journal* in 1912, the Mutual Movies campaign late in 1913, and especially newspaper fictionalisations of serial films, beginning with *The Adventures of Kathlyn* in January 1914.[28] The idea that distributors needed to promote and advertise only first-run, downtown feature films at movie palaces followed a logic initially articulated in serial-film promotions in metropolitan newspapers.

Identifying this shift through newspaper advertising makes vivid how the transition from the cinema of attractions to classical cinema was precisely laid upon the foundational emergence of a mass market in cinema, in which a regional run-zone-clearance system of distribution gradually rationalised the distinct character of disparate movie theatres, and stripped away their cultural specificity in a pattern that is characteristic of the production of space in modernity more generally (Harvey, 1989; Lefebvre, 1991). This system took about a decade to develop, and first required each theatre showman and audience member in the mass public – as local newspaper readers – to understand cinema as a mass culture. The 'modernity' of filmgoing had less to do with the perception of urban modernism on the screen than it did with an awareness of filmgoing as a practice that embedded its viewers in metropolitan modernity, not least through its capitalist mass market. This was not restricted to perception-in-viewing, but started with an awareness of cinema as an option in daily life: a commercialised pastime and form of consumption that was somewhat similar everywhere, and that connected life in the town or village to the metropolis, and indeed to the entire mass-marketed network of popular culture that animated modernity. The region in turn became an important mediating scale between the local and the global.

Conclusion

The local case study is obviously important for grounding our understanding of cinema in experience, while theory or generalised history is important for understanding the complex industrial context. Mediating these two positions, the region provides a scale in which embodied experiences of cinema are made cultural. This culture became a mass culture precisely because the region had a metropolis. Regional practices are metropolitan, not cosmopolitan: experienced and interpreted by audiences and publics, but not considered in isolation or as a pointed, individuated case study. The cultural basis of the region admits a scale between the local and the global that is both grounded and yet strongly related to mass practices in the sense of activities open to everyone, and to all places. Thus, small towns treated the arrival of cinema as a sign of their modernisation and how they were part of the zeitgeist of common culture. Cinema gave local publics a strong relation to the metropolis and to modernity at large, and yet always grounded in a specific place, through a particular showman-entrepreneur, and focused on a precisely timed, promoted, and priced show.

Acknowledgements

Hailey McCron assisted in coding the cache of research into a database. The presentation of the preliminary version in Ghent was supported with a travel grant from the Faculty of Arts at Ryerson University.

Notes

1 'Social Biograph', *Fort William Times-Journal* from 6 August 1904.

2 My own concern is for the cultural and architectural history of cinemas and theatres throughout Canada, compiled into a nascent Canadian Theatre Historical Project (www.mapleleafmarquee.ca). My research assistant, Nikesh N. Bhagat, single-handedly designed and created the database and its web-based interface.

3 For an excellent history of Toronto's urban geography in a North American context, see Richard Harris, *Unplanned Suburbs: Toronto's American Tragedy 1900 to 1950* (Baltimore: Johns Hopkins University Press, 1996). For more contemporary implications in the multiplex era, see Charles Acland, *Screen Traffic: Movies, Multiplexes, and Global Culture* (Durham, NC: Duke University Press, 2003).

4 The model general history of the nickelodeon period remains Eileen Bowser, *The Transformation of Cinema, 1907–1915* (Berkeley: University of California Press, 1990). Local case studies are numerous, including those compiled in Fuller-Seeley (2008). For exhibition on an overall industrial level, the key achievement of Richard Abel's last few books has been to bridge the national, indeed nationalist, with

local casework in *The Red Rooster Scare: Making Cinema American 1900–1910* (Berkeley: University of California Press, 1999); *Americanizing the Movies and "Movie-Mad" Audiences, 1910–1914* (Berkeley: University of California Press, 2006). Abel, too, has increasingly made newspapers themselves the subject of his research, not just his method. His forthcoming book is prospectively entitled *Menus for Movieland: Newspapers and the Movies*.

5 Such an emphasis on the region has been cited as commercially important, especially because of railroad distribution networks. See Alfred D. Chandler Jr, *The Visible Hand: The Managerial Revolution in American Business* (Cambridge, MA: Belknap-Harvard University Press, 1977). On mass marketing, Susan Strasser, *Satisfaction Guaranteed: The Making of the American Mass Market* (New York: Pantheon, 1989).

6 Indeed, histories of production and distribution in the transitional or nickelodeon period 1907–1913 argue against the idea that these branches of the film industry were any more centralised or 'vertically integrated' than exhibition. Keil (2001); Rick Altman, *Silent Film Sound* (New York: Columbia University Press, 2005); Scott Curtis, 'A house divided: the MPPC in transition', in Keil and Stamp (2004), pp. 239–284.

7 The cultural particularity of regions has been noted vital to their independence-yet-integration into the continental mass market. See John C. Teaford, *Cities of the Heartland: The Rise and Fall of the Industrial Midwest* (Bloomington: Indiana University Press, 1993).

8 The best discussion of newspapers as foundational to urban modernity is Gunther Barth, *City People: The Rise of Modern City Culture in Nineteenth-Century America* (New York: Oxford University Press, 1980). Emphasising an earlier connection to democratisation as well as the 1890s 'yellow press' period of modernisation is Michael Schudson, *Discovering the News: A Social History of American Newspapers* (New York: Basic Books, 1981). A classic essay is Robert E. Park (1923) 'Natural history of the newspaper', *American Journal of Sociology, 29*, 273–289.

9 The mass market is a key part of modernity for historians such as Eric Hobsbawm, *The Age of Empire 1875–1914* (London: Weidenfeld & Nicolson, 1987). Others define modernity in terms of concepts like interdependence, which connotes the mass market without focusing on it. See, for example, Thomas L. Haskell, *The Emergence of Professional Social Science: The American Social Science Association and the Nineteenth-Century Crisis of Authority* (Baltimore: Johns Hopkins University Press, 2000 [1977]); David Frisby, *Cityscapes of Modernity* (Malden, MA: Polity, 2001); Thomas Bender, *Community and Social Change in America* (New Brunswick, NJ: Rutgers University Press, 1978), and of course Ferdinand Tönnies, *Community and Civil Society – Gemeinschaft and Gesellschaft* (New York: Cambridge University Press, 2001 [1887]).

10 Respectively, advertisement in *Seaforth Huron Expositor*, 19 March 1909; advertisement in *Fort William Times-Journal*, 22 September 1908.

11 Advertisement in *Galt Reformer*, 29 July 1907. Note: Berlin is now named Kitchener; Galt is now named Cambridge.

12 'Week's Local News', *Newmarket Era*, 1 November 1907.

13 Respectively, advertisement in *Peterborough Examiner*, 23 January 1907; advertisement in *Collingwood Bulletin*, 31 August 1907.

14 Allen's essay was revisited by Ben Singer, prompting a sustained debate in *Cinema Journal* from 1995 to 1997, beginning with Ben Singer (1995) 'Manhattan nickelodeons: new data on audiences and exhibitors', *Cinema Journal*, 34 (3), 5–35.

15 Giorgio Bertellini (1999) 'Shipwrecked spectators: Italy's immigrants at the movies in New York, 1906–1916', *Velvet Light Trap,* 44, 39–53. Judith Thissen, 'Charlie Steiner's Houston Hippodrome: moviegoing on New York's Lower East Side, 1909–1913', in Bachman, G. and Slater, T.J. (2002) *American Silent Film: Discovering Marginalized Voices*. Carbondale: Southern Illinois University Press, pp. 27–47. See also Melvyn Stokes and Richard Maltby (eds) *American Movie Audiences: From the Turn of the Century to the Early Sound Era* (London: British Film Institute, 1999). On the immigrant press and its importance in America, see Peter Conolly-Smith, *Translating America: An Immigrant Press Visualizes American Popular Culture, 1895–1918* (Washington, DC: Smithsonian Books, 2004).

16 On the *Chicago Defender*, see also Armistead Pride and Clint Wilson, *A History of the Black Press* (Cambridge, MA: Harvard University Press, 1987).

17 'Theatre Burned Out', *Toronto Globe*, 30 April 1906; 'Two Firemen Injured', *Toronto Globe*, 15 November 1906.

18 Advertisement for Theatorium, *Brantford Courier*, 10 November 1906.

19 'Local News', *Paris Star-Transcript*, 1 May 1907; 'Local and General News', *Petrolia Advertiser*, 7 Sept. 1907; 'News About Town', *St. Mary's Journal*, 10 October 1907.

20 'Small Locals', *Owen Sound Advertiser*, 5 March 1907; 'New Wonderland', *Owen Sound Sun*, 11 June 1907; advertisement for Star Theatre, *Owen Sound Advertiser*, 25 June 1907.

21 On the dramatic dispersal all over the United States see Charles Musser, 'Introducing cinema to the American public: the Vitascope in the United States, 1896–97', in Gregory Waller (ed.) *Moviegoing in America* (Oxford: Blackwell, 2001), pp. 13–26. My research on the similar dispersal of cinema in Canada is summarised in 'Mapping early cinema's mass public: film debuts coast-to-coast in Canada in 1896 and 1897', *Canadian Journal of Film Studies* (forthcoming).

22 The terms metropolis, city, town, and village are my codes for the distinctions among types of community–newspaper–cinema relations, and are not legislated or official. Populations and newspaper circulations from *McKim's Canadian Newspapers Directory* for 1907. A relatively comprehensive list of Canadian (and American) picture shows is printed in *Billboard* between September 1910 and February 1911.

23 The four metropolitan cities and their 1907 populations are Toronto (340 000); national capital, Ottawa (80 000); steel-mill city, Hamilton (70 000); and farm country marketplace, London (50 000).

24 On fire safety, see my chapter 'Socially combustible' in Moore (2008). On the discourse over the juvenile, immigrant and gendered audience, see Lee Grieveson, *Policing Cinema: Movies and Censorship in Early Twentieth Century America* (Chicago: University of Chicago Press, 2004).

25 The two places with daily papers but populations below 7000 were Lindsay and Port Hope, historically important towns whose regional position was slipping as other places industrialised more thoroughly. The two cities without daily papers were the suburb of West Toronto, and Owen Sound.

26 Advertisement for Wonderland, *Goderich Signal*, 12 September 1907.

27 'Everybody's Column', *Toronto Star*, 19 February 1908, p. 14. Estimates for American cities are from 1909 city directories for each. The count of 26 from Montreal is from *Montreal La Presse*, 12 Octobre 1908, cited in Germaine Lacasse, *Histoires de scopes: Le cinéma muet au Québec* (Montréal: Cinémathèque Québécoise, 1988).

28 This point draws primarily upon feminist research critical of how women were incorporated as foundational to the 'low culture' of mass-marketed entertainment: Andreas Huyssen, *After the Great Divide: Modernism, Mass Culture, Postmodernism* (Bloomington: Indiana University Press, 1986); Moya Luckett (1999) 'Advertising and femininity: the case of Our Mutual Girl', *Screen*, 40 (4), 363–383; Barbara Wilinsky, 'Flirting with Kathlyn: creating the mass audience', in David Dresser and Garth Jowett (eds), *Hollywood Goes Shopping* (Minneapolis: University of Minnesota Press, 2000), pp. 34–56; Jennifer Bean (2001) 'Technologies of early stardom and the extraordinary body', *Camera Obscura*, 16 (3), 9–56.

References

Allen, R.C. (1979) Motion picture exhibition in Manhattan: beyond the nickelodeon. *Cinema Journal*, 18 (2), 2–15.

Allen, R.C. (2006) Relocating American film history. *Cultural Studies*, 20 (1), 48–88.

Allen, R.C. (2007) Race, region, and rusticity: relocating U.S. film history, in *Going to the Movies: Hollywood and the Social Experience of Cinema* (eds R. Maltby, M. Stokes and R.C. Allen), University of Exeter Press, Exeter, pp. 25–44.

Fuller-Seeley, K. (ed.) (2008) *Hollywood in the Neighborhood: Historical Case Studies of Local Moviegoing*, University of California Press, Berkeley.

Fuller-Seeley, K. and Potamianos, G. (2008) Introduction: researching and writing the history of local moviegoing, in *Hollywood in the Neighborhood: Historical Case Studies of Local Moviegoing* (ed. K. Fuller-Seeley), University of California Press, Berkeley.

Harvey, D. (1989) *The Urban Experience*, Johns Hopkins University Press, Baltimore.

Keil, C. (2001) *Early American Cinema in Transition: Story, Style, and Filmmaking, 1907–1913*, University of Wisconsin Press, Madison.

Keil, C. and Stamp, S. (eds) (2004) *American Cinema's Transitional Era: Audiences, Institutions, Practices*, University of Chicago Press, Berkeley.

Lefebvre, H. (1991) *The Production of Space*, Blackwell, Oxford.

Moore, P.S. (2008) *Now Playing: Early Moviegoing and the Regulation of Fun*, State University of New York Press, Albany, 2008.

Stewart, J.N. (2005) *Migrating to the Movies: Cinema and Black Urban Modernity*, University of California Press, Berkeley.

16

Modernity for Small Town Tastes

Movies at the 1907 Cooperstown, New York, Centennial

Kathryn Fuller-Seeley

Organisers of the August 1907 Centennial Celebration in Cooperstown, a village of 2500 tucked in the hills of rural upstate New York and famous for its scenery and literary heritage, paid $150 to itinerant movie showman B. Albert Cook to exhibit his 'Cook and Harris High Class Moving Pictures' on six of the seven nights of the festival. Local resident Bert Cook projected films outdoors on a canvas screen stretched across the side of the First National Bank on Main Street, while his wife Fannie 'Harris' Cook played piano accompaniment.[1] The historically focused Celebration was a rousing success by small town standards. *The Otsego Farmer* reported that 15 000–20 000 visitors were on hand for Thursday's historical parade and speeches. More than 10 000 people viewed the spectacular fireworks display that evening, and many lingered afterwards to watch the Cooks' film exhibition, creating the largest audience of their 40-year career.[2]

Although it might not seem an especially noteworthy event when placed in the sweeping context of American culture at the turn of the century or the development of early cinema, the Cooperstown Centennial's inclusion of motion pictures was one of the earliest municipal recognitions of films as suitable entertainment for provincial viewers. While motion pictures were beginning to attract censorship and legal controversy in Chicago and New York City, it is difficult to imagine the movies attaining clearer evidence of acceptance than by being officially sponsored by the village fathers and projected against the side of a bank.

Many film historians continue to view early cinema as an essentially urban product, a harbinger of modernity, a new media form that embodied the speed, dislocation and dangers of city life (Charney and Schwartz, 1995). From this perspective, movies might seem to be out of place at the backward-looking Cooperstown Centennial, which focused almost exclusively on history, conservative Anglo-American culture, and the literary heritage of the town's most famous native son, novelist James

Explorations in New Cinema History: Approaches and Case Studies, First Edition.
Edited by Richard Maltby, Daniel Biltereyst and Philippe Meers.

Fenimore Cooper. Unlike the World's Fairs being held in major cities in this era, the Cooperstown Centennial did not highlight visions of the future, celebrations of new inventions, manufacturing might or consumer culture. Instead, it featured a historical parade, military manoeuvres, a regatta, dances, baseball games, band concerts and a fireworks display over Lake Otsego that featured giant pyrotechnically illuminated heads of Cooper and the village's most famous living citizen, Henry Codman Potter, Episcopal Bishop of New York.[3] Motion pictures were nevertheless positioned as the equal of the other, more traditional spectacles and had an accepted and even largely unremarked-upon role at the Centennial as a source of historical representation, education and amusement fit for small-town families, women and children.[4]

Bert and Fannie Cook's Centennial film programme featured a recent Edison one-reel historical drama, *Daniel Boone: or Pioneer Days in America* (1907), as the centrepiece of their show, which also combined light comedies and romantic melodramas with patriotic and documentary scenes. The plot of *Daniel Boone* complemented the conservative themes of the Cooperstown Centennial, celebrating the courage and perseverance of white pioneers to tame the wilderness, subdue Indians and establish patriarchal order. Despite relating the time-honoured story of a revered founding father and pathbreaker, *Daniel Boone*'s narrative nevertheless also incorporated hints of new ideas, new gender roles and changing types of power relations into the movie's plot and characters' actions.

In the summer of 1907, a similarly unlikely combination of film and traditional culture was transpiring 500 miles south of Cooperstown at the Jamestown Ter-Centennial Exposition, which was held outside the small southern city of Norfolk, Virginia. Larger in scope but parallel in purpose, this provincially focused historical exposition explicitly avoided promoting urban or contemporary social issues, dwelling instead on white colonial and naval heritage, celebrating a mythical past of pioneers conquering wilderness, eradicating Indians, and bringing European civilisation to America. At Jamestown, the only Big City represented at the Fair was destroyed daily – shaken and burned to the ground at the 'San Francisco Earthquake and Fire' exhibit. Yet cinema also had a place at the Jamestown Exposition. Entrepreneurs commissioned the Edison studio to produce two one-reel films, *Pocahontas, Child of the Forest* and *Scenes in Colonial Virginia* (1907), to be shown in a purpose-built theatre (Musser, 1991, pp. 333, 424, 526). These films share many narrative and ideological similarities with the Boone picture that the Cooks exhibited in Cooperstown. While the subject matter of the festivals at Cooperstown and Jamestown reinforced traditional themes of the Anglo-Saxon foundation of American civilisation, the narrative of the Boone film, like the two Virginia subjects, opened small spaces for readings that allowed modernity to be adapted to provincial tastes and some modern ideas to slip quietly in through the back door (Fuller-Seeley, 2009, pp. 59–68).

Aspects of these film narratives moved beyond the traditional, white, paternally dominated history that most Americans learned in school. Instead, they emphasised family building over the exploits of individual male pioneers. Young women were the active protagonists – Boone's daughter and her Indian friend straddling steeds to race through the wilderness in the first film, Pocahontas halting executions in the Jamestown movie. They energetically rescued family members, friends, lovers and settlers, anticipating the serial movie queens to come. 'Great white men' became vulnerable actors who ultimately triumphed not by natural inevitability, but through trickery, talented horses, knowledge of other cultures, and through their partnership with spunky women. These films presented new images of the past.

This chapter seeks to re-evaluate exhibition and reception practices at the dawn of the 'transitional era' of American cinema, when narrative films were growing in complexity and length (Fuller, 1997; Fuller-Seeley, 2008). The interactions of cinema and modernity in this time represented, as film historian Ben Singer suggests, a 'complex, dynamic process in which disparate forces – competing paradigms and practices – overlap and interact' (Singer, 2004, p. 76). In the larger American culture as well, nineteenth-century and twentieth-century ideals coexisted and competed with one another. Film scholars contend that motion pictures of this period embodied the idea of modernity produced by urban cultural change. If so, then at the Cooperstown Centennial, this cinema intermingled change with cultural continuity, in a melding of new media form and cultural/ideological tradition. The films Bert and Fannie Cook exhibited turned old stories into new ones, and linked the past with the speed, dislocations and dangers of the present for the provincial middle- and working-class audiences who viewed them (Fuller-Seeley, 2009).

This historical case study of local film reception endeavours to understand the cultural and social context in which motion pictures were chosen as an appropriate public entertainment in one village, and the contexts in which several films were understood by the film industry, exhibitors and local viewers. I draw on records of the Cooperstown Centennial organising committee, local newspaper coverage of the festivities, the business records of itinerant film exhibitor Bert Cook, and reviews, synopses and advertisements of these historically focused films published in the film exhibitors' trade press. Working outwards from a microhistory of one small town event, I place it within the contexts of American film historians' and cultural historians' concerns with urban modernity and its impact across the breadth of American society in the early twentieth century. Cultural transformations are the aggregate of many thousands of such small occurrences.

Planning the Centennial Celebration

Examining the inclusion of the movies in the Centennial programme gives us insights into turn-of-the-century Cooperstown as a community that struggled to balance culture and commerce, older rural ways of living and new urban technologies, and traditional social practices and 'modern' entertainments. World's Fairs and massive expositions were hugely popular across the United States at the turn of the century, and often combined exhibitions of industrial manufacturing with historical commemorations: the Columbian Exposition in Chicago in 1892–1893 feted the 400th anniversary of Columbus's voyage, and the St Louis World's

Fair of 1904 celebrated the centennial of the Louisiana Purchase. Visually, physically and symbolically, these expositions taught civic lessons in patriotism, providing their visitors with a more grounded sense that this still-young nation had a history, and was anointed by higher powers to fulfil its manifest destiny by growing into an economic and military world power (Rydell, 1993). They showcased the growing consumer bounty created by American manufacturing, with fairground buildings serving as gigantic advertising displays for everything from steam engines to pickles, steel girders to soap.

At the other extreme of expositions during this era was the 1907 Jamestown Exposition, which steadfastly declined to promote commerce or consumer culture. In this unsettled time of rapid industrial growth, some were wary of the wholesale rush into the 'modern' world of goods. One commentator noted that the best thing about the Jamestown Fair was that it was not a 'tomato can' exposition, with 'enormous aggregations of canned fruits and other mercantile products, familiarly known as "exhibits", bordering its aisles'.[5] Here the spotlight was primarily on the heritage of colonial settlement and on the strength of the US Navy, with a nodding reference to the status quo of contemporary Southern agriculture (Fuller-Seeley, 2009). The Cooperstown festival organisers largely embraced the model of the Jamestown Fair but, as the economic downturn of 1907 became a recession, bringing poor business and widespread unemployment, they also gave some thought to how local merchants might benefit.

Although motion pictures were a significant component of the Cooperstown Centennial festivities, there was little official provision for other commercial entertainments. There was no boisterous, bustling Midway area as at the World's Fairs, and the gaudy dancing girl sideshow found each September at the local county fair was also absent. This drew praise from a number of conservative local critics, such as the editor of the *Cherry Valley Gazette*, who wrote, 'The whole affair was free from the obnoxious features which too often mar such occasions'.[6] Centennial organisers kept the commercial aspects of the festival to a minimum, allowing just a few booths to be erected, from which visitors might purchase postcards, lemonade or ice cream.[7] 'Mayor Francis has made no concessions for souvenir stands, etc. on Main Street during Centennial week', the *Otsego Farmer* noted. 'He is of the opinion that the village people, who are paying the expense of the Celebration, should be protected from outside competition as far as possible.'[8] Nevertheless, Centennial sponsors did pay to have Bert Cook entertain the villagers with motion pictures, and commemorative postcard sales must have been brisk, for the Cooperstown post office reported dispensing 13 300 one-cent stamps during the festival week.[9] Although not sponsored by the Centennial organisers, the William C. Wild Stock Company performed its repertoire of popular melodramas at the old Village Opera House on the third floor of Main Street's Bowne Hall. Their feature play was *Shadows of a Great City*, popular since the 1880s, a crime drama exploring the seamy side of urban life that told precautionary tales to rural audiences.[10] In the midst of bucolic Cooperstown's historical festival, movies, plays and picture postcards were a taken-for-granted part of the proceedings, mingling unease about urban life and increased commercialisation with hints of acceptance of new ways of thinking and behaving.

Beginning their planning in April 1907, the festival organisers raised $6000 to mount a small-scale historical extravaganza. Donations came from all sections of the village, even from many of the working class. Donating one third of the total was the prominent Clark family, heirs of the Singer Sewing Machine Company, who maintained summer homes and a large presence in the village. Bishop Henry Codman Potter, who three years before had wed the widowed Elizabeth Clark, waived his speaker's fee to stretch the funds further. Summer resident Augustus Busch (prominent beer manufacturer) and representatives of the village's largest firms (banks, hop merchants and a cheese manufacturer) gave a combined $1200. In a broad show of civic support for the Centennial, the other half came from small merchants (grocers, fruit sellers, milliners, hotel owners and bar-keepers). About one-quarter of the village's 800 families donated money in smaller amounts such as the $1.00 contributed by Ah Choy, who operated a small laundry in the basement of the Iron Clad building.[11] Civic pride and the spirit of boosterism may account for the democratic breadth of the list of local donors to the Centennial funds, but many probably calculated that much of the money raised was going to be spent in the village, distributed back to merchants and workers as supplies were purchased, costumes and decorations created, and visitors fed, housed and amused.

The grandest event of the Fair was the parade down Main Street, which almost exclusively focused on historical topics. Horse-drawn floats depicted such themes as Indian life 'Before the White Man', Cooper's fictional hero Natty Bumppo and other mythical and actual pioneers, and George Washington and Revolutionary war soldiers. Civil War veterans rode on a float, while their sons marched in vintage uniforms along with volunteer fire brigade members and a military band imported from the state capital at Albany. Fair planners included parade displays tracing the early development of the region's transportation, which pointedly omitted any mention of the area's thriving railroads, trolley lines or new automobiles. The only bow to commercial culture in the parade was also set in the past. A float carrying hop-pickers was titled 'When Otsego controlled the hop market of the world', but it also featured a prominent logo of a flying eagle and red letter A, representing the still-prominent local interests of the Anheuser-Busch brewery.

About two-thirds of the sum raised for the Centennial Fair was expended on big-ticket items imported from outside the community: banners, special electric lights to illuminate Main Street, the 10th Regiment of Albany military company and band, and the fireworks. Among the local entertainments and events, the $150 paid to Bert Cook was roughly equivalent to the outlays for the regatta, the athletic events, the parade, and the rental of chairs for the bandstand grounds.[12]

Bishop Potter, widely recognised to be America's most prominent churchman, and second husband of Mrs Elizabeth Clark, had been a prominent member of Cooperstown summer society since their marriage in 1904. They shared an interest in Progressive reform, especially in cleaning up corrupt urban government and helping poor workers improve their communities. Potter had been a leading figure in the reform campaign that elected Seth Low mayor of New York in 1900, and in 1902 Clark had donated Lower Manhattan real estate valued at $500 000 to the City of New York to found the East Side Community House, modelled on Jane Addams' Hull House in Chicago. Unusually for a clergyman of his position, Potter thought safe saloons for working-class men and their families were far more beneficial than harmful, arguing that for the 'multitude of people who work hard and live in small rooms' in the city, the saloon was their only 'place of resort and recreation' (Hodges, 1915, pp. 368–369). Known for their concern for the quality of the amusements available to working people, Potter and Clark may well have had at least a benign tolerance of the movies. Since they could easily have taken action to bar motion pictures from the Centennial Celebrations, we must assume they had no objection to the prominent part that movies played in the programme.

The Cooks and the Movies in 1907

Bert Cook had been involved in motion picture exhibition since 1899, and he and Fannie became full-time movie show people in late 1903. Their troupe was named 'The Cook and Harris High Class Moving Picture Company', for they were keenly aware that many conservatives objected to the movies and other cheap amusements. The Cooks tried to head off opposition by advertising that their show was '100% moral' and contained 'Nothing to offend'. Their advertising posters declared their exhibition of moving pictures and illustrated songs to be 'Pre-Eminently the most successful Exhibition in America! Travel – Science – Comedy – Drama. The whole world before your eyes. Beautiful Illustrated Songs! Miss it, and you're missing the Greatest event of your life!'[13]

In 1907 there were several competing models of travelling movie shows on which the Cooks could pattern their programme. Some, like those of area movie showmen Edwin Hadley or J.P. Dibble, featured filmed prize fights, violent slapstick, risqué glimpses of women's ankles and pyjama-clad schoolgirls engaging in pillow fights mixed in with more mundane comedies and dramas. Others, like that of 'high class' exhibitor Lyman Howe, who had introduced the first movies to Cooperstown at the Bowne Hall Opera House a full decade before, focused exclusively on educational scenes of foreign travel, and did not so much entertain as instruct. The Cooks' programmes took a middle path, showcasing films and songs concerning family-centred comedy, romance and melodrama, and sentimental scenes of animals and children. They also rarely performed in towns of population more than 4000. While urban nickelodeons offered movie shows as brief as 15 or 20 minutes for their 5-cent admission charge, the Cooks assembled a two-hour programme of film and song for 25 cents per ticket. Adding to the strength of their reputation in Cooperstown, the Cooks were also hometown talent, for Fannie Shaw Cook was born and raised in Cooperstown, and Bert Cook grew up in the nearby Otsego County communities of Little Falls and Richfield Springs (Fuller, 1997).

The Cooks' August 1907 film exhibitions occurred at a pivotal moment in the development of American cinema. No longer novelties or single scenes, by 1907 most of the motion pictures that the Cooks exhibited were one-reel story films, collections of scenes building a not-terribly-complicated narrative lasting from 3 to 12 minutes (Fell, 1983; Bowser, 1990; Musser, 1991; Fuller, 1997; Keil, 2001). Major changes were also occurring in the way people across the United States viewed motion pictures, as stationary, storefront movie shows – 'nickelodeons' – began to spread beyond the larger cities to smaller towns and residential neighbourhoods, until by 1907 there were between 6000 and 10 000 of them across the nation (Fuller, 1997). Nickelodeons had recently opened in Ilion, Oneonta, Herkimer and Little Falls, larger manufacturing centres surrounding Cooperstown, and in 1907 the Cooks began to find it more difficult to locate provincial sponsors for their shows and venues in which to perform. Like the Cooks, most itinerant movie show people in the more thickly-populated Eastern half of the United States were being forced to decide whether to leave the road and open a stationary nickelodeon theatre themselves, to relocate to more open territories in the West, or to scrape for diminishing returns in saturated markets.

The Cook and Harris exhibition incorporated a mixture of entertainment forms: not only the motion pictures with musical accompaniment and realistic sound effects, but also their performance of illustrated songs, sentimental Tin Pan Alley songs sung by Bert, accompanied by Fannie on the piano and with Bert's projection of glass slides picturing the narrative of the song. For the Cooperstown Centennial festivities, Bert and Fannie Cook featured the newest film in their collection, a melodrama of the early frontier called *Daniel Boone, or Pioneer Days in America,* released in January 1907 by the Edison film studio. As a travelling exhibitor, Cook still purchased his films outright and needed them to find favour with audiences for as many months or years as possible, so he strove to select films that would have broad and lasting appeal with their provincial audiences. The Edison Company charged $150 for a print of the 1000 foot-long film, equivalent to the entire fee the Cooks earned for their week of Centennial shows.[14] Each film was thus a carefully considered investment for these exhibitors.

Daniel Boone, Mingling Pioneers with Modernity?

Daniel Boone, depicting a fictional episode in the life of the historical pioneer, told its story in ways that reshaped traditional narratives. Most discussions of the frontier in the late nineteenth century, such as Theodore Roosevelt's four-volume *The Winning of the West* (1889) centred on 'heroic accounts of settlement' by 'men who created the national destiny by their own deeds' (quoted in Kasson, 2000, p. 115). Daniel Boone, Kit Carson and Buffalo Bill were among Roosevelt's models. Film historian Richard Abel has noted that Western heroes in histories, novels, paintings and films were increasingly being depicted as 'the masculine advance guard of civilization', and white male supremacy was becoming 'the core of a new national identity'

(Abel, 1999, p.159). In this cinematic version of the frontier legend, however, the power of white Anglo-Saxon men was decentred, and women played much more active roles in frontier events than they had in more traditional tales.

Like other early American attempts at making Western-themed film subjects, *Daniel Boone* was set in the heavily wooded East in an earlier historical period when the trans-Allegheny territory (and upstate New York) had been the wild frontier. Produced at a time when the US film studios were based in New York City, these 'Eastern Westerns' were most often filmed in parks or rural areas outside the metropolis, in New Jersey or the Bronx (Simmon, 2003). If the West of dime novels, genre paintings and later cowboy and Indian films featured the wide-open landscapes of the Plains and Rockies as well as nonstop action and constant fighting and heroic male activity, the Eastern Westerns took place in forested areas, dotted with lakes and small clearings, and were perhaps more able to include a wider range of characters and glimpses of Indian and white domestic life.

The plot of *Daniel Boone* has much in common with James Fenimore Cooper's Leatherstocking novels of the 1830s and 1840s; not only was it a romantic, thrilling theme that would have resonated with Bert and Fannie Cook's audiences everywhere they showed the film, but it was particularly appropriate to show in Cooperstown at a Centennial celebrating Cooper the author and the town's frontier past. In its unusual features, *Daniel Boone* also shared similarities with several other historical dramas that Edison Company director Edwin Porter was producing and showed glimpses of modernity, especially the film *Pocahontas, Child of the Forest*, which Porter produced for the Jamestown Exposition. Both drew on widely shared public knowledge of American popular culture and familiarity with American founding traditions and myths. The plots of both movies were loosely adapted from theatrical melodramas regularly performed in American opera houses. Several popular nineteenth century stage melodramas drew on the Daniel Boone legend, and would almost certainly have been performed by travelling theatrical troupes at the old Bowne Opera House in Cooperstown.[15] Porter, the probable scenarist for both films, incorporated the melodramatic plot elements of nineteenth century theatrical productions and novels: romance, peril, rescues, happy endings, and then added an additional layer of new twentieth century sensibilities. The heroes are not solely sufficient and infallible, and have to be rescued from danger just as often as they rescue the heroines; the women are not passive victims waiting to be saved, but assertive multidimensional characters who take important and active roles in the narratives. Boone is shown in a domestic setting, living in a cabin with wife and two daughters, pioneering a settlement rather than blazing a trail. Boone's daughter makes cross-cultural friendships with the Indian girl, fights off the attacking Indians, hunts for her captured sister and father, and rides pell-mell through the forest on a galloping horse. The film ends with the reunification of the Boone family (minus the mother, who had perished in the cabin fire). Film historian Scott Simmon has found that women rarely play major roles in early Western films such as those directed by D.W. Griffith. Closer examination of Porter's film *Pocahontas* and the other film commissioned from the Edison studio to show at the Jamestown Exposition, *Scenes in Colonial Virginia,* shows a different trend, however.

In all three of these Porter/Edison films, serious depictions of historical events are interspersed with humorous incidents that work to undercut the idea of unquestioned Anglo-Saxon male authority and allow brief moments for viewers to contemplate the roles of women and family building in the film narratives and even possibly to question the history of race relations (Fuller-Seeley, 2009). These films seem as much progenitors of the 'serial queen' melodramas that would become phenomenally popular within four or five years, as they are of the typical cowboy and Indian movie Western that would become a staple genre by 1910. While Westerns would be very popular with cinema audiences of boys and men, the serial queens drew in many girls and women to nickelodeon movie shows. Bert and Fannie Cook strove to create a family-centred film programme that could interest all their audience members, male and female, young and old. To attract enough provincial moviegoers to make a profit, film exhibitors in small towns would aim to assemble a balanced programme that offered some attraction for every viewer. This might introduce them to new stories, and new variations on accepted narrative genres, along the way (Singer, 2004; Mahar, 2006).

Daniel Boone was an ambitiously complex piece of film-making in 1907, and this may have led to some problems in how audiences interpreted it. Film historian Charles Musser notes that *Boone* was one of the Edison Studio and Porter's most complicated narratives up to that time, requiring a larger cast and more scene settings than usual (Musser, 1991, p. 331). Although the one-reel, 12-minute film's plot relied more on the conventions of melodrama than those of documentary history, Porter aimed for as much historical atmosphere as he could achieve, and shooting on location in harsh winter weather created lengthy delays in filming (Musser, 1991, pp. 338–339). Porter's cast included several members of the 'Pioneer Days' Wild West show, a huge extravaganza then appearing at New York's Hippodrome, and teenage stage actress Florence Lawrence in her first screen appearance as Boone's daughter (Musser, 1991, p. 336).[16]

Like so many early films, *Daniel Boone* exists today only in small fragments and still photos, and in written advertising and plot descriptions published in the film exhibitor trade journals. The 29 scenes described in the Edison Company advertisement give modern readers an indication of the nonstop action and dizzying succession of desperate chases that would have excited viewers in 1907, but which in their sparseness might have left some audience members wondering who is chasing whom and why.[17] The elaborately detailed synopsis of the plot provided by the Edison Company to the *Moving Picture World* was a hefty 1036 words long, at a time when the narratives of many films of the era could be fully explicated in a paragraph.[18] The ambitious story development and character interactions would have challenged the most gifted of silent film directors, especially in an era without dialogue subtitles or sophisticated editing or mobile camerawork to help direct viewers to understand the intricacies of the plot.

A review of *Daniel Boone* in the entertainment trade paper *Variety* noted that 'There are interesting moments in the story of frontier Indian fighting but the clearness of the story is clouded by a mass of superfluous matter.'[19] Charles Musser suggests that to many viewers, the 1907 film may have resembled a collection of scenes rather than a narrative and that some audience members might have been unable to link the scenes of Porter's films together without extra added title cards on screen or a lecturer on stage describing the action to smooth over the gaps in the story. Bert Cook did not incorporate lecturing into his entertainment programme, so he most probably showed this film with only a word or two of scene-setting, if that much. Given that most audiences at the Cooperstown Centennial knew the Cooper pioneer novels and these kinds of melodramatic stories so well, they might not have needed much extra help to understand the *Daniel Boone* film plot (Musser, 1991, p. 360).[20] Film historian Janet Staiger argues that middle-class audiences would similarly have been culturally equipped to decipher an early Edison film version of *Uncle Tom's Cabin* (Porter, 1903) that seemed more like a collection of scenic tableaux that illustrated the play or novel rather than a connected and developing cinematic plot (Staiger, 1992).[21]

Edwin Porter's desire to tell complicated stories in a one-reel format perhaps limited the success of all three of these historical films, which only allowed for 12 to 14 minutes of on-screen action. When the film trade journals reviewed *Pocahontas* and *Scenes in Colonial Virginia* in fall 1908, critical reactions were mixed. In the spirit of uplifting the appeal of motion pictures to an audience of educated middle-class viewers, critics applauded the historical and educational focus of both films. 'It is not too much to say that such films as this [*Scenes in Colonial Virginia*] ought to be more numerous. They would attract a desirable class of patrons to the theater showing them and the profits would be immeasurably increased,' noted the *Moving Picture World* reviewer.[22] Indeed, films such as these and *Daniel Boone* were precursors of the serious, 'quality' films drawing their plots from Shakespeare, literature, history and the arts that studios such as Edison, Vitagraph, Thanhouser and Biograph would begin featuring in their output in the years ahead (Gunning, 1991; Musser, 1991; Uricchio and Pearson, 1993; Bowers, 1997; Fuller-Seeley, 2009).

The balance of the Cook and Harris Centennial programme consisted of older Edison Company films in their collection, including *Dream of a Rarebit Fiend* (1906), a fantasy film adapted from a popular newspaper comic strip about an urban fellow who has crazy dreams after overindulging at dinner in champagne and rich cheese, and *The Ex-Convict* (1905), about a poor father, who as an ex-convict, cannot find any work. When his child is very ill, he is driven to rob a rich man's home and is discovered, but is spared when the wealthy man's daughter identifies the robber as the Good Samaritan who had saved her from being run over by a wagon. *The Train Wreckers* (1905) was a melodrama about a girl's attempt to intercept thieves trying to hold up a train. *Romance of the Rail* (1903) was based on popular advertisements for the Lackawanna Railroad, and concerned a romance involving a handsome man and Phoebe Snow, 'who wore a gown of white on the road of anthracite'.[23]

The Cooks showed a group of three to five one-reel films, each running for 12 or 13 minutes, then Bert would sing an 'illustrated song' such as 'The Tale the Church Bell Tolled', a currently popular sentimental Tin Pan Alley tune. As he sang, Bert projected the accompanying glass slides reflecting the song's narrative on the screen, while Fannie played accompaniment and encouraged audience members to join in the singing of the chorus. The show concluded with a brief finale film, such as *Three American Beauties* (1906), a brief montage in which a lovely rose (the film hand-painted in colour for fancy effects) fades to a picture of a beautiful girl, who gives way to a big American flag unfurled in the breeze. The Cooks' moderate programming philosophy did not feature the very latest, most exciting, or most newsworthy or most controversial film subjects, but they did regularly select films that featured especially visible and active heroines and modern modes of transportation. These choices earned them the general acceptance of conservative small town Central New York State audiences.[24]

Conclusion: The Movies Continue in Cooperstown

How popular were the Cooks' Centennial movie programmes at the Cooperstown Centennial? Locating any lengthier published reviews or mentions of the shows in diaries or letters has been difficult; in all my searching I have located one advertising flyer preserved in a scrapbook, which promoted 'outdoor exhibition of moving pictures each evening during the band concerts'.[25] Apparently, movie shows, even in small, conservative towns, were coming to be taken for granted in 1907. The Cooks received notice from one out-of-town source, for *The Utica Daily Press* gave the movies a brief mention in their review of the Centennial week's festivities, noting in the first paragraph of its report (after describing the main speeches), 'There was an illuminated launch parade on Otsego Lake last evening, a band concert on the lake front, and an exhibition of moving pictures on Main Street'.[26] The *Cooperstown Freeman's Journal* reported of Monday's programme, 'The moving pictures thrown by B. Albert Cook of Cook and Harris against the First National Bank building were excellent, and pleased a large crowd.'[27] The *Otsego Farmer* added that 'During the evening a large crowd that filled the street from one side of the street to the other was attracted by the moving pictures, which held the interest of the spectators until their end.' On Wednesday, 'increased crowds watch the moving pictures in the street, which is proving one of the most popular of all the attractions.'[28]

The Daughters of the American Revolution Ball was held for the wealthier fairgoers on Tuesday night, with tickets costing $2.00. On Wednesday night the Ladies of the Maccabees hosted a second Centennial Ball, with tickets at $1.00. Bert Cook's movies, shown on both of those evenings, represented the entertainment alternative for those too poor or otherwise disinclined to attend the balls. Thursday was the busiest day of speeches, parade and fireworks. On Saturday, the concluding night of the Centennial, the main (and only) entertainment was the Cooks' moving picture show at 8.00 pm.[29] On a self-congratulatory note at the end of the Centennial celebration week, an editorial in the *Cooperstown Freeman's Journal* commented, 'The [whole] affair was carried on in a most dignified and commendable manner, that must have left a good impression of Cooperstown in the minds of our thousands of visitors.'[30] Motion pictures were in the midst of that 'dignified and commendable' programme. The movies had achieved wide acceptance in conservative small town upstate New York.

The Cook and Harris programme might also be considered a success as it further laid a foundation for Cooperstown's acceptance of regular exhibitions of motion pictures in the village, as opposed to just the occasional movie programmes put on by itinerant exhibitors who happened through the area. The evolution of movie shows and entertainment culture in Cooperstown would continue after the Centennial Fair's conclusion. Within a month of the festival's close, the *Otsego Farmer* wondered, 'Is Cooperstown to have a nickel theater?' 'The Village Hall has been rented for an indefinite period by Oneonta parties for a moving picture entertainment at minimum prices.'[31] This first iteration of a nickelodeon in the village lasted only a few weeks, closing by November. A second group of entrepreneurs tried again in July 1908, inaugurating 'a continuous moving picture show' in the 60-year-old Bowne Opera House. George Carley, editor of the village newspaper *Freeman's Journal*, purchased a half-interest in the show and renamed it the Star Theatre. Bert and Fannie Cook operated their itinerant movie show for four more years before managing a nickelodeon in Richfield Springs. They came back to Cooperstown in 1914 to manage the Star for Carley, and then became its owners. The place of Cooperstown in popular culture also began to shift from memorialising James Fenimore Cooper the nineteenth century novelist to celebrating professional baseball as a historic and modern amusement.[32] In August 1908, the Spaulding Base Ball Guide reported that it had been 'determined' that General Abner Doubleday had invented the game of base ball in 1839 while attending school in Cooperstown, starting in motion the movement to establish a Hall of Fame in the sport's 'hometown'.

Despite the efforts of Cooperstown Centennial Celebration planners and their colleagues at Jamestown to keep the spectre of modernity at bay in 1907 by focusing on history, tradition and the status quo, new ideas and alternative points of view would not stay shut out. Regardless of organisers' plans to keep 'tomato cans', consumer culture and urban ideas to a carefully controlled minimum, festival-goers in Cooperstown and Jamestown voted with their feet to explore the offerings of movie shows, consumer product manufacturers and retailers, and amusement vendors. It is possible that even at as unlikely an event as the Cooperstown Centennial in 1907, modernity seeped through the cracks and fissures of the exhibits and films on display, presenting itself for consideration to the visitors (Fuller-Seeley, 2009).

Notes

1 The Cook and Harris performances took place in an empty lot along Main Street, next to the First National Bank of Cooperstown building. One photograph in the Hagerty scrapbook in the New York State Historical Association collections, contains a partial view of the bank that shows a large square white canvas tied up on the angled exterior bank wall. Celebration organisers paid $20 to rent a piano from one of the local hotels and have it moved into place alongside the bank for Fannie Cook to play musical accompaniment to the films and illustrated songs.

2 'Centennial Closes', *Otsego Farmer*, 16 August 1907, p. 5.

3 'Cooperstown is prepared', *Otsego Farmer*, 2 August 1907, p. 5.

4 'Cooperstown Historically', *Utica Daily Press*, Tuesday 6 August 1907, p. 8.

5 Robertus Love, 'An Exposition with a Warpath: What the Jamestown Fair Means and Why It is a Milepost in American History', *Newark* [Ohio] *Daily Advocate*, 23 April 1907. Found at 'Worlds Fairs and Expositions; defining America and the World', ed. Jim Zwick. (www.boondocksnet.com/compos.index.html), accessed 1 June 2007.

6 Quoted in *Otsego Farmer*, 16 August 1907, p. 5.

7 During the Centennial celebrations, the cellar of a burned out hotel on Main Street was covered over and booths were erected there to sell postcards drinks and treats. *Main Street Cooperstown: A Mile of Memories* (New York State Historical Association, 1992), p. 57.

8 *Otsego Farmer*, 19 July 1907, p. 5.

9 *Otsego Farmer*, 16 August 1907, p. 5.

10 They also performed *Camille, The Two Orphans, Jesse James, Wedded but no Wife* and *The Little Red School House. Otsego Farmer*, 2 August 1907, p. 5.

11 *Main Street, Cooperstown*, p. 33.

12 *The Cooperstown Centennial Celebration 1907* (Cooperstown: Cooperstown Republican, 1907).

13 Cook and Harris papers, New York State Historical Association, Cooperstown NY, file1907 May-Dec Expenses.

14 *NY Clipper*, 13 July 1907, p. 572.

15 In 1907 and 1908 one typical group, the Daniel Boone Amusement Company, from Bloomington, Indiana, advertised its theatrical production of a western extravaganza titled *Daniel Boone on the Trail*, featuring 'a band of genuine Sioux Indians and 100s of Siberian Wolves' (notwithstanding the fact that Boone's exploits occurred in Kentucky). This stage show apparently mixed violent, virile physical action with music and comedy, for the company manager sought actors to play Boone the heroic lead, a 'straight heavy' or villain, an Indian heavy, a blackface comedian who could sing and dance, two young women to play emotional juvenile and ingénue, three or four additional Indians with long hair, musical and sketch teams and a piano player. *NY Clipper*, 21 August 1908, p. 717.

16 Florence Lawrence recounted her first motion picture experience in an interview in *Photoplay Magazine*, November 1914, pp. 40–41, reprinted in Musser (1991), pp. 337–339. She moved to the Biograph Studios in 1909 and, working with D.W. Griffith, became famous as 'the Biograph Girl', before moving to Carl Laemmle's IMP company in 1910, where she became the first American film performer to have her real name advertised.

17 Edison advertisement, *Moving Picture World*, 20 April 1907, p. 98; 'Great Historical Production; Daniel Boone, or Pioneer Days in America. Synopsis of scenes; Boone's Daughter befriends an Indian Maiden – Boone and Companion start out on a hunting expedition – Boone's cabin attacked by the Indians – The desperate defense – Burning cabin – Abduction of Boone's daughters – Boone's return – The oath of vengeance – On the Trail – The Indian camp – Escape of Boone's daughter – Discovery and Pursuit – A Friend in Need – The Fight – Defeat of the Indians – Capture of Boone –Surprising an Indian Picket – The Fight on the cliff – Death of the Indian – Shoots the burning arrow into the Indian camp – Boone tied to the stake – War Dance – Torturing Boone –

Burning arrow lands in the Indian Camp – Indians become panic stricken – Rescue of Boone by his Faithful horse – Desperate Bowie knife duel between Boone and Indian Chief – Death of Indian Chief – Tableau.'

18 'Film Review', *Moving Picture World,* 6 April 1907, pp. 74–75. Edison advertisement, *Moving Picture World*, 20 April 1907, p. 98.

19 *Variety,* 1 June 1907, p. 10, quoted in Musser (1991), pp. 366–367.

20 In 1908, Bert would call *Daniel Boone 'The Great Pioneer Picture'*; it is also known as *Pioneer Days in America* according to the Edison catalogue.

21 Edison advertisement, *Moving Picture World*, 20 April 1907, p. 98.

22 'Comments on Film Subjects', *Moving Picture World*, 28 November 1908, p. 422.

23 'Sidney News and Notes of Interest', *Binghamton Press*, 4 April 1907.

24 Cook and Harris papers, file 1895–1906.

25 Hagerty Centennial scrapbook, New York State Historical Association (NYSHA).

26 'Cooperstown Historically', *Utica Daily Press*, Tuesday 6 August 1907, p. 8.

27 'The Centennial Opens', *Freeman's Journal*, 8 August 1907, p. 1.

28 'Cooperstown Celebrates Centennial', *Otsego Farmer*, 9 August 1907, pp. 1, 4, 5 in Hagerty scrapbook, NYSHA.

29 *Cooperstown Centennial Celebration 1907; History of Cooperstown*, pp. 152–153.

30 *Freeman's Journal,* 15 August 1907.

31 *Otsego Farmer,* 20 September 1907, p. 5; *Freeman's Journal*, 29 August 1907, p. 4; *Freeman's Journal,* 19 September 1907, p. 5. On 19 September 1907 the newspaper announced: 'M.N. Goodrich and A. Sergeant of Oneonta have rented Fireman's Hall for an indefinite period to have there a moving picture entertainment every night at small prices.'

32 *History of Cooperstown*, p. 154.

References

Abel, R. (1999) *The Red Rooster Scare: Making Cinema American, 1900–1910,* University of California Press, Berkeley.

Bowers, Q.D. (1997) *Thanhouser Films: An Encyclopedia and History* (CD-ROM), Thanhouser Film Company Preservation.

Bowser, E. (1990) *The Transformation of Cinema 1907–1915,* Scribner, New York.

Charney, L. and Schwartz, V. (eds) (1995) *Cinema and the Invention of Modern Life,* University of California Press, Berkeley.

Fell, J. (1983) Motive, mischief, and melodrama: the state of film narrative in 1907, in *Film Before Griffith* (ed. J. Fell), University of California Press, Berkeley, pp. 272–283.

Fuller, K.H. (1997) *At the Picture Show: Small Town Audiences and the Creation of Movie Fan Culture,* Smithsonian Institution Press, Washington, DC.

Fuller-Seeley, K. (ed.) (2008) *Hollywood in the Neighborhood: Historical Case Studies of Local Moviegoing,* University of California Press, Berkeley.

Fuller-Seeley, K. (2009) Provincial modernity? Film exhibition at the 1907 Jamestown Exposition, in *Media Convergence History* (eds J. Staiger and S. Hake), Routledge, London, pp. 59–68.

Gunning, T. (1991) *D.W. Griffith and the Origins of American Narrative Film: The Early Years at Biograph,* University of Illinois Press, Urbana.

Hodges, G. (1915) *Henry Codman Potter, Seventh Bishop of New York,* Macmillan, New York.

Kasson, J. (2000) *Buffalo Bill's Wild West,* Hill and Wang, New York.

Keil, C. (2001) *Early American Cinema in Transition: Story, Style and Filmmaking 1907–1913,* University of Wisconsin Press, Madison.

Mahar, K. (2006) *Women Filmmakers in Early Hollywood,* Johns Hopkins University Press, Baltimore.

Musser, C. (1991) *Before the Nickelodeon: Edwin S. Porter and the Edison Manufacturing Company,* University of California Press, Berkeley.

Rydell, R. (1993) *World of Fairs: The Century of Progress Expositions,* University of Chicago Press, Chicago.

Simmon, S. (2003) *The Invention of the Western Film: A Cultural History of the Genre's First Half Century,* Cambridge University Press, Cambridge.

Singer, B. (2004) *Melodrama and Modernity: Early Sensational Cinema and Its Contexts,* Columbia University Press, New York.

Staiger, J. (1992) *Interpreting Films: Studies in the Historical Reception of American Cinema,* Princeton University Press, Princeton.

Uricchio, W. and Pearson, R. (1993) *Reframing Culture: The Case of the Vitagraph Quality Films,* Princeton University Press, Princeton.

17

Silent Film Genre, Exhibition and Audiences in South India[1]

Stephen Putnam Hughes

During the 1920s, exhibitors and film critics in south India classified film genres to help them imagine, cultivate and socially differentiate the steadily growing audiences for cinema. This chapter examines how the emergence of film genre categories and their subsequent refinement through the 1920s addressed and articulated a stereotyped sociology of local film audiences in Madras, now officially known as Chennai. Insofar as film genre categories helped to classify audiences, their use in the local contexts of exhibition offers a useful entry point to the difficult historiographical problem of examining audience composition for silent cinema in India. As there are few sources and little scholarship that can help deal with early film audiences, the history of film genres provides unique insights into how those in colonial Madras discursively constructed the always indeterminant social reality of film audiences.

As an object of enquiry, film audiences will always by circumscribed by indeterminacy. As Robert Allen and Douglas Gomery point out, 'the "audiences" for movies in any sociological or historical sense are really only an abstraction generated by the researcher, since the unstructured group that we refer to as the movie audience is constantly being constituted, dissolved, and reconstituted with each filmgoing experience' (Allen and Gomery, 1985, p. 156).[2] Film audiences are never present as a totality, but only in geographically dispersed, unique and fleeting social events. When speaking about film audiences, we can therefore only refer to abstract and constructed social categories, which should not be confused with the empirical reality of those who actually attended films. However, the indeterminacy of the film audience made categories of film genre an important means by which exhibitors and historians alike might imagine the social reality of audiences. In this chapter I consider film audiences as a many-sided discursive category as it is constructed by the Madras film trade and film critics.

Explorations in New Cinema History: Approaches and Case Studies, First Edition.
Edited by Richard Maltby, Daniel Biltereyst and Philippe Meers.

The focus of this chapter is primarily on the 1920s because this is the period in which genre classifications first emerge as an important means of understanding cinema audiences in south India. At the beginning of the 1920s there were three main classifications of films recognised in the local cinema market of Madras: serials, short dramas and Indian films. For about a decade these three categories encompassed the range of films available in Madras. Local exhibitors and film critics saw each type of film as part of a changing system of complementary and contrasting entertainment alternatives that corresponded to identifiable kinds of local audiences. During the 1920s these main three genre categories were continually refined, until they were eventually replaced by a proliferation of other generic categories for both foreign and Indian film productions. With the introduction of Indian sound cinema from 1931 onwards, the problem of genre quickly moved in other directions. My argument, however, is less concerned with how and why genre classifications change over time than with how contemporary discussions of film classifications can suggest a local sociology of genre, and illustrate the historiography of cinema audiences in colonial Madras.

Genre as Part of the Historiography of Audiences

Although the vast majority of films screened in Madras were titled in English, silent cinema did not demand any primary linguistic identification from its public, and film viewing cut across all language groups: preponderantly Tamil and Telugu, but also Hindi, Urdu, Malayalam, Kannada, Gujarati and English. Rather than operating as a medium of some already existing linguistic group, silent cinema constructed its own public through the practices, institutions and spaces of exhibition, and innovated its own language of address. Compared to other cultural forms of music, literature and drama, the emerging public institutions of the cinema in south India worked to allow castes, classes and communities as well as women, children and families to mix in a new kind of public social space. Writing about Tamil cinema after sound had divided Indian cinemas linguistically, Karthigesu Sivathambi emphasised the distinctive role of the exhibition space as 'the first social equalizer' in the history of Tamilian arts:

> The Cinema Hall was the first performance centre in which all the Tamils sat under the same roof. The basis of seating is not on the hierarchic position of the patron but essentially on his purchasing power. If he cannot afford paying the higher rate, he has either to keep away from the performance or be with all and sundry. (Sivathambi, 1981, pp. 18–19)

Sivathambi's comments can also inform an understanding of silent film exhibition, where the democratic promise of a socially equalised audience was tempered by the economic hierarchy of ticket prices creating distinct seating classes.[3] As exhibitors organised audiences spatially according to price, they created a space in which existing relations of caste and class could be 'both *enacted* and *transgressed* at the same time'

(Liang, 2005, p. 369). Genre was an important component of the processes by which these publics were identified and positioned in a distinctively cinematic hierarchy.

My approach to genre is based on the work of Valentin Volosinov, Pavel Medvedev and Mikhail Bakhtin.[4] As an analytic concept, genre commonly refers to the classification of conventionalised forms of language, literature or films. According to a formalist reading, genres variously limit, define, order or unify a diverse range of film texts through a relatively stable set of rules, which can be ascertained from the accumulated analyses of individual film texts. In this sense we can understand genre as oriented from *within* as a unity of thematic determinations. But as Bakhtin and Medvedev argue, genre is also oriented *outward*, socially toward an addressee, a listener and a perceiver (Bakhtin and Medvedev, 1985, p. 131). The analysis of film genre cannot, therefore, be limited to how its rules and limits impose order on a group of films, but should also consider how genre classifications articulate a sociological relationship between exhibitors, audiences and a social hierarchy amongst audiences. From this perspective, each film screening of genre is like an utterance, a performative act that presupposes a particular audience at a specific time and place, under specific historical conditions.[5] Film performances are constructed through the socially organised and reciprocal relationships between the exhibitors who promote them and their paying audiences (Volosinov, 1973, pp. 85–86). This is why Bakhtin and Medvedev claim that 'a genuine poetics of genre can only be a sociology of genre' (Bakhtin and Medvedev, 1985, p. 135).

Although genre has a long-held and important place within film studies, there has been comparatively little such work done on the case of cinema in India.[6] The relatively undeveloped study of Indian film genre results, in part, from the emergence of stars as the more important element of audience address in Indian sound cinema. Addressing this absence goes beyond filling a gap in the scholarship to suggest a major reorientation for Indian cinema history, moving the history of films to their sites of exhibition, where films and audiences came together. This move transfers the analysis of film genres into the historically contingent and culturally specific locations, institutions and practices of exhibition, where genres play an important role in the discursive construction of audience typologies. Once genre is understood as a mode of address, film classifications can be seen as a kind of social imaginary based on a presumed hierarchy of film tastes. By posing the issue of how films and audiences relate, a sociology of genre opens the possibility of understanding how film genres classified local audiences, countering widely held assumptions about Indian film audiences being an undifferentiated category conceived variously as the masses, the working classes or a public sphere.[7]

From Variety to Featured Attraction

Cinema started in south India around 1900 as a European form of itinerant variety entertainment, with films from Europe shown by Europeans for predominantly European audiences. The first touring cinema exhibitors in India were part of a world market in variety entertainment that circulated throughout the colonial outposts of Africa and Asia. At first films were introduced as part of a mixed programme that included live music hall or vaudeville performances. From about 1905, touring exhibitors increasingly began to specialise in shows dedicated exclusively to film screenings, using the same venues, formats and standards as had already been used for variety performances. Within this variety format every cinema show was itself a composite of all film genres, so that the variety format can be seen as in its own way a celebration of film genres.

The changing trends in world film production during the 1910s and 1920s also set constraints on what Madras exhibitors offered their local audiences. Before Indian films reached the cinema halls of Madras Presidency around 1920, south Indian audiences were fed an exclusive diet of films from abroad. As world cinema production shifted away from the variety format of short attractions, multiple reel narrative feature films emerged as a new standard for cinema entertainment, in India as elsewhere. The transition to a featured attraction format can be discerned in changes in local cinema advertising: instead of listing seven or eight different kinds of films, one film title and a descriptive label became the norm in newspaper advertisements in the late 1910s, even though exhibitors continued to offer a variety of comic and topical shorts as part of every film programme. Once individual film titles were used to form the main attraction at cinema shows, however, generic classifications came to be used in new ways. Designations of genre were no longer confined to describing the variety within a film programme, but were used to identify the particular appeal of one programme by comparison to others, and to distinguish one cinema offering from another.

Silent film serials

The first kind of film to be recognised as a featured genre in Madras was the action serial. Serials comprised a succession of films with a continuous story, usually screened over the course of a few weeks or months. They relied on an entertainment formula of fast-paced action and melodramatic scenarios to build up a climax of suspense and anticipation strong enough to bring audiences back for the next instalment. As the *Madras Mail* described them:

> Unscrupulous men heavily masked, slink about by-ways and kidnap girls and carry them off to mountain fortresses in the wilds. Every instalment has a motor smash, a fight, a robbery and at least one murder. The bedroom scene is favourite and frequent.[8]

Until recently, European and US film scholarship has routinely ignored or discounted the significance of silent film serials as a low-budget, unsophisticated and transient phenomenon that lost popularity as filmgoers' tastes matured.[9] In south India, however, action serials were, with Indian films, the most consistently profitable, reliably popular and dominant film category to be screened throughout the 1920s.

The success of serials undoubtedly played an important part in helping film companies from the United States accomplish a rapid and comprehensive takeover of the Indian cinema market during and immediately after World War I. The Universal Film Company, which opened its first distribution offices in Bombay in 1916, dominated the Indian market by the late 1910s and supplied the majority of serials screened in south India throughout the 1920s.[10] The success of their serials demonstrated to exhibitors how 'a feverish interest could be aroused and sustained in the desire of the people for seeing a story continued on the screen for a number of weeks'.[11] For a period during the early 1920s, all the cinema halls in Madras screened serials.

Two of Universal's star attractions were the serial actors Elmo Lincoln and Eddie Polo, the first film personalities to be widely recognised by name, with a loyal fan following in the region. Polo, who starred in a series of loosely autobiographical serials about life in the circus, probably achieved the most enduring local popularity. According to one journalist, 'Eddie Polo is a name to conjure with in Madras. One has only to mention his name to his devotees to hear him acclaimed as their idol.'[12] At a time when there was virtually no Tamil-language film journalism, there were a series of numerous and widely published pamphlets in Tamil about Eddie Polo and his serials from about 1919 until about 1930.[13] In 1928, one Madras distributor claimed that along with Pearl White, Polo was still the most popular star in south India.[14] Elmo Lincoln established himself as a star in the title role of the first film version of *Tarzan of the Apes* in 1919. Describing the local reception for *Elmo, the Fearless* (1920), the *Madras Mail* observed that:

> Hundreds flock to see him perform wondrous feats of strength in rescuing the heroine from danger and cheer themselves hoarse whenever he comes off on top. The size and enthusiasm of the audience serve to prove what a great hold the serial film has obtained in Madras and also what a popular actor Elmo Lincoln is.[15]

Polo and Lincoln both inspired committed devotion amongst some of their fans. In his autobiography, Tamil dramatist T.K. Canmukam recalled how his young actor friends divided into opposing camps over which star was the stronger or the better actor, and these disputes sometimes resulted in fights among the friends (Canmukam, 1986, pp. 180–181).

Part of the serials' appeal to exhibitors was that they were more readily available and less expensive than other films, particularly as action serials fell out of favour in the West. Amongst Madras cinema halls, R. Venkiah's Gaiety Theatre (seating 885) gradually gained a reputation for screening serials. Located in the prestigious European shopping district of Mount Road in close proximity to south India's most up-scale cinema venues, the Gaiety showed the first run of all the Universal serials. After Venkiah went bankrupt in 1924, the new management at the Gaiety tried unsuccessfully to change the established film programming policy at the cinema hall from Hollywood serials to Indian films, but attendance fell substantially and the management shifted a policy of showing imported Western films, both features and serials.[16] When the Gaiety was leased and sold to Madan's exhibition circuit chain in 1926, the stable film programme switched back with great success to the older standard of action serials.[17]

Madras exhibitors screened serials in a more condensed pattern than was the habit in Western countries, where one episode was normally exhibited each week as part of a programme, so that one serial would continue over the course of several months. In contrast, Madras exhibitors tended to screen serial films as the featured attraction, with as many as six episodes shown during every film show, so that an entire serial would be screened in no more than 4 or 6 weeks. Exhibiting serials in this condensed fashion helped to concentrate and intensify the experience of watching these films, as well as indicating their relative importance in the local market.

According to exhibitors, serials constituted a film genre well suited to the majority of south Indians, appealing especially to poor, uneducated and young audiences, known as 'the two *anna* crowd'.[18] Action serials were the one imported film category most likely to transcend the linguistic and graphical limitations of English inter-titles and be comprehensible to non-English-speaking audiences. Their pronounced plot and fast-paced action did not require reading complicated inter-titles in a foreign language that most Indians did not understand. Canmukam claimed that the general public (*potumakkal*) avidly followed film serials every week for a month and were able fully to understand the entire story (Canmukam, 1986, p. 179). For south Indian exhibitors in both urban and rural areas, the visual immediacy of serial film stories made this genre, more than any other, important for cultivating new 'low class' and illiterate audiences, but attendance at serial films was never limited to poorer and uneducated Indians. In 1928, Madras exhibitor A. Narayanan explained with remarkable confidence to the Indian Cinematograph Committee (ICC) that in Madras the crowd for serials was made up of 70% wage earners, 20% middle-class and semiliterate, and 10% rich and literate.[19] While Narayanan's statistical breakdown of audience composition may have been, at best, a well-informed estimate, its precision indicates the extent to which exhibitors related a sociology of genre to their perception of the social composition of their audiences.

Short drama

Because serials dominated the south Indian film market during the 1920s, other film categories were defined against them. The serial form was one of the last holdouts against the emergence of Hollywood's commercially dominant feature film format, which rose to prominence in part because of the American industry's efforts to improve its cultural status by adopting high-brow entertainment forms such as literary and stage adaptations (Uricchio and Pearson, 1993). In current usage the category 'feature film' is not normally recognised as a genre, but as a narrative format shared across a wide range of genres. In south India in the 1920s, however, feature films were identified as a distinct category, marked by unique narrative conventions and a class-based audience appeal. Distinguishing them from the serials viewed over several weeks, Madras exhibitors referred to feature films as 'short dramas', because they could be seen in their entirety over the course of one show. While serials generally ran from 4 to 6 weeks and were often immediately recycled to other local cinemas, short dramas had a comparatively brief screen life, often only playing for half a week in one of the Madras cinema halls.

Most of the major feature films produced during the 1920s made their way to the screens of south India sooner or later, although exhibitors often had difficulties obtaining their pick of films available in the print markets of the world, and major Hollywood productions routinely screened in Madras one year or 18 months after their American release.[20] A small number of imported features, especially those of the most famous stars, routinely drew full houses from all classes and all cinemas: Douglas Fairbanks' lavish action romances were said to have universal appeal, and never failed to fill south Indian cinema halls. *The Thief of Baghdad* (1924) was reportedly the most popular silent film ever screened in India.[21] In general, however, Madras exhibitors considered that American and European short dramas appealed to more educated and elite audiences, and that they only did well when exhibited in more European-oriented cinema halls. These venues actively cultivated young, relatively affluent and educated Indians, such as the students at Presidency College and Queen Mary's College, by offering occasional concessions on ticket rates and special showings of feature films with historical, literary or dramatic interest.[22] Multiple reel dramas based on literary adaptations and complicated romances were, however, considered too difficult for most Indians to follow without prior knowledge of the story. Although these films attracted a higher proportion of their audiences from the wealthy and educated classes, elite filmgoers never constituted a majority of those attending high-class foreign short dramas. A. Narayanan informed the ICC that 'a western film of a famous literary work or a high-class feature film' would attract 50% wage earners, 35% middle-class people and students, and 15% rich and educated.[23] Despite their greater prestige and the opportunities they presented for reaching a more attractive market segment capable of paying higher ticket prices, short dramas in Madras had difficulties in consistently attracting enough audiences from all classes to make their exhibition a profitable venture.

Serial or drama?

From 1921 onwards, in a weekly feature entitled 'Stage and Screen' in the *Madras Mail*, Madras's only film columnist lobbied on behalf of short dramas and against the dominance of serials in local cinema halls.[24] He made two main complaints. The first was that serials were all too predictable and boring, always following 'a common plan ... we have the same situations with a different atmosphere, different artistes, different accessories as to scenery and location'.[25] The second was that serials attracted the wrong kind of audiences: lower class patrons – 'the poor folk who are content with serial fare' – whose addiction to serials was held responsible for preventing quality short drama films from playing in local cinema halls: 'Once having acquired a taste for the serial the masses find that they cannot shake it off.'[26]

Six months later, the *Mail* published an article titled 'Serial or Drama?' written under the pseudonym 'Aah Fan' and extending the familiar criticism of serials by claiming that the serial craze was a direct consequence of the contemporary political agitations of colonial Madras:

> The present craving for serials is, I think, a reflex of the unsettled state of the national mind. Men and women and youths are all seething with excitements as a result of the political and other movements now being sedulously propagated. They want adventure, movement, life at ninety miles an hour and since they cannot get it in their daily round, they seek for it in their amusements and especially on the screen.[27]

Aah Fan was not explicit about which contemporary 'political and other movements' – the Nationalist Non-Cooperation movement, the agitation for a pan-Islamic Khilafat, a 4-month industrial labour strike in the textile mills of Madras, the picketing of liquor shops in the south, the Moplah revolt on the west coast, left-wing militants in the Punjab or the constant threat of Bolshevism – he held responsible for the serial's appeal (Geetha and Rajadurai, 1998, pp. 206–208; see also Sarkar, 1983, pp. 204–226). While this equation of film serial audiences with political sedition and the 'unsettled state of the national mind' was undoubtedly an extreme position only possible for the most loyal of British colonial residents, its publication articulated a broader notion of cinema audiences participating in the social and political movements of the day. Police authorities and colonial government viewed the daily collecting of crowds outside the theatre with concern, particularly after they had been emotionally galvanised through the collective experience of film watching. The very idea of collective gatherings, even at places of public entertainment, evoked anxieties of the crowd as a potentially uncontrollable threat to the political and social order.[28]

The *Madras Mail* not only criticised serials but also did its best to promote the cause of short dramas as a superior choice of films pairing the serial and the short drama as part of an opposition of high and low culture:

> It is good to know that the Wellington and Elphinstone managements are reverting to short drama programmes for the coming week. I confess frankly that I am not a friend of the serial. The sameness of the average serial appals me. But short dramas do not have such an inevitable character. I hope that patrons of all classes will give the short dramas at the Elphinstone and Wellington good support. I would like to see the patrons of the dearer seats turn up in great force for these films are such as they are more likely to please them than the masses who throng the cheaper seats. The short drama appeals more to one's sense of beauty and dramatic effect than the serial and the masses are, at present, mainly interested in the fighting and thrilling stunts, which the serial contains.[29]

In advocating greater attendance in the higher priced seats as the best way to prove to local exhibitors that short dramas were worth booking, the film correspondent appealed to the readers' sense of social hierarchy and cultural superiority in contrast to the 'masses who throng [to] the cheaper seats'. The thematic contrast of genres in terms of beauty and dramatic effect against thrilling action articulated a distinction of the classes against the masses. The newspaper's relentless criticism of 'the blood-curdling serial' did not, however, have any impact on the parade of serials through Madras cinema halls, and the *Mail*'s critic eventually capitulated to the inevitability of serials, reluctantly concluding that 'As with governments, so with cinemas, the people get that which they deserve and Madras cinema-goers demand serials'.[30] Except for the first- and second-run cinema halls, serials continued to be the basic fare at most cinema shows in the districts and touring cinemas until the 1930s. Although elite and educated audiences in urban areas lost interest in the genre, their sustained popularity contributed a very significant action element to early Indian cinema. As the only locally published film criticism, the *Madras Mail*'s campaign would have played a significant role in defining the public recognition of how film genre categories mapped social hierarchies, but the characterisation of generic affiliation based on a notion of high and low class was only one of many ways that film genre was being articulated as a kind of social relation.

Mythological cinema

Indian silent films comprised the third of the main film genres, but unlike the class-based appeal of serials and short dramas, Indian silent cinema was constructed on a Hindu religious address. This was most obviously typified by the films of Dadasaheb Phalke, a Maharastrian Brahmin who established Hindu mythological film as the first indigenous and self-consciously nationalist cinema genre. What distinguished Indian mythological films from foreign counterparts were that they were either based on stories taken from the Hindu *puranas* and epics, or were about religious saints and devotees. With their distinctive appeal for Indian audiences already familiar with the stories, mythological subjects were an obvious choice for creating a commercially successful Indian cinema, and until 1923 about 70% of all Indian silent films produced were based on mythological stories (Dharap, 1983, p. 79).

Hindu mythological cinema did not, however, initially affect all parts and peoples of India evenly. Phalke's first five feature films were screened to enthusiastic Indian audiences throughout western and north India from 1913, but they do not seem to have been exhibited much, if at all, in the south. Phalke's sixth film, *Sri Krishna Janma* (*The Birth of Shri Krishna*, 1918), depicting a series of well-known episodes from young Krishna's life, was the first to attract much attention.[31] Because the stories were familiar to all, including most non-Hindus, most viewers could follow the films without needing to read the Hindi or English captions. Produced and distributed on a larger scale than his previous films, *Krishna Janma* was first screened in Madras in January 1919. Coinciding with the Tamil festive season of Pongal and the Hindu holiday of Vaikunta Ekadesi, the film's premiere at the Wellington theatre drew unprecedented crowds, with over 200 000 people attending shows running from 10 a.m. to 3 a.m. over a one-month period. According to an editorial in Annie Besant's *New India*, these crowds were 'intensely moved by the show', testifying 'to the very deep religious feeling that underlies Hindu life', and 'the deep love for Shri Krishna that abides in the South'.[32]

A year later, the film again did record business at the Crown Theatre in George Town, and almost a decade after its debut in south India *Sri Krishna Janma* was still drawing large crowds and doing good business for exhibitors throughout south India.[33] The total production of Indian silent films was, however, still small enough that the screening of an Indian film was a rare occurrence anywhere for several years to come. In 1919, only eight films were produced throughout all of India, and only half of these were screened in Madras. In 1920, perhaps 8 of the 18 Indian productions played in Madras.[34]

When compared to the usual fare of serial films and short dramas, exhibitors considered Indian mythological films to be more respectable and morally unobjectionable for Hindu audiences. These *purana* films even attracted religiously orthodox people who would never otherwise attend public entertainments unrelated to worship or festivals.[35] For many Indians, including many of those in the cinema trade, mythological films were a celebration of India's spiritual superiority and an affirmation of a distinctive Indian national culture. They also provided a successful way to compete with Hollywood films at the box office. Indian cinema exhibitors and distributors advertised that the seeing of mythological films was an act of religious duty and merit (*puniyam* in Tamil). For example, when Phalke's *Lanka Dahanam* was screened at the Wellington Cinema in Madras in 1919, a newspaper advertisement for the engagement claimed that, 'It is the sacred duty of every Indian to see this religious film'.[36]

Many exhibitors who catered primarily to Indian audiences preferred mythologicals because they felt that they drew more respectable crowds of family audiences and especially women. With the exception of Anglo-Indians, Indian women did not attend the cinema in large numbers, and few women went alone. One Madras government education official explained that 'Hindu women have a natural reluctance to go to any public affair, to attend any show in a public place.' At any given film show, 'at most there are about a dozen [women] sitting in a roped off section or behind a *purdah* [screen] if there is one.'[37] At mythological films, however, women could account for as much as a quarter of the entire audience, usually coming with their families and children or in groups.[38] According to A. Narayanan, the social breakdown of a typical audience for an Indian mythological film was 60% poorer classes and wage earners, 25% ladies and 15% literate Indians.[39] One distributor even claimed that most men did not want to see *purana* films, 'but with every woman six gentlemen are going due to the force of the ladies'.[40] Whether or not Narayanan's statistical calculation was exact, it indicates that mythological films played a significant role in identifying women, as well as religious groupings, as important categories within the local sociology of film audiences.

Mythological films could, however, only be promoted as the Indian national film genre on the basis of a series of social, religious and cultural exclusions of Muslims, Christians, Anglo-Indians and Europeans as well as educated elite

Indians.[41] As the production of Indian silent films increased in the 1920s, a number of mythological films proved to be failures, and the Indian production industry responded by experimenting with other genres, particularly romantic costume dramas 'presented with all the adventure and thrill of a Wild West film', and 'social' films featuring contemporary settings and costumes, usually focusing on the life-styles of wealth and luxury enjoyed by new classes of the social elite, but some-times advocating social reform of contemporary problems such as child marriage, dowry or untouchability (Shaw, 1950, p. 29).[42] While mythological films had com-prised some 70% of all Indian silent film productions up to 1923, they accounted for only about 15% of the total output after then (Dharap, 1983, p. 79). Although social pictures became increasingly popular in urban areas, mythological films continued to be by far the most successful in *moffusil* [rural] stations.[43]

Cinema Halls, Genre and the Local Sociology of Film Audiences

By the end of the 1920s, Madras cinemas had become readily distinguished by the kinds of films they screened and their corresponding clientele. Genre also helped to classify the social space of cinema theatres, so that most cinema halls gained a settled reputation based on their locality and film programming policy. Each exhibitor had to work out the best possible match of films for his local patrons from the affordable and sometimes limited options available to him. Given these overriding constraints, exhibitors in Madras did not always have much choice in what kinds of films they had to offer. Even so, Madras exhibitors established their own local address, at least in part, through a series of programming decisions and changes made over time.

Among cinema halls in Madras, the Wellington Cinema and Elphinstone Picture Palace specialised in screening the high-class imported silent feature films from the mid-1910s through the 1920s. Along with the more downmarket Gaiety Theatre, the Wellington (seating 1800) and the Elphinstone (seating 1200) were located within one block of each other in the prestigious European shopping district in the northeast corner of Mount Road.[44] These two cinema halls were the grandest and most luxurious in south India, constructing their reputations as high-class enter-tainment venues through a combination of architectural opulence, elaborate décor and quality film programming. Even though other genres were screened at both the Wellington and Elphinstone during the 1920s, these two venues exclusively offered the first runs of the high-class feature films, including the best and most popular the United States and Europe had to offer.

The frequency and number of Indian silent films shown at Madras cinema halls became an important way in which exhibitors distinguished their venues as being for Indian audiences. The Cinema Majestic, in the densely populated Indian neigh-bourhood of George Town was the first Madras cinema hall to show exclusively Indian films from 1924. More than any other in the city, this venue succeeded in acquiring and maintaining a regular programme of Indian films.[45] A rival exhibitor claimed that the Majestic, 'always had a steady house, whatever Indian films they put on, good, bad or indifferent.' Had the management tried to change the Majestic's programme to Western film serials, for example, their business would have suffered because, it had 'an established reputation for a particular film and a particular set of audiences go to them'.[46] Another George Town venue, the Crown Theatre, had done well in the early 1920s by screening Indian silent films, but its business suffered when its owner, Raghupathi Venkiah, could not acquire a continuous supply and it was forced to show mostly foreign films and serials. Competition for Indian films intensified, with some cinema halls entering into exclusive collaboration with major Indian film producers. In 1924 Venkiah was forced into bankruptcy and the Crown Cinema itself was eventually purchased by Madan and Company who, on the basis of their own film productions and an all-India chain of cinema theatres, were able to maintain a guaranteed regular supply of Indian silent films.[47]

Matching films with the tastes of paying audiences could be a matter of survival in the exhibition business. The Kinema Central (seating 650) in George Town opened in the late 1920s with the declared purpose of exclusively screening Indian films for Indian audiences. Eventually it also had to show Western films occasionally because of the difficulties in obtaining a steady supply of Indian silent films, but it continued to generate good business, particularly with Indian social films of high quality, such as Kohinoor's *Gunsundari or Why Husbands Go Astray* (1927).[48] On the other hand, the Liberty Theatre, also located in George Town, gained a reputation for routinely screening serials. According to rival exhibitor S.K. Vasagam, the Liberty was a 'low class' cinema hall that only drew a crowd when they screened 'serials of the sensational type'. He claimed that the popularity of serials at this hall was a function of the fact that 'no decent people' would go to the hall, as was evidenced by the fact that the Indian mythological films occasionally shown at the Liberty 'did not pay nor attract on account of the locality', although the same films did extremely well at other nearby cinema halls.[49] What Vasagam failed to mention was that the Liberty's audiences were predominantly middle and lower class Muslims who 'do not care much for Indian pictures', as former Liberty employee N.R. Desai, manager of the Universal Pictures distribution office in Madras, explained to the ICC.[50]

Conclusion

From the beginning of the 1920s the generic equation of films and south Indian audiences was an important way of understanding cinema as a set of social relations. By looking at the emerging relationships between the main silent film categories, I have shown some of the ways in which genre was used to construct, imagine and address the filmgoing publics of colonial Madras. As the film critic for the *Madras Mail* clearly expressed in his simplified sociology of film genre dividing audiences into classes and masses, the cinema in south India had acquired a reputation as being an entertainment medium for the urban working classes and among the poor. It was also clear to those working in the Madras cinema trade that their business was best sustained by the far more numerous lower, uneducated and working classes. For some cinema halls the elite classes were always part of the audience equation, but their patronage was never enough to keep the two- and four-*anna* crowds from being the primary audience target.

A much more detailed and complex sociology of genre was needed for the work of film exhibitors and film agents, who used genre categories to classify and cultivate paying audiences, and to address an array of class, gender, community and generational differences depending on location and clientele. Drawing on their own practical experience and their sense of business success, exhibitors created their own working sociology of genre to manage and calculate local audiences as part of their business practices. Over the course of the 1920s the generic equation was greatly complicated by increased film production and the proliferation of both foreign and Indian genres. Yet throughout the period genre categories helped the film trade address, understand and create multiple constituencies for the cinema in urban Madras.

Notes

1 This chapter is a revised version of a paper originally published as 'House full: film genre, exhibition and audiences in south India' in *Indian Economic and Social History Review*, 43 (1) (2006), 31–62.

2 See also Ien Ang, *Desperately Seeking the Audience* (London: Routledge, 1991) for a similar argument in relation to television audiences.

3 For another view of Sivathambi's analysis see S.V. Srinivas, 'Gandhian nationalism and melodrama in the 30's Telugu cinema', *Journal of the Moving Image*, 1 (1) (1999), 14–36.

4 The following account of a sociological approach to genre is roughly drawn from Bakhtin and Medvedev (1985); M.M. Bakhtin, 'The problem of speech genres', in M.M. Bakhtin, *Speech Genres and Other Late Essays* (trans. Vern McGee) (Austin, TX: University of Texas Press, 1986), pp. 60–102; and I.R. Titunik, 'The formal method and the sociological method', in V.N. Volosinov, *Marxism and the Philosophy of Language* (Cambridge, MA: Harvard University Press: 1973), pp. 175–200.

5 I have developed this argument in more detail in Stephen Hughes (2003) 'Pride of place', *Seminar* (525), 28–32.

6 For example, in their comprehensive overview of Indian cinema, Ashish Rajadhyaksha and Paul Willemen complain that the study of film genre for Indian cinema has been left relatively undeveloped. Ashish Rajadhyaksha and Paul Willemen, *Encyclopedia of Indian Cinema* (London: British Film Institute, 1994) p. 13. Within film studies I have found two general accounts of genre particularly helpful. See Rick Altman, *Film/Genre* (London: British Film Institute, 1999), and Steve Neale, *Genre and Hollywood* (London: Routledge, 2000). The other important film studies contribution to genre, which most closely corresponds to my approach, is Richard Maltby, 'Sticks, hicks and flaps: classical Hollywood's generic conception of its audiences', in *Identifying Hollywood's Audiences: Cultural Identity and the Movies* (eds M. Stokes and R. Maltby) (London: British Film Institute, 1999), pp. 23–41.

7 For other scholarship on the relationship between exhibition and urban histories of India, see S.V. Srinivas, 'Is there a public in the cinema hall?', *Framework*, Summer (2000); and E. Grimaud, 'Reshaping the vision: film scraps, middlemen and the public in a Bombay motion picture theatre', *Homme*, 164 (2002), 84–104. Bhrigupati Singh is

currently producing important research on local histories of the cinema in Delhi in conjunction with SARAI-CSDS research project, 'Publics and Practices in the History of the Present'.

8 *Madras Mail* (hereafter *MM*), 9 April 1921.

9 Singer makes this point in 'Female power in the serial-queen melodrama: the etiology of an anomaly', *Camera Obscura* 22 (1990), 91–129. For what little scholarship there is on this largely ignored part of film history, see Lahue, *Bound and Gagged: The Story of the Silent Serials* (New York: Barnes, 1968); Alan G. Barbour, *Days of Thrills and Adventure* (London: Collier, 1970); and Singer, 'Serials', in *The Oxford History of World Cinema* (ed. Geoffrey Nowell-Smith) (Oxford: Oxford University Press, 1996), pp. 105–111.

10 Universal opened distribution offices in Calcutta in 1917 and Madras in 1922. Kristin Thompson, *Exporting Entertainment* (London: British Film Institute, 1985), pp. 43, 48, 72 and 144. Also, see the Madras List of Trades. *Asylum Press Almanac*, 1923.

11 S. Devasankar Aiyar, a self-described amateur cinematographer who worked as a clerk for the Maharastra and Southern Railways, as cited in *ICC Evidence*, vol. 3, p. 338.

12 *MM*, 21 May 1921.

13 See the *Fort St. George Gazette Supplement, Catalogue of Books*, Madras, for the years 1919–1930 for details on the various Eddie Polo publications in Tamil, which ranged from serial story synopses, biographical sketches to folk songs in praise of his strength. During the silent period, these materials were some of the very few items about the cinema published in Tamil.

14 Thomas H. Huffton, film distributor and sole proprietor of the Peninsula Film Service, *ICC Evidence*, vol. 3, p. 357.

15 *MM*, 22 January 1921.

16 See the oral statement of F.H. Wilson, official assignee in charge of liquidating R. Venkiah's holdings after bankruptcy. He took over the Gaiety along with the Crown and the Globe in November 1924. *ICC Evidence*, vol. 3, pp. 150–158. A.A. Hayles, Representative, European Association, Madras, *ICC Evidence*, vol. 3, p. 274.

17 Along with the Crown Theatre, also originally owned by R. Venkiah, the Gaiety is still in operation in Chennai.

18 An 'anna' was a currency unit formerly used in India, which was worth 1/16 of a rupee.

19 Ananthanarayanan Narayanan was a pioneer of the Tamil film industry, operating as a distributor and exhibitor in Madras before founding the General Pictures Corporation in 1929 and establishing a film production industry in South India. *ICC Evidence*, vol. 3, p. 284.

20 *MM*, 15 January 1921.

21 See Joseph A. David, Cinematographer, Madras, *ICC Evidence*, vol. 3, p. 320; and U.B. Romesh Rao, Manager of the Radha Picture Palace, Calicut, *ICC Evidence*, vol. 3, p. 442.

22 Sambandam Mudaliar, *ICC Evidence*, vol. 3, p. 238.

23 *ICC Evidence*, vol. 3, p. 284.

24 During the early 1920s there was very little in the way of film journalism in south India. The *Madras Mail* was the only local newspaper to cover regularly cinema-related news until the late 1920s. The other main dailies, *The Hindu* and *Swadesamitran* (in Tamil), only started weekly cinema columns in the late 1920s.

25 *MM*, 5 March 1921.

26 *MM*, 23 April 1921.

27 *MM*, 1 October 1921.

28 I discuss this issue in more detail in Stephen P. Hughes, 'Policing silent film exhibitions in colonial south India', in Ravi Vasudevan (ed.) *Making Meaning in Indian Cinema* (New Delhi: Oxford University Press, 1999), pp. 39–64.

29 *MM*, 2 April 1921.

30 *MM*, 28 May 1921.

31 For a detailed description of the surviving portions (about 500 feet out of 5500 feet) of this film see P.K. Nair, 'Those illuminating aspects', *Cinema In India*, 3 (9) (1992), 21–28.

32 *New India*, 20 January 1919.

33 *MM*, 19 January 1920, p. 3.

34 Production totals used here are drawn from Firoze Rangoonwalla, *75 Years of Indian Cinema* (New Delhi: Indian Book Co., 1975). The number of Indian films screened in Madras is an estimate based upon my survey of contemporary newspapers.

35 V. Venkataramama Aiyangar (B.A., B.L.), Member of the Legislative Council in the *ICC Evidence*, vol. 3, p. 211.

36 *New India*, 4 April 1919.

37 Miss I.H. Lowe, Deputy Directress of Public Instruction, *ICC Evidence*, vol. 3, p. 82.

38 A. Narayanan, *ICC Evidence*, vol. 3, p. 284.

39 *ICC Evidence*, vol. 3, p. 284.

40 Thomas H. Huffton, Proprietor, The Peninsula Film Service, Madras, *ICC Evidence*, vol. 3, p. 355.

41 Somnath Zutshi develops this point further in questioning the limits of Phalke's inclusive project of Hindu cultural nationalism. See Zutshi, 'Women, nation and the outsider in Hindi cinema', in *Interrogating Modernity: Culture and Colonialism in India* (eds T. Niranjana *et al.*) (Calcutta: Seagull, 1993), pp. 83–141.

42 For more details about some of the key Indian silent films, see Rajadhyaksha A. and Willemen, P. (1994) *Encyclopaedia of Indian Cinema*, British Film Institute, London, pp. 106, 219, 242–252.

43 U.B. Romesh Rao, Manager of the Radha Picture Palace, Calicut, *ICC Evidence*, vol. 3, p. 442.

44 The seating capacity figures are based on a government survey. See Tamil Nadu Archives, Law (Gen) G.O. no. 1545, dated 29 September 1921.

45 This claim is made on the basis of advertisements in the *Swadesamitran* (Madras).

46 A. Narayanan, *ICC Evidence*, vol. 3, p. 284.

47 According to F.H. Wilson, the official assignee in charge of liquidating Venkiah's holdings after bankruptcy, his financial failure was due to the large amounts spent on building the theatres, large loans and high interest rates, bad management and robbery on the part of the staff. The problems the Crown had in maintaining a steady run of Indian films was, no doubt, symptomatic of these other problems. *ICC Evidence*, vol. 3, p. 156.

48 *ICC Evidence*, vol. 3, p. 316.

49 S.K. Vasagam, *ICC Evidence*, vol. 3, p. 317.

50 *ICC Evidence*, vol. 3, p. 376.

References

Allen, R. and Gomery, D. (1985) *Film History: Theory and Practice,* Knopf, New York.

Bakhtin, M.M. and Medvedev, P.M.(1985) *The Formal Method in Literary Scholarship: A Critical Introduction to Sociological Poetics* (trans. Albert Wehrle), Harvard University Press, Cambridge, MA.

Canmukam, T.K. (1986) *Enatu Nataka Vazhkkai,* Vanathi Press, Madras.

Dharap, B.V. (1983) The mythological or taking fatalism for granted, in *Indian Cinema Superbazaar* (eds A. Vasudev and P. Lenglet), Vikas, New Delhi.

Geetha, V. and Rajadurai, S.V. (1998) *Towards a Non-Brahmin Millennium: From Iyothee Thas to Periar,* Samya; in Association with Book Review Literary Trust, Calcutta.

Liang, L. (2005) Cinematic citizenship and the illegal city. *Inter-Asia Cultural Studies, 6* (3), *366–385.*

Sarkar, S. (1983) *Modern India, 1885–1947,* Macmillan, Dehli.

Shaw, P. (1950) *The Indian Film*, Motion Picture Society of India, Bombay.

Sivathambi, K. (1981) *The Tamil Film as Medium of Political Communication,* New Century Book, Madras.

Uricchio, W. and Pearson, R. (1993) *Reframing Culture: The Case of the Vitagraph Quality Films,* Princeton University Press, Princeton, NJ.

Volosinov, V.N. (1973) *Marxism and the Philosophy of Language,* Harvard University Press, Cambridge, MA.

18

The Last Bemboka Picture Show

16 mm Cinema as Rural Community Fundraiser in the 1950s

Kate Bowles

As Australian cinema history has become more sensitive to the history of film exhibition, its keynote stories have come under review. The assumed impact of television on theatrical exhibition, after its launch in Sydney and Melbourne in 1956, is one of these stories; related to it is the more long-standing assumption that an exhibition market dominated in the 1950s by Hollywood product was the outcome of coercive business practices that had all but crushed local production. The impression left by this account is that Australian audiences were unwilling accomplices to America's success, and that Australian communities were culturally diminished by this. This larger argument about the effect of media consumption on audience preferences is easy to assert but difficult to prove. As yet, we know relatively little about the social and emotional impact on 1950s audiences of their long-term diet of foreign product, both in theatres and via imported television shows, and a substantial investment in oral history will be needed to address this.[1]

The Australian trade press does, however, provide us with some interesting evidence of the mutual engagement between Australian theatre entrepreneurs and American distributors, which had resulted in this dominance of foreign product. The scale of the activity in the exhibition industry across Australia and New Zealand suggests a wider context for the specific anxieties generated in the 1950s by the problem of Australia's limited production capacity, or the impact of television. Both of these were talking points in the trade press, for obvious reasons. Nevertheless, the Australasian regional market was too diverse at this time for these two totalising accounts of the industry's concerns to dominate, as we might with hindsight expect. Rather, the trade press continued in the 1950s to illustrate the very complicated internal segmentation of the market: between states, between country, city and suburban exhibitors, between hard-tops, outdoor shows, itinerants and drive-ins and, consistently, between the theatrical and non-theatrical. This internal diversity derived from

Explorations in New Cinema History: Approaches and Case Studies, First Edition.
Edited by Richard Maltby, Daniel Biltereyst and Philippe Meers.

the challenging geography of Australasian distribution, rather than from language or cultural diversity, which might have been factors in European or subcontinental film markets at the time, and in simple terms it meant that the impact of key transitions, and key internal conflicts, diffused through this market at an uneven pace.

This presents an Australian version of the challenge that confronts every historian of cinema exhibition and reception: where is the locus of national typicality? Is it always in the cities, where things tended to happen first, or to happen with the greatest economic consequence for the industry as a whole? Is it always in the mainstream, 35 mm theatrical sector, with its predictable concentration of industry power and government interests, including through systems of licensing, taxation and the management of public safety? If we allow metropolitan case studies to dominate for this reason, we need to think carefully about the kind of attention we should pay to the case study that is not by these standards typical. We might treat it as a potential challenge to the dominant account, but there are risks associated with this kind of romanticism. In a diverse market, the development of particular tactics at marginal locations in the network does not in itself contradict the evidence of broad strategies at the centre. We might therefore suggest that the strength of cinema exhibition history is constituted in its aggregation of detail, and this compilation and comparison of results across locations benefits from *any* expansion of the field (Fuller-Seeley, 2008, p. 4). This is a less romantic argument, analogous to the way in which the history of film analysis, for example, has accepted the proposition that the more individual films we unearth and study, the more we know about films in general.

There is, however, a third reason why we might take an interest in the smallest and most remote microstudies. What makes these particularly valuable to historians is that the gap between the local expectations attached to a particular picture show, and the regulation of those expectations from the distant perspective of industry headquarters, is often at its widest in the most marginal cases. As exaggerated instances of the tension between local consumption and national management of supply, they provide an exceptionally clear demonstration of the maturity and elasticity of the business culture surrounding cinema distribution and exhibition in Australia in the 1950s and 1960s, a culture that was capable of accommodating a surprising degree of misunderstanding, incompatibility, and mutually non-aligned exploitation.

This observation has arisen from reflection on a small collection of bank books, distributor invoices and correspondence relating to a volunteer-operated weekly picture show that entertained the Australian rural community of Bemboka from 1956 to 1967.[2] Bemboka is a village on the main rural highway that connects the harbour towns on the far south coast of New South Wales (NSW) to the inland farms and towns of the Monaro plains. Although its population had once been as much as 600, in the late 1950s it was closer to 300. It is not remote by Australian standards, but it is now an hour's drive from the nearest regional town, Bega, and at least 5 hours from the state capital, Sydney. In the 1950s, when the district's roads were still unsealed, both these journeys would have taken much longer.

There is, moreover, no rail access into Bemboka; goods delivered via rail from Sydney require collection and a further journey by road. This combination of factors put the nearest fixed picture theatres, in Bega and Narooma, beyond the reach of casual weekly attendance and made it genuinely difficult for film prints to reach the village, thus making a fixed show in the village an equally challenging commercial proposition. Nevertheless, the movies had come to Bemboka. Like the other similarly sized villages in the district, Bemboka had entertained a succession of passing picture show operations since the silent period. After World War II, it was part of the territory served by the local itinerant exhibitor Mr Allan Jamieson, whose Jamieson's Country Pictures was the last touring show in NSW, operating until the late 1960s (Bowles, 2008, p. 89).

In 1956, however, a licence was obtained from the Chief Secretary's Department of the NSW Government for the Bemboka community to run their own show. A 3-hour programme of two 16 mm features plus shorts or a newsreel was screened each Saturday night in the local School of Arts hall, and the purpose of this programme was to raise funds to build the new Bemboka Memorial Hall.[3] The instigators of the show were 19-year-old Mr Doug Chapman, who had arrived in Bemboka the previous year to take up a teaching position at the local school, and Mr Jack Hobbs, who had taken over the Bemboka general store and post office from his father. The last Bemboka picture show therefore commenced in the same year that Australian television broadcasting began in Sydney and Melbourne. However counterintuitive this may seem from an urban perspective, this is in fact one of many rural case studies that challenge the pervasive belief that television immediately and comprehensively reduced the cinemagoing market throughout Australia. In partnership with postwar suburbanisation, television certainly put pressure on cinema exhibitors in cities, in Australia as in the United States, with the result that exhibitors who were already attuned to seasonal fluctuations in demand caused by holidays, weather, war or the economy quickly had to develop their understanding of the scheduling rhythms of television. As one US drive-in exhibitor put it in 1965:

> A year, year and half after they have the TV it's 'I like it, but Tuesday nights there's nothing on.' And if you look at television, Friday and Saturday nights are their miserable program nights. And these are the nights that these people can go out and they have two and three and four kids and the husband comes home Friday and she says we're going to get out of this damn house tonight or I'm going to jump out of the window.[4]

This type of accommodation would have been premature in Bemboka in 1956, however. The intransigence of Australian geography hampered the national rollout of the new medium, and although television had been demonstrated locally by 1961, regional reception problems would continue throughout the 1960s (Hanson, 2008). As Kathryn Fuller-Seeley has demonstrated, the occurrence of similar delays in the availability of television in rural America undermines the national myth of television's sudden and widespread impact on the habit of cinema attendance (Fuller-Seeley, 2004). So the decision of the Bemboka Memorial Hall Fund Committee to take advantage of the Bell & Howell 16 mm projector at the school, and to strike up a commercial relationship with the remote representatives of the even remoter Hollywood majors, can be explained as a straightforward exploitation of the lag between television's celebrated arrival in Sydney, and its delayed and continually troubled reach into rural NSW. When we consider the operation of the show within the large network of Australian distribution and exhibition and its internal divisions, however, we can see that there were factors other than poor television reception that shaped the brief history of the last Bemboka picture show.

The Australian Country Picture Show: Theatrical or Non-Theatrical?

The Bemboka committee's fundraising motivation was not unusual. Other shows in the same district had linked specific fundraising efforts, often for the upkeep of the premises in which motion pictures were screened, to the more general project of promoting and boosting the local community (Bowles, 2007, p. 250). Exhibition of this nature, and for this reason, has been dominant in many remote Australian rural contexts, for the obvious reason that many widely dispersed rural towns and villages have a population too small to justify the construction of a permanent picture theatre. Most rural operators in the early twentieth century borrowed time in existing community halls, which were used for other purposes for the rest of the week. Some travelled around a district bringing both projectors and films with them. Others took advantage of permanent projectors and even projection booths as they became an increasingly common feature in rural halls after 1928. Many operators also had other jobs, and those who were working in fundraising operations often took on the task of arranging the supply of films, or even managing the projection, much as they might undertake other forms of civic duty related to church, committee or Lodge membership. The scale of activity in rural cinema exhibition in Australia was therefore not exactly coterminous with the 'country' sector imagined by the annual summaries of business activity to be found in the trade press, nor does it slot neatly into categories organised around a distinction between theatrical and non-theatrical. 'Country' was a messy designation, covering fixed and touring shows in both gauges, encompassing both shows run along commercial lines and community-run operations.

In the cities, meanwhile, the ingenuity and resilience of the rural showmen was viewed as both opportunity and risk. The expansion of the 16 mm sector, and its possible impact on nearby 35 mm operations, was regarded with particular ambivalence. Both in the United States and Australia, 16 mm was a difficult development to classify, as it ranged from home projection within a family setting to the screening of adult movies to a quite different audience. In both adult and arthouse sectors, themselves often perceived as competing with non-specialist programming in the mainstream theatres, 16 mm was becoming associated with unfair internal competition from interests that were increasingly labelled 'amateur', 'non-professional' or non-theatrical (Schaefer, 2002, p. 7; see also Twomey, 1956; Zimmerman, 1988). We still tend to associate 16 mm historically with non-commercial screenings of non-Hollywood products, but in 1950s trade discourse equal attention was being paid to the growth of a new tier in mainstream theatrical programming, where 16 mm represented a potentially cost-effective means of increasing print run, reaching a wider audience, and significantly extending the shelf-life of product.

Theatre owners using the traditional 35 mm gauge were burdened with the debts incurred in the purchase of expensive projection equipment, the higher cost of prints, the maintenance of large buildings, the payment of overheads, including the wages of unionised staff, and the need to meet the standards on which their licences depended. Their profits depended in part on protecting their business from *arriviste* operators offering the same or similar experience at lower cost, and from the general risk to quality associated with these lower cost operations. Reports of new 16 mm shows in the early 1950s had emphasised that they were sufficiently remote to cause no concern – 'one at Marree, in the far, far north'.[5] Likewise, as more US companies expanded into the supply of this new market, their reassurances focused on the protection of established interests, both by emphasising that 16 mm prints would be held back for up to 2 years following 35 mm theatrical release, 'to ensure no unfair competition with regular 35 mm theatres, whose interests would be protected', and by promising equivalent quality in service and prints to that offered to the 35 mm operation.[6] The third strategy of reassurance was to stress the novelty of the 16 mm projector and its use either in direct support of theatre business, or in promotional activity far removed from the traditional interests of the cinema owner:

> MGM has used 16 mm film trailers most effectively in stores and shop windows ... Several theatres have run these small-gauge trailers in their foyers as a 'come on' to passers-by. I pushed to the front of a large crowd outside Hartley's Sports Store window in Flinders-street [sic] last fortnight for further evidence of 16 mm's successful uses. On the face of an outside tennis racquet, being used for a screen, a well-handled piece of back-projection was demonstrating sporting events, and detailing various stages of tennis racquet manufacture ... much to the street audience's interest. A perfect piece of salesmanship (hidden loud-speakers provided accompanying sound and commentary), it was proof of the infinite value of a 16 mm projector.[7]

Nevertheless, the visit to Australia in December 1951 by Orton H. Hicks of Loew's International 16 mm department disrupted the rhythm of these reassurances. Hicks toured Australia for a week, and then announced that the future of exhibition lay in the smaller gauge. He suggested that the 16 mm format was only held back by the fact that its projectors were less robust than larger models, and while this might mean a delay in full implementation of up to 10 years, even US exhibitors were 'seriously considering (for the first time) making a wide change to

16 mm'.[8] A critical element in Hicks' pitch lay in his acknowledgement of the grumbling discontent concerning competition between the new commercial 16 mm operators, and their established 35 mm rivals:

> Hicks was anxious to settle the question of 16 mm versus 35 mm. 'There is no such things as a 16 mm market as opposed to a 35 mm market,' he said. There's been confusion because some industry men think of the non-theatrical market as being synonymous with the 16 mm market. 'The fact that most non-theatrical shows are in 16 mm is only incidental. There are only two real markets in the motion picture field. They are the commercial and the non-theatrical.'[9]

In fact, the shared obligation to the quality and public reputation of the cinema-going experience that lashed together the commercial and the non-theatrical operator continued to rankle. The following month, Ernest Turnbull, managing director of the theatre chain Hoyts, responded that Australian investment in developing the 35 mm theatrical sector to a standard appropriate to urban audiences must not be 'jeopardised by the unbridled exhibition of 16 mm in all kinds of make-shift theatres and halls in the suburbs'.[10] In 1952, a promotion for the smaller gauge enquired whether 16 mm was 'a threat to current standards of presentation? Is it essentially an insidious, non-theatrical patron-stealer? Or is it an answer to mounting costs of exhibition and distribution?' The purpose of this article was to persuade in favour of the latter conclusion by arguing that 'savings in installation and film print costs, up-keep, freight and insurance premiums could make a substantial difference to the economic structure of the industry.'[11] The rhetorical questions it posed, however, reveal the nature and extent of ongoing industry concern as the 16 mm commercial sector continued to expand, not reaching outwards from the city, but encroaching on the city from the remote and rural situations where it had been a tolerable competitive presence. Continued alarmist lobbying for greater regulation of the 16 mm sector drew attention to the plight of licensed operators, such as Mr Henry Joseph of Oaklands, NSW, who found himself having to share the local hall with a 'non-professional' screening in aid of the local football club. *The Film Weekly* appealed publicly to the distributors who were supplying the rival outfit:

> Our opinion, without being partisan in any way, is that distributors who rent entertainment films for use in competition with licensed showmen are being disloyal to the men from whom the vast bulk of their revenue stems. They are doing a disservice to the industry by undermining the habit of attending commercial screenings. Ultimately this must reflect on themselves as well as on the exhibitor.[12]

The Film Weekly had begun to track the expansion of the 16 mm commercial sector in its annual survey of activity in 1950–51, when it found 112 shows nationally, with 4347 16 mm films having been imported in the previous year. These figures remained reasonably steady until 1955, when a sudden increase in the number of 16 mm titles imported led to a doubling of the number of shows nationally by 1958–59.[13] While this represented a fraction of the overall business activity in the

Australian market, its growth, coupled with the hyperbolic nature of claims made by the 16 mm departments of the majors as they pursued their new market, heightened the sense of risk at a time when all levels of industry were apprehensively anticipating the spread of television from the United States to Australia. In 1956, when the Bemboka Memorial Hall Fund Committee applied for their 16 mm picture show licence, therefore, there was a clear trade discourse surrounding 16 mm screenings, focusing on unfair competition and the protection of quality, and a brisk and pragmatic intolerance of shows operating as fundraisers.

Why did the major distributors engage with fundraiser operations under these circumstances? Surely they had as much to lose as their 35 mm exhibitors if a programme of indifferent quality was put before an audience, or an overcapitalised 35 mm theatre nearby was put in harm's way by this move? One simple explanation is that the threat of internal competition was radically altered by the geography of cinema attendance in many remote country areas, as well as by the small size of the likely potential audience in these situations. The collision of a licensed and a non-professional operation in the same hall, as in the Oaklands case, would not necessarily have been the common experience. In any case the small audience in many local situations might not have discouraged distributors from dividing the market, since the 'market' in a village of 300 fell below any sensible standard of economic significance, while even a small audience would prolong the life of the kinds of titles that were typically sent out into these situations, at least by the amount of a weekly booking fee. Families who did not attend a weekly screening in a community like Bemboka were unlikely to travel further afield, so the threat of an apparently non-theatrical show in the territory was lessened by this limited mobility. In other words, if there was no show in Bemboka, its audience was more likely to spend the night in listening to the radio, or to join some other kind of community entertainment at the hall, than to set off to Bega or Narooma unless they already had business in town – and so the existence of a Bemboka show would not necessarily draw off patronage from the larger show.

Everyday Operating Problems: Negotiation and Making do

If the distributors had sufficient reason to support marginally theatrical enterprises such as the Oaklands or Bemboka shows, this did not always result in harmonious dealings with the operators of those shows. Correspondence between the Bemboka Memorial Hall Committee and the full range of Hollywood 16 mm distribution interests in Sydney concerning the running of the Bemboka show reveals some significant friction. The gap between distributor and exhibitor aspirations demonstrates in quite practical ways how the business culture of cinema distribution operated to contain the risk of conflict and discontent, as part of a wider public relations exercise of considerable scale that encouraged the continued smooth accommodation of American commercial interests to Australian consumer culture.

Whether country exhibitors were running a dedicated theatre with usherettes in full uniform, or managing a weekly fundraising programme in the local hall, their engagement with Hollywood via its city-based distributors confirmed the positioning of cinema among the predictable patterns of social and business experiences by which Australian rural communities defined themselves and were defined. The commercial and legal requirements related to picture show operation recruited the schoolteacher and the general store manager into a relationship with the distant metropolitan business culture that supported the supply, transport, insurance, promotion and projection of motion pictures. The straightforward practical difficulties involved in organising a weekly show for a small population in a remote place sustained a particular style of mutual exploitation between the radically disproportionate businesses of supply and demand, in which the goals served at the point of exhibition were entirely different from the goals expressed at the commercial centres of production and distribution.

The Bemboka Memorial Hall Fund Committee were dealing directly with the 16 mm departments of MGM, Columbia, Paramount and Fox, as well as with their trade association, the Film Renters' Association of Australia Ltd. They were also supplied with both motion pictures and projector maintenance by Sixteen Millimetre Australia, which represented the Rank Organisation, Bell & Howell, Encyclopaedia Britannica Films, Universal Pictures and, eventually, Disney. The Sydney company Hamilton & Baker, which specialised in 'Projection, Sound and Theatre Equipment', supplied technical advice and additional spare parts, as well as the special labels that the Sydney distributors required to be used on film cans travelling throughout the state by rail. Weekly correspondence arriving at the Bemboka Post Office under the lavishly illustrated letterheads of the Hollywood majors conveyed the values, aspirations and expectations of a global metropolitan corporate culture into a rural business community where the terms of trade in the local store were established by personal reputation (particularly in terms of credit and integrity), negotiation and making do. This fundamental cultural incompatibility led to three closely linked points of tension that characterised the relationship between Bemboka and Sydney. These related to the commercial or non-commercial status of the Bemboka operation, the terms of payment for film programmes, and the quality and reliability of the film programmes supplied to country exhibitors.

In the first place, the standard contracts and terms of supply devised by the distributors could not easily accommodate a 16 mm picture show run for profit but not as a commercial proposition. This definitional awkwardness and resulting contractual inflexibility extended to other significant costs incurred by the committee. In 1957, for example, the committee wrote to the Norwich Union asking for some reconsideration of the terms of their projector insurance:

> We note you quote 30/-% [sic] for an all risk policy this being the rate of professionals. This machine is used to show features for profit by the above organization. However all the operators and persona helping are acting in a voluntary capacity. In view of this my committee suggests that you consider charging us amateur rates.

The insurer took a disappointing view of the definition of amateur, however, replying 'that it is our normal practice to charge the professional rate for any Projector etc. which is used for public screening'. Despite this crisp rejection, the status of the Bemboka picture show continued to cause confusion. In November 1957, Mr Gow, the Australasian manager of Columbia's 16 mm distribution stressed that their agreement was to supply films 'to screen commercially', but in 1959 sent them a form for the particulars of 'non-commercial situations', which included screening to family, friends, relatives and club members. The nature and varying forms of club membership in Australia still remain the hinge between public and private for many forms of leisure and entertainment, and in this case the difficulty revolved around whether or not members of the Bemboka community could be said to be participating in a commercial form of movie attendance if the show was run by members of the Memorial Hall Committee and the school P & C (Parents and Citizens) committee, none of whom were paid. Indeed, the show's status seems to have remained unresolved throughout its operation: in 1964 and 1965, Sixteen Millimetre Australia produced a succession of contradictory invoices defining the show variously as 'screening to members', 'private' and 'commercial'.

The appeal by the show's operators for some consideration of their volunteer effort and fundraising goals was part of the broader campaign they pursued over their terms of trade. While they were charged as commercial operations, they were treated as somewhat subcommercial in terms of their credit status, and were therefore required to pay their accounts in advance of the screening date. This may have related to the fact that the rural banking sector was highly localised, and so the financial affairs of many country businesses could not readily be guaranteed by the normal means used in cities. As an experienced and respected rural trader, however, Mr Hobbs complained consistently against this imposition, and it is hard not to see this as a clash of cultural principles as much as a commercial dispute. The committee took up their cause directly with the individual distribution companies, and were referred back to V.T. Jeune at the Film Renters' Association, who managed the awkwardness of credit rating on behalf of the major distributors. By this time, however, the question of credit rating had become entangled with the Memorial Hall Committee's dissatisfactions concerning irregularities in the supply of prints.

These complaints arose from problems of late programme substitution and print quality, which risked the show's good name with its local audience. In July 1957, for example, Mr Chapman wrote to Sixteen Millimetre Australia concerning the soundtrack of *The Third Man*: 'There was a constant roar through the speakers and the speech was often not able to be understood. Another such film would considerably reduce our takings. One patron – her first night at our show was heard to remark "That is the first and last …"' The response from the company was both conciliatory and evasive, taking the standard line of defence that distributors and exchanges could not be held responsible for checking picture quality:

> We do agree that the sound reproduction on this film is below standard. It would appear that some damage has been sustained to the film whilst in the care of

> another exhibitor. Unfortunately, we had received no previous complaint concerning the sound on this film and since this is the only way by which the standard of prints may be determined, we naturally assumed it to be in good condition and forwarded it to you on that assumption. We sincerely regret that this fault appeared in one of your first programs and assure you that no further programs will be supplied in inferior condition.

Blaming other country showmen for lost or damaged prints was a common strategy used by the exchanges in response to problems of picture quality or irregular picture supply. Part of the problem lay in the tight schedules for the collection and return of films. A film that screened in Bemboka on a Saturday night was despatched from Sydney the previous Wednesday, collected by car service from the railway station at Nimmitabel or Cooma on Friday, and could not have returned to Sydney before the following Wednesday. This meant that for one screening, a film print was away from the exchange for a week or more, and that the margin for error in return and re-despatch of the programmes was very slim. If one consignment missed a train somewhere in the country, the exchange had to act quickly to send a substitute to the next operator, followed by a new set of invoices. The Bemboka correspondence suggests that these problems, and the confusion they caused, were common. Some of the distributors' waste of profit caused by the transit time was offset by displacing all the costs of freight and cartage onto the exhibitors, but the exchanges could not reasonably charge for the lost time and still expect the participation of rural exhibitors who were already struggling to maintain profits from small audiences.

A series of problems with film quality and supply in 1958 led to increasingly testy correspondence between Bemboka and Sydney. In October, for example, Columbia responded to a report of another difficult screening: 'Dear Sir, We acknowledge your letter of the 14th instant, and we deeply regret the inconvenience to you on screening the feature "ROCK AROUND THE CLOCK," this particular print has been screened at 29 situations and this is the first complaint of this nature we have had.' Following similar complaints about other titles made to Fox and MGM, V.T. Jeune, seemingly oblivious to the fact that the print had been on the road for almost 6 months, suggested on behalf of his members that the Bemboka projectors might be at fault. Jeune's letters dealt with the issues of picture quality and credit status together, apparently acknowledging the committee's suggestion that there was at least an ethical link between the two, and the Bemboka show was finally removed from the Film Renters' Association Payment in Advance list in January 1959. This enabled them to pay for both film programmes and playbills 7 days after delivery, a significant and hard-won concession that gives us a clear sense of the difficulties facing both the Sydney distributors and their country exhibitors in managing the physical and commercial challenges of the rural cinema sector.

If this was so difficult for both parties, why did they persist? The distributors were demonstrably tolerant of the logistical difficulties and the conflicts involved, not to mention the marginal profits from these temporary fundraising shows, in a way that suggests that the primary benefit of their participation lay in other outcomes. As foreign stakeholders already dealing with local resentment from the production industry, the Hollywood majors would have understood that the reputational battle could be won or lost according to the quality of their commitment and service to rural and regional Australia, and their willingness to supply entertainment to small, remote communities like Bemboka. This is at least a partial explanation for their patience. Meanwhile, if the quality of the prints was so poor, the titles so out of date, and the venue so uncomfortable, was the simple absence of television enough to explain why the Bemboka community supported this operation in return? The answer to this part of the question lies in the local community goal that Hollywood was recruited to serve: the memorialisation of Bemboka's losses to wars in places as remote as Hollywood from the everyday life of this small community. Over a 14-year fundraising campaign, including eight years of the picture show's operation, the committee eventually raised over £16 000, and with the assistance of three other small loans and the raffling of a new Holden car, the picture show enabled the new Memorial Hall to be built in 1962. The weekly show continued for a few years, no doubt partly because the television signal was still unimpressive, but when it wound up in 1967 this was at least partly because its job was done.

The last Bemboka picture show was therefore not a failed or inconsequential operation, but a tactically successful temporary engagement between the global American motion picture industry and a local community seeking to address needs that had nothing at all to do with motion pictures. Indeed, what makes this case interesting to cinema historians is that the local goals sustaining the last Bemboka picture show had so little to do with cinema itself. It helps us to understand the historical development of Hollywood's global commercial advantage, in its willingness to entertain even the most marginal proposition, and to take each dollar of profit equally seriously. Precisely because the two parties involved had so little in common, the Bemboka picture show exemplifies the attitude and the approach taken by Hollywood's distributors to the management of diverse regional markets, and the construction of a global business – one small contract at a time.

Notes

1 Scott McKinnon, 'Australian youth, modern teens: the Hollywood teen film and Australian teenage culture in the 1950s and 1960s', unpublished thesis, held in University of Technology Library, Sydney.

2 I am very grateful to Mr Jack Hobbs of Bemboka, New South Wales, for sharing his recollections of the management of the Bemboka picture show, and particularly for the donation of his surviving correspondence and other records. All information on the Bemboka show has been taken from these two sources.

3 The Schools of Arts and Mechanics Institutes that are common in Australian country towns were nineteenth century institutions set up to provide community education programmes, and often included small libraries and other meeting rooms. In the early twentieth century many of them became de facto part-time picture shows, and

their buildings were upgraded to accommodate projection equipment and to meet fire safety standards.

4 Bart Pirosh, quoted in David Paletz, Michael Noonan, Bart Pirosh, Max Laemmle, Shan Sayles, 'The exhibitors', *Film Quarterly*, 19 (2) (Winter 1965–1966), 14–40.

5 *The Film Weekly*, Sydney, 31 May 1951.

6 *The Film Weekly*, 30 August 1951, p. 1; *The Film Weekly*, 20 December 1951, p. 5; *The Film Weekly*, 13 December 1951, p. 13.

7 *The Film Weekly*, 8 November 1951, p. 12.

8 *The Film Weekly*, 3 January 1952, p. 3.

9 *The Film Weekly*, 3 January 1952, p. 3.

10 *The Film Weekly*, 21 February 1952, p. 1.

11 *The Film Weekly*, 29 May 1952, p. 20.

12 *The Film Weekly*, 21 August 1952, p. 5.

13 These data are taken from *The Film Weekly* 'Easy reference statistics: theatres of Australia' annual summaries of theatre openings and closings; *The Film Weekly* recorded activity in the 16 mm sector separately between 1950–51 and 1962–63.

References

Bowles, K. (2007) 'Three miles of rough dirt road': towards an audience-centred approach to cinema studies in Australia. *Studies in Australasian Cinema*, 1 (3), 245–260.

Bowles, K. (2008) 'All the evidence is that Cobargo is slipping': an ecological approach to rural cinema-going. *Film Studies*, 10, 87–96.

Fuller-Seeley, K. (2004) The video divide: unequal diffusion of early US TV ownership 1945–1955. Society for Cinema and Media Studies conference paper.

Fuller-Seeley, K. (2008) Introduction, in *Hollywood in the Neighbourhood: Historical Case Studies of Local Moviegoing*, University of California Press, Berkeley, pp. 3–19.

Hanson, S. (2008) Snow falling on Bega: early television reception on the far south coast of New South Wales. Unpublished report (http://www.uow.edu.au/content/groups/public/@web/@arts/documents/doc/uow019605.pdf).

Schaefer, E. (2002) Gauging a revolution: 16 mm film and the rise of the pornographic feature. *Cinema Journal*, 41 (3) (Spring), 3–26.

Twomey, J. (1956) Some considerations on the rise of the art-film theater. *The Quarterly Review of Film, Radio and Television*, 10 (3) (Spring), 239–247.

Zimmerman, P. (1988) Hollywood, home movies and common sense: amateur film as aesthetic dissemination and social control, 1950–1962. *Cinema Journal*, 27 (4) (Summer), 23–44.

Index

Explorations in New Cinema History: Approaches and Case Studies, First Edition.
Edited by Richard Maltby, Daniel Biltereyst and Philippe Meers.